The Demjanjuk Affair

The Demjanjuk Affair
The Rise and Fall of a Show-Trial

YORAM SHEFTEL

Translated from the Hebrew by Haim Watzman

VICTOR GOLLANCZ
LONDON

First published in Hebrew as Parashut Demjanjuk:
Aliató unfilato shel misphat ra'ava
in Israel in 1993 by Adam Publishers, Tel Aviv
This revised edition first published in Great Britain 1994
by Victor Gollancz Ltd
A Division of the Cassell group
Villiers House, 41/47 Strand, London WC2N 5JE

Copyright © Yoram Sheftel 1993
Translation copyright © Haim Watzman 1994

The right of Yoram Sheftel to be identified as author of
this work has been asserted by him in accordance with
the Copyright, Designs and Patents Act, 1988.

A catalogue record for this book is
available from the British Library

ISBN 0 575 05795 5

Photoset in Great Britain by
Rowland Phototypesetting Ltd, Bury St Edmunds, Suffolk
Printed in Great Britain by
Mackays of Chatham plc, Chatham, Kent

דאס בוך ווידמע איך מיין איין איינציגע
טייערע יידישע מאמע, בריינדל שפטל

This book is dedicated to my
one and only dear Yiddisher mama,
Briendel Sheftel

Contents

	Acknowledgements	ix
	List of Illustrations	xi
	Preface	xiii
1	Defence Attorney for the 'Phoney Satan'	1
2	Let the Show-Trial Begin	26
3	The Prosecution Case	38
4	*Kalt und Fest*	61
5	O'Connor is Dismissed	90
6	The Collapse of the Defence Case	115
7	Out of Thin Air	139
8	Dovele	186
9	To the Gallows	209
10	Judge Dov Eitan Joins the Defence	227
11	Acid Attack	248
12	A Precedent	264
13	The Appeal	273
14	The Turning Point	288
15	The Demjanjuk Affair	324
16	The Final Appeal Hearing	338
17	From the Gallows to Cleveland	347

Acknowledgements

This book would never have looked as it does had it not been for the initial editorial assistance of attorney Doron Beckerman, who worked on the first draft, making constructive and useful comments throughout, almost all of which I agreed with.

Tzvia Weiss, in addition to her hard work typing up the book, constantly made helpful observations, as with everything I do.

Eyal Megged encouraged me at every step of the way to believe in my ability to meet the challenge of writing this book.

For the excellent editing which transformed my original manuscript, my thanks are due to Yoram Verteh, who had a gargantuan task.

Liz Knights and Vicki Harris of Victor Gollancz toiled ceaselessly to ensure that the British edition of this book would be even better than the Hebrew. For this I owe them my most grateful thanks.

Illustrations

Following page 176

The page of photographs including Demjanjuk and Federenko from which Demjanjuk was identified

The Travniki document

Judges Dov Levin, Zvi Tal and Dalia Dorner

Mark O'Connor, the author and Michael Shaked

Demjanjuk in the dock during Professor Smith's testimony (*Associated Press*)

Ivan Marchenko on his wedding day

Ivan Marchenko on the day of his arrival at the Travniki camp

Ivan Marchenko with Ivan Takchuk, at Travniki

Dov Eitan

Eti Yisrael nursing the author's eye

Demjanjuk, holding his release papers, shakes hands with a prison guard at the Supreme Court on 29 July 1993 (*Associated Press*)

Preface to the British Edition

In 1976 a New York Communist newspaper called the *Ukrainian Weekly* published a document that was apparently an ID card from the Travniki camp in Poland, a training centre for ex-prisoners of war who had volunteered for the German SS auxiliary forces. This card came to be known throughout the world as the 'Travniki document'. The accompanying article named the man in the ID photograph as Ivan Demjanjuk, labelling him a Nazi war criminal living in the US. It is largely due to this document – now known to be a crude forgery – that people have been left with the impression that Demjanjuk, if not the infamous Ivan the Terrible, was at least a Nazi camp guard of some description.

The American authorities opened an investigation into Demjanjuk and Fyodor Federenko, also mentioned in the article. They badgered the Soviets for a copy of the Travniki document, meanwhile sending photographs of Demjanjuk and Federenko to Israel and asking the authorities there to find some Holocaust survivors and see if anyone recognized Federenko as a guard from the Treblinka death camp, and/or Demjanjuk as a guard from Sobibor. The Israeli police composed 'photo spreads' – sheets of paper with several photographs pasted on to them – one of which showed both Demjanjuk and Federenko with overwhelming prominence. The first survivor to look at the photo spreads, his eye naturally drawn to the two 'target pictures', unexpectedly named Demjanjuk as the dreaded Ivan from Treblinka. From this moment, the Israeli investigation was aimed at identifying Demjanjuk as Ivan the Terrible, operator of the gas chambers at the Treblinka extermination camp, the murderer of some nine hundred thousand Jews.

In 1981, the Travniki document was presented at Demjanjuk's denaturalization trial; after being shown to the judge it was transferred to the Soviet Embassy in Washington. The prosecution were able to examine it there, but it was swiftly returned to the USSR before the defence could see it. Demjanjuk was extradited to Israel on 28 February 1986, but the Soviet Union held on to the Travniki document until December.

As soon as he was extradited Demjanjuk was condemned by the

Israeli public and media. As a result of the atmosphere surrounding the case, the Minister of Justice began to press the Chief Justice of the Supreme Court to agree to hold Demjanjuk's trial in a specially leased theatre hall. The Chief Justice acceded to this request and even agreed that the entire trial be broadcast live on television, making it the first televised trial in Israel's history. For this reason, it was clear even before the trial began that the court, like the media, would find him guilty at the end of the show-trial it was planning. After all, the theatre was not rented to provide live TV coverage of his acquittal.

In the mid-1970s the British public was shocked by a series of deadly terrorist attacks perpetrated by the IRA, in which dozens of innocent people were killed. A large number of suspects was quickly rounded up. Their interrogations were conducted with little regard for accepted procedure; in practice, the object was not to find out whether these people committed the crimes, but to find them guilty. The evidence produced by the police investigations rested in large part on the confessions forced out of the subjects by improper methods. These confessions were corroborated by flimsy and ambiguous forensic evidence. Charges were pressed, leading to the trials of, most famously, the Guildford Four, the Birmingham Six and the Maguire Seven.

By now there was a furious public atmosphere that for all practical purposes prevented the possibility of the defendants being acquitted, in spite of the unpersuasive nature of the evidence against them. As expected, the defendants were convicted and their appeals rejected. As time passed, however, doubts began to arise about the soundness of the evidence for these convictions. The press and public began to question the justice of the convictions. After seventeen long years, the establishment (the police and judiciary, including the Crown Prosecution Service) deigned to admit their combined error and set the victims free.

These cases exposed the weakness of many of the judicial procedures in Britain, particularly with reference to crimes that inflame public opinion. But the public fury surrounding the trials of the Guildford Four, the Birmingham Six and the Maguire Seven was a gentle rebuke compared to that awakened by the Demjanjuk affair in Israel. This affair shows that public opinion, ignited by dreadful crimes and fanned by the media, drastically reduces the ability to hold a proper, fair trial. Such a mood may pave the way to the conviction, even execution, of innocent people.

There is nevertheless a fundamental difference between the two legal establishments. While the British judiciary felt itself obliged, following the quashing of these convictions, to establish a royal commission of inquiry to look into the functioning of the entire system, the Israeli judiciary remains too arrogant and self-satisfied to do likewise.

Not only did Israel fail to appoint an independent national commission of inquiry, but, in an astounding display of callousness, it rewarded two of the judges who sent Demjanjuk to the gallows for crimes he never committed. They were appointed to the Supreme Court bench.

1 · Defence Attorney for the 'Phoney Satan'

In the first week of March 1986 I was in the throes of a case dubbed 'the Billion-Shekel Robbery'. I appeared for the principal defendant of a group charged with armed robbery of a billion shekels, a sum that at the time was equivalent to a million US dollars.

My days were crammed with dozens of phone calls, meetings and court appearances. But as I hurriedly scanned the week's papers, one item caught my eye: 'Ivan' John Demjanjuk had been brought to Israel as a result of extradition procedures sought by the Israeli government from the US authorities. This same Demjanjuk was said to be none other than that inhuman Ukrainian monster known as 'Ivan the Terrible', who had perpetrated the most heinous crimes at the Treblinka extermination camp. Truth to tell, I did not give too much thought to the reports at the time. Certainly it never occurred to me that our paths might ever cross. Yet the story did lodge in my mind.

Looking back, it now seems to me to have some similarity to another news item casually spotted in the daily paper that had embedded itself in my mind. On the eve of the Jewish New Year, Rosh Hashanah, in 1970, the papers reported that Meyer Lansky, who was reputed to have played a leading role in organized crime in the US over the previous fifty years, had arrived to spend the festive season in Israel, and also to stay on a while afterwards. I was then a first-year student at the Law Faculty of the Hebrew University in Jerusalem, and no one could have anticipated that within a few years, a close and special relationship would develop between this ageing, warm-hearted, sharp-witted Jew and me. Though Lansky was shamefully expelled from the country he loved so deeply and supported so generously, I later instigated a complex series of moves that culminated in a successful petition to the Supreme Court. As a result he was permitted to return to Israel whenever he wished, with tourist status.

Several weeks later, at the end of March 1986, John Demjanjuk's defence attorney, Mark O'Connor, arrived in Israel, with blanket media coverage – articles, news reports and photos. Even though I was still deeply absorbed in the Billion-Shekel Robbery and other cases, I gathered a great deal of new information about the Demjanjuk case from the media.

I learned that the Nazi Crimes Investigation Division of Israel Police had started to investigate him ten years earlier. The evidence was based entirely on photo spreads, sent by the American authorities to Israel Police in 1976. Another document was said to exist in the Soviet Union that would provide proof against Demjanjuk – but the Russians were none too keen to hand it over to the Israeli state prosecution.

I found even more intriguing the report that Chief Superintendent Alex Ish-Shalom had been appointed head of the special investigation team responsible for the interrogation of Demjanjuk. Ish-Shalom had taught me criminology at the law faculty in Jerusalem; among some criminal lawyers, there is a distinct feeling of unease over the way he conducts his investigations. Everyone agrees however that Ish-Shalom is a highly successful investigations officer with a credible record of serious crimes solved.

By the beginning of 1986, I had ten years' experience of almost continual court appearances in criminal cases behind me. Constant friction with police personnel and lawyers at the State and District Attorneys' offices led me to develop a basic distrust of the authorities responsible for criminal investigations, particularly the police. In this case too, on the basis of the news items that happened to catch my eye, I began to feel distinctly uneasy, and to view the 'Ivan the Terrible affair' as another of those innumerable acts of folly perpetrated by the establishment. However my reaction was just the way one feels about any other irritating newspaper report. I put the matter out of mind – though not for long.

At the end of April O'Connor returned to Israel; once again he was the focus of media attention, and once again I found a certain fascination with reports about the case. At a press conference given by O'Connor, it was said that certain survivors from the Treblinka death camp had given evidence indicating that Ivan the Terrible was killed in the revolt that erupted at the camp on 2 August 1943. But among the plethora of reports and interviews, I read that when John Demjanjuk was extradited to Israel, another order was pending against him – a deportation order from the United States to the Soviet Union. In other words, if he had not been extradited to Israel, Demjanjuk would have been sent straight to the 'socialist paradise' of the Soviet Union. This fact bothered me, for I realized that if Demjanjuk had been deported to Russia in February 1986, within two months at the most his body would have swung from a Soviet gallows. It seems that the Israeli application for his extradition was not out of concern that the man identified as Ivan the Terrible might continue to live a peaceful life in Seven Hills, a suburb of Cleveland, Ohio, while the blood of his victims cried out from the earth; but that the sole purpose of getting Demjanjuk handed over to Israel was to conduct a show-trial.

Israel's attitude to the trying of Nazi criminals is astonishing. The state of the Jewish people, of whom more than one-third were massacred in the Holocaust, was involved in shameful tacit agreements with West Germany, to enable Israel to receive German money in the framework of the 'Reparations Agreement'. Under this agreement (called in German *Wiedergutmachung*), which was signed in 1952, the Israeli government received $800 million from the Germans. The calculation is horrifying in its stark simplicity: $150 per Jewish head.

I recalled the case of Hilmar Schacht, a member of Adolf Hitler's cabinet. In November 1951, the Israeli authorities allowed him to leave the country unharmed after he had spent fourteen hours here, in transit on a journey from India to Germany. Although reports of Schacht's presence in Israel spread throughout the country like wildfire within minutes of his arrival at Lod Airport, the authorities did not make the slightest effort to arrest him and put him behind bars. Negotiations over the Reparations Agreement were then in progress, and our government figured that if Schacht were arrested those talks might come to an abrupt end.

Even where Adolf Eichmann was concerned – the only Nazi criminal tried in Israel since the establishment of the state – it is highly unlikely the trial would ever have taken place were it not for the 'Kastner trial'. During that trial, in 1954, embarrassing facts came to light concerning the behaviour of the socialist leaders of the Zionist movement in respect to the Holocaust of European Jewry. The trial exposed their helplessness and their unforgivable failure to act. Only after the Kastner trial was over, and apparently in order to erase the horrific picture it had painted, was the search for Eichmann launched.

To explain their shameful failure to bring Nazi criminals to trial, the Israeli authorities tend to advance the pretext that no state would agree to extradite Nazi criminals to Israel; particularly not Germany, where thousands of those responsible for the massacre of European Jews live out their lives in peace. But the state of Israel has proved that when it is truly determined, it does not need the acquiescence of any country. The capture of Eichmann in Argentina is a case in point. More recently, the kidnapping by Mossad of Mordecai Vanunu, who had exposed Israeli nuclear secrets abroad, made a mockery of the authorities' repeated claim that it is vital to get the consent of the state in which the criminal happens to be hiding.

These thoughts simmered in my mind, until it became increasingly clear to me that it was not a wish to see justice done to the murderers of the Jewish people that was behind the plea for the extradition of John Demjanjuk – nine years after the gruesome crimes attributed to him had become known to the Israeli authorities. The one and only purpose of this move was to conduct a special 'Israeli-style' show-trial, to teach Israeli children the story of the Holocaust and heighten 'Holocaust awareness' among the public. And all this was to be achieved by means of putting in the dock, and then hanging, a retired mechanic from a Ford automobile plant. The opportunity was supplied by a Treblinka survivor, called to identify another Treblinka guard in 1976, who had pointed to Demjanjuk's photograph and unexpectedly named him as Ivan the Terrible.

I was still preoccupied with the Billion-Shekel Robbery, where I had discovered defects in the procedures of identifying the accused. Throughout my ten years of work, I had not come across a single instance when Israel Police had conducted a proper photo spread in the absence of a defence lawyer on behalf of the suspect. Furthermore, whenever I challenged the admissibility and evidential value of such photo spreads, I was able to persuade the court that they carried no weight whatsoever. The most recent was the case of the Billion-Shekel Robbery.

One day, mulling over the Ivan the Terrible story, it occurred to me that it was highly unlikely that, in the case of Demjanjuk, Israel Police would conduct a fair photo spread with no defence lawyer being present, given that this basic right had been denied to so many ordinary, petty criminals. They would not grant this right to the man they suspected of being Ivan the Terrible from Treblinka. Therefore it seemed inconceivable to me that the evidence against Demjanjuk would carry any legal weight. The mysterious involvement of the Soviet Union – which hoped to destroy the good (and anti-Soviet) relations between the Jewish and Ukrainian communities in North America – only intensified this bleak view.

It suddenly occurred to me that perhaps I should join Demjanjuk's defence team. Why should I not try to undermine this shameful spectacle that the authorities were planning to mount? As I turned this crazy idea over and over in my mind, I could see no reason not to put out feelers, to see which way the wind was blowing.

In mid-May, on my way to the Tel Aviv District Court with my partner Doron Beckerman, I asked him bluntly: 'What would you think if I undertook the defence of Demjanjuk? Instead of the wretched show-trial planned by the authorities, I'd give them a new Kastner trial. I'd make them so ashamed they'd wish they'd never got themselves into this business.' I elaborated my thoughts. As far as I can remember, Doron gave a non-committal reply. But I noticed that he did not seem at all surprised by the idea itself. Doron has known me well since I was thirteen, and he must have seen immediately that my analysis of the case tallied with my general views about the activities and motivations of our establishment.

Towards the end of May, the press gradually reduced its coverage of the Demjanjuk case. The summer recess of the courts was approaching, and I was increasingly absorbed by thoughts of exotic places in the Far East, where I was planning to spend the vacation months of July and August. I can put up with my continual feuds with the state prosecutors, the arrogance of police personnel and a lot of 'pestering' from my clients, their families and peculiar friends only if every few months I can cut myself off, far far away from my professional work. During such trips I do not even phone my office, for what is the point of staying on a wonderful, frick island such as Borakai in the Philippines if you don't get right away from your work? When I am in Borakai, my work seems trivial, irrelevant, even annoying. And yet, even during the two wonderful months I spent in the Far East, the Demjanjuk affair refused to stay out of my thoughts. Gradually I came round to the view that I must try to get involved and join the defence team.

When I returned to Israel early in September, I caught a severe cold and sore throat. I had to stay in bed for ten days and again found myself preoccupied with the Demjanjuk case. I realized that his defence could not possibly be conducted without an Israeli attorney, and that most criminal lawyers were too conformist, too inclined to play safe, to undertake an adventure like this. I gathered from news reports that O'Connor had not yet managed to find an Israeli attorney to work with him. I felt that I had the necessary chutzpah and determination, and that my chances of getting on to the case were pretty good.

A few days after I returned to my office, I asked Tzvia Weiss, who is in charge of everything but legal work there, to ask the Ministry of Justice where she might find O'Connor, but without revealing that she was enquiring on my behalf. To her total astonishment, I explained that I intended to look into the possibility of joining the defence in the imminent trial of Demjanjuk. Tzvia said straight out that she had strong reservations about this new 'madness' plotted by her boss. She declared that she would refuse to do any work connected with the case; and even if she personally were to agree to do so, her family and friends would not allow her to. But after a silence she said, with a glimmer of understanding, 'Only a madman like you could think up such a crazy idea.'

Towards the end of September, O'Connor again returned to Israel.

Despite her threats, Tzvia found out that he was staying at the American Colony Hotel in East Jerusalem. I was later to spend the best part of fourteen months at that hotel. When O'Connor had finally been ousted from the position of defence attorney, the Demjanjuk family would joke that there were two good things O'Connor had obtained during the five years he was their lawyer: Sheftel and the American Colony. The hotel is indeed a delight, and greatly helped me survive the tension and tempestuous events of the long months of the trial.

Seven months after he was brought to Israel, on 29 September 1986, Demjanjuk was at last indicted; only after the court, in one of many hearings on requests for extension of remand, stated that it would refuse to grant any further extensions if no indictment were filed against him.

Now that I had discovered how to get in touch with O'Connor, and there was an indictment, doubts began to assail me. Was this really what I wanted to do? Was it right for a nationalist Israeli like myself to undertake the defence in a case in which the accused was charged with playing a major role in the massacre and destruction of one-quarter of the Polish Jewish population? Was it conceivable that I, who had read books, articles and the poems of Zeev Jabotinsky (the great Zionist leader) from the age of eight, would undertake such an assignment? What about my family? My mother had two sisters and one brother. One of her sisters, Fania, used to live in an apartment in Tel Aviv. Though they were relatively well off (even possessing a car), she and her husband decided, in August 1939, to return to Poland. For all we know, that journey may have ended at Treblinka: all trace of them was lost. Whatever their precise fate, there is no doubt they were murdered in the Holocaust. My maternal grandmother had thirteen brothers and sisters. Each was married and had many children, a total of approximately a hundred. Yet after the Holocaust, fewer than ten survived. How could these anguished feelings tally with undertaking the defence of this Ukrainian goy who was charged with such heinous crimes?

Conflicting thoughts raced around my mind, and I was painfully aware of the gulf between theoretical deliberations and actually taking the practical measures to which such deliberations lead. My doubts increased, but finally I became annoyed with my pathetic emotionalism about my family's fate in the Holocaust: What you are about to do is in no way tantamount to denying the Holocaust, I said to myself; nor are you going to defend Ivan the Terrible. What you are going to do is to defend a goy – not just a goy, but a Ukrainian goy – who for the past ten years has been vigorously denying that he is Ivan the Terrible. Furthermore there is no realistic probability that the police could possibly have any valid and convincing evidence to disprove his innocence. *Because* so many members of your family were massacred by the Nazis, you are duty-bound to join the defence team on the case. What the authorities plan to stage is a cynical show-trial, and that would indeed be a desecration of the memory of your family. So no more cold feet, Yorichka [that is my parents' nickname for me, and the one I use in my innermost thoughts]: pick up the phone and be a man; do what you, with your character, your concept of truth, peculiar as it may be, know perfectly well to be your duty.

I decided to pick up the phone, but stopped before it connected. This time it was not concern over my strategy, but tactics. I thought that if I simply offered myself as defence attorney, O'Connor, and especially Demjanjuk and his family, might well suspect that I had come not to help them but to foil their efforts. Who knows how much anti-Semitic venom lurked in the souls of the people to whom I was about to offer my services? I might fail completely in the initial phone conversation, and that would put an end to the whole idea. What then was to be done? I pondered the question for several days without arriving at a satisfactory answer.

Meanwhile Yom Kippur was approaching. No hearings take place in Israeli courts the day before Yom Kippur. There was no pressing work to be done at my office, so I thought this was a good opportunity to visit the Ayalon Prison and meet clients incarcerated there whose appeals were pending before the Supreme Court. I handed the duty sergeant the list of prisoners I wanted to see, and entered the canteen to wait for them to be brought in.

As I was walking through the canteen, whom did I see but Mark O'Connor himself. A sentence flashed through my mind with which my mother used to needle me: '*Seichel host du nisht, ober mazel host du vi a goy*' ('You don't have much brain, but at least you have the good luck of a goy'). At that moment I sensed with absolute certainty that I would appear as a defence attorney in the case of John Demjanjuk.

Without thinking I said *shalom* to him, and he replied with a polite *shalom*, and we shook hands. I sat down by him and he asked whether I knew who he was. I replied that one could hardly open a newspaper or watch television without seeing his handsome face. O'Connor asked me what I was doing in the prison. 'Apparently the same as you,' I replied, 'I've come to visit clients.' O'Connor said he understood I was a lawyer.

'Correct,' I replied. 'And my only area of specialization is in criminal cases.' O'Connor then went on to ask me whether I didn't have reservations about talking to him, since he was defence attorney for the man accused of the murder of nearly a million Jews. 'You do not relate to the defence attorney as to his client,' I replied – an answer that greatly pleased him.

While we were talking, my clients were brought in. I decided to use this meeting with them to make an impression on O'Connor. As soon as they arrived, I shook hands with them and went out to the small anteroom to ask the duty sergeant – whom I had known for ten years – to delay O'Connor's meeting with Demjanjuk for the next half-hour, and make sure I was served two cups of coffee, at fifteen-minute intervals, while talking to my clients. I explained that I needed time to talk to O'Connor before he met his own client. The duty sergeant gave me an understanding smile and said: 'For you, Sheftel – whatever you say...' I went back to the canteen, shook hands with O'Connor and said that if he was still in the prison when I had finished talking to my clients – of course he would be – I'd be delighted to continue our conversation.

The show began. One after another my clients approached my table, and with each of them I spoke with very decisive facial and manual gestures. The duty sergeant served me cups of coffee at the intervals requested. I noticed the curious and admiring glances cast by O'Connor.

It took me about forty minutes to finish with my clients. Then I went over to O'Connor, and before I could open my mouth he said, 'You must be a big shot.' He began to ask me about my work and I told him in considerable detail about representing Meyer Lansky, and mentioned that I had appeared in many cases in which the principal legal question was one of identification. O'Connor asked for my card. 'Even if your client is indeed the monster he is made out to be – and that is very far from certain – the pleasure of meeting you was all mine,' I said. I gave him my card and we shook hands warmly and agreed to get in touch again immediately after Yom Kippur.

Two days later, O'Connor phoned me at home asking whether I did not regret giving him my card. Once more I reassured him, but said I was surprised to hear from him so soon. O'Connor said he had to leave the country in a few days, and would very much like to meet me before then to discuss the possibility of my joining the defence team as the Israeli attorney. I could hardly conceal my delight, but in a matter-of-fact tone suggested he bring to our meeting the pictures used in the photo spreads; a photocopy of what I called the 'Soviet rag', by which I meant the famous Travniki document; and a copy of the indictment. O'Connor asked me what I wanted all these exhibits for. Feeling pretty confident, I said it would all become clear to him when we met.

I hardly closed my eyes that night; my head was full to bursting with different scenarios and ways of handling my conversation with the American attorney. By dawn I had mapped out my path, and knew just how I would conduct myself.

I set out for the meeting at the hotel in my Porsche 914. As I arrived, I spotted O'Connor waiting for me at the entrance. I waved and honked the horn to make sure he noticed my car, and parked right in front of the hotel. As we shook hands, O'Connor voiced his admiration, and was impressed when I told him it was a Porsche.

We entered the magnificent lobby with its arches, illuminations and oriental carpets. Without preliminaries I asked O'Connor whether he had brought the documents I requested. He drew out a sheet with eight photos from among the note-filled pages of his pad. 'I gave the indictment to someone who has not returned it,' he said, adding, 'and the only copy of the Travniki document available is in my office in the United States.'

At that stage I had confidence in, and a great deal of respect for, O'Connor, convinced that I was dealing with a serious, erudite, reliable and honest attorney; I believed him unhesitatingly. But with hindsight, it seems very likely that he did have both the charge sheet and a photocopy of the Travniki document with him. He simply did not want to show me much of the important information concerning the case at such an early stage of our acquaintance. O'Connor drew my attention to the sheet of photos, saying that all the photo-spread identifications in the case had been conducted on the basis of these. I could not believe my eyes. Not even in my wildest imaginings would I have believed it possible that Israel Police would use such a biased set of pictures for the identification of a man thirty-five years after the crimes attributed to him were committed, knowing that just one finger pointed at his photo could place a noose around his neck.

The photos of Demjanjuk and the only other 'target picture' – of Fyodor Federenko – were next to each other. They were twice the size of any of the other photos, and brighter and clearer. In the other stills, facial features were hardly distinguishable. Demjanjuk's was the only one in which one could clearly see a round-faced, almost totally bald man. The other photos were of men with full hair. Everything was done in this combination to focus attention on to the picture of Demjanjuk, short of a caption actually stating *This is Ivan the Terrible*. Later on I learned, to my great astonishment, that in spite of all this most of the Treblinka survivors (forty altogether) who were shown this set of photos did not identify Demjanjuk's portrait as that of Ivan the Terrible.

My assumptions concerning the identification procedures in the case of Demjanjuk thus proved to be correct. I lost no time in sharing my thoughts with O'Connor. First, I said, these photos, the very core of the case, showed without doubt that Demjanjuk was identified through improper procedures; and secondly, 'If the defence, from the beginning of the trial, admits to all the facts in the indictment, apart from the identity of John Demjanjuk as Ivan the Terrible, and if I were given the chance to meet Demjanjuk for a few hours of conversation and become convinced that he isn't lying when he claims he never set foot in the Treblinka extermination camp – if these two conditions were met, I would not hesitate to join the defence. But do not delude yourself that, even if Demjanjuk were to make an explicit admission of all the facts, the evidence would then focus solely on the question of identity. The Israeli authorities don't see this as a criminal case, but plan a show-trial in order to teach the public – particularly the young – a lesson about the Holocaust. You should know that, unlike usual criminal court proceedings, where there is no necessity to prove facts which have been explicitly admitted, in this trial indisputable facts will have to be substantiated and proved in court. When the authorities rent a theatre to stage a trial, nothing the defence can do must be allowed to ruin the show. To justify the expense of hiring the premises for this trial, they will feel obliged to spend time on proving facts which no one is disputing.'

O'Connor was taken aback. He liked my analysis and asked if I was not afraid to face a hostile reaction from the public and the media once my position became known. I told him that I had only contempt for cowards and hypocrites who avoid doing what they should out of fear of public opinion. I then gave a detailed description of identification in Israeli law, emphasizing the various defects in the procedures used for Demjanjuk. At the time I knew little about such procedures, but it seemed that many more defects were yet to come to light. I told O'Connor that in every case in which I had achieved the disqualification of identification procedures, the defects I exposed had been minor compared to those already obvious in the procedures for Demjanjuk.

O'Connor was impressed and encouraged. Nevertheless he thought I might still change my mind. 'It is not my style to back out,' I emphasized.

I led the conversation to more casual subjects, to try to impress him with other aspects of my personality and my working life. I sensed that he was listening attentively and I was making an excellent impression. I came away with the feeling that he was an exceptionally gifted lawyer, and a sensitive, kind, restrained person. When we said our goodbyes after two hours it was very cordially, and we resolved to stay in close and frequent contact.

I had no doubt that my two meetings with O'Connor had been successful far beyond my expectations, and would lead directly to my joining the case. I was also pleasantly surprised by the ease and simplicity with which everything had seemed to fall into place.

Two days went by without a sign from O'Connor. I rang the American Colony Hotel, and the receptionist informed me that he had left the country. It had never occurred to me that O'Connor might leave Israel without informing me, or telling me where I fitted in with his plans. It seemed like a slap in the face, but there was nothing I could do about it except wait.

Contrary to appearances, in those months I did not devote most of my time to O'Connor and Demjanjuk, but to the regular work of my office: frequent appearances in the courts; meetings with my clients on remand, in prison or (the more fortunate ones) in my office; writing appeals; and all the usual activities which fill the days of a busy criminal lawyer.

Three weeks later, in mid-November, just as I was beginning to kick myself for my over-generous evaluation of O'Connor and my imagined successes, he returned to Israel in the usual blaze of publicity. I decided to wait a few days to hear from him, and make no move to re-establish contact. And indeed, within a couple of days he phoned me, starting the conversation in his polite manner, with no hint that he was aware of the effect of his sudden disappearance – as if such strange, not to say rude, behaviour were perfectly normal.

I arrived at my third meeting with O'Connor racked with doubts. But he gave me a warm and cheerful welcome, and introduced me to his wife, Joyce. After some polite conversation, Joyce got up and left; she had a great deal of work to do, O'Connor explained.

Without beating about the bush, O'Connor now asked me what fee I was asking for my services. I was astonished. Though I had given some thought to the matter after our second meeting, the timing and manner of the question took me by surprise. I thought O'Connor's sudden departure from the country without telling me meant he had no serious desire for my participation; yet here he was, suddenly springing upon me, 'How much will the pleasure cost me?' Since I had already reached a decision concerning my fee – that it must be neither too high nor too low – I overcame my surprise and blurted out the amount.

I must mention, in parentheses, that all kinds of guesses appeared in the press concerning my fee, with crude hints that money was my principal reason for taking up the case. I have never defended an Israeli Jew without charging a fee and it certainly never occurred to me to defend a Ukrainian goy for nothing. But I can say definitively, with a clear conscience, that it was not money that motivated me, neither when I first had the idea of joining Demjanjuk's defence, nor at any other time.

O'Connor (though, as anticipated, he said it was somewhat high) accepted the sum I mentioned, complimenting me on the logic behind my demand, so that I immediately began to wonder whether I was asking too little. I told him I did not expect it to be paid all at once; it could be paid in monthly instalments.

I now went on to expand some of the ideas that had been formulating in my mind. I explained the importance of the testimony to be given by Dr Arad, Director of Yad Vashem, and of the defence's response to this testimony, which would be confined solely to describing facts that were not in dispute. It was essential for the defence not to allow his testimony to be given. In other words, it had to be stressed in every possible way that the court's approach to this testimony would determine whether the hearings were to become a much-publicized show-trial or be conducted in accordance with accepted Israeli legal practice. I suggested certain practical steps we could take to back up this demand.

O'Connor expressed his appreciation for my ideas and the original thinking behind them. I went on elaborating my views, and after two hours we got up to go our separate ways. O'Connor promised that 'this time really' he would keep in constant touch with me. Ostensibly it seemed as successful a meeting as the previous ones, but I was sceptical about this now.

A few days later O'Connor phoned to say that the first court hearing was scheduled for 26 November, just a week away. He was referring to the arraignment, when the accused is called to plead guilty or not, and the defence can argue any preliminary pleading. At that hearing the accused also states his alibi, if he has one, and must declare whether he objects to the submission of statements he made to the police in the course of his interrogation. O'Connor said he would like to meet me as soon as possible. We decided to meet for dinner at the American Colony the next day.

O'Connor's first question was what he should do at that hearing. I was surprised, as it seemed rather strange, so close to a hearing that might prove to be of crucial importance, that the lawyer who had been handling the case for over four years did not know what to do. But I said to myself, What do you want from the poor guy? If you were in a similar situation in the United States, would you know what to do? So I began a detailed explanation of the nature, status and purpose of the initial hearing and the legal procedures characteristic of these occasions in Israel. I advised him to seize the opportunity at this hearing to admit all the facts contained in the indictment, apart from those relating to the identity of Demjanjuk as Ivan the Terrible. In light of this confession, he would have to stress, courteously, that the court should instruct the prosecution to call only those witnesses whose testimony was about the identification of Demjanjuk as Ivan the Terrible. I advised him to be ready to spell out Demjanjuk's alibi which, I had no doubt, he knew well by now. As to Demjanjuk's statements to Israel Police, I suggested he ask to present his position on their submission at a later stage, as he had not yet had a chance to study them thoroughly. He was grateful for my advice and said he would act accordingly.

By this time it had been reported that the hearing of evidence would begin on 19 January 1987, and that the judges would be Dov Levin, a Supreme Court justice, as presiding judge; and Judges Zvi Tal and Dalia Dorner, both judges at the Jerusalem District Court. (The composition of the bench was exceptional, since only such a bench could hear cases under the Law for the Punishment of Nazis and their Collaborators.) The trial was due to start in two months' time, and even if O'Connor decided to hire my services I would not have the time to prepare adequately for it. For I had not even seen any of the material in the file, apart from the photo-spread pictures.

I told O'Connor that I did not want to rush him but he ought to make up his mind about my services as quickly as possible. It would not be fair for me to accept substantial fees if I could not be of any real help, not having enough time to study the evidence thoroughly. O'Connor replied that the trouble was that the Demjanjuk family still had doubts as to whether there was any need to hire an Israeli attorney. He was pressing them to do so, and a little more time was needed. Only later was I to learn that in fact the very opposite was true: it was O'Connor who was resisting the demand of the family to retain an Israeli attorney at once.

At the first hearing, O'Connor put up a ludicrous performance. In fact he did not put a single coherent sentence together. I attributed this to a feeling of vulnerability at appearing in a foreign court with no one on hand to advise him. In the televised footage, Demjanjuk appeared to be in acute pain, almost weeping in front of the judges. The whole scene was an embarrassment.

A few days after the initial hearing, reports began to appear in the press saying that O'Connor was in contact with several lawyers recommended to him by the Jerusalem Bar Association. One morning I was listening to a radio interview with Dr Gershon Orion, lecturer at the Law Faculty of Bar-Ilan University, and learned to my amazement that he had been appointed by O'Connor as the Israeli defence counsel for Demjanjuk. Seized by rage, astonishment and disappointment, I determined not to seek any further contact with O'Connor. After all, he had the right to hire anyone he wished, and if he thought it right to act so rudely he was certainly not worthy of any approach from me. If that was the way O'Connor was going to behave, I would be a great deal better off not working with him, however great the disappointment might be. Doron and Tzvia both thought this ended any possibility of my appearing as defence counsel in the case.

But the same evening another volte-face occurred. O'Connor rang me at home and began with an apology and flattery; for the first time he called me by my nickname Shefy (at our first meeting at the prison I had told him my friends call me Shefy – a nickname that even appears on my card, in both Hebrew and English). He explained that the business with Gershon Orion was not serious, and he only intended the latter to assist him in an appeal he had lodged against the decision to keep Demjanjuk in custody until the end of proceedings. I then asked why he believed Orion would be able to give him better counsel on this appeal than I could. He said he thought I was too busy and that he had taken up enough of my time. He did not feel comfortable about intruding further on my time before we had come to an official agreement on my terms and fee. I thought this a satisfactory argument.

O'Connor added that he was due to leave Israel for the US at once, and would contact me immediately upon his return, when we could at last draw up an agreement on my participation in the case.

When I told Doron and Tzvia of this latest development, both were dubious. Doron had begun to suspect O'Connor of being unreliable and rather distasteful, and came increasingly to mistrust his character and motives. In this he was ahead of me by more than three months. Only much later was I to learn from John Gill, the attorney who had assisted O'Connor in the US at various stages of the proceedings from 1984 onwards, that O'Connor had refused to ensure that an Israeli attorney would appear beside him. For this purpose he misled the Demjanjuk family and everyone else connected with the case. But his plans went awry. On 19 December 1986, the Travniki document was brought to Israel through the good offices of oil magnate Armand Hammer and Shimon Peres, then Foreign Minister. O'Connor panicked at this development and hastily approached Gill, asking him to come in on the case itself, concentrating on all aspects concerning the Travniki document. Gill made his acceptance conditional upon O'Connor hiring 'that same Shefy' of whom he had told him so much. At the time, of course, I knew nothing of the real intentions of Mark O'Connor.

The Travniki document was immediately leaked to the media by the prosecution. A photocopy of it appeared in the papers, in flagrant violation of the *sub judice* rule. Three days later, on 22 December,

O'Connor rang me from Tel Aviv to tell me that he had just arrived in Israel and wished to come and see me immediately in my office, together with advocate Gill, so that we could come to a final agreement. It was not hard to work out that O'Connor had brought Gill along to hear his opinion before signing any agreement with me.

I began in a matter-of-fact tone: 'It would be inconceivable for the hearings in the case to begin on 19 January as scheduled. We have less than a month to prepare, and I haven't a clue about the material in the file, apart from my casual glance at the photos used in the identification procedures. I think we could get a postponement without difficulty, even though the bench, particularly Justice Levin, won't be too pleased at the idea. The judges know enough about the case to understand O'Connor's difficulties in finding an Israeli lawyer. It should also be clear to the court that no attorney could possibly master the huge quantity of material well enough to be able to represent Demjanjuk effectively within such a short period of time.' My joining the defence team officially ought to provide a convincing pretext for the motion to postpone, which should be lodged without delay. O'Connor explained that he had already filed such a motion, though not for my reasons, and it was to be heard on 29 December. I was delighted, since it would be no problem to add the fact that I was joining the case as another reason for the request.

I repeated my opinion on the best line of defence, stressing that we should do all in our power to ensure that the only question to be decided was the identity of the accused. I added that experience had shown however that the chance of acquittal in trials of this nature is entirely theoretical. When I had finished I turned to O'Connor and said, 'As far as I am concerned, the very latest date for drawing up an official and binding agreement for my services is this weekend' (our conversation took place at the beginning of the week). 'Otherwise, even if the trial is postponed, I won't have time to prepare myself properly. If I am not prepared, at least minimally, there will be no Sheftel in the case.'

O'Connor agreed, and we went over the terms once more. Afterwards O'Connor and Gill drove me home, and we talked and joked about what awaited us; I stressed my expectation of uproar in court on the 29th.

At about one a.m. on Christmas Eve, the phone rang. Over the years I've got used to phone calls at strange hours. Intuition told me that this was O'Connor, and that something of great significance had happened. I picked up the phone and O'Connor's voice said: 'For reasons I cannot reveal on the phone, Gill and I have to leave the country immediately for the United States, and we won't even be able to return for the hearing on our motion for a delay; I've made up my mind to hire your services, and you are to appear for the defence at that hearing.' I asked him whether he had drawn up a contract as agreed, but he said no, and suggested we meet at five a.m. at the airport; his flight was due to take off at seven-thirty. It all seemed crazy and sudden, but I said I would show up for the meeting, adding that he should bring a power-of-attorney with him so that I could appear on his behalf. He promised to do so.

I arrived at the airport five minutes earlier than we had agreed and headed for the TWA counter to wait for O'Connor. He arrived at five-thirty and said the reason for his sudden departure was the urgent need to meet elderly alibi witnesses who might die at any moment; he wanted at least to get affidavits from them. All this he said in the presence of John Gill, who kept smiling ironically at me. I thought he was trying to encourage me, but he told me three months later how shocked he had been by O'Connor's lies, and he had instinctively winked to signal that the man was bluffing. When O'Connor said he had not brought the power-of-attorney with him, I asked Gill to draw one up there and then, and have O'Connor sign it. Gill did the best he could, scrawling a few lines on a piece of yellow paper – hardly the kind of document that I could present as power-of-attorney in order to appear on O'Connor's behalf. It was applicable to a single court hearing – something I insisted upon, as I most certainly did not wish to be obligated to any commitment beyond that. Imperfect as it was, it empowered me to seek a postponement of the start of the hearings.

I made some points clear to O'Connor: 'I will appear in court only if you promise me that you will pay my first instalment by 8 January, by banker's draft.' (Though I still put my trust in O'Connor at the time, my trust in a banker's draft was considerably greater.) 'The cheque must reach my office immediately, together with an agreement about the terms of my engagement, with your signature. Otherwise you will not hear from me again.'

I felt I had perhaps been a little too harsh, so I tried to soften the impression somewhat (without appearing to diminish my resolve). I told Gill and O'Connor a famous Jewish joke: twenty minutes before the start of the Sabbath, the cantor asked the rabbi for a five-thousand-zloty loan; and the rabbi gave it to him. Twenty minutes after the Sabbath ended, the cantor returned the entire sum to the rabbi, who asked in astonishment, 'Why did you ask for the loan in the first place? After all, you've not been able to do anything with the money.' The cantor replied, 'I just sing better when there are five thousand zlotys in my pocket.' They both laughed, and O'Connor agreed to all my demands.

I added another request – that he send me all the evidence dealing with identification proceedings by express mail, as well as all the verdicts pertaining to Demjanjuk in the US. He said he would.

I was taking a tremendous risk in agreeing to appear in court under such circumstances. First of all, I was presenting myself for the first time as defence counsel for a man perceived by one and all as the personification of Satan himself. Even now there was still the possibility that nothing would come of all this, and I would be exposed to derision and contempt without ever actually appearing in the case proper. Second, even the hearing on a postponement could be a great embarrassment for me, because hardly any information on the case was at my disposal at the time. Third, I had not yet met Demjanjuk, and was determined not to act as his defence counsel if he left me with the slightest impression that he had actually been at Treblinka. However, it would be far from easy to withdraw on these grounds once I had appeared on his behalf at an official court session.

Fourth, Justice Levin would be delighted to learn that at last the problem of an Israeli attorney ready to appear in the case had been solved. (Although not required by law, an Israeli attorney was crucial; it would be unthinkable to conduct a trial of this nature without one.) He would undoubtedly do everything possible to bind me to the case irrevocably, to make sure this problem did not arise again.

Fifth, I had agreed to appear at an official hearing before receiving any of my fee, which could lead to considerable difficulties concerning payment. Finally, I might fail to gain a postponement, and O'Connor would regard this as a sign of poor performance and happily forgo any further appearance of mine in the case. All these difficulties presented themselves to me straight away, and I began to plan ways to overcome them.

I decided to approach Michael Shaked, acting head of the prosecuting team, to tell him that I would appear at the postponement hearing and discuss the possibility of a joint request for a postponement. I rang him that morning and explained the situation. He was very courteous, and agreed to meet the following day. I asked him to keep my involvement secret from the media. He promised to do so – but that did not stop the news from spreading like wildfire. That evening the news agencies and radio correspondents began to phone me, seeking confirmation. I refused to answer them, but the item was broadcast on radio and television that evening, and appeared in all the dailies next morning. The media onslaught had begun.

Given all the criticism I had directed against the police and the State and District Attorneys' offices over the years, I never expected any sympathy from them. Despite the short time between my phone call to

Shaked and my scheduled meeting with him, he was sure to hear a good deal of malicious gossip about me. I thought it best therefore to touch on this at the beginning of our meeting.

We met at the Justice Ministry offices in Jerusalem. I opened by saying, 'I am sure you've heard all kinds of weird stories about me in the last twenty-four hours. I'd like you to know that they are misleading. I've never *started* a quarrel with anybody in my life and all my quarrels, even the worst of them, have been in response to intolerable behaviour towards me. I can assure you that if you treat me fairly, there won't be any problems between us. On the contrary, we can enjoy a productive and stimulating working relationship.'

Shaked, visibly surprised, replied that he would be glad to co-operate with me. I asked how much time he thought I would need to get a reasonable grip on the evidence in the file. About a month, was his reply. I asked him whether he would be prepared to join me in the request to get the hearing postponed till the beginning of March. He said that, while he would not explicitly join the motion, he would put no obstacles in my way and 'it will be all right'. I let him know that if the court did not agree to postpone the start of hearings until at least mid-February, I would not be in a position to join the defence.

I understood that the excitement surrounding the case would make it impossible to concentrate, and that extremely difficult days lay ahead. I would have to give up my annual skiing holiday in late January or early February, in Romania. But then suddenly I decided that I would go after all. I would take all the material with me, spend only two hours a day on the slopes and devote the rest of the time in the calm of the village of Poiana in the Carpathian mountains to studying the case far from the madding media crowd at home.

I left for Jerusalem on the 29th, preoccupied all the way with the court session, the questions likely to be put by the judges and my answers. I decided to drop altogether the unconvincing arguments that O'Connor had presented in his motion, and concentrate solely on my own belated co-option to the defence team. From time to time the holiday in Romania pushed itself to the front of my mind. When I reached the Jerusalem District Court, I was met by dozens of reporters and cameramen, and I rather liked it. The hearing was to take place in the chambers of one of the judges, and on such occasions sessions are usually held in the presence of the attorneys alone. But I saw at once that this horde of reporters, or at least a great many of them, were about to crowd into the chambers for the hearing.

I swallowed the protest that sprang to my lips, for the presence of the media might actually be helpful in getting the judges to accept my plea, particularly since the request was so well justified. I entered the chambers with Shaked and several other prosecutors from the State Attorney's office. Behind the table sat Justice Levin, flanked by Judges Dorner and Tal. My glance fell upon Justice Levin. I had appeared before him dozens of times before, and it occurred to me that he would have been a lot happier if someone else had entered his chambers as defence counsel in this case.

Levin greeted me with a courteous *shalom* and invited us to take our places at the table facing the judges. He began by asking me what my precise status was in appearing at the session. I showed him the scrap of paper from O'Connor and said I had been given power of attorney to participate on his behalf for that session only, but the idea was to continue to appear in the case as the Israeli defence counsel alongside O'Connor. This had already been agreed between O'Connor and me, and I would receive all the relevant documents by 8 January 1987.

As anticipated, Justice Levin responded by saying he was prepared to appoint me right away as defence counsel on behalf of the court; this was meant to bind me to the case so that I wouldn't be able to drop out of it later without his consent, even if I wanted to. For that very reason (and because on principle I never act as a court-appointed, hence court-paid, attorney) I turned the offer down. Justice Levin then asked me to state the reasons for my request.

'First of all,' I began, 'as a Jew and an Israeli, it is a fundamental condition, as far as I am concerned, that the defence admits to all the facts in the indictment, apart from those facts that pertain to the question of the identity of Demjanjuk as Ivan the Terrible. This is also accepted by O'Connor, and, in so far as it is up to the defence, this would make it possible greatly to curtail the duration of the trial.' I went on, 'The case is apparently so complex that three prosecution lawyers are needed to answer the simple questions posed by Justice Levin. That being so, in order to adequately represent Demjanjuk, at least two defence attorneys are obviously necessary, and one an Israeli.

'Even though I am ready to do my utmost to study the case from all its aspects, for me to be able to do this I must seek a postponement of the hearings. In the opinion of my learned friend attorney Shaked, who is very well versed in the case, I need at least one month beyond the date originally scheduled in order to master the material reasonably. I therefore request that the trial be postponed to mid-March. Given the importance of the case, and the extensive publicity to which I am likely to be exposed because of my participation, I cannot possibly join the defence team if I am not adequately prepared. And I cannot possibly be prepared unless the hearings are postponed.' I repeated that I was confident that by 8 January I would be able to file a power-of-attorney on behalf of O'Connor for the case (whose number I now learned for the first time: Criminal File 373/86 at the Jerusalem District Court, sitting as the Special Court, under the Law for the Punishment of Nazis and their Collaborators, 1950). Justice Levin asked us all to leave his chambers, and said that he would announce the court's decision in a few minutes.

During the recess I thought of the ski slopes at Poiana and the growing likelihood that I would shortly spend a holiday there with my friends. Soon we were summoned back to the chambers, and told that the trial hearings would begin on 16 February 1987. I ran at once down to the payphone and joyfully told Tzvia that Poiana was saved. I went back to take my leave of the others and told Shaked that I would stay in touch with him. In very high spirits I drove back to Tel Aviv, and within a few minutes heard a full report of the hearing on the radio news bulletin.

That evening, I had a phone call from O'Connor, who had given no sign of life since leaving Israel. He congratulated me on my success and said that he had been briefed by a reporter who'd told him I'd made a creditable appearance. I asked whether he had sent me the material I requested. He said he would, within two days. I told him that as far as the court was concerned if I did not have his power-of-attorney by 8 January I would be off the case, and demanded that he mail the necessary papers without delay and maintain daily contact with me. This he promised, as usual.

The time had now come to put my thoughts in order. It seemed that most of the details were being taken care of and I had no doubt that the documents and the first payment would arrive on time. There was only one thing that kept me from giving my final consent: I had not yet met Demjanjuk. For the first time since I first entertained the thought of becoming his defence counsel, the decision was entirely in my hands.

Another two days went by with no word from O'Connor. I phoned his office in Buffalo, and his wife answered. When I identified myself and asked whether O'Connor was there, she asked me to wait. I could hear her talking to him; he was instructing her to say he was out of the office, which she promptly did. I asked her very politely to tell him to contact me immediately.

After hanging up, I realized that if I waited for O'Connor to send me the evidence I might never get to know the first thing about the case. So I decided to go directly to Shaked, explain the embarrassing situation and ask for his help. Next day I phoned his office and asked whether he would be kind enough to have copies made of the identification procedures. I realized that the prosecution had already given all this material to the defence, and that he was under no obligation to grant my request, but I had no alternative. He agreed at once. Over the ensuing months, I was often to thank him for this, and made sure it appeared on the record. We agreed that when I came up to Jerusalem to file the power-of-attorney on 8 January I would collect the material at the Ministry of Justice.

Meanwhile 8 January was drawing near, yet there was no power-of-attorney and no fee agreement; no payment had been made and there was still no word from O'Connor. I called his office again, and again his wife asked me to hold. A few seconds later I heard his voice at last. He apologized for not contacting me, because he had left town to deal with alibi witnesses. He also said he had already sent all the documents and a bank cheque, and that he had no doubt everything would arrive at the time agreed. I suggested he return to Israel as soon as possible since we had to roll up our sleeves and get down to work together.

I was due to meet Shaked at the Ministry of Justice at noon on the 8th; I would have to file the power-of-attorney with the court before then. But by ten that morning I had still received nothing from O'Connor. It never occurred to me to doubt him when he said all the documents had been mailed. I therefore wrote a statement to the court saying O'Connor had told me on the phone that he had mailed the power-of-attorney. I saw no reason not to inform the court that I was ready and willing to join the defence officially.

When I reached the secretariat of the district court, I was told I should contact my office urgently. The long-awaited envelope had arrived. I changed the wording of my statement, handed it over to the secretariat and had Tzvia forward the power-of-attorney to the court. Pleased with developments, I crossed the road and entered the Justice Ministry building. Within a few minutes Shaked handed me a bulky parcel of papers, which I knew was only a small part of the evidence.

As I began to study the evidence I thought of my meeting with Demjanjuk which, under pressure of events, had been somewhat delayed. Now I became increasingly preoccupied with this 'decisive' meeting. I was greatly troubled by fears that I might come away from the meeting with the impression that he was lying shamelessly when he categorically denied that he was Ivan the Terrible. While it appeared perfectly evident, given the identification procedures used, that it would never be possible to prove by accepted legal standards that he *was* Ivan the Terrible, in this particular case that was not enough. Unlike other criminal cases I had handled, the question of whether my client had actually perpetrated the crimes attributed to him was now of cardinal importance to me. Under no circumstances would I have been capable of defending Demjanjuk if I were to sense that he was indeed Ivan the Terrible.

These misgivings, as well as the constant stream of phone calls from journalists, distracted me from concentrating on the evidential material. When I contacted O'Connor – once again he was 'very busy' – I had to remind him that I was still waiting to meet Demjanjuk. I insisted that the meeting should take place as soon as possible, that he should be present, and that it would be best if he would come back to Israel without delay. Time was running out, a great deal had to be done and it could not be accomplished separately in Buffalo and Tel Aviv. We should tackle it together, in Jerusalem. O'Connor promised he would be in Israel on 20 January, with John Gill.

This promise he kept. He contacted me as soon as he arrived and we arranged to meet at the Ayalon Prison. The next day I got into my beautiful, new, dazzling white Porsche 924. When I arrived at the prison to admiring cheers from O'Connor, he made me promise to let him have a drive sometime soon. We entered the prison gate and were soon in the canteen where we had first met. The circle was closed, and I could not resist mentioning it to O'Connor. His response was that that first meeting between us had been his most successful and important encounter since he first came to Israel.

I was calm and concentrated on the imminent meeting. It occurred to me that I might speak to Demjanjuk in Russian; that would enable him to express himself in a language with which he was far more familiar than English, and it would also prevent O'Connor from interrupting too much. While it might not have been polite, there are times when I am prepared to sacrifice courtesy in the name of expediency.

At last we were ushered into the room containing Demjanjuk's cell: a most peculiar room, about six yards long and three wide, divided by grilles set at ten-centimetre intervals. The section furthest from the entrance was Demjanjuk's cell, and the other half the guard-room of his warders, who maintained a twenty-four-hour watch. At all times there had to be at least two guards, the main point being to ensure that the prisoner did not attempt suicide – a possibility that, in my opinion, had never crossed his mind since he was brought to Israel. The toilet and shower were at the far end of the cell behind felt screens, in each of which was cut a large window. Thus the guards could see a part of Demjanjuk's body at all times, even when he was using the toilet or shower; at the same time he had a certain measure of privacy. A lamp in his cell was always lit, so that a video camera could follow his movements at all times. The shape of the room and the bars give an impression of a cage in a zoo; Demjanjuk paced up and down like a caged animal in front of his keepers.

O'Connor introduced us and we sat down at a table attached to the grating – Demjanjuk on one side and us on the other. O'Connor began with a long speech extolling my virtues, calling me 'magic Shefy' (quoting one of the newspaper reports about me). When he had finished enumerating my professional qualifications, adding that I had courage to match, I said he was greatly exaggerating, and switched immediately to Russian, asking whether we might converse in that language. Demjanjuk, taken aback, asked whether I was from the Soviet Union. I said I was not, but was a native Israeli who had been taught Russian by my parents. Demjanjuk said in fairly good Russian, interspersed with Ukrainian words, that he could talk to me in Russian if that was what I wanted.

But O'Connor cut off the conversation, protesting loudly to Demjanjuk that payments due to him had not been made, and that this undermined his ability to conduct the defence. He had heard too many promises from Demjanjuk's family, and seen too little cash. I could hardly believe my ears and saw that Demjanjuk too was astounded. He murmured something about not being able to do anything about it from his prison cell. Then O'Connor reassured him that, despite the financial difficulties, all was going well – particularly where the witnesses for his alibi were concerned. When Demjanjuk asked for more details, O'Connor said he would brief him only when the picture was complete. When I saw that he had said all he wanted, I asked him whether I might proceed, and restarted my conversation with Demjanjuk.

After our talk, which lasted two and a half hours, I came to the following conclusions. First, Demjanjuk was the simplest of individuals, with a quite limited intellectual capacity. He seemed to personify the descriptions I had heard from my mother of the large-limbed, weather-beaten Ukrainian peasants who lived in the villages near Rovno, the town where she was born; so much so that I felt as though I had met this *muzhik* ('peasant') somewhere in the past.

Second, I found that either Demjanjuk had a very bad memory, or was utterly confused. He had difficulty remembering many details about his own life and those of members of his family. I ruled out any possibility that this forgetfulness might be deliberate, because he would simply be incapable of such finesse. Third, while Demjanjuk's head might be filled with prejudices about the Jews, he is no more anti-Semitic than the average east European goy. Fourth, I found that he was so much under the influence of O'Connor as to be emotionally dependent upon him. Fifth, Demjanjuk talked with no hesitation whatsoever about the period from his enrolment in the Red Army in 1941 up to his arrival in the United States in 1952. Yet he would forget many details and become confused even when referring to events in which he had undoubtedly participated, events which he had no reason to pretend not to remember or conceal the truth about.

Sixth and most significant of all, I sensed that he was speaking the truth when he flatly denied the allegation that he was Ivan the Terrible, or that he had ever been to Treblinka. In this he seemed completely plausible, giving a clear impression of honesty and sincerity.

When at last I felt that I could rely on my intuition I took leave of Demjanjuk. On our way out I said to O'Connor, 'Within less than a minute I shall be outside the prison and have both feet planted firmly in this case.' We shook hands warmly and parted. I got into my Porsche, promising O'Connor I'd let him drive it one day.

I felt confident and reassured. It was now definite that I would be defence attorney for the 'phoney Satan' and I felt that my entire professional life had been a preparation for this watershed in my career. I remembered when I was a student, wondering about my career and dreaming of a case that would take me above the mediocrity and dullness of run-of-the-mill law to break into the headlines. 'With very little brain and a great deal of luck', that happened just ten days after I passed my bar exams. In 1976 I represented Sarah Alkanovitz, who was on trial for firing pistol shots into crowds. Her senseless cruelties brought both of us into the headlines. Since then I had appeared in several cases that received extensive media coverage, the most outstanding being Meyer Lansky's. So I was fully aware of the impact of the tremendous press and television coverage that awaited the lawyer who undertook to defend John Demjanjuk. I realized that there would be extraordinary exposure in both the national and international press, and that it would not subside quickly but go on and on, because of the nature of the case. I knew that because of this exposure I would be recognized wherever I went, people would point at me and whisper. I confess I rather liked the idea.

But I also realized that within a few days the publicity in Israel would become negative and hostile, and I was not at all sure that it would fall on deaf ears. In anticipation of malicious attacks and a lynching atmosphere, I resolved to be guided by the motto of Jabotinsky, *'kalt und fest'* ('cool and determined'), throughout the vituperative attacks that lay ahead.

I had reached the outskirts of Tel Aviv when I finally asked myself what the true motive was for my apparently insane decision to represent

Demjanjuk in spite of the considerable risks involved. If not the money or the media coverage or even the 'chance to get into the history books', then what was it all about? Gradually I began to perceive what was a vague feeling for the past few months, and now was sharp and clear: the Demjanjuk case, for a criminal lawyer, had everything, and in generous measure. I realized that if I did play a role in it, mine would be a significant and decisive one.

This case would be the realization of the dreams of any criminal lawyer (anyone who would deny that is deluding himself). Since the three *sine qua non* conditions I had set for my participation in the defence team had been fully met, I was firmly resolved to go ahead. In retrospect, I can say that this was the wisest decision I have ever taken in my life.

2 · Let the Show-Trial Begin

At about midnight on Sunday 15 February, I went up to my room at the American Colony. I had no illusions about being able to sleep.

I can never get to sleep the night before any particularly exciting event. I switched off the reading lamp and closed my eyes, but a confused rush of thoughts crowded my mind. What if I am wrong after all? I thought. What if my intuition is wrong and that Ukrainian goy really is Ivan the Terrible? This notion had never penetrated my consciousness with as much force as on that night. Graphic descriptions of the atrocities perpetrated by that inhuman creature known as Ivan the Terrible sprang to mind, descriptions whose veracity I had never doubted for a moment. And these descriptions came from the mouths of the very people who were to step into the witness box in the coming days, to swear that John Demjanjuk was none other than Ivan the Terrible. For when all is said and done, it was Pinhas Epstein, Eliahu Rosenberg, Josef Charny and the other witnesses who were actually in Treblinka, and if only for that reason are they not more likely to be right than I? If so, would it not be terrible beyond words for me of all people, an ardent admirer of Menachem Begin, to find myself defending Ivan the Terrible – even in error? The thought sent shivers down my spine. I remembered the fiery speeches made by Begin, branding that disgrace we call the 'Reparations Agreement' in the harshest terms. Was it conceivable that the next morning I would get up in court to defend one of the most abhorrent of those involved in the situation which gave rise to the Reparations Agreement?

The image of my aunt Fania, whom I had never met, now flashed before my mind's eye. I saw her slowly walking down the narrow alleys of the ghetto, her glance fixed upon me. In my ears now rang the stark warnings my mother had so often repeated over the past few weeks, 'With your own hands you are about to destroy the successful career you have built up with so much hard work in the past ten years.' The next image to appear was of Justice Levin, looking at me with contempt and disgust. I tossed from side to side, trying to escape the nightmare, but the pictures continued to flash before my eyes. In each of them I looked humiliated, persecuted, helpless, as though my whole world had collapsed. I got up – it was three a.m. I felt weak and confused, and wished that morning would never come. I went back to bed, clenched my fists and said to myself, Enough of this wallowing. Nothing unpleasant has happened so far, yet you are lying here in despair and gone all to pieces. If that's how you react before anything has happened, how are you going to face up to things that actually do happen? In such a mood you would never have coped with any of the difficulties you've faced in the past. If you're going to be so defeatist and cowardly you should never have entertained the idea, even in your wildest dreams, of acting as Israeli defence counsel for Demjanjuk. Yet for months now you've been working to achieve that aim.

And as to that cynical and malicious team of prosecutors who were not ashamed to file an indictment and plan a show-trial on the basis of such unconvincing and disgraceful evidence – aren't they enjoying a peaceful and untroubled sleep? What's got into you, letting yourself be overwhelmed by pessimism? Remember the truth you have known from the day you first entered this profession: doubt always works to the advantage of the accused, and not against him.

I got up at five. I felt stronger and my good spirits were restored. I went back to bed once more, and told myself, One thing is for sure: no one is going to break me. And I'm certainly not going to do it to myself. Encouraged at last by this resolute thought, I felt my eyelids grow heavy and sank into a deep sleep.

At six-forty-five came the receptionist's wake-up call. In a state of great agitation I quickly showered and dressed, and checked my appearance in the mirror before leaving the room. The shower had done me a world of good. By seven o'clock I was in the hotel dining room. Johnny, Demjanjuk's son, was already sitting at one of the tables and I joined him.

We were joined by Gill and O'Connor and other friends of the Demjanjuk family who had come over specially to attend the opening day of the trial. I was increasingly agitated but made great efforts to hide my feelings. I think I managed to appear calm, relaxed and even somewhat indifferent. We finished our breakfast and after a short drive arrived at Binyanei Ha'uma, where the trial was to take place in a theatre auditorium. We went straight up to the defence counsels' offices on the second floor. I noticed that both O'Connor and Johnny were quite tense; I suggested we go down to the hall in order to get a sense of the place and arrange our seats on the defence side.

We entered the theatre hall in the basement of the building, which had been hired by the Israeli courts' administration as a setting for the show-trial that was to begin in a few minutes. The hall was already packed with what looked like several hundred people, and our entrance caused a considerable stir. The prosecution team were already seated in their places when we arrived. I went over and shook hands warmly with each of them, particularly Shaked. I told him I hoped we would keep up our good professional relations throughout the duration of the trial.

I returned to the defence benches and reminded O'Connor that as soon as he had finished putting the preliminary points concerning the court's lack of jurisdiction to try Demjanjuk on the charges filed against him, I would rise to give the defence's specific response to those charges. I would place particular emphasis on the unqualified admission of all the facts, the only point of contention being the identity of Demjanjuk. O'Connor agreed, though not hiding his impatience, and added that he was disturbed by the absence of a television monitor on the defence table, which would have let him know at once how he looked on TV. I was taken aback and distracted myself by turning to look at the audience. There wasn't a single empty seat in the gallery set aside for the press. Dozens of TV cameras were positioned there on tripods, the cameramen making their final preparations to shoot. I also spotted two radio booths that had been specially constructed at the far end of the press gallery, to enable reporters to broadcast directly from the court. Several cameras had been set up in the hall itself, only about ten yards from us. Flashes from stills cameras continued non-stop, from both the press gallery and the hall.

A large number of visitors and official representatives of many countries, including Germany and Poland, were present. In the front rows sat Holocaust survivors and their relatives. Justice Ministry officials were running to and fro. Police personnel were on duty at every corner of the hall to maintain order, but they all looked pretty bored. Various politicians, among them Knesset Members who were themselves Holocaust survivors, were conspicuous in the audience. The attorneys for the defence and prosecution, the witness box, the dock where Demjanjuk was to sit and the table for his interpreters as well as the judges' bench were all on the dais, which was three feet above the floor of the hall. It was a dramatic décor, carefully designed by the prosecution with the full consent of the court. Beyond all this, I was able to discern the looks of hostility directed at me from the rows occupied mainly by Holocaust survivors and their families. I also spotted Doron and Tzvia, and it was with some relief that I stepped down into the hall to shake hands with them; they wished me success and good luck. Their words gave me true encouragement and made me feel stronger in those most difficult moments, when I felt an unbearable tension growing within me.

Returning to my place, I felt like a gladiator in a Roman arena, where the grandiose surroundings had the sole purpose of providing a setting for the ordeal he was about to face. I imagined the vituperative press coverage to which I was about to be subjected. It came to me all of a sudden that in this televised show-trial, with everyone baying for the blood of Demjanjuk, there was not the slightest glimmer of a chance that the verdict could be anything other than guilty, with a sentence of death. I was deeply scared and agitated.

I ordered myself to stop bothering with these foolish defeatist scenarios, to grab the bull by the horns and tackle the legal issues, and reminded myself that there was a huge amount of work to be done – so as to get the most and the best out of myself. I reminded O'Connor for the umpteenth time that, in stating the case against the jurisdiction of this court to hear this case, he must at all costs refrain from using the argument that it did not have a mandate to try anyone charged with Nazi crimes against the Jewish people. He must concentrate solely on the contention that its lack of jurisdiction stemmed from the fact that Demjanjuk was extradited to Israel to stand trial on a murder charge but that the indictment against him was actually on a charge of genocide, and these are two different crimes. Although he nodded in agreement, I got the impression that his mind was somewhere else entirely.

While we were talking, there was great commotion and noise in the hall; the cameras began to roll and the flash bulbs explode; and police formed a buffer between hall and platform, and some of the audience rose to their feet. I realized that Demjanjuk, handcuffed and with legs chained, had just been brought into the hall through the stage door behind me. Two policemen led him to the dock behind the defence bench. In recent weeks I had given a great deal of thought to the moment when Demjanjuk would be led into the court, to a seat just behind me and only inches away. O'Connor would naturally shake hands with him, and so would Gill, but what was I to do? If I shook his hand, it would look like an intolerable action designed to provoke the audience. But to refrain from doing so would be just as unforgivable, as it would imply that I too believed the man in the dock to be Ivan the Terrible. Would Demjanjuk himself not see in it a sign of weakness? In the end I decided to do what was fitting for the role I had chosen to assume. As soon as the policemen had finished removing Demjanjuk's handcuffs, O'Connor went over to hug him. Gill got up and embraced Demjanjuk too, but without O'Connor's dramatics. Next I got up and shook hands with Demjanjuk, confident that a real difference would be perceived between my cool, formal handshake and the demonstrative hugs of my colleagues.

But the audience burst into a roar at the sight, with shouts of 'Disgrace!', 'Shame,' 'Disgusting.' The pandemonium intensified, the shouting coming from all sides. Again I felt weak and helpless. Though I had anticipated hostile reactions, I had certainly not foreseen such noisy and constant shouting from the hall itself.

Within a moment I recovered and resolved not to let audience reaction dictate my responses. My confidence was restored and I felt I had come through my baptism of fire relatively unscathed. It was noticeable that no one from the Justice Ministry or the police had made the slightest effort to silence the voices raised against me. There's nothing to be done about it, I told myself. This must be the way show-trials are conducted.

Before I had had time to come to grips with the drama of Demjanjuk's first entrance into the hall, one of the junior clerks gave the traditional call 'The court!' (Hebrew equivalent of 'All rise'). Now I felt calm; I rose to my feet like everybody else. The three judges made their way to their table. The hall was brightly illuminated to allow the dozens of TV cameras to work; the still cameras flashed continuously for several long moments. Whispers and murmurs rippled through the audience, a little like the opening of a circus performance. The outcome of this trial will be determined not at its ending, I said to myself, but right now, in these very moments. Would it be at all conceivable that these same judges, who have given their blessing to this shameful piece of theatre, could do anything but find Demjanjuk guilty?

I carefully studied the face of Justice Levin. Ever since the day, ten years earlier, when I had first appeared before him, I had had a horror of repeating the experience. Most of the country's criminal lawyers have a hearty dislike of Dov Levin, who they feel has a tendency to make petty comments, and is of an intolerant character. I looked into his eyes and saw that unpleasant expression that never seems to leave them.

The judges took their places and Justice Levin said, 'Good-morning, please take your seats.' When at last relative silence descended upon the hall, a clerk rose to announce 'Criminal File 373/86 – the State of Israel versus John Ivan, son of Nikolai Demjanjuk. Appearing for the State: State Attorney advocate Yonah Blatman; and advocates Michael Shaked, Michael Horowitz and Dennis Goldman. On behalf of the accused: defence counsels advocate Mark O'Connor and advocate Yoram Sheftel. Court session of 16 February 1987 – morning session.' The trial was under way.

Levin invited O'Connor to put the defence's case on the issue of the jurisdiction of the court. O'Connor began with a long, confused, irrelevant and unprofessional lecture, with no reference whatever to legal precedent, even though the subject was of a purely legal nature. It was torture to sit and listen to this nonsense. I noticed that Gill too was suffering.

At last my eyes were opened, and I perceived O'Connor's worth – his *lack* of worth. I remember thinking to myself, Good heavens, this man doesn't know what he is talking about; he can't even put a proper sentence together. This entire case will fall upon my shoulders; yet I can't *begin* to tackle it because I don't know the first thing about it.

All of a sudden I felt convinced that I must find a way to get off the case as quickly as possible; otherwise a catastrophe would befall me from which I would never fully recover. Nevertheless every now and then I listened to what O'Connor had to say, and after an hour realized that he had not even touched the one point that he was supposed to argue. All my attempts to whisper to him to come to the point fell on deaf ears.

There was no alternative but to scribble quickly for myself the legal arguments on the jurisdiction issue; however, I felt I must begin with a few opening words that would appeal to everyone. When O'Connor wound up his address, I asked Justice Levin for permission to 'clarify' the case expounded by my learned colleague.

I began by saying, 'First of all I have to say that I stand before you in all due humility, but I believe from the bottom of my heart in the innocence of the accused. I am aware of the awesome grandeur of the fact that this case is being dealt with in a court of law whose seat is in the united Hebrew city of Jerusalem. I am overwhelmed by the presence in this hall of Knesset Members who are Holocaust survivors, and there is remarkable historical significance to the appearance of representatives of the government of Poland, a country whose native sons hardly lifted a finger when the events described in the indictment took place.'

This was a very poor showing, and quite superfluous. In fact I myself did not believe a single word I said; I stooped to flattery – of the court, the public and the media. It was a display of weakness; I had succumbed to the nature of the occasion, to the hostility and my own mixed feelings. This was one of two occasions when I stumbled because of the circumstances and the general pressure I was under, and said things that I most definitely should not have said.

Next I presented the defence's point of view on aspects of the question of jurisdiction, and then sat down. O'Connor rose once more and again made some fairly meaningless remarks. When at last he had finished, advocate Goldman replied on behalf of the prosecution, although his reply responded only to my remarks. He argued that there was no essential difference between the various categories of murder: genocide was a form of murder, and therefore the court had the right to try Demjanjuk on a charge of genocide. In this argument there was a combination of deception and stupidity. Goldman was clearly aware that the US Federal Appeals Court had explicitly ruled that 'Although these allegations would certainly appear sufficient to support a charge of genocide, until the United States and Israel amend the extradition treaty to include a crime of genocide and make genocide a crime under their respective domestic laws, genocide does not provide a basis for extradition.'

Goldman concluded his argument and the court declared a half-hour recess. Immediately after the judges had filed from the hall, Demjanjuk was taken to a special cell built for him just outside. I headed for the door facing me, to escape the public eye for a while. But before I could get out, cries rose from every direction, particularly from the front rows of the hall. I could make out 'Kapo,' 'Nazi collaborator,' 'Nazi,' 'You piece of filth,' 'They should kill you' and 'It's a shame you're alive.'

For a second I froze; a policeman leaped on to the stage and tried to drag me to the exit. I resisted him vigorously, telling him that those curses did not scare me and would not drive me out of the hall. The shouting crescendoed, and was now accompanied by aggressive gestures. The television cameramen, particularly the Israelis, began filming the people shouting and gesturing, the entire shameful spectacle, while the print journalists started questioning them, so encouraging them to continue. The many policemen in the hall did nothing to control the chaos, and not one of those responsible was removed.

Eventually I got away, seething with rage, not only because of the shouting and the disturbance, but also because of the media reaction and the inertia of those responsible for keeping order. But I resolved not to show my feelings or be deterred by what had happened.

Some minutes later I returned ostentatiously to the hall. To my surprise O'Connor was in the middle of a press conference. I looked around for Tzvia and Doron, spotted them and climbed down from the platform to talk to them. A policeman offered to escort me but I shook him off and went ahead on my own. Tzvia and Doron complimented me on my presentation and encouraged me to continue. I did not tell them I had toyed with dropping the case altogether because of O'Connor's weak arguments. As I always did in those days, I gave him the benefit of the doubt, since the issue of jurisdiction pertaining to extradition laws is very complex and arises so infrequently. I was pleasantly surprised that my reappearance in the hall had not caused a renewal of the commotion. I went up to the defence offices while O'Connor continued with his press conference in the centre of the hall. In the office I met Johnny Demjanjuk, who shook hands warmly with me, expressed his admiration and said how pleased he was with my performance. The other friends of Demjanjuk's family also shook my hand and made encouraging remarks, particularly so after the unpleasant incident at the end of the hearing.

I hardly had time for a sip of a cold drink before it was time to return. When the hearing began O'Connor got up to respond to Goldman. All he did was repeat his earlier arguments; what he said could in no way be construed as a negation of Goldman's contentions. Again I felt obliged to get up and ask the court to allow me to clarify. This time the bench replied with obvious reluctance, and Justice Levin said it was unthinkable that two defence counsels should get up one after the other to make the same contentions with minor variations. But in the end he gave in and allowed me to have my say. I needed just ten minutes to dismantle Goldman's argument.

Seconds after the judges had left the hall for the lunch recess, even greater pandemonium broke out than during the morning break. Hysterical shouting came from every side, accompanied by waving fists. Hate-filled glares were turned on me and full-throated cries of 'Sheftel is a kapo,' 'Hang your head in shame,' 'Shameless bastard,' 'Nazi' and 'You should be killed' reverberated through the courtroom.

Once again the local media hastened to record the event, and once again none of those responsible for law and order made the slightest effort to put an end to the disturbances. I stood on the platform and watched what was happening. I did not feel threatened and assumed a deliberate air of indifference. I told myself that if the guardians of the law ignored their actions, as before, these people would take that as tacit approval and repeat them over and over. Indeed such outbreaks continued throughout the entire trial, with only two or three mild rebukes from the judges – and then only when the noise had not abated by the time a court session had begun.

I stood and watched the audience for about forty minutes, until the rowdy elements grew tired of shouting and fist-shaking. When the commotion had died down completely, I calmly left the hall to go up to our offices. O'Connor, Gill, Johnny and Demjanjuk's supporters were already sitting there heatedly analysing the day's events. Johnny asked for a literal translation of the remarks shouted at me downstairs in the hall. An expression of shocked consternation spread across his face when I translated them, but he encouraged me and said he hoped I would have the strength to continue and would not break down. I hastened to reassure him that, unlike the first time it had happened, I was not at all upset by the whole scene and my breaking down was the last thing that would happen.

At about two o'clock the entire group (we were twelve) walked over to the Hilton Hotel, just a few hundred yards from Binyanei Ha'uma, for lunch. During the meal I mentally re-enacted all the tempestuous events of the morning, noting with satisfaction that it had not been as bad as it might have been, and I could be quite pleased with my performance, apart from my superfluous opening remarks. But I had better watch out not to repeat such a mistake.

I also tried to arrive at some evaluation of the Ukrainian goyim who had rallied to the help of the Demjanjuk family, but it was rather difficult to do in the relaxed atmosphere of the meal.

At four o'clock precisely the court hearing began again – but not before another outburst against me. The session began with a reading of the court's decision on the issue of its jurisdiction to deal with the charges in the indictment. The court rejected the defence argument, and ruled that it undoubtedly had the jurisdiction to try charges of genocide. The judges showed no compunction about distorting the decision reached by the United States Federal Court, when it had ruled on Demjanjuk's appeal against his extradition to Israel.

The decision read out by Justice Levin contained the following sentence: 'The position taken by the learned judge Battisti, that all murder offences are the same, was ratified also, in very clear terms, by the appeals court, which was asked to review and examine the verdict of the district court.' Yet the US appeals court to which Levin referred had ruled explicitly in Demjanjuk's appeal that 'Genocide does not provide a basis for extradition.' (Genocide does not exist as a crime in the USA.)

I got up and told the court I wished, on behalf of the accused, to admit to the many facts contained in the indictment. I began by saying just that, and in particular that the accused admitted the description of the annihilation of European Jewry by the Nazis, including the facts pertaining to the Treblinka extermination camp and all that happened there and to the atrocities perpetrated by Ivan the Terrible at that extermination camp. The accused, then, admitted all the facts contained in the indictment – with one exception: that he was the monstrous creature known as Ivan the Terrible.

Here I drew the attention of the court to the specific article in the law which stipulates that a fact admitted by the defendant is to be considered proven. With these remarks I had hoped to set the court on the course along which criminal cases are normally conducted. But I had also implied arguments against running a show-trial, the principal purpose of which was clearly to drive home lessons about the history of the Holocaust.

Justice Levin discerned this, and it immediately became clear that he would not allow me to ruin the best show in town, but would do everything he could to thwart my efforts. Again and again he interrupted my presentation with petty comments, even going so far as to declare that the court had no judicial knowledge about the Holocaust, and it would therefore be necessary to prove every detail of this matter. Any first-year student of the laws of evidence would have been astonished by these words, yet no one in Israel's legal community found the courage to speak out.

When I had finished, Justice Levin decided there was no need to ask the prosecution to respond. In the decision he dictated to the court record, he said, *inter alia*: 'We believe that, in relation to this most complex and grave set of circumstances, it is not enough to confine ourselves to the brief statements contained in the indictment; instead it would be fitting for the court to hear the facts ... We allow the prosecution to act as it sees fit and put forward evidence as it requires with respect to facts which are not in dispute.'

I had never deluded myself into thinking I could dissuade the court from halting a show-trial. All the same, when Justice Levin had finished reading this shameful decision, I was in shock. I had expected a more sophisticated and less abrasive ruling, and could not believe that Israeli judges would, in the full glare of publicity, discard the rules of court and statutory laws, and distort their very essence, as these three judges were now doing. When I recovered from the shock, there was an even more significant point that suddenly became clear to me: just as this court had deviated from the rules of extradition and jurisdiction, and then deviated from the procedural laws and the laws of evidence to enable the prosecution to conduct a show-trial, by the same token, when the time came, it would also trample underfoot all the proper legal procedures and laws pertaining to identification.

The first day of this trial, I said to myself, is in effect also its last. And so at five o'clock in the afternoon of the first day of the trial of Demjanjuk, I was convinced that his fate had already been sealed. No legal argument, however brilliant and appropriate, would stop his conviction and sentencing to the gallows, a depressing conclusion for any defence attorney. However, strange as it may seem, this analysis inspired in me a measure of calm and self-confidence. You have nothing to lose, I said to myself. Your client won't be sent to the gallows because of any mistake you might make, but only because of the determination of the court to send him there.

Now it was advocate Blatman who was addressing the court – he had launched into the opening speech of the prosecution. It was a smooth but long and uninspiring address. In describing the Nazi crimes, Blatman spoke of the superb railway system without which so efficient a mass slaughter could not have been accomplished. Then he went on to describe the Nazi hierarchy of command responsible for the extermination. Then on to the atrocious deeds in the death camps themselves. He droned on, giving a very long speech but saying no word about the nature of the evidence pertaining to Demjanjuk's identity as Ivan the Terrible. The three judges listened attentively to this boring presentation on the history of the Holocaust.

Shaked rose to speak next. His opening address was matter-of-fact, yet his powers of rhetoric were remarkable compared to Blatman's. Shaked described the body of evidence the prosecution would present in the course of the trial. He believed it would convince the court that Demjanjuk was indeed Ivan the Terrible; that it was he who had operated the gas chambers in Treblinka, and tormented his victims with such cruelty in their last living moments.

Shaked spoke briefly, concluding his address shortly after six o'clock. Justice Levin thanked him, adjourned the session and declared the trial would resume the following morning, when the evidence would begin. The judges filed out of the hall and the crowd began to disperse. Several of those who had caused disturbances earlier in the day once more raised their voices against me with the familiar slogans. But these were isolated incidents, and they quickly abated.

Thus ended the first day of the trial. I had found time to hold brief conversations with representatives of both foreign and local media and had promised several interviews. As we left the hall, O'Connor asked me what my plans were for the evening, and when I told him I would spend the next hour or so giving interviews to the US media, I saw his disappointment, but he said nothing. On my way to the defence office quarters I tried to put some order in my thoughts.

I decided that in the interviews I was about to give, I would express my views freely on the course of events and not try to hide behind vague formulas. Johnny and the friends of the Demjanjuk family watched me all the time, and afterwards expressed their admiration for the way I had handled the questions.

During the first week of the trial I thought, erroneously, that I should be able to get home to Tel Aviv every evening and come back to Jerusalem in the morning. After all, it was only an hour's drive. So I said good-night to them all and headed for my car. All the way home I felt wide awake despite my great fatigue. My mood improved, and the more I pondered the events of the day the more strongly I felt I had coped pretty well. I fell asleep the moment my head hit the pillow and it was a struggle getting up next morning.

3 · The Prosecution Case

Over the course of the trial I would come to realize that O'Connor was not really up to the job. He never seemed to have prepared very thoroughly for the sessions; he ignored my advice on which points to raise; his cross-examinations were lengthy, wandering affairs that achieved little. Yet O'Connor frequently boasted about his performance and also assured Demjanjuk and his family that he would get Demjanjuk released – something that was impossible under the circumstances. In fact, he did much damage to Demjanjuk's defence.

I *wanted* to believe O'Connor was capable, although I had every reason to doubt it. I am confident that normally I am a good judge of character and legal ability: I need only hear five minutes of a lawyer's arguments to appraise his professional abilities. The story of my relations with Mark O'Connor is a notable example of how this ability may fail me. Had I seen him for what he was from the start, I would never have joined the 'phoney Satan's' defence team. Had I done so shortly after joining, I would clearly have come into conflict with him and found myself unceremoniously kicked off the case. I was struck blind when it came to judging O'Connor, a case of my *mazel* of a goy working for me while my intelligence failed. This combination prevented conflict with O'Connor at an unhelpful time for me, and promoted it at the worst possible time for him. So at first I made excuses for O'Connor's failings, to myself and even to others who attacked O'Connor – Doron, for example, and especially an American lawyer who insisted that this must be O'Connor's first criminal trial. As well as being incompetent, O'Connor was given to unpredictable outbursts of rage. He also appeared to resent the amount of attention that the media paid to me and to Johnny Demjanjuk.

O'Connor not only disregarded my advice on how to conduct the defence, but interfered with my own performances. I tried to avoid public argument, but O'Connor could not always be silenced; there were quite a few arguments between us in the defence offices too. The family were witnesses to this; although they had been depending on O'Connor for five years, they eventually had to face the possibility that he was damaging their case and they would have to put their trust in me alone.

By the end of the prosecution's presentation of its case, Gill, the family and I were convinced that O'Connor had to go; initially we did not want to 'sack' him outright but diminish his influence to a point that he was bound to find unbearable. Finally we had no choice but force his resignation.

Having first met O'Connor in mid-October 1986, at the Ayalon Prison, in retrospect I had plenty of opportunity to assess him before the trial opened in mid-February 1987. During the period that led up to my joining the case, O'Connor's behaviour was very strange, to put it mildly. There was his severance of contact after our first two meetings; his brief and incomprehensible association with Dr Orion, who became Demjanjuk's Israeli attorney for a week; his botched appearance at the first hearing on 26 November, and the misleading television interview he granted thereafter; the strange meeting in the airport, after which I was suddenly and irresponsibly thrown into the arena. All this should have been enough to warn me of what lay ahead.

There is one factor that helps excuse my blindness. When in good faith you join the defence of an accused man in order to assist a foreign attorney who has been working on the case for five years, the possibility that he is not doing his work properly does not occur to you. Even if doubts arise, you tend to reject them on the grounds that they must be the product of insufficient acquaintance with the evidence and of the short period you have been on the case. This is, however, no more than an extenuating circumstance, since Doron, solely from what I told him about Demjanjuk's lawyer, reached the correct conclusion about O'Connor's character and professional competence almost immediately.

A most serious incident took place on 13 February, the Friday before the trial began. We were eating breakfast together at the hotel and chatting about nothing in particular. O'Connor suddenly said that he had just remembered something very important. 'Actually, the most important thing,' he added. 'My wife is arriving in Israel soon. I want immediately to draft a motion to the court that she be allowed to sit on the defence bench during the trial. Her status will be defined as "paralegal".' I was astounded, but O'Connor had yet another idea. 'I also want you to request that a television monitor be placed on the defence table, so that I will be able to see in real time how I look on the screen.' I could not believe my ears. To this day I don't know where I found the presence of mind to respond, after a long pause, 'There is absolutely no chance that the court will allow your wife, who is not a lawyer, to sit on the defence bench. It's simply not accepted practice in

Israel. There is no precedent for it, and it won't be set in this trial. As for the monitor, such a request will make the court think you're more concerned with how you look on TV than how you look to the judges. It will give a negative impression of you right from the start.' O'Connor was not convinced, and insisted that I submit the request. Calmly but firmly I repeated that I, unlike him, would have to continue to appear in Israeli courts after the Demjanjuk trial. It was not fair to force me to submit the motion, since it would seem ridiculous to everyone, and to the judges especially. I gave further reasons for my refusal, and O'Connor finally closed the conversation, saying he'd come back to it later.

The fact that O'Connor's mind was occupied with such nonsense less than seventy-two hours before the trial began should have led any reasonable person to doubt him. Yet this incident also failed to open my eyes. I convinced myself that the magnitude of the responsibility lying on his shoulders and the approaching trial were making him nervous and tense, and this was being expressed in these ideas – which were, perhaps, normal practice in the US.

All of this might give the impression that during the period before the trial opened O'Connor and I were busy discussing the trial from early in the morning to late at night. This is far from correct. True, at O'Connor's request I arrived at the American Colony Hotel on the Thursday before the trial began, so that we could, in his words, 'polish what needs polishing' before the hearing. However, O'Connor spent most of the next four days granting interviews to the media, devoting no more than a few hours to discussions with me.

The echoes of O'Connor's abortive arguments on the matter of jurisdiction had barely faded when another wheel fell off the defence's wagon. We had decided that if the court were to allow Dr Arad's testimony (on the facts which the defence had admitted), we would boycott the session. Yet O'Connor left me to voice the objection to hearing this testimony, as if he'd forgotten everything we had agreed.

In my argument I emphasized the severe implications of hearing the testimony of an expert on an issue that was not under dispute. I made it clear that the prosecution's attempt to admit Dr Arad's testimony would turn the proceedings into a show-trial. As expected, this prompted a fierce response from the bench, and later from the media. No attempt was made to confront the substance of my argument.

On Tuesday, just before six in the evening, Arad concluded his lecture on the extermination of Polish Jewry. O'Connor's useless, tiresome cross-examination began immediately thereafter. Whilst I never thought it effective, I tried my best to find good points in it. Furthermore, in order to boost O'Connor's self-confidence, I complimented him on his performance.

Towards the end of that week, we had our first serious collision. Two days into his cross-examination he demanded that I participate as well. He wanted me to cross-examine Dr Arad on the question of Ivan the Terrible's death in the Treblinka rebellion. I tried to explain that there was no need for this, since Arad's expert testimony had no bearing on Ivan the Terrible's death. This, I emphasized, had to be proved or disproved by direct evidence during the case. O'Connor insisted, and in the end I had to comply with his instructions.

The next day, I grudgingly conducted the cross-examination, finishing in less than half an hour. As I turned to sit down, O'Connor pushed a heavy book towards me. It was *The Black Book*, by Ilya Erenburg and Vassily Grossman, and it contained a description of Ivan the Terrible that was slightly incompatible with that given by the survivors. O'Connor demanded that I submit the entire book immediately as an exhibit. This is not allowed even under Anglo-American rules of procedure and evidence, most of which are also in force in Israel, as any novice lawyer knows.

During Dr Arad's re-examination by State Attorney Yonah Blatman, O'Connor and I had a sharp exchange. When I said that the submission of the book as evidence had been totally inappropriate, he hissed: 'Maybe you can work with me, but *I* can't work with *you*.' This comment was recorded by the press, because O'Connor had failed to turn off the microphone on our table, and a few hours later it was on the radio.

That evening I told Doron what had happened. The radio had broadcast additional news about the disagreement between me and O'Connor. Doron's opinion was unequivocal: 'You can't think of leaving the case at such an early stage. True, this was a very unpleasant incident, but it's not the end of the world. Leaving the case would be a much greater disgrace than your shame at O'Connor's behaviour.' I was still not convinced, but I decided to have a meeting with O'Connor over the weekend to clarify matters.

As soon as O'Connor saw me next day, he greeted me with a warm and heartfelt *shalom*, as if nothing had happened, and invited me to sit with him in the dining room. I told him: 'I would like to clarify the events of last week with you, in detail.' O'Connor answered with great friendliness: 'There's no need for that. Everything that happened is simply the result of natural tension that resulted, apparently, from the pressure of the beginning of the trial. I am willing to forget the whole matter without dredging through it again.' All of this was said so amiably that my anger was deflated completely. Everything seemed fine again.

* * *

On the day the trial began, O'Connor discovered that a large part of the media's attention was focused on Johnny Demjanjuk, on me and to a certain extent on Gill. He told Johnny that he was absolutely forbidden to give interviews to the press, threatening that, if he did not obey him, Johnny himself would be responsible if his father was hanged. Only O'Connor knew what should be said to the media, and he could not take responsibility for Demjanjuk's life if Johnny would not stop giving interviews.

At the beginning of the trial, Gill did not have a permit to appear in court as a non-Israeli defence attorney. O'Connor apparently hoped that Gill would reach the obvious conclusion and return to Cleveland. As for me, he planned to create dissension between us, hoping that I would resign from the case, or that he would have an excuse to fire me. His plans were foiled by Johnny, who insisted that O'Connor take immediate steps to obtain a permit for Gill. He also made it clear that he and his father would not be happy with any situation that could result in my leaving the case. This conversation between Johnny and O'Connor took place on the evening before I met O'Connor to clarify my position; I later discovered that it was behind the sudden reversal in O'Connor's attitude to me.

Among the many people who came to watch the Demjanjuk trial was a retired attorney named Paul Brifer. Brifer, a genial and popular American Jew, had served as defence counsel in hundreds of criminal trials in California. He was also staying at the American Colony. At the end of the trial's second day, when I returned to the hotel, Brifer approached and asked if he could speak to me privately.

'I can hardly tell you how much trouble you're in,' he began.

'What do you mean?' I asked.

'Your boss, O'Connor, doesn't know what he's doing. He's a complete rookie, and he's appearing in a criminal case for the first time in his life.'

I was astounded and took exception to what he had said. 'How do you know that it's his "first" criminal trial and not, for instance, his third?'

Brifer, sounding with his Jewish Lower East Side accent like someone from a gangster movie, replied: 'The way he talks in court shows it. For example, for two days he's been repeating the line: "I take exception to the court." An American lawyer who's appeared in even just one criminal trial would not dare let a sentence like that loose. I just think it's my obligation to give you my opinion, so that you know who you're dealing with and so that you can plan your steps accordingly.'

I rejected what he said. Two months later, when I realized the truth about O'Connor, I joked about it with Brifer and reminded him of our first conversation.

At the beginning of the second week, the first of the identification witnesses, Treblinka survivor Pinhas Epstein, took the witness stand. The courtroom was full. The testimony was broadcast live on television and caused an outpouring of emotion. All the plans we had worked out together about our handling of those parts of Epstein's testimony that did not deal with Ivan the Terrible had already been abandoned by O'Connor. Nevertheless I reminded him again of our position on this issue and called his attention to his change of policy. He answered dismissively that I would have to get used to it. He plunged eagerly into the cross-examination of Epstein. We had resolved from the first that he would conduct the cross-examination on all issues except Israel Police's identification procedure, which was to be my responsibility.

The cross-examination was pathetic. It dwelt largely on unimportant details such as the colour of the Ukrainian camp guards' uniforms and the shape of the buildings in Treblinka. Every lawyer knows very well that one should not base a cross-examination on contradictions or inaccuracies in such details of the testimony if many years (in this case forty-five) have passed since the events in question took place. In any case, such contradictions would not cast doubt on Epstein's identification of Demjanjuk's picture as a photograph of Ivan the Terrible, or on the weight of his testimony. Moreover, meticulous cross-examination on such details, by nature shocking and heart-rending, only fuelled the blaze of emotions and primal instincts surrounding the trial. O'Connor's mind was not on such fine points. He referred constantly to 'history', and I knew that what concerned him was the period of time he would star on the stage of history.

Epstein's testimony and O'Connor's cross-examination thus inflamed public passions about the trial in general, and the defence in particular. The audience in the courtroom frequently directed curses at us, at me especially. The press was also hysterical, and swift to pass judgement on Demjanjuk. One newspaper, for instance, printed the headline 45 YEARS ON, EPSTEIN FACES EXECUTIONER AGAIN. Many reporters asked me when I would finally leave the defence bench. I tried to explain that I had no quarrel with Epstein's shocking testimony about the outrages that had occurred at Treblinka, and about Ivan the Terrible's horrible deeds. The only matter I was contesting was the identification of Demjanjuk as Ivan the Terrible. No one, however, was prepared to listen.

O'Connor had no conception of the significance of his actions, and was delighted by the furore that he had helped to create. Without batting an eyelid he boasted to Demjanjuk Senior and Junior and to anyone else who would listen that he had succeeded in 'absolutely destroying' Epstein's testimony. Yet I would be lying if I were to say that O'Connor's performance seemed so awful to me then. In telephone calls I made to my office during recesses, Doron was deadly critical of the cross-examination. I remember one conversation in particular: 'Your boss looks like someone who doesn't know where he's coming from or where he's going. He really isn't interrogating at all – he's just standing in front of the witness, lecturing to him and asking for his response, instead of asking questions. When he finally gets around to asking something, it's always a long question compounded of many other questions, which is totally improper in cross-examination.' While I understood all that, I emphasized to Doron the few reasonable questions O'Connor had asked. Paul Brifer also had harsh words: 'As far as Demjanjuk is concerned, it would be better not to be represented at all than to be represented by O'Connor.' But I found excuses to counter this too.

My own cross-examination of Epstein was extremely brief and touched only on Israel Police's identification procedure. Its aim was to draw attention to the procedure's many flaws, flaws repeated in the identifications made by the other survivors who were to appear as witnesses. I tried to conduct the questioning with great delicacy, and took care not to attack Epstein directly. There really was no need to do so, since most of his answers were in keeping with my expectations. Even so, there was great tension in the courtroom. One could sense the great indignation of the onlookers at the chutzpah of my even addressing Epstein.

The most significant fact that emerged from his cross-examination was that, when eight pictures that included the 'Travniki picture' were placed before him, he identified one of the pictures as that of 'Nikolai' (Shelaiev), Ivan the Terrible's murderous partner in operating the Treblinka gas chambers and in torturing the victims on their way into them. Both the prosecution and the defence agreed that this identification was erroneous. The man whose picture Epstein pointed to was not Shelaiev but another murderer, a German by the name of Schmidt. The obvious conclusion was that if Epstein had misidentified Shelaiev his identification of Demjanjuk could not be trusted.

Epstein's testimony lasted two whole days, and then the stand was taken by Eliahu Rosenberg. Everything that had happened during Epstein's testimony recurred, only it was worse. Rosenberg was on the stand for three days. O'Connor's method was again to deliver long lectures to the witness. He stooped so low as to ask Rosenberg about the colour of the flames given off by the burning bodies of his murdered brothers after they were removed from the gas chambers. Rosenberg's testimony charged the atmosphere in and out of the courtroom even further. The media's assault on the defence team reached unbelievable dimensions: DEMJANJUK, YOU ARE THE KILLER; THE KILLER SITS AND LAUGHS WHILE WE SAY NOTHING; THE DEFENCE, SPECIFICALLY SHEFTEL, MAKES THE SURVIVORS' BLOOD FLOW ALL OVER AGAIN. Yet O'Connor kept going.

The most severe courtroom clash between me and O'Connor took place during the cross-examination. In 1947, Rosenberg had given a statement to Tuvia Friedman, one of the first documentalists of the Holocaust. This was in Vienna, and the statement includes the story of how Ivan the Terrible was killed during the Treblinka revolt of 2 August 1943. According to Rosenberg's statement, he saw the killing with his own eyes. He had made the statement in Yiddish, and Friedman had translated simultaneously into German, with someone typing the translation. It takes no legal skills to realize that, given his 1947 statement about Ivan the Terrible's death, his 1987 identification of Demjanjuk as Ivan the Terrible should be rejected.

When he was interrogated by O'Connor, Rosenberg tried to excuse these problems by claiming he had actually said in Yiddish that 'they dealt him murderous blows [*tseharget*]', not that they had killed him, and that the German translation had mistakenly stated that they had really killed him. During the course of the examination a question arose as to what was actually written in the German version of the statement that O'Connor had submitted. There had not been any reason for him to submit this version, since the court's Hebrew translation, which the prosecution had agreed was accurate, stated explicitly that Ivan had been killed, and not that he had been 'dealt ... murderous blows'. Shaked and I were asked to examine the German statement, to see whether we could reach a consensus on its contents. Shaked immediately said that he accepted that what was written was 'killed' and not 'murderous blows'. He then declared that the defence and prosecution agreed that the German version of the statement referred to the killing of Ivan.

The simultaneous translation that O'Connor received via earphones apparently said that Sheftel and Shaked had 'come to an agreement' about the German version. He jumped from his seat as if he had been stung and shrieked hysterically, 'Sheftel makes no agreements for the defence. Sheftel will not stand on his feet in this trial any more. Only I, O'Connor, the lead counsel, am authorized to make agreements on behalf of the defence!' I could sense the audience's satisfaction at the insult inflicted on me. Shaked, though, was not pleased by this serious blow to my honour. Judge Levin's features were completely dispassionate, as if nothing had happened.

At the next recess I made it very clear to O'Connor, in Johnny and Gill's presence, that I would under no circumstances agree to be the target of such demeaning insults. O'Connor, who apparently understood that he had gone overboard, had nevertheless not expected such a direct attack, certainly not in the presence of others. He was shocked for a moment, recovered, apologized, and promised that as soon as the court reconvened he would find a way to apologize publicly, which he did.

Johnny later told me that he had relished my onslaught on O'Connor. O'Connor had lorded it over him and his family for five years. At that time, however, O'Connor could have insisted that I be dismissed from the case, and Johnny's joining in would not have helped anyone.

One of the most dramatic and unnecessary moments of the trial took place during Rosenberg's evidence in chief. It began when Shaked asked: 'Mr Rosenberg, I would like you to look at the defendant, if you can; scrutinize him.'

Rosenberg responded: 'I request that the honourable court order him to take off his glasses.'

Judge Levin: 'His glasses? Why?'

'I want to see his eyes. May I get a little closer?'

'No.' There was an exchange between O'Connor and Levin over O'Connor's consent to Demjanjuk's removal of his glasses. The atmosphere in the courtroom, which was always tense, became more and more charged each moment. A murmur passed through the audience. This is the last thing that the defence needs in such a case, and at such moments the defence attorney should make every effort to cool tempers.

O'Connor did precisely the opposite, intentionally. His design was to shock, to heighten the drama, so as to focus attention on himself. He addressed the witness: 'Mr Rosenberg, would you please approach?' Rosenberg was still walking when shouts of 'Murderer!', 'He should be killed!', 'Enough of the trial, take him to the gallows!' began coming from all directions in the audience. Judge Levin, who understood very well what was going on, not only failed to stop Rosenberg and to silence the audience, but actually allowed Rosenberg to get as close as three feet from Demjanjuk and to fix his gaze on him. Demjanjuk responded by holding out his hand and saying, '*Shalom*.' Rosenberg pushed the hand aside and began shouting: 'You murderer, how dare you offer me your hand?' In the mean time the catcalls from the audience grew so loud that they almost brought an end to the session. Rosenberg's wife, who was in the audience, started screaming and fainted. Only at this point did Judge Levin attempt to restore order in the courtroom: 'Mr

Rosenberg, Mr Rosenberg, I must call you to order. Agitated as you are, difficult as this is for you, you must be more restrained in expressing yourself.'

I could not believe what I was seeing. I was furious with O'Connor for having fanned the flames by inviting Rosenberg to walk up to Demjanjuk. He should have stuck to his objection to Demjanjuk removing his glasses, because this was obviously an attempt by the prosecution to create an unnecessary dramatic effect typical of show-trials. I was even more furious with Levin, who knew exactly what was going on, yet allowed the scene to proceed.

When Rosenberg got close to Demjanjuk, he said: 'Beyond a shadow of doubt – it's Ivan from the Treblinka gas chambers. The man I'm now looking at. I saw the eyes. Those murderous eyes.' 'Murderous eyes' – *merderische oygen* – is a common Yiddish expression used of goyim by Polish Jews. Rosenberg knew that the eyes he saw were not the murderous eyes of Ivan the Terrible. One could say, however, that he said this under the influence of the show-trial being stage-managed by the prosecution with the court's full approval. It should hardly come as a surprise, then, that the verdict was based in part on this disgraceful scene, explicitly referring to it as another reason for ruling that Demjanjuk was Ivan the Terrible.

O'Connor did not stop there. While I was cross-examining Rosenberg on Israel Police's procedures, he began tapping on his legal pad with his pen, to attract my attention. I turned to look, and was stupefied to see that he had written in red ink, across an entire page, the word BULLSHIT. Furthermore, he did this in such a way that everyone in the courtroom could see that he was expressing his displeasure with me.

I swallowed my surprise, and proceeded at once with my interrogation. This revealed two important points. First, when in 1976 Rosenberg had pointed to Demjanjuk's 1951 photograph as a picture of Ivan the Terrible, he had not been entirely certain that it was indeed Ivan the Terrible. He was finally convinced of this only when he saw Demjanjuk in 1981, when he testified against him at the denaturalization trial in Cleveland. The implication was that it had been easier for him to identify Demjanjuk as Ivan the Terrible in 1981 than it had been to identify a photograph taken thirty years previously, only eight or nine years after Demjanjuk had allegedly been in Treblinka, which is absurd. Second, in 1978 precisely the same pictures were shown to him and he was asked to point out Ukrainians known to him from Treblinka. On this occasion Rosenberg failed to single out Demjanjuk's picture. (This fact was later confirmed by the testimony of the policeman who had been in charge of the 1978 photo spread, Martin Kolar.) According to criteria set by the Israeli Supreme Court, either one of these points was sufficient to reject Rosenberg's 'identification' on the grounds that it was unreliable evidence. The district court ignored this, and its judgement attached great weight to this 'identification'.

When we reached our offices after the end of my cross-examination, I turned straight to O'Connor. 'It is now clear to me that your goal is to undermine my self-confidence so that I perform badly, even if you hurt our case. You're not bothered by that since you just want to be the only defence attorney who comes out looking good. But you won't succeed. You won't succeed in undermining my self-confidence.'

When I returned to the hotel, I sat down on my bed and considered the situation at length. I was facing a combined force of O'Connor, who was doing all he could to break me; the media, which were calling for my blood with unconcealed glee; and a court that was staying aloof from all this malpractice. How could I withstand it? I remember very well how I worked on myself in those days. *Kalt und fest* – I recited these words of Jabotinsky's over and over to myself. Soon the testimony of the survivors will be over. Then my hour will come, when I interrogate Ish-Shalom, Radivker and Kolar, the people who conducted the photo spreads. If I do my work well, I'll win esteem, my indispensability to the defence will be recognized and O'Connor will not be able to keep harassing me.

The fourth witness was Josef Charny. During his time at Treblinka, Charny had not been in 'Camp 2', where Ivan the Terrible committed his crimes. He had been a slave labourer in 'Camp 1', which served as a preparatory camp for those who were sent to the gas chambers. This meant that Charny had seen Ivan the Terrible only infrequently.

Charny had testified in 1978 at Federenko's trial in Florida. Federenko had been a Ukrainian camp guard at Treblinka; and had been identified, along with Demjanjuk, from one set of pictures, during an investigation by the Nazi Crimes Investigation Unit of Israel Police. The upshot of the trial was that Federenko's American citizenship was revoked and he was deported to the Soviet Union, where he was hanged in 1986. The American judge described Charny as the most unreliable of the witnesses in the Federenko trial, so it was hardly surprising that the American prosecutor did not summon him to testify at the 1981 trial aimed at denaturalizing Demjanjuk. The Israeli state prosecution was not troubled by Charny's unreliability.

O'Connor failed to present these facts in spite of their manifest importance to the cross-examination. At this point I did not know about the Federenko trial, so I was unaware of O'Connor's incompetence. I first heard of Federenko purely by chance, during a conversation I had with Johnny immediately after Charny's testimony. He mentioned offhandedly that Federenko had been tried in the US. When I pressed him, I discovered to my dismay that the Federenko trial was of great importance to the entire issue of identification in the Demjanjuk case. Even though the trial was now reaching the end of its third week, and despite the many conversations I had had with O'Connor on the identification issue, he had not bothered to tell me that Federenko's case had been deliberated exhaustively in American legal proceedings. Johnny himself had trouble believing this when I told him.

The very next day I began studying the Federenko proceedings. The verdict stated explicitly that the procedures that led to Federenko's identification lacked any legal weight or substance, since the pictures from among which he had been identified – the same pictures from which Demjanjuk had been identified – were 'impermissibly suggestive'. My argument that the photo spreads used by the Israeli police in the Demjanjuk case were of no value had thus been given full legal substantiation by an American court decision that related to the very same pictures.

I was overjoyed at this discovery, but I was furious with O'Connor. I now realized, for the first time, that he had decided not to offer me any information at all about the case. I would have to trust to myself alone. Even after his botched cross-examination of Charny, I was still not persuaded that O'Connor was doing his work improperly. In my conversations with Doron I continued to dig up points in his favour. I went so far as to term O'Connor, I am embarrassed to say, as 'one of the world's great experts on Treblinka'. This unfortunate phrase perfectly illustrates how unaware I was of what was going on under my nose. As with the others, I cross-examined Charny only on the police identification procedures. This also took less than half an hour. The cross-examination showed, among other things, that according to the 1976 photo-spread reports the set of pictures containing Demjanjuk's photograph was first shown to Charny in the context of the Federenko investigation, when he failed to identify Demjanjuk's picture as one of the Ukrainians he recognized from Treblinka. This fact did not prevent Charny, and later Maria Radivker, who conducted the photo spread, from claiming resolutely during their testimony that what was written in the 1976 reports was the opposite of what had actually happened. Judge Levin did not refrain during the course of my cross-examination of Charny, nor during the entire trial, from interjecting into the questioning, especially when a prosecution witness was having trouble. This did not, however, prevent the facts from emerging. In any proper legal proceeding these facts would have been sufficient to rob Charny's testimony of any value as evidence. O'Connor, who continued to distract me during this cross-examination, claimed afterwards to have 'completely destroyed' another witness's testimony. He proclaimed this with great enthusiasm to anyone who would listen to him, Demjanjuk especially.

The next identification witness was Gustav Boraks, another survivor of Treblinka. At this time Boraks was eighty-six years old and almost completely senile. When he was asked how he had reached the Florida court in 1978 to testify in the Federenko case, he said that he had made the journey from Haifa to Florida by train. Judge Levin quickly came to his assistance, to minimize the damage done by this remark to the testimony as a whole. He asked Boraks if he was really sure that he had travelled to Florida by train. This time Boraks responded that he had actually gone there on a plane from Katowice in Poland. Then he changed his mind again and said that he had really flown to Florida from the city of Czestochowa. When Levin asked him why he had to travel to Florida from these places, Boraks answered that he had lived there in 1978. (In fact he had been living in Israel since 1948.) All Levin's attempts to put Boraks on the right track were in vain; this elderly, amicable witness was senile. His testimony, given in Yiddish and translated into Hebrew by Judge Tal, created a heavy, uncomfortable feeling in the courtroom.

Shaked now informed me that three of the eight identification witnesses whose names appeared in the charge sheet would not testify at the trial. This meant that there was to be testimony from only one other identification witness, Yehiel Reichman, also a Treblinka survivor, who had lived in Uruguay since the beginning of the 1950s.

It was at this point that we finally received a permit from the Ministry of Justice allowing Gill to appear as an additional foreign defence counsel in the case.

Now the time had also come to hear the testimony of Commander Alex Ish-Shalom. He had been in charge of investigating Demjanjuk after he was extradited in February 1986. According to an agreement between me and O'Connor, I was to conduct the questioning of Ish-Shalom. Right after the conclusion of Bourkas's testimony, O'Connor announced to me that he had decided to cross-examine Ish-Shalom as well. I made no real effort to keep him from doing so, but I reminded him that he should leave anything bearing directly on the identification issue to me. He promised he would.

The defence's interrogation of the police officer responsible for investigating the case against the defendant is one of the most important cross-examinations in any criminal trial. This was especially so in Demjanjuk's trial. There was no guiding principle behind O'Connor's cross-examination, which lasted from Thursday to Monday, 5–9 March.

He spent his time on irrelevant matters, such as questions about the nature of and reasons for the special investigation team being code-named Tsedek ('Justice'). He asked questions about the personal lives of Ish-Shalom and the other members of the special investigation team. The possibility that Brifer and Doron were correct in their evaluation of O'Connor's abilities began to nag at me. Perhaps this really was his first criminal trial.

At the end of the first session I commented to O'Connor that this was not the way to conduct the cross-examination of the head of a special investigation team. I explained that he had to concentrate his efforts on trying to show that Ish-Shalom had not conducted the investigation in good faith, since it had not been aimed at discovering the facts but rather at confirming Demjanjuk's guilt. This had meant deliberately avoiding any inquiries in directions suggested by the evidence, lest doubts were raised about Demjanjuk's guilt. O'Connor listened impatiently and answered angrily that he knew very well what to do.

For the first time, I was unable to find a single good point in O'Connor's cross-examination. But I tried again to convince myself that I could not completely dismiss his abilities as a result. After all, this is a subject that is unique to each country and its legal system, I said to myself. O'Connor does not know, nor can he know, the chicanery and unscrupulous methods of many of Israel Police's investigators. This is a clear reason for his failure in the cross-examination. This time, however, the attempt to reassure myself did no good. This uncomfortable feeling only grew during the rest of O'Connor's cross-examination of Ish-Shalom on Monday. During a break in the morning session, while I was drinking coffee in the court snack bar, Paul Brifer appeared behind me and began badgering me about my inability to see how worthless O'Connor was. Instead of taking exception to this, as I had up until then, I replied that I was beginning to think he might be right after all.

As mentioned in Chapter 1, I had once been a student of Ish-Shalom's. Among other things, he had taught us how to conduct a proper photo spread. Yet there was only the vaguest of connections between his academic doctrine and his actions as head of the investigation team working on the Demjanjuk case. It was no great problem to demonstrate that he had consciously refrained from carrying out investigative work to confirm or dismiss the identification of Demjanjuk as Ivan the Terrible.

During the course of my questioning, Ish-Shalom confirmed that he had been aware of the verdict in the US in the trial of Federenko that characterized the photo spreads conducted in his case as 'impermissibly suggestive'. In other words, he knew very well that his photo spreads were worthless as evidence. Ish-Shalom also confirmed that he had had pictures of Demjanjuk from 1941 to 1947, while the picture from which Demjanjuk was identified was taken in 1951. Finally, he admitted that he had made no attempt to conduct additional photo spreads using the pictures of Demjanjuk from the 1940s; he was also forced to agree that these pictures were much more fitting for use in a photo spread than the 1951 picture.

Ish-Shalom's explanation of his actions was that there was no point in conducting additional photo spreads with different pictures before witnesses who had previously taken part in identification proceedings for the same suspect. I referred him to the fact that, during his investigation, he himself had conducted additional photo spreads with witnesses who had taken part in the previous identification proceedings. Here Ish-Shalom made use of the same picture of Demjanjuk that had already been presented to the same witnesses. Ish-Shalom had no real answer for this. In distress, he shunted responsibility for his actions off on to others: the state prosecutors. Members of the prosecution team, he claimed, had forbidden him, for 'tactical' reasons, to do what he should have done.

The cross-examination lasted about forty minutes, and Ish-Shalom's answers were so evasive that he was even mildly reprimanded by Judge Levin. This was the only time that a court reprimand given during one of my interrogations was directed at the witness and not at me. The general impression left by Ish-Shalom was completely unconvincing. The facts revealed during his testimony should have been sufficient to negate the value as evidence of all the photo spreads in which Demjanjuk had been 'identified' as Ivan the Terrible. Moreover, it should have been sufficient to pave the way for his acquittal without him even having to answer the charges. When the session was over I called Doron, who praised my cross-examination. He thought Ish-Shalom looked very unconvincing, which was pleasing, since I considered Ish-Shalom's interrogation a dress rehearsal for the examinations of Radivker and Kolar.

That same week O'Connor's wife and their three children arrived in Jerusalem. Demjanjuk and his family were not at all pleased. First, they understood immediately that they would have to foot the huge bill for their trip and their stay in Israel (in the end it cost them more than $20,000). Second, the family were afraid that it would hurt their efforts to raise additional funds for the defence, if the people asked to contribute wondered why they had to finance a trip to Israel for O'Connor's family. O'Connor's mind was not on such 'trivialities', and his family spent several long weeks with him in Jerusalem, until their presence became completely intolerable to the family. When they left, the Demjanjuk family breathed a sigh of relief.

After Ish-Shalom's testimony, the last of the identification witnesses took the stand. Yehiel Reichman had been interviewed and shown a photo spread, not by Israel Police, but by the Office of Special Investigations (OSI) of the American Department of Justice. This unit was assigned to investigate American residents suspected of having committed war crimes in the service of the Nazis during World War II. Reichman testified in Yiddish, and his memory was notably weak. So, for instance, he stood for ten minutes facing a huge blueprint of Treblinka, and after a careful examination of it declared that he could not find his way around the diagram and that he could not match what he saw there with his memories of the extermination camp.

The identification procedure in which Reichman participated was performed by the American authorities, and it became clear in my cross-examination that this procedure had been even more flawed than that of the Israelis. For instance, Reichman was not given any identification report to sign. The reason was simple – the Americans did not write such a report until seven years later. According to Israeli legal precedents, this itself should have been sufficient to invalidate Reichman's identification of Demjanjuk. The connection between the report written by the Americans for the trial in Jerusalem and what really happened was tenuous in the extreme. It stated, for instance, that Reichman had needed only a few minutes to identify Demjanjuk's picture as Ivan the Terrible. Reichman, in contrast, testified that it had taken him three hours, and that he had examined each picture ten times before deciding.

The report also stated that Reichman's interview had been conducted in English, and emphasized that there was no interpreter. Reichman, however, testified that he did not know a word of English, and the entire interview had been in Yiddish. As if this were not sufficient, the report also indicated that Reichman had not even identified the Travniki photograph as a picture of Ivan the Terrible. All these flaws were revealed in my twenty minutes of cross-examination.

The fourth week of the trial concluded with the testimony of another, completely unimportant witness, a police officer named Kaplan who was insinuated among Demjanjuk's guards at the Ayalon Prison in order to fish for more incriminating evidence, but failed in his mission.

Because of the Purim holiday the trial's fifth week opened on Tuesday, 17 March 1987. On the witness stand was Maria Radivker, a woman of eighty-two, who had directed the investigation of Demjanjuk eleven years previously. She had conducted most of the photo spreads in which the Treblinka survivors had identified the 1951 Demjanjuk photograph as being of Ivan the Terrible. According to our original plan, O'Connor was not to cross-examine Radivker at all. The issue of the identification process was, after all, my responsibility. But O'Connor ignored this, while promising that he would not encroach on my field. For nearly two whole days he conducted a senseless and embarrassing interrogation of Radivker about various odd subjects, such as the date she came to live in Israel, the circumstances of her husband's death in Siberia, her occupation in Poland.

By legal standards, the cross-examination of Radivker on the identification process was the defence's most important cross-examination in the entire trial. If we can show that in conducting the photo spreads she did not act in accordance with the court-mandated guidelines, I had said to myself dozens of times over the past weeks, that would in itself be sufficient to topple the entire house of cards the prosecution has built. True, there would have to be a miracle for the case to be decided on its legal merits, but you can only do your best.

I had in my possession dozens of documents written by Ms Radivker following photo spreads she had conducted, as well as large portions of the record of her testimony in the 1978 Federenko trial in Florida and in Demjanjuk's 1981 denaturalization proceedings. I considered this to be the most important cross-examination in my entire career, and I prepared accordingly. Throughout the night before, I went over and over the contents of the many documents I would use in my interrogation, and only when I felt I had a perfect grasp of the material, at nearly four a.m., did I go to bed. Johnny approached me before I left the hotel in the morning and wished me luck.

As soon as the cross-examination began, I felt it could not be going better for me. Ms Radivker quickly lost her composure and tried, without much success, to navigate the flood of questions I asked her and to avoid giving direct answers. Judge Levin quickly noticed her distress and interfered continually with the cross-examination, sometimes with the help of his fellow judges. I had not imagined he would try to subvert the defence in such a blatant way, in front of the microphones and cameras broadcasting Radivker's testimony live. After each interjection I had to work to minimize the damage it caused, and I did not hesitate, on occasion, to confront Judge Levin. Even though I was furious at his behaviour, I think I succeeded in preserving a veneer of serenity and composure throughout the cross-examination. The audience also began to sense that Ms Radivker was having great difficulty. I felt more than ever the malicious glares directed at me by some of the observers in the courtroom. The looks were accompanied by almost constant noise from the audience, but Judge Levin did not seem to be disturbed by this.

The picture that emerged from the four hours of cross-examination was that the record of the identification process did not coincide, in many cases, with what had actually happened. In some instances, there had been an attempt to correct the record ten years later by making an additional written statement different from the original.

Radivker admitted that she had determined the order in which the pages of pictures were presented to the witnesses, and in particular the page containing the photograph of Demjanjuk from which he was identified as Ivan the Terrible. She confirmed that Demjanjuk's photograph was the only one on this page with advanced balding; the rest were of men with full heads of hair. Radivker also confirmed that the photographs of Demjanjuk and Federenko were about twice as large as the other pictures on the same page. They were also by far the clearest. She agreed that there was no similarity at all between Demjanjuk's picture and the others shown to the survivors. Her only explanation for the crude suggestiveness of the photo spread she conducted was: 'I am not responsible for Demjanjuk's baldness.'

Radivker's testimony also revealed that some of the witnesses had not identified Demjanjuk as Ivan at the first opportunity. She also confirmed that she had given no weight to their failure to identify him as Ivan the Terrible; neither had she made any attempt to analyse this failure. Many additional facts emerged in the cross-examination to cast an extremely negative light on Radivker's conduct of the photo spreads. It is important to emphasize that these botched photo spreads were the prosecution's only evidence that Demjanjuk was Ivan the Terrible.

Immediately after the session was over dozens of journalists and television reporters pounced on me for interviews. This was the first time that an Israel Television correspondent saw fit to broadcast an interview with me. While I was talking to the reporters on the stage in the auditorium, the audience was yelling at me: 'You should be ashamed of yourself, the way you interrogate an old woman for a Nazi!', 'How many millions have they paid you for those questions!', 'You interrogate like the Gestapo,' 'It shows you're a Nazi!' These were the cruellest and loudest insults so far, and they obviously expressed frustration at my productive cross-examination. O'Connor, Gill and especially Johnny commended me heartily. I was soon on my way to Tel Aviv, in a very good mood.

Along the way an idea started pricking my brain and would not leave me alone the entire weekend. Levin hasn't stopped impeding the defence, I said to myself. Each time he does it to a greater extent and in a blunter way. He thinks he can get away with it because the reactions of the defence attorneys, myself included, are not forceful enough. If there's any chance of making Levin stop this intolerable behaviour, it can only be by our asking the bench to disqualify itself from hearing the case further, on the grounds of bias of the court. Even if Levin doesn't change his ways, the trial record will at least show that the defence protested, and that will make a huge impression, particularly on the international media.

I met with Doron as soon as I arrived in Tel Aviv. We traded opinions about the last session, and he thought it had been most successful for me. I told him my idea about asking the court to disqualify itself and explained my reasons. Doron was sure this was the right move to make. The problem was to persuade Gill and, especially, O'Connor. I called Gill that same evening, spoke to him about my plan and emphasized that I should be the one to make the arguments for this request, because of my knowledge of the relevant Israeli court rulings. Gill expressed great enthusiasm and assented without reservation. He and I agreed that I would come to Jerusalem the next day and that we would together try to persuade O'Connor. Gill said that he would talk to Johnny and enlist him as well.

When we proposed the idea of moving for disqualification to O'Connor, he did not say a word, but it was very clear that he had no misgivings about it. I began to explain to him what such a procedure involved. The longer I spoke, the more I felt he was being persuaded. Then suddenly he asked who would present the disqualification motion for the defence. When I said that I would, as it was a question dealing with Israeli substantive law and procedure, O'Connor's expression quickly changed. He asked: 'Isn't it my job, as lead counsel, to ask for the disqualification myself?' I explained that it was just not practical for me to convey to him, in the space of two days, all the ins and outs of the law and previous rulings necessary to make an effective argument. Gill supported what I said. O'Connor changed tack, saying it might be too extreme a step, and only make the court's attitude towards the defence worse. Before I even had a chance to answer, Gill interrupted pointedly: 'The court's attitude towards the defence can't *get* any worse – it hit rock bottom in the last session.'

After a few moments of silence, O'Connor proposed an alternative. 'Look, almost every day we enter the judges' chambers with the prosecution to work out various procedural problems. We should, during one of these meetings, draw their attention to the fact that the unrelenting intervention in the proceedings by the judges is damaging the effectiveness of the defence's cross-examination.'

'Levin will interpret it as weakness,' I quickly responded. 'He'll take the fact that we raised it in chambers as a sign that the defence is afraid to bring up the matter directly, in the courtroom. The very fact that it happens in chambers will make his response more furious. Besides, we've already expressed our displeasure to the judges in chambers, in various ways, but nothing has come of it.'

As the discussion went on, O'Connor's reservations grew. Gill and I did not let up, however. As we stood O'Connor summed up: 'It's a very complicated matter and I'm the lead counsel. The responsibility for Demjanjuk's life rests on my shoulders, and we need to think about this a great deal.'

Over the weekend I asked several lawyer friends of mine what they thought in principle about asking at some point for the judges to disqualify themselves from the case. I refrained from giving any indication that such a measure was really being considered. Most of them said the idea was worth pursuing. On Sunday I drove to Jerusalem for the opening of the sixth week of the trial. I went to Gill's room as soon as I arrived. I was happy to see Johnny there as well; I gave a detailed report on the argument I had prepared. I emphasized that there was no chance that the judges would accede to the motion. Its importance lay in its very suggestion, because of the great reverberations it would set off. O'Connor's opposition gradually softened and in the end he agreed.

On Monday morning, Judge Levin opened the court session as usual, asking, 'Mr Shaked, do you have a witness?' 'Yes, Your Honour,' Shaked answered; 'we have a witness, but I see that the defence has risen.'

I began: 'We, meaning the defence, have spent the weekend going over the record of last Thursday's session. We have consulted with each other and with attorneys outside the defence, and I am sorry to report that we have reached the conclusion that we find it necessary – for the reasons I will present forthwith – to request that Your Honours disqualify yourselves from continuing to hear this case.'

It was like a thunderbolt. I studied the judges' faces, especially Levin's. Their expressions were of utter astonishment; Levin even fell back in his chair. Only with great difficulty did I manage to hide a smile of satisfaction. Looking at the court out of the corner of my eye, I could feel that the entire room was in suspense. There were shouts of surprise and mutterings from all directions. The cameras began flashing at a rate reminiscent of the trial's first day. People shifted in their chairs; the policemen were tense and began pacing the hall. You wanted a show-trial, my dear judges and prosecutors, I said to myself. And now I am going to expose you in all your ignominy.

I paused for a few seconds then continued, presenting a long chain of arguments peppered with quotes from the judges from this trial. I gave some examples of unacceptable behaviour by the judges during meetings in chambers. I also protested that the court had not taken upon itself to reprimand the media for their reporting of the trial, reporting which bordered on prejudgement and which was manifestly illegal. The bench's thunderous silence on this point amounted to encouraging the media to carry on in this flagrant violation of the law. I did not take my eyes off the judges the entire time. I enjoyed seeing that my words were not pleasing them, to put it mildly. I felt that my argument was well constructed, which further increased my self-confidence and contributed to the fluency and potency of my speech. I concluded by saying that the reason for the court's behaviour was simply 'boundless hostility to the defence and to the defence case'.

I finished speaking and sat down. Judge Levin turned to Shaked and asked: 'Does counsel wish to respond?' Shaked said briefly that the defence's arguments were merely subjective. He quoted two precedents of the Israeli Supreme Court which determined that a defence attorney's subjective feeling of being discriminated against is not cause for disqualifying a judge. According to legal procedure the defence has the final word, so Judge Levin gave me the floor again. I repeated concisely that the many examples I had quoted were sufficient to show, objectively and not subjectively, the court's improper and unbalanced treatment of the defendant and the defence.

Levin called a recess and announced that a decision would be handed down after that. As soon as the judges left the hall, I was surrounded by scores of Israeli and foreign correspondents who peppered me with questions from all sides. I answered in Hebrew and English, setting out our reasons for requesting the disqualification. When the reporters dispersed, Johnny came up and embraced me; Gill shook my hand warmly. I quickly went up to the defence offices and called my own office in Tel Aviv. I was answered with a cheer. Tzvia and Doron told me how great an impression the request had made, and about the media's instant reaction to the bombshell I had dropped in the courtroom.

I returned to the courtroom and the judges entered a few minutes later. Judge Levin began reading their decision: that the court's attitude to the defence was not only extremely fair, but fairer than it had to be. As an example, they pointed to the great amount of time they had allowed O'Connor to cross-examine the prosecution witnesses, even when his examination had dealt with irrelevant subjects. There was therefore no basis for the defence's request and it was denied.

The decision was not the end of the matter however. The law states that, other than in exceptional instances (which must be mentioned explicitly), when a court rejects one side's petition for disqualification and that side announces it intends to appeal to the Supreme Court, proceedings must halt until a decision is handed down on the appeal. Immediately after Judge Levin finished reading his decision, I therefore rose and announced that we intended to appeal to the Supreme Court, and basing my argument on the relevant law, I asked that these proceedings be suspended until the Supreme Court had ruled on the appeal. I explicitly noted that the appeal would be submitted the next day, and that there was no doubt that the hearing would be concluded that same week.

Once again Judge Levin and his colleagues ignored the law. They rejected my request without even asking for the prosecutor's opinion. They cynically stated that 'delaying the trial will mean a travesty of justice for the defendant, who has been imprisoned for an extended time'.

So the proceedings returned to their normal course, and Martin Kolar took the stand. Had the Demjanjuk trial been a proper one, Kolar would have been the most important witness in the trial after Radivker. He had also organized several photo spreads with Treblinka survivors. His involvement in the investigation began after Ms Radivker retired in 1978. O'Connor again disregarded the understanding between us and decided to cross-examine Kolar himself, leaving questions on the identification procedures to me. That week Demjanjuk's two daughters, Irene and Lydia, had arrived in Israel, and Irene had brought Eddie, her eighteen-month-old son. With the Demjanjuk family present in the courtroom at almost full strength and the television cameras continuously running, someone like O'Connor could not possibly forgo conducting a cross-examination. The fact that the cross-examination was totally pointless, and could even hurt Demjanjuk's case, did not bother him in the least.

O'Connor's examination lasted for about two days, the vast majority of it questions that would have been better not asked. Then the baton was passed to me. This time I was less tense than I had been before Radivker's testimony: my questioning of Radivker had gone well, and my confidence had increased after the successful impact of my argument on the disqualification petition.

The cross-examination went very well, revealing many facts indicating that Kolar had ignored, sometimes knowingly and sometimes unknowingly, most of the guidelines established by Israeli court rulings for conducting a photo spread. He had also failed to keep records of some of the identification procedures. The records he *had* kept did not always correspond with what had actually happened. As a result, there were many contradictions between his testimony in the US on some of the photo spreads he had conducted and the memos he had written about them. There were also contradictions between the memos and his present testimony. He confirmed what already emerged from Rosenberg's testimony (that when, in 1978, he had been shown Demjanjuk's picture he had not identified him as Ivan the Terrible, nor even as a Ukrainian known to him from Treblinka). It also emerged that Kolar had never told any of the identification witnesses that a picture of the man they had been asked to identify might *not* be among the photographs they had been given. According to Israeli law, this in itself is an invalid form of suggestiveness to the witnesses. This collection of facts, or even a fraction of them, were theoretically sufficient to disqualify his photo spreads from being used as evidence.

Even though less than a week had passed since the court had been asked to disqualify itself, it did not change its ways. Judge Dorner, taking her cue from Judge Levin, intervened in the cross-examination almost every time Kolar became disconcerted, and consistently kept the defence from exercising its right to conduct an undisturbed, continuous cross-examination. The disqualification petition had heightened tensions between the bench and the defence. Even O'Connor got into a sharp exchange with the judges during his cross-examination of Kolar.

When Kolar descended from the witness stand, my defence colleagues and the Demjanjuk family thought I had done my job well. I estimated that from now on I would have little work until summing-up time. I would be able to concentrate on making a workable summary of the record, which already covered 2,600 pages. I was filled with a deep sense of contentment. I would never have imagined that that very day, just a few hours later, I would feel like someone whose career was in shreds.

4 · *Kalt und Fest*

With the completion of Kolar's testimony, the trial's first chapter was almost closed. From now on, most of the testimony would focus on the Travniki document. John Gill had been hired by O'Connor first and foremost to deal with the experts testifying on this document. Travniki was a camp where Soviet prisoners of war who had volunteered for this purpose were trained to serve as auxiliary forces for the SS, stationed in the ghettoes and death camps. The central question to be decided was whether the document was truly Demjanjuk's ID card or a KGB fabrication. Despite the central importance of this question to the prosecution, it had no connection to Demjanjuk's identification as Ivan the Terrible. The Travniki document contained no reference to Treblinka, so that, even if the document's authenticity were proved, it would only show that Demjanjuk had been a member of the SS Ukrainian auxiliary forces. It could not prove that he had been Ivan the Terrible at Treblinka.

Why, then, was the prosecution working so hard to prove that the Travniki document was Demjanjuk's ID card? They believed that such proof would reinforce the testimony of the identification witnesses. It would show that they had not simply singled out some Ford factory labourer from Cleveland, but someone who had been in the SS auxiliary forces. The Travniki document, so the prosecution argued, could disprove Demjanjuk's alibi – that during the period in question he had been a German prisoner of war in Chełm, Poland.

The first witness would be a German lawyer, Helga Grabitz, retired Attorney for the State of Hamburg. Ms Grabitz had conducted, over a period of many years, criminal proceedings against Karl Streibel, the Commandant of Travniki, as well as officers of other ranks who had been stationed in the same camp. Because of the way German courts deal with such cases – looking for any reason to acquit – and apparently also because of Ms Grabitz's shortcomings as a prosecutor, all the defendants, including Streibel himself, were acquitted on all counts.

It turned out that Grabitz was intended to present at length (in response to Shaked's questions) all she knew about the training camp at Travniki. These facts were not in dispute. The only relevant question was whether or not Demjanjuk had been there, and Grabitz could make no contribution to settling this point. I therefore decided, after about fifteen minutes, to rise and object – at least for the record – to the last question asked by the prosecution. This directed Grabitz to identify pictures of SS officers from Travniki. I rose and asked: 'Is there any dispute over the fact that Globochnik [the commander of Operation Reinhard, the 1942–43 campaign to exterminate the Jews of Poland] was there, how he looked, who his assistant was, and what he did? Why do we need to hear all these stories that are not in dispute?' Before the prosecutor could open his mouth, Judge Levin said, 'Why do you express yourself that way, "these stories"?' He repeated these words for about two minutes, at the end of which he told me to 'Continue with your argument.' I went on: 'I accept the correction of my style. Still, the substance is valid. It is not proper for the prosecution, which drew up its list of witnesses before the defence admitted ninety-nine per cent of the facts, to continue proving facts as if this admission had not been made.' I gave several other arguments and concluded: 'I request that the court not allow the questioning of the witness in this direction to continue.' Judge Levin did not even bother to ask for the prosecution's response. 'Your objection is denied. Refer to our previous decisions on similar arguments made by the defence.'

That would seem to have been the end of it. But then Judge Tal suddenly interjected, asking me: 'I've noticed that the defence has been conducting a most precise, detailed and lengthy cross-examination about facts that are ostensibly undisputed. How can that be reconciled with counsel's claim that there is no need at all for these facts?' The bench was again using O'Connor's superfluous cross-examinations to justify its policy of allowing the prosecution to present evidence that was clearly irrelevant. I responded: 'The precise and detailed cross-examination by my learned colleague O'Connor is meant to test the witness's memory and not to dispute the fact that 870,000 Jews were killed at Treblinka. We, after all, proposed to the prosecution before the trial that it submit the survivors' statements, and that the prosecution ask these witnesses questions about the extent of their contact with, and specifically how and when they saw, Ivan the Terrible, and to leave it at that. Because we acknowledge the rest. Then the cross-examination would also have been very limited. The prosecution, however, was not interested, for reasons it knows best.' Everything was fine up until this point. But then I made a horrible mistake. I added: 'But then that is not why this hall has been rented. But –'

One does not talk that way in court, especially in such a hostile one.

I should have restrained myself from uttering such a sentence, especially during a week when I had caused the court great discomfort by asking that it disqualify itself. Levin needed nothing more. His face red with anger, and in a loud, strident voice, he lashed out at me: 'I ask, Mr Sheftel, that you withdraw those words. If you continue in this way we will have to take measures against you, counsel, and put you on trial for contempt of court.' He added: 'We call counsel to order. We call counsel to order. Take what we have said seriously, with all the severity in our words. What kind of talk is that?'

While I should not have used those words, Judge Levin's response was disproportionate. He went so far as to threaten me with criminal sanctions because I had hinted that the judges were accessories in the staging of a show-trial. He attacked me because my comments were justified. I tried to repair the damage, but only made it worse. 'Your Honours, first, I accept . . .' but Levin cut me off.

'Please answer my colleague's question to the point. If counsel wishes to respond.'

But I had already answered Judge Tal's question. I tried to conciliate Judge Levin – something I should not have attempted to do. 'I would like to note that it is absolutely clear to me that this court did not rent the hall, absolutely not.' What I wanted to say was that the prosecution *had*. But it was stupid of me to repeat the words 'rent the hall'. Levin dealt me another heavy blow:

'I call on counsel. I call counsel to order for the second time. And if counsel repeats this behaviour, he will find himself outside the court. I have a very high estimation of attorneys O'Connor and Gill who, with their good manners, apparently bestowed by the education they received, do not dare make such charges. I request, no more arguments.'

The world went dark. I was humiliated, disgraced. My most pessimistic thoughts had never included finding myself in such a situation. I felt my face going red and my vision blurring. I did not know what to do with myself, and in a desperate attempt to recover I turned to Judge Tal and said: 'So, with regard to Judge Tal's question . . .' Tal, who had without a doubt been the least hostile of the three throughout the trial, dealt me an additional blow. 'I think I've already been answered by counsel, thank you.' I had no choice but to respond: 'Thank you, Your Honour,' and then I finally sat down. I slipped into a deep depression. I glanced at the audience and could not help but notice the great satisfaction many people felt at the indignity I had just suffered. I sat for many long minutes, wishing that the earth would swallow me up. I could not even respond to Gill's and Johnny's attempt to encourage me.

After half an hour of total paralysis, I began to think practically and logically about what had happened. I had obviously acted like an idiot when I spoke explicitly about the rental of the hall, I thought to myself, but Judge Levin's outburst was an act of unparalleled severity. I should make that clear to him, and quickly. Shaked's questioning of Grabitz was continuing, but I did not listen. I turned to O'Connor and whispered: 'As soon as the recess begins we've got to go to the judges' chambers, and you as lead counsel have to explain that, if there is another outburst like that by the judges against any member of the defence team, all the defence attorneys will leave the hall and not return. The rest of the trial will be conducted between the bench and the prosecution.' O'Connor responded, 'Don't worry, I'll make Levin very sorry about this.'

The recess finally arrived. On the way to the chambers I told O'Connor once more what he had to say. He reassured me again. The atmosphere was tense; the judges seemed very agitated. Levin's face was pale, his expression baleful. O'Connor began to speak in a hesitant, almost apologetic voice: 'I don't understand why the court is treating the defence so harshly.' Levin did not wait for him to finish. 'The defence? The court is treating the defence with great respect. The problem is not the defence, the problem is Mr Sheftel, who does not know how to behave and who dares accuse the court of conducting a show-trial.' I expected O'Connor forcefully to reject Levin's crude attempt to drive a wedge into the defence team and to warn him that if he continued to treat me in this way, in the courtroom or in chambers, the defence would walk out. Instead he said: 'I didn't know that counsel Sheftel said anything like that, I didn't understand. It really is a serious matter if he said that.' I could not believe my ears. O'Connor was deliberately playing the fool, and he actually seemed to want Judge Levin to continue to treat me with disdain. I looked into O'Connor's eyes, but he did not meet my gaze. I was enraged. I felt my face turning red again. Levin took advantage of the situation and addressed me. 'Sheftel, after the recess you will apologize straight away and beg the court's pardon.' Then he added, in a somewhat more conciliatory tone: 'This is the trial of your life. Don't ruin yourself. Listen to what I'm saying and apologize.'

But that was exactly what Levin intended to do – to ruin me. He knew very well how humiliating the apology would be. Especially since I had to apologize to him, as if he had not pounced on me so rudely as to require an apology to *me*. I felt crushed, beaten into the dirt. Gill did not say a word, and his silence angered me. I felt I had no choice but to agree to Levin's demand; I wanted to conclude this horrible scene quickly, since it was only making my situation worse. 'I accept Your Honour's suggestion and I will apologize immediately the session opens.'

In spite of this the exchange went on for a few long minutes more, both sides merely repeating themselves. The nightmare finally came to an end, and we left the chambers. I went off to one side in an effort to pull myself together.

I don't think I have ever been so angry with anyone as I was with O'Connor at that moment. I really despised him. I must pay him back for this, I said to myself. And I'll do it in a way he'll never forget until the day he dies. The only thing that could satisfy my appetite for revenge was to get O'Connor dismissed from the case. I swore to myself that I would reveal my thoughts to no one, not even Doron and Tzvia. I did not want them to think I had lost my mind as a result of the knocks I had taken.

Now I began to think about my 'walk to Canossa', and the apology I would have to make, and I sank once more into a state of gloom. The judges entered the courtroom and Levin spoke. 'Please be seated. I would like to declare that we have come to the courtroom late because of a discussion in our chambers with the attorneys.' Then he added, in a tone of forced curiosity, steeped in pleasure: 'Mr Sheftel, does counsel wish to say something to the court?' I rose. 'Your Honours, there was indeed a consultation in your chambers during the recess, during which I apologized to Your Honours; and I wish to apologize once more in this courtroom for a comment that I uttered, during the course of my objection to the continuation of witness Grabitz's testimony, about the rental of the hall, which could indeed have been understood to mean that I was accusing the court of conducting a show-trial. I believe I should, especially in light of the heartfelt and paternal comments meant to help me and not hurt me voiced by the presiding judge during the discussion in chambers, express my apology from the depths of my heart and with all sincerity and to make it clear that there was no such intention in the said comment or in earlier comments I made at other times. I sincerely hope that my apology will be accepted.' Judge Levin did not hide his satisfaction at my humiliation: 'We have heard you, have noted what you have said, and we hope that such unnecessary comments will not be heard in future.'

I sat down. Again my face was reddening and my head was spinning. Every word I had said cut me like a knife. I felt helpless, unable to fight back at Levin. Within a few seconds I began to regret apologizing, and especially that I had been broken. I was filled with anger at myself, and I could think of nothing but what I *should* have said: 'There was a consultation in chambers, in the wake of which I once more considered what was said, and I have nothing to tell the court.' Judge Levin would have been shocked, but could not have said anything. The entire scene would have made him look ridiculous, and as a result he would have learned, the hard way, that he had not succeeded in frightening me. These thoughts only aggravated my sense of helplessness. I glanced at the audience and could sense their smugness and satisfaction at my humiliation. I was in utter despair. The idea of getting O'Connor dismissed from the case seemed like a child's response. How did it happen? I kept asking myself. After all, I finished cross-examining Kolar only a few hours ago. Even now, more than seven years later, I feel ashamed and furious as I recount these events.

When the session was over, I swiftly arranged my papers and went out to my car. Within the minute I was driving madly home to Tel Aviv. Along the way, I heard on the news a detailed report on events in the courtroom. The commentary that followed was a single sentence: 'He deserves it.' I was home in less than an hour, tired, broken, debilitated. I unplugged the telephone and went to sleep, waking up two hours later. Within minutes of my reconnecting the phone, calls began coming in from my closest friends, all trying to comfort and encourage me. These kindnesses improved my mood a little. The two television stations rebroadcast my whole apology several times. The accompanying commentary amounted to *Schadenfreude*.

On Friday morning, Johnny called. 'Gill told me what happened in chambers,' he told me emotionally. 'I was just shocked. I told my sisters, and they could not believe their ears. On Sunday, when you arrive at the hotel, I'd like you to go straight to Irene's room. Everyone will be there without O'Connor and we'll discuss the matter.' I was surprised and felt, for the first time, that Johnny had more confidence in me than in O'Connor. Johnny ended the conversation with warm words of encouragement.

Over the weekend, as I recovered, I reviewed the ups and downs of my relationship with O'Connor, from the time we first met in the Ayalon Prison. I turned his professional functioning over and over in my mind, and for the first time I reached the categorical conclusion that O'Connor was out of his depth. I could not understand how I had failed to reach this conclusion weeks before. How could I have remained so insensitive to what Doron and Brifer had told me? What had happened to my powers of judgement? I gave some more thought to the idea of getting O'Connor dismissed. If my plan were to succeed, I could not be seen to want that. I had to plan my steps wisely and craftily.

On Sunday, at six in the evening, I knocked on the door of Irene and Lydia's room. Johnny and Gill were already there. Demjanjuk's daughters did not conceal their great curiosity about me, and within seconds began showering me with questions. They especially wanted to know what had motivated me to defend their father. They repeatedly asked if I was not regretting it, given the court's treatment of me and the hostility of the media and the public. I repeated for them what I had said to so many others before. Lydia, however, did not hide her doubts as to whether I could hold up.

Irene changed the subject and asked: 'What exactly is the division of duties between you, the lawyers, in the case?'

'I'm responsible for the subject of the identification procedure as it took place with Israel Police, and in my opinion this is the heart of the case,' I answered. 'Gill is responsible for the subject of the Travniki document, and O'Connor for the rest.' I wished to lead her to the conclusion that there was really no need for O'Connor, and in fact she instantly said:

'If that's the case, O'Connor is completely unnecessary.'

'That's not correct,' I said, in order to take stock of her determination. 'When it comes down to it, he has been conducting this case for five years, and it would be hard at this stage to define him as unnecessary.'

Irene stood her ground. 'He's been on the case for five years and he has done nothing but damage. I saw all last week how O'Connor functions in court and my impression is that everything he does is causing my father the greatest possible harm.' Here Johnny intervened in the conversation and asked Gill's opinion.

'O'Connor's work is undoubtedly faulty,' Gill responded, 'but it would not be wise to dismiss him from the case at this point.' This was a pleasant surprise for me: he rejected O'Connor's dismissal from the case 'at this point'. It was clear to me, then, that it *was* possible to dismiss O'Connor, though it would not be easy.

Irene summed up: 'We have no confidence in O'Connor, and the problem is that, unfortunately, our father has great confidence in him. Father is also psychologically dependent on him, and we hope that the day will soon come when he realizes that O'Connor is leading him to disaster.' Gill and Johnny remained silent.

I called Paul Brifer and he invited me to his room. I told him in detail about how things had gone since the miserable meeting in the judges' chambers. He turned out to have heard about this already from Johnny. He did not hide his joy when he heard about my meeting with Demjanjuk's daughters. I told him that my eyes had finally been opened about O'Connor, and that I was now in total agreement with everything he had told me about the man. I expressed my astonishment and anger at having needed so long to be finally convinced he was right. Brifer, good-tempered and perceptive, tried to minimize my failure, and said that only because he himself was an American lawyer could he see so quickly how worthless O'Connor was. Obviously, I told him nothing about my plans. On the contrary, I took pains to emphasize that I had no intention of lifting a finger to bring about O'Connor's dismissal. I sensed that it was still too early to reveal my real intentions, even to Brifer.

The trial reopened on Monday and Shaked continued to ask Ms Grabitz questions irrelevant to the trial, but this time I made no attempt to object. When she had finished the evidence in chief, O'Connor rose and announced, to everyone's astonishment, that he was not prepared for his cross-examination because of the large quantity of documents that had been submitted during the evidence in chief, and that he needed a recess until the next day. Shaked did not object, and Judge Levin had a nice opportunity to display his generosity to the defence. During the rest of the trial he remembered, of course, to cite this instance, among others, to show how far he had gone on behalf of the defence. The situation as a whole did not create a good impression, implying that the defence was not properly prepared. O'Connor even said that, although Gill was responsible for the Travniki document, he himself would undertake most of Grabitz's cross-examination, with Gill only opening it.

That evening I was invited to be interviewed on a popular television talk show. I saw this as a good opportunity to correct the bad impression left by the previous Thursday, and to respond to the deluge of castigation and indignities that had been my lot in the weekend press. The interview was very successful and I received many compliments about it. None of this, however, kept the newspapers from shredding me when they wrote about it. The reporters again proved that they were not open to considering facts that were likely to confuse them and spoil their image of me.

The next day Gill launched our cross-examination of Ms Grabitz. I have to admit that it was not brilliant, but it was many times better than O'Connor's ridiculous effort. When it came down to it, the defence had no need to cross-examine Grabitz, but the chief defence counsel had decided to do so, and after the morning break O'Connor began his exhausting and pointless interrogation. He quizzed her for hours about the Vanza conference, which had decided on the Final Solution; the extent to which SS men were enthusiastic about the extermination programme; and other odd subjects irrelevant to the trial.

An idea came to me the next day, during the lunch break. If the useless cross-examination of Grabitz was taking so long, it was only fitting to use it to show the fundamental contradiction between the Travniki document and the identification testimonies. According to the Travniki document, its holder had on 22 September 1942 been transferred to an SS farm called Uksau for an unknown period of time. Jews were used for slave labour at this farm, where they were kept in inhuman conditions, abused by the SS guards. It also showed that on 27 March 1943 the holder of the document was transferred, again for an unknown period of time, to the Sobibor death camp.

According to the testimony of the survivors, they saw Ivan the Terrible in Treblinka uninterruptedly from July 1942 to the day of the Treblinka revolt on 2 August 1943. Even without this testimony it was obvious that Ivan the Terrible, one of the two gas-chamber operators in Treblinka and a key participant in the extermination process, would not be transferred, at the height of the extermination campaign, to a farm, certainly not for an unlimited period of time. In other words, the Travniki document did not support the survivors' testimony as the prosecution claimed, but actually contradicted it. Even if the Travniki document was not forged, it could not have belonged to Ivan the Terrible. I presented this reasoning to O'Connor and explained that we should take advantage of Grabitz's testimony to demonstrate the contradiction. This would cast doubt on both the document's authenticity and the quality of the identification witnesses. I pointed out that, since this was a matter with direct bearing on the nature of the identification process, it was only proper for me to conduct this part of the cross-examination. O'Connor did not fully understand me, but after additional explanations he agreed, once Gill had put the weight of his influence behind my proposal.

On Wednesday afternoon O'Connor resumed his vapid cross-examination of Grabitz. This time his questions were on matters such as the nature of the legal proceedings carried out in the Soviet Union at the West German prosecution's request, and any number of other such ridiculous questions. The members of the Demjanjuk family did not conceal their displeasure with the futile and unnecessary cross-examination, but Demjanjuk himself remained faithful, mainly because of the fanciful tales O'Connor told him during the recesses.

The next day, as soon as the session opened, I began my cross-examination. To be honest, this also was unnecessary, since everything I wanted to prove with it could have been proven from the document itself. When Grabitz, in answer to my questions, confirmed the facts about the apparent contradiction between the Travniki document and the identification testimonies, the bench, led by Judge Dorner, was quick to intervene, inadmissibly and repeatedly. I was nevertheless able to get Ms Grabitz to agree that the contradiction existed. When I concluded my questioning, Shaked began his re-examination. Basing himself on my questions, he tried to use Ms Grabitz in order to submit the Travniki document as evidence for the prosecution. This pathetic attempt was cut off by a recess.

Whereupon another tempest struck. We were all heading up to the defence offices when O'Connor suddenly attacked me in front of the Demjanjuk family. He accused me of having made a deal with Shaked, allowing the Travniki document to be accepted as prosecution evidence at this stage in the trial. I was too shocked to speak for a moment. Then I recovered and reminded him that my questioning of Grabitz had been exactly in line with what we had agreed. I added that it was disgraceful that he, as lead counsel, was now washing his hands of responsibility and even accusing me of conspiring with the prosecution. Gill, who had been present when O'Connor and I had reached the agreement, confirmed that I had questioned Grabitz on precisely those points. The expressions of Demjanjuk's daughters revealed their disgust with O'Connor's action; and only Johnny's face remained frozen: he was apparently still not completely sure of me. I said pointedly that I would not tolerate such accusations, and that if O'Connor wanted the defence team to function properly he would have to restrain himself, immediately. Realizing that no one at all was behind him, O'Connor backed off. 'OK. Let's see how we can prevent Shaked from submitting the document through Grabitz.' 'Don't worry,' I said immediately. 'Even Levin and his colleagues would not dare at this stage to include the document as evidence in the case.'

Over the weekend I spoke to Paul Brifer on the phone. He told me about the no-holds-barred conversation he had had with Demjanjuk's children when he learned of O'Connor's latest move in the defence office. He also told me that Demjanjuk's daughters wished to dismiss O'Connor from the case as quickly as possible. I told him that the matter was not my business, since the question of O'Connor's performance in the case was a Demjanjuk family matter.

The trial's eighth week was the week of Professor Shefler, a German professor whose expertise was the history of the Holocaust, and especially of Operation Reinhard. He had been called on to testify that the Travniki document was authentic from a historical point of view. Yet in a criminal trial there is no place for making such an argument, because the determination of a document's authenticity is done only by forensic experts, who can examine the quality of the paper, the handwriting, the kind of ink, the colour on the document and other related matters. Shefler could say nothing about this issue. Yet the evidence in chief went on for two entire days. He answered questions on the methodical murder of the Jews among the Soviet soldiers imprisoned by the Germans, on the procedures at the Travniki camp, on the chain of command for Operation Reinhard, and other subjects irrelevant because the defence had admitted them when the trial opened. Professor Shefler absent-mindedly said, however, that as a historian he did not have the capacity to evaluate the authenticity of documents from the Travniki camp, including the guards' personal files. In saying this, the learned witness admitted, of course, that his entire testimony was worthless.

The cross-examination of Shefler should have been over in two hours. But O'Connor again dragged out his questions. Throughout Shefler's testimony, Demjanjuk displayed an unusual interest in the proceedings. At several points he told O'Connor to ask questions about 'the top button on the guard's shirt in the Travniki document picture'. O'Connor ignored this foolish question and went on with his superfluous interrogation.

Gill tried to be more to the point in his cross-examination, but for some reason was led to ask Shefler questions relating to forensic science, a field about which the witness knew nothing. Despite this, he astutely drew Shefler's attention to the fact that it was a highly reputed historian, the British professor Hugh Trevor-Roper, who mistakenly certified that the 'Hitler diaries' in *Stern* were authentic. Gill then asked Shefler, in light of this, for his opinion on the overall value of his own testimony. At this point Shefler lost his composure and responded: 'The man who made a pretence of being a historian in the matter of *Stern* was not a historian at all.' In any court that was doing its job properly, such an unfortunate remark would have been sufficient to cast a pall over his entire testimony.

About half an hour after Gill began his cross-examination, O'Connor visibly lost his patience. He began talking to himself, spitting incomprehensible words while banging his fist on the defence table. His face turned red; he was behaving like someone mentally disturbed. I tried to calm him, but to no avail. Shaked also noticed what was going on and we exchanged perplexed glances. O'Connor grew yet more agitated, commenting to Demjanjuk about Gill and the quality of his cross-examination. He stressed, quite loudly, that if he had continued to interrogate Shefler he would have broken him completely. Demjanjuk nodded in agreement every so often, and continued to demand that Shefler be asked about the button. When I could no longer bear this embarrassing scene, I addressed Demjanjuk in Russian, so that O'Connor would not understand. I told him that Gill was performing much better than O'Connor, and asked him to pay no attention to the latter's comments.

Suddenly, Demjanjuk demanded to consult with his attorneys. O'Connor rose and asked the court to declare a short break immediately, for a consultation in the courtroom. Demjanjuk then demanded that O'Connor get up and ask questions about the button. To our utter surprise, O'Connor rose and, emphasizing that he was acting in accordance with Demjanjuk's express wish, asked the court for permission to pose questions 'about the uniform'. Permission was granted, and he asked a long and involved question about the top button appearing on the shirt in the Travniki picture. Shefler responded no less intricately, saying in effect that he could not answer the question because it all depended on the angle from which the photograph was taken. Demjanjuk's patience ran out and he announced to O'Connor that he wanted to ask the questions himself. Embarrassed by Demjanjuk's open lack of confidence in him, O'Connor addressed the court: 'We have here an exceptional request. While my client, John Demjanjuk, has full confidence in his lawyer, under the circumstances perhaps it would be best if he asked the question. You have said that this is possible, so he will take advantage of this opportunity and will become his own lawyer in this interview.' Judge Levin pounced on the opening and, completely ignoring the abnormality of the situation, asked O'Connor: 'In what language would he like to ask his question, in English or Ukrainian?' 'In Ukrainian,' O'Connor answered. The audience and journalists began to realize that here was a dramatic and unexpected event. The familiar murmur began to pass through the courtroom, and the cameras snapped and flashed at a frantic pace. Within seconds the hall was electrified. Everyone was tense, the air was thick with expectation. Shaked rose and objected to Demjanjuk asking questions in person. But Levin was not about to pass up the opportunity to prove his fair-mindedness and simultaneously make the defence look ridiculous. He interrupted Shaked: 'The defendant feels that the defence attorneys have not succeeded in presenting his question . . . this is a very important trial for the defendant. If that is how he feels, we are prepared to allow it. We allow it in other cases as well.'

Demjanjuk rose to his feet and said: 'I thank the court,' and immediately added, ineptly and confusedly: 'I would like to emphasize that the questions that should be asked now are of the greatest importance for me. I would like to ask the honourable Professor Shefler a few questions I heard while he gave his testimony, and there are a few questions on which I do not agree with the testimony given by Shefler. The first question to Professor Shefler: you had a question about the uniform, you said that the black uniforms were instituted in the Travniki camp afterwards, and at first there were yellow uniforms. I heard here that this is not true, so I am waiting for your answer.' The question was, of course, incomprehensible, and O'Connor ought to have made it very clear to Demjanjuk that he should not be intervening in the questioning. There must have been a reason for him to allow such a pathetic scene to occur. Shefler, in any case, responded: 'I did not mention yellow. I only know that at the beginning they wore black, and afterwards changed to a different colour. I don't recall that I said yellow.'

Demjanjuk continued. 'Are you sure that the black uniforms were the first ones and that afterwards there were different-coloured uniforms?' The tone of his question could have given the impression that he was basing it on personal knowledge, from having been a guard at Travniki. This is what happens when a simple man of limited intelligence and education decides to be his own lawyer, and no one prevents him. Shefler responded: 'I can only say that, according to all kinds of statements that we have heard from people who were at Travniki, they more or less point in the direction that I have indicated.' Then the mask of the objective expert fell from Shefler and he asked Demjanjuk: 'Perhaps you can tell us what the uniforms were like?' This was a vile remark. As an expert witness, Shefler was prohibited from making it, since it clearly demonstrated his bias in favour of the prosecution. Demjanjuk's foolish question and Shefler's heinous remark unsettled the audience even further, and the noise in the hall increased.

It was clear that this spectacle had already caused enough damage, so I decided to intervene. I addressed Demjanjuk in Russian and told him that we had to have a consultation immediately. He agreed. I told O'Connor that Demjanjuk wanted to consult with us, right away. O'Connor again addressed the court and asked for an additional short recess for consultation. I told Demjanjuk: 'You asked the question in such a way that implies that you were at Travniki yourself. At least, there's a big danger that the court will understand it as such. You must immediately make it clear to the court that you asked the question only on the basis of the testimony you have heard during the trial.' I repeated this several times, until I was convinced that Demjanjuk understood it. I did not leave it at that, however. I phrased for him, in Russian, exactly what he was to say after the consultation. When we were through, Demjanjuk rose to make a clarification. 'Mr Shefler, you must take into account that I am asking questions, only those questions I heard from the witnesses who have testified here in the trial.' I was pleasantly surprised by his ability to repeat my words, more or less. Then he went back to the matter of the button. 'Mr Shefler, you must take into account. Regarding the picture. I don't see any uniform in this picture, and as for the button, and the white stripe, I don't think that has anything to do with a uniform.' This was, of course, still not a question. Levin intervened at once to explain this, and Demjanjuk asked: 'I would like to get an answer from the professor, if the button he sees here in the area of the Adam's apple, is that a button from the coat, or is it a button from the shirt?'

Shefler responded: 'It's a little hard to tell from the picture. I think you can see that this is a point on which I have trouble giving a historical opinion.'

There was now a consultation between the attorneys and the court, at the end of which it was decided to end Demjanjuk's questioning. We informed Demjanjuk and he rose. 'I would like to thank the respected professor, as well as the honourable court, and all the people who heard me. I am very thankful for this opportunity to listen and speak, and I would like to give my thanks to all who participated in this event.' This was the end of Demjanjuk's role as a defence attorney in the case. A recess was declared immediately after this, whereupon the journalists charged at O'Connor and showered him with irritating questions about what had just transpired. It was 9 April, and the court began its Passover recess, which lasted until the 21st. The court record now filled 3,550 pages.

Over the course of that week Demjanjuk's daughters had several times expressed to me their dissatisfaction with O'Connor and the way he was handling the case. They were especially vocal about the conspicuous presence of his family, the huge expense this involved and the damage this was doing to the fund-raising efforts. Irene said she simply hated him: 'I know that he is doing my father serious harm each day he continues to be his defence attorney.' I did not support what she said, but neither did I make any protest. Johnny's confidence in O'Connor was also dwindling. He decided that before leaving for Cleveland that weekend he would photocopy the entire court record in English so that he and his brother-in-law, Irene's husband Ed Nishnic, could study it carefully. His reason was 'because we're no longer sure of O'Connor'. I concealed the great satisfaction this brought me. In the mean time, Paul Brifer continued to inveigh against O'Connor. This *dybbuk* ('*idée fixe*') would not let him go, and he repeated his allegations over and over again to Demjanjuk's three children.

Gill and O'Connor remained in Jerusalem, while I planned to spend most of my time in Tel Aviv, studying the record. I spoke with O'Connor about meeting to discuss the case, then I said goodbye to everyone.

After two or three days in Tel Aviv, the feelings that had been growing over the last eight weeks became more decisive. I had become the most hated man in Israel. For two months the media had heaped so much calumny on me that it sometimes seemed that I, and not Demjanjuk, was the one accused of operating the Treblinka gas chambers. Everyone recognized me on the street, because of my daily, hours-long appearances on television. People glared at me with loathing from every direction. Still, on rare occasions someone would come up to me and, after checking that I was indeed 'defence attorney Sheftel', compliment me on my steadfastness in the face of the media and the judges, and even tell me to keep at it. These times gave me great pleasure and made it easier for me to cope. Being the most despised man in the country certainly brought me no pleasure, but it had no effect on my determination and my performance. I told myself over and over: You should have taken this into account. Shame on you if you can't take the pressure.

Doron told me that almost everyone he saw said something like 'Sheftel must be depressed.' When he told them, 'You'd be surprised, Sheftel is in an excellent mood, he's just like normal and shows no signs of depression,' he would be met with astonishment and disbelief.

According to my contract with O'Connor, on 16 April I was to receive an instalment of my fee. We arranged that I would come to Jerusalem so that we and Gill could discuss our next steps, and that at this same opportunity I would be paid.

O'Connor immediately launched into a sharp attack on Demjanjuk's children. 'That piece of nothing, Johnny, that overgrown child, is starting to poke his nose too far into what's going on in the case. Demjanjuk's daughters are also suddenly putting their two cents in. When the trial resumes, I will not allow Johnny to enter the defence offices any more. John is the only one who does what he's supposed to all the time.' Gill winked at me, and I almost burst out laughing. The scene was pathetic, but also very funny. I told O'Connor: 'Practically speaking, I don't think that you can prevent Johnny from entering the office. After all, the case belongs to Demjanjuk and his family. We are no more than their representatives.'

I decided to lead the conversation in an entirely different direction. 'Mark, is it clear to you that within a short time the prosecution's case will come to an end and the defence will have to present its case? What do we have ready?' O'Connor stared at me, apparently astonished: 'What witnesses do you think we need?' I suspected at once that he had not yet begun preparing the defence case. I began to speak about the need for testimony from an experimental psychologist with a reputation in assessing the evidential value of photo spreads, in order to challenge the weight of the procedures used to identify Demjanjuk as Ivan the Terrible. I then spent some time detailing the significance of the evidence the prosecution had already presented, and that which it still intended to bring, and enumerated the types of testimony that the defence had to present to the court. At the end I asked, 'Do you have witnesses for all or some of the subjects I have mentioned?' To my astonishment, O'Connor answered: 'No, I don't have a single witness.' He added: 'If you tell that to the family I'll fire you on the spot.'

This hit me like a bolt from the blue, but I tried to respond quickly. 'What are you waiting for? Where do you think you'll find witnesses? Do you think they'll come on their own?' O'Connor's answer was a sentence that Gill and I, and later the Demjanjuk family, repeated dozens of times over the next few months. 'The wind will bring the witnesses,' he said, and fell silent. Gill and I stared at each other in disbelief. In an attempt to change the subject, Gill said that he was devoting all his time to preparing his cross-examination of Amnon Bezaleli, head of Israel Police's document-examination laboratory. Bezaleli was the prosecution's central witness in its attempt to prove the authenticity of the Travniki document. Gill's stratagem succeeded, and the rest of the conversation was calmer. I talked about the homework I was doing in order to master as much material as possible, and that I had completed a summary of all 3,550 pages of the Hebrew court record, something that would be of great help to the defence as the trial progressed.

After the meeting I arrived at the hotel and went to Brifer's room, whence I telephoned Gill and asked him to come over. I told Brifer in detail about the meeting that had just ended. Brifer said: 'You've got to remove him from the case, and fast.' Even at this point I did not want fully to reveal my thoughts, and I said non-committally: 'We've got to neutralize O'Connor, but not remove him from the case entirely.'

The next day, the three defence counsels met again in Binyanei Ha'uma. O'Connor told me he had spoken the previous day with Ed Nishnic, and that in the wake of the conversation he could immediately pay me all I was owed. He held out a cheque. I did not want to ruin the atmosphere, so I launched a conversation on the testimony anticipated from Bezaleli, presenting Gill with a number of questions. O'Connor declared that this time he would leave the entire cross-examination to Gill.

The trial was set to resume on Monday, 22 April. On Sunday, towards evening, Johnny arrived back in Israel and invited me over to his room. When I arrived, he said without preliminaries: 'Ed and I spent a lot of time in Cleveland discussing what is going on and we reached the conclusion that O'Connor is not living up to our expectations. His performance is very flawed, and as a result the defence is in a very bad position.' I fanned the flames by telling him in detail about the meeting at which we discovered that the defence had no witnesses. 'I am convinced that O'Connor has not even begun discussing your father's anticipated testimony with him. This testimony is most complex and demands a great deal of very precise preparation.'

'I'm not at all surprised by what you're telling me. I no longer have any expectations of O'Connor,' Johnny said. 'Ed will call you during the course of the week. Tell him in detail about all the facts touching on O'Connor's performance, and especially how at this moment the defence does not have a single witness.'

'I'll be glad to,' I said with a smile.

'Ed is unsure about whether to come to Israel right away,' Johnny continued. 'A lot depends on his conversation with you. He appreciates you a lot, and if you can persuade him, I have no doubt that he will.' I promised Johnny that, to the extent that it depended on me, he could already consider Nishnic as having arrived in Israel. I mused that O'Connor's dismissal was becoming more inevitable by the minute. Still, I had to continue acting as if I had no interest in the matter. I would make my contribution without anyone noticing it.

Amnon Bezaleli explained at length why, in his opinion, the Travniki document was not a forgery. Two points in particular stood out. First, he based his conclusion about the general authenticity of the document on the fact that the signatures of Streibel (the Commandant) and of Toyfel (the quartermaster) were authentic. But Professor Shefler's testimony had shown that the Soviets entered the Travniki camp in July 1944 and captured thousands of documents and office equipment. Under the circumstances, one could not reject the possibility that when they arrived in Travniki the Soviets found, among other things, forms of the type from which Travniki documents were issued, some of which were already signed by Streibel and Toyfel. Similarly, it was possible that at some later date, in the mid-1970s, the KGB added Demjanjuk's personal details to one of these forms.

The second point was Bezaleli's unwillingness to state that the signature *Demjanjuk* on the Travniki document was definitely the signature of Demjanjuk the defendant. Bezaleli was prepared to say only that 'it is possible that the signature on the document is that of the defendant'. Such a statement cannot, however, serve the prosecution as proof 'beyond a reasonable doubt'.

Towards the end of the evidence in chief, Shaked asked to submit the Travniki document as a prosecution exhibit through Bezaleli. I objected strongly. In a fairly long argument that I had prepared in advance, I presented the reasons one by one, with references to the relevant rules of evidence, jurisprudence and Supreme Court precedents. The main thrust of my objection was that it was not possible to accept the document as what the law defines as a 'public' or 'ancient document', because there was no formal certification of where it had been kept and by whom until it was brought to Israel by Hammer and Peres. Nor could the document be submitted in any other way, because there were no details about the document's 'chain of custody', no chain of facts describing its progress from the Travniki camp to the court. The existence of such a 'chain of custody' is a condition of a document being accepted as evidence, when it is not submitted as a 'public' or 'ancient' document.

I was sure that these arguments had no chance of being accepted in the Demjanjuk show-trial. A clear indication of this was given by Judge Levin: 'A wind out of the east blew through the country and brought the document to Ish-Shalom's room. The name of that wind out of the east is Hammer.' This was reminiscent of O'Connor's style. But Armand Hammer was no 'wind out of the east', and he himself did not appear to submit the document and to be interrogated about the circumstances under which it came into his hands. Judge Levin's mind was not, however, on such details. In a brief decision that he dictated into the record, he said: 'The document, according to the evidence presented to us at this stage, would seem to be not only a document of importance and relevance to the trial, but also one that would seem to have components that grant it the status of a public document, as defined in Section Twenty-nine of the rules of evidence.'

This decision was both mistaken and legally unfounded, just like many dozens of other interim decisions of this type made by the judges. If the Travniki document was indeed a 'public document', why was it necessary to wait for Bezaleli's testimony in order to submit it? There would have been absolutely no need to submit it via a witness if it had borne a legal confirmation of its originality: the prosecutor could have submitted it at any time. He did not do so because he did not have such certification. Without this, no witness could orally certify the document without a chain of custody. Despite all this, I accepted the court's decision serenely. I had long since ceased expecting it to make its decisions according to the law.

Gill prepared well for his cross-examination of Bezaleli, and conducted it acceptably. He succeeded in showing that there were conspicuous differences between the way Demjanjuk writes the letters D and M in his undisputed signatures that served as a basis of comparison, and the way these letters were written in the signature *Demjanjuk* on the Travniki document. He even demonstrated that Bezaleli had omitted this fact in his report and in his earlier testimony. This itself prejudiced his findings, both the conclusions derived from them and his own reliability. It had, after all, been his fundamental duty as an expert witness to make note of all the facts, even if disadvantageous to the side that had invited his opinion. Gill's cross-examination also revealed that Bezaleli lacked any experience in examining documents suspected of being forged by government agencies. Bezaleli, despite having served as head of Israel Police's document-examination laboratory, had not received systematic professional training of any sort, and had never taken a professional course of any kind in the examination of documents.

Bezaleli failed on another central point. There were two holes in the picture on the Travniki document, holes that even a non-professional eye could tell were made by a staple. The picture itself was attached to the document with glue, not with a staple. This indicated that the picture was not originally on the card. It had been attached to some other document, from which it was taken and glued on to the Travniki document. In other words, it was clear that there had been tampering, at least with regard to the picture. Gill succeeded in showing that Bezaleli had not examined these holes because, in his view, they were of no importance. At this point in the questioning it was perfectly clear that Bezaleli was in very serious trouble. Judge Levin, as usual, came to his aid, interrupting his answers, interfering with Gill's interrogation, even preventing him from asking further questions about the holes.

On Wednesday evening, at close to eight o'clock, Johnny invited me over to his room. Locking the door, he said: 'At around eight-thirty Ed will call from the US, and I want you to tell him everything about O'Connor, as we agreed. Give him all the facts on O'Connor's failure to perform, his lack of preparation in the case, and especially his failure to prepare even a single defence witness so far.' 'With pleasure,' I responded. We exchanged opinions about the way Bezaleli's cross-examination was going, and I praised Gill's interrogation. A short while later the telephone rang; first Johnny told Nishnic about the cross-examination of Bezaleli, and then handed me the receiver. Nishnic began by saying: 'It is a great honour for me to speak to the bravest man in Israel.' I was surprised, but flattered.

'Your opinion of me is greatly exaggerated,' I blurted out.

Nishnic added by way of apology: 'If it had been up to me, I would have called you a long time ago, but O'Connor warned me not to do so under any circumstances. Until recently we accepted without reservation whatever O'Connor told us, but no more. I would like to hear your opinion of him, in detail.'

I launched into a long lecture that took nearly half an hour, about O'Connor's misconduct, his obsessions, his blunders. Nishnic made almost no attempt to interrupt me, only asking a few times for clarification. When I had finished, he asked:

'What do you suggest?'

'I suggest you get on the first plane to Israel,' I said without hesitation. 'Stay here for a week and see what is happening with your own eyes. On that basis you can make decisions.'

Ed tried to press me. 'What decision do you suggest we make?'

'I don't think it would be wise to discuss such important issues on the phone, and before you've had the opportunity to form an unmediated impression.'

Nishnic realized that he would not get anything else out of me. 'I'll be with you, at the latest, this coming Monday.' Johnny did not try to hide his joy.

The next day there was no court session and the continuation of the Bezaleli cross-examination was postponed to the Monday. During the morning I noticed that O'Connor was nowhere to be seen in the hotel grounds, but I did not attach much importance to it. I spoke with Johnny and Gill and found out that the night before, O'Connor had learned about Nishnic's expected arrival from Johnny. He had reacted strongly to the news and had seemed very confused. By evening he was still not around. I tried to find out where he was from his wife, but she responded evasively.

The following day I devoted much thought to O'Connor's dismissal, which had become imperative and urgent. I decided I had to engineer a situation during this visit in which O'Connor would cease being chief defence attorney. My proposal would be that in any situation where the defence team was in dispute, the majority would decide. O'Connor would never accept such an arrangement, especially not if it were made public. He would start to act in such an unacceptable way that he would eventually bring about, with his own hands, his humiliating sacking from the case.

On Saturday night, Johnny called me and said indignantly: 'O'Connor's gone to America. He wants to stop Ed's visit. He spoke with my mother and told her that if Ed comes to Israel, it would be utterly impossible to prevent her husband's hanging. My mother went into a panic just because O'Connor came to America in such a surprising and unexpected way. She tried to speak with Ed, but he was already on his way to Israel. Now O'Connor is also on his way back to Israel.' I could not believe my ears. In addition to considering O'Connor a bad and lazy lawyer who did not know his craft, who did not devote enough time and effort to the case, I also thought he had an unstable and unpredictable personality. Still, I had not imagined, even at this point, that he was capable of such lunacy. It was really hard to believe what I heard.

I returned to Jerusalem on Sunday afternoon. I was just crossing the hotel's courtyard when a cab pulled up, with O'Connor inside. He got out, noticed me, waved and, with a friendly smile, asked how I was. He acted as if nothing had happened, and gave no hint that he had just been in the US.

In Johnny's room, he, Gill and Brifer were discussing O'Connor's trip with great excitement. I informed them that he had just returned. Briefer emphasized during the conversation that O'Connor had to be removed from the case immediately because, beyond his lack of professionalism, he had completely lost the mental balance needed to function in such a trial. Johnny told us that Nishnic would not arrive till the next afternoon.

The trial's tenth week began with Gill continuing his cross-examination of Bezaleli, ably raising many questions regarding the weight and general value of Bezaleli's evidence. The next witness was Reinhard Altmann, a German police sergeant from their forensic department. The prosecution wished to prove, through him and its next witness, that the photograph on the Travniki document was of Demjanjuk. Altmann was meant to demonstrate this by making a complicated comparison between the Travniki picture and undisputed photographs of Demjanjuk. The prosecution needed this proof very badly, since two of the survivor witnesses, Epstein and Rosenberg, had in December 1979 identified the Travniki photograph as that of Ivan the Terrible. There had never been an attempt in an Israeli court to prove the identity of a disputed picture by comparing it to other photographs; the prosecution's notion that it could do so was dubious, at the least. They should not be blamed for this, however, since it was inevitable that the court *would* hear these testimonies and base its judgement on them. It soon became clear that there was no accepted theory, certainly not one 'recognized by the international scientific community' (a precondition, according to Israeli Supreme Court precedents, for accepting the testimony of an expert witness), that could endorse Altmann's testimony. This focused on an album of photographic comparisons that he had prepared, which was submitted as an exhibit. This album made a detailed analysis of various features in known photographs of Demjanjuk and in the Travniki photograph. Likewise, it contained composite photographs of half of the face from the Travniki photograph and halves from known photographs of Demjanjuk. It was just a tiny leap from these to 'proof' that the man depicted in the Travniki photograph was Demjanjuk.

Altmann admitted in the evidence in chief that his method could not provide a conclusive finding, but only one that was in his words 'probable, bordering on certain'. As for the Travniki photograph, he said that he had reached a conclusion that he defined as 'very high probability'. Despite his linguistic contortions, this does not meet the level of certainty required to prove any and every fact in a criminal trial. Altmann's conclusion was insufficient to remove a reasonable doubt that the Travniki photograph was *not* of Demjanjuk. As a result, his testimony lacked any value as evidence but, as I have noted, in this show-trial it was clear that it would be seriously considered.

When we returned to the hotel, Gill and I headed for Johnny's room. Nishnic was there and immediately sprang forward, shook my hand warmly and said, 'I am very happy to finally meet you face to face, it is a great honour for me. I admire your determination to continue with the case despite everything you are going through.' 'It is very nice to hear such things,' I said, 'even if they are highly exaggerated.' There was an immediate rapport between us. Nishnic was then in his early thirties, a tall, plump man, energetic in his movements, with a full head of black hair and a black beard. He told us in detail about O'Connor's frantic trip to the US the previous weekend, and especially about the trying conversation between O'Connor and Demjanjuk's wife. He expressed his opinion that 'O'Connor has simply lost his mind.' Afterwards he related how O'Connor had, for years, misled his entire family, the Ukrainian community and Demjanjuk himself.

I now understood two things: why O'Connor feared Nishnic's arrival; and that it would not be long before O'Connor was off the case. All I had to do was make an occasional move that would advance this – to make it not only happen, but also happen at the most appropriate juncture in the management of the case.

At that time, despite all the meetings, I was very much occupied with an assiduous study of the case. I did not imagine, even at this point, that within just a short time most of the responsibility for running the defence would fall on my shoulders. I simply felt obliged to extend and deepen my knowledge. Furthermore, the case and everything connected to it fascinated me. I felt I had to know everything possible about it. Johnny later told me that my mastery of the material was a decisive factor in the decision to dismiss O'Connor.

The next day, Nishnic came to Binyanei Ha'uma for the first time. The entire morning was devoted to Shaked's continued questioning of Altmann; the cross-examination was to begin in the afternoon. Gill was meant to cross-examine Altmann, of course, but during the break O'Connor announced that he would conduct the cross-examination himself. 'I have spent all of the last few days studying Altmann's testimony,' O'Connor said in explanation of his decision. 'Because of its great importance and because I am the lead counsel, and therefore directly responsible for John's life, I have decided to cross-examine Altmann.'

Gill was stunned; he blushed. He looked disappointed, but he didn't say a word. Nishnic asked somewhat worriedly, 'Is this how things are run? Is that the way you decide which lawyer cross-examines for the defence?' I decided not to say anything, contenting myself with a wink at Nishnic. His complete lack of confidence in O'Connor and their mutual antipathy were blatantly obvious. O'Connor stood his ground. 'In such matters, on which John's life hangs, I am the only one who decides.' He had a foolish hope that he could impress Nishnic with a cross-examination that he did not have the slightest idea how to conduct.

In asking his questions, O'Connor treated Altmann the police sergeant as if he were a scientist, thus lending credence to the witness's professional expertise, instead of minimizing it, as any defence attorney must when cross-examining an expert witness. O'Connor's questions and style of interrogation were just as feeble as during his other cross-examinations. He made a very bad impression. As if this were not enough, he kept waving his pencil threateningly at me, while facing both Nishnic and the audience. This was meant to convey that I was doing something improper. My entire 'sin' was that I continued, as I always did, to summarize the record of the morning session. O'Connor was never able to understand how important this was. I looked carefully at Nishnic's face and could make out his distaste for O'Connor's behaviour.

As soon as the session was over Nishnic bounded up to the stage, and said to me: 'I feel really embarrassed for what you have to suffer, in front of everyone, from your colleague on the defence bench. Let's go out into the corridor, I want to speak to you right now.' We left the courtroom: 'I want to throw that lunatic off the case right away. I'm sick of him. I simply can't look him in the eye any more.' I was very happy to hear this, but since we could not afford to dismiss O'Connor rashly, I decided to tell Nishnic something of what I was thinking. 'It's not practical to dismiss O'Connor immediately, in that way,' I began. 'However, it is urgently necessary to neutralize him, to reduce the damage he is doing.' I paused in order to focus his attention on what I was about to say. 'You must notify him, with the consent and knowledge of the entire family, including Demjanjuk himself, that it has been decided that he will no longer serve as chief defence counsel. In any disagreement among the attorneys about any given step, the majority rules. That way, Gill and I will be able to direct the defence as we see fit, and O'Connor won't be able to do anything by himself. You should know that dismissing the chief defence attorney, however necessary, will always cause some damage, especially as the media will lick its lips at such a chance.'

This cooled Nishnic's fervour, and after some further exchange of ideas he agreed to proceed according to my plan. We then went up to the defence offices, where the atmosphere was thick with the animosity between Nishnic and O'Connor. O'Connor began, as he always did, with a series of commendations for himself, claiming to have almost destroyed Altmann's testimony, and that tomorrow he would destroy it entirely. The whole scene was pathetic and ludicrous.

At eight in the evening Nishnic and I set out, unseen, in my car, driving to the restaurant in the Notre Dame Hotel, a few dozen metres from the northern wall of Jerusalem's Old City. We talked for some three hours, Nishnic trying for most of the conversation to take stock of me and my motives for taking such an active part in his father-in-law's defence. I answered all his questions coolly, and went out of my way to emphasize my nationalist views. In the end I felt I had gained his full confidence. I spoke at length about what could be expected as the trial proceeded, and what its final result would be. I repeated without any attempt at embellishment: 'Nothing we can do will help. This is a show-trial, and in such a trial with such a case only conviction and the death penalty are possible. However, things are likely to look completely different in the Supreme Court. So we must make every effort to be prepared for the moment when we present our case on appeal.' Nishnic was very impressed by my not hesitating to give him the truth as I saw it, even though it was painful. He commented that this was the direct opposite of what O'Connor had been telling the Demjanjuk family for years. We concluded that we should set up a meeting between the three defence attorneys, Nishnic and Johnny, at which they would notify O'Connor that he was being ousted from his position as chief defence attorney, and that he would be subject to the majority of the team's decision whenever there was a dispute. Now Demjanjuk's consent to all this had to be obtained. At eleven we got up and went back to the American Colony. The excellent meal, the understanding we had achieved and the firm trust fostered between us made us feel as close as two old friends.

The next day, before the morning session ended, Judge Levin read into the record a decision about carrying out a special procedure in Germany and Belgium in May and June. The subject was the testimony *in absentia* of two SS men who had been clerks at the Travniki camp – Heinrich Schaeffer and Helmut Leonard – and from Otto Horn, an SS sergeant in Treblinka's Camp 2, where the gas chambers were situated. Another such procedure was to be conducted in Belgium, to receive the testimony of a Lithuanian named Vladas Amanavitsious, who had been a Travniki guard.

This decision, handed down in the wake of a hearing in chambers (the judges categorically refused to conduct it in the courtroom), was completely irregular from a legal point of view. Such procedures are conducted outside the country only when the witness is unable to come to Israel, and proof of this must be presented. The prosecution presented no such proof for any one of these four witnesses. The only document presented was a cable from the German police, according to which Otto Horn did not feel well. No medical certification was attached. Clearly the prosecution wanted to engage in this procedure in order to save itself the embarrassment of having to rely on the testimony of four foul SS men, broadcast live on television, in the framework of a Holocaust trial. Moreover, everyone would see the prosecution attending to the needs of these Nazis, putting them up in luxury hotels, providing them with food and drink, and finally sending them home without putting them on trial.

The judges took another unprecedented step. They decided that they would themselves go to Berlin for Otto Horn's testimony, because he was an identification witness. They said this was being done at the express request of both sides, but this was untrue: the defence had never requested it. Since the hearing had taken place in chambers, it was impossible to refute what the judges said in their decision.

The next day's testimony was to be given by Patricia Smith, a professor of dental morphology at the Hebrew University of Jerusalem's Faculty of Dentistry. She too was called by the prosecution in order to prove that the Travniki photograph was of Demjanjuk. To do so, Smith took eight pairs of identical twins and made measurements of different morphological features in their faces. She did the same with regard to features in the Travniki photograph and in two known photographs of Demjanjuk. She argued that the extent to which these features converged on each other in the known photographs of Demjanjuk and the Travniki photograph was greater than the average convergence in the pictures of the eight pairs of twins. The prosecution had informed the defence of all this, and had shown us the witness's visual aids, only four days before Smith's testimony began. Her expert opinion on the Travniki photograph had been given to the prosecution back in February, but this had been based only on superimposition – that is, placing a transparency of a known photograph of Demjanjuk over one of the Travniki picture.

The evidence in chief did not end that day. Over the weekend, Shaked provided the defence with a video cassette which contained superimpositions of Demjanjuk's face, as photographed with his full consent in the Ayalon Prison, on the Travniki photograph. Minimal fairness required that this cassette be given to the defence weeks before.

Meanwhile I waited impatiently for a call from Nishnic. On Friday night, at almost ten, he finally rang and announced that Johnny, Gill and O'Connor were gathered in his room and that it would be best for me to get to Jerusalem quickly. I jumped into my car and was in his room in less than an hour. An extremely tense atmosphere pervaded the room, and I noticed that my entry had only added to it. O'Connor immediately blurted out, his face red with anger: 'What's he doing here, he always spends his weekends resting in Tel Aviv while I'm working my ass off here.' I did not react, but exchanged winks with Nishnic. I sat down on the floor and leaned back against the couch. Nishnic asked me to detail my criticisms of the defence's performance. I spoke for about an hour; O'Connor interrupted me angrily many times with cries of 'Liar!', 'Playboy!', 'You and your Porsche,' and other such idiocies that made him look pathetic. At one point I addressed him in his usual truculent way, 'Now sit down and shut up. For months we've all had to listen to the nonsense that comes out of your mouth. Now shut your mouth, open your ears, and listen to what a lawyer in this case should and should not do.' With help from Johnny and Nishnic, who joined me in demanding firmly that O'Connor allow me to speak, he fell silent for a while.

It was clear that this speech would lead to a definite rift with O'Connor. But I was convinced that the time had come to pressure him explicitly. I concluded by saying: 'There is only one way out of this predicament, and that is removing O'Connor from his position as lead counsel. The working arrangements from here on will be that, in any case of a dispute among the defence attorneys, the majority will decide. To avoid embarrassing O'Connor, there is no need to make this decision public, if he accepts it and abides by it.'

The floor was given to O'Connor. 'There's no need to pay any attention to what Sheftel says. It's all the result of the pressure he is under because of the media's attacks on him. Sheftel is on the verge of mental collapse. He can't hold up. Neither can he face up to the continual pressure from his mother to leave the case immediately.' Then he began praising himself, emphasizing continually that he had completely devastated all the testimony against Demjanjuk. He repeated his stupid charge that my devoting a great deal of time to summarizing the court record was proof of my poor performance.

O'Connor talked for a long time, but never responded directly to a single one of my arguments. His speech quickly began to bore everyone in the room. In the end Nishnic silenced him: 'OK, we've understood what you want to say. I agree with everything Shefy said, especially his conclusion about the defence's working procedures. As far as Johnny and I are concerned, O'Connor is no longer chief defence attorney. Tomorrow I will see my father-in-law and notify him that this is what the family wants. When I get his consent, the new arrangement will take effect.' I knew O'Connor would never acquiesce to this arrangement, and it would lead to the family dismissing him from the defence bench. He must have seen that Johnny and Nishnic, who represented the whole family, had absolutely no confidence in him and were disgusted by his behaviour and his speech. It is surprising that he did not submit his resignation immediately after this humiliating meeting.

On Monday evening Nishnic informed me that he had seen Demjanjuk in prison and that he was inclined to agree with the change in O'Connor's status. He added that O'Connor had also seen Demjanjuk and was putting heavy pressure on him not to agree to the new arrangement. Nishnic expressed his confidence that Demjanjuk would prefer his family's advice to O'Connor's.

The trial's eleventh week began, unusually, on Tuesday, with Smith on the witness stand again. After about half an hour the prosecutor asked to present the video cassette that had been given to us only three days previously. He asked to play it on screens that had been prepared in advance for this purpose. It was possible to object to this only on the grounds that the cassette had been given to the defence at too late a date, and we had not had time to prepare our cross-examination on this point. O'Connor jumped to his feet and began a formless, meaningless babbling. For some fifteen minutes he argued that the cassette was a serious libel against Demjanjuk. Among other things, he said, 'When the subject is the loss of a man's good name, over the generations that has been the equivalent of declaring him fair game. When a man's face is whitened and the blood actually leaves and you don't see the blood any more, that is the equivalent of declaring him fair game, which is a crime in the Bible and in the Talmud as well. This is actually a horrible libel, to whiten a man's face, to slander him. It breaks every rule, both in the Bible and the Talmud. And with all due respect I will give the example of Miriam and Aaron. Miriam and Aaron, when they turned against Moses when Moses took an Ethiopian woman, and then he heard himself slandered by Aaron and Miriam, and of course Miriam soon received a divine scourge and she fell ill with leprosy, and only after Moses prayed to God was she cured.' He went on and on with such inanities that it was hard to believe this was a lawyer speaking in court. This nonsense made a (justifiably) bad impression on the judges; the defence was exposed in all its weakness. I tried to hint to O'Connor that he should cut himself short and finish. When he finally sat down he told me: 'Put yourself in your Porsche and go to Tel Aviv and don't come back here any more.'

The video was submitted as an exhibit, of course. After the morning break Gill began his cross-examination by strongly but politely protesting that the defence was forced, without any preparation, to conduct a cross-examination about material of a type that had never before been presented to a court in Israel or elsewhere. This argument made no impression on the judges. In contrast, Levin later ordered the defence, in a formal decision dictated into the record, to provide the prosecution with every expert opinion that it intended to present, at least fifteen days before the beginning of the witness's testimony.

In February 1987, when the defence had received a part of Professor Smith's opinion, I had made it clear to O'Connor that he had to ensure we had an opposing opinion before she testified. I also said that such an opinion had to be given by an expert of stature, and must be the foundation of the cross-examination of Professor Smith. O'Connor had promised me that 'You can consider it done.' Like other promises, it was broken. The defence had no contradictory opinion; Gill stood there empty-handed as a result, and could not challenge Smith's testimony.

When Gill had finished his cross-examination, on Wednesday evening, Nishnic summoned us all to his room. As soon as we sat down he said: 'I spoke with my father-in-law again today, and he has agreed that from here on out there is no longer a chief defence attorney, and that if there is a dispute among the defence attorneys the majority will decide. There is no need to make the matter public.' Then he addressed a warning to O'Connor. 'If you dare try to influence my father-in-law to change his mind, things will finish badly for you.' O'Connor looked agitated and angry, but except for hissing, 'OK, OK,' did not say a word.

Nishnic announced that he was returning to Cleveland the next day, and we arranged to meet alone at ten, in my room. Nishnic asked me what I expected from O'Connor. I said I had no doubt that he would renege on the agreement and would continue to do as he pleased. Nishnic's response was: 'If that's what happens, we will kick him the hell out of here, and my father-in-law will agree.' He then thanked me warmly for facing up to O'Connor and for having saved his father-in-law and the entire family from his incompetence. He declared that henceforward he would be directly responsible for paying my fees, and that if O'Connor failed to make any given payment, he would pay me the entire sum. At this point I was already aware that Nishnic had established an efficient and sophisticated organization for collecting contributions from all over North America, and I believed he could keep his pledge. We parted and promised to meet again many times.

5 · O'Connor is Dismissed

On the morning of Thursday 7 May, it was Gideon Epstein's turn to take the witness stand. Epstein was an American forensic expert who had testified at Demjanjuk's denaturalization hearing in Cleveland in 1981. Based on almost the same evidence that the prosecution in Jerusalem was using, Demjanjuk's citizenship was revoked because the court ruled that, when he applied for and received American citizenship, he had not truthfully disclosed his actions during the war. Epstein had examined the original of the Travniki document for the first time in the Soviet Embassy in Washington in 1981. He had not, in his written report, addressed the question of whether the signature *Demjanjuk* on the Travniki document was in fact the signature of Demjanjuk the defendant.

Epstein's testimony in Jerusalem was virtually identical to Bezaleli's, although his answers were more intelligent. Shaked also tried to ask him about the *Demjanjuk* signature on the Travniki document. I rose and objected strongly. Shaked's attempt was so blatantly unfair, and contrary to legal procedure, that he decided to retract the question without waiting for the court's formal decision.

Gill was well-prepared for the cross-examination and did a good job. The results were by and large similar to those of his cross-examination of Bezaleli. We were now at the beginning of the trial's twelfth week and the record was at page 4,450.

Next, Professor Matityahu Meizel of Tel Aviv University, an expert on Soviet history, began his testimony. This opened what the prosecution called the 'historical evidence' stage, during which attorney Yonah Blatman, the State Prosecutor, returned to the scene. Its primary object, as described by Shaked's opening presentation, was to show that Demjanjuk's alibi (that he had been a prisoner-of-war in the Chełm POW camp from the autumn of 1942 to the spring of 1944) was historically impossible. Meizel was also supposed to show that when Demjanjuk filled out forms in 1948 to receive refugee status, and entered incorrect facts and omitted many others, he was hoping to conceal his being Ivan the Terrible from Treblinka and not to avoid, as he claimed, being forcibly repatriated to the Soviet Union.

According to Meizel's testimony, the 'Vlasov army' was not formed until November 1944, while its second division, based near the German city of Hoiberg, was formed only in January 1945. The Vlasov army was made up of Soviet, primarily Russian, prisoners of war who had been captured by the Germans and agreed to fight on their side against the Allies. It was conceived and founded by General Vlasov, taken prisoner by the Germans in the summer of 1942. The prosecution wished to discredit Demjanjuk's claim that he had joined the Vlasov army in the spring or summer of 1944 in Hoiberg, after he was freed from the Chełm camp. They hoped that this would help persuade the court that Demjanjuk's whole alibi should be rejected.

O'Connor began his cross-examination, after telling us all that he had spent months preparing for it. He promised 'to tear Meizel to shreds'. When he voiced this boast, Gill and I knew he was fantasizing again. But Gill was not familiar with the material, and I – despite my extensive knowledge of the Second World War – did not consider myself sufficiently prepared to cross-examine an expert witness on this subject in a criminal case that was liable to end with a death sentence. It was soon clear that O'Connor was on his usual form. He interrogated Meizel on the notorious murder in 1941 of some fifteen thousand Polish officers by the KGB in the Katyn forest, about the annals of the Vlasov army, about the conditions of imprisonment in German camps, all without presenting any counter-position, anchored in fact, to Meizel's claims.

At the end of Meizel's testimony the court announced an official adjournment until 22 June, in order to hear the witnesses in Germany and Belgium. Gill, Johnny and I had already formulated our work programme for the immediate future. O'Connor would appear for the defence at the overseas proceedings. Gill would return to the US and put together expert evidence about the Travniki document. I would begin preparing Demjanjuk for his own testimony. At that point it was confirmed that, during the five years O'Connor had been responsible for the case, he had never sat down with Demjanjuk to draft a detailed response to the charges against him. I was astonished to discover that this had not even been done during the 'deportation trial' in Cleveland in 1984. We had likewise agreed together that a series of documents would be submitted from both the prosecution and the defence, in order to save us all much precious time. It was clear that O'Connor would object energetically to this, with no well-founded reason, but now it was sufficient for Gill and I to agree to this action.

The following morning I went over the material that O'Connor intended to take with him for the proceedings in Germany. I realized that several things were missing – statements by and evidence from Otto

Horn, who was to be questioned in Berlin. That evening Johnny and I approached him as he sat alone in the hotel dining room. We asked him whether all of Otto Horn's statements, in their English translations, were in his possession. He replied, 'That's none of your business. I, not you, will be in Berlin to examine Otto Horn.'

'The question is not who will examine him,' I answered calmly but firmly, 'but whether whoever does examine him will have all the necessary material, including Otto Horn's statements.'

O'Connor was infuriated: 'You're fired!'

Johnny turned to me swiftly: 'And you're hired.' A moment later he explained that from that minute onward I was no longer O'Connor's employee; I was now retained by the Demjanjuk family.

Johnny and I then went out to a Jerusalem pub. We spent several hours there talking, the first occasion when the two of us had sat alone together for such a long time. The atmosphere was pleasant and open. I marvelled at Johnny's persistence in believing that his father was innocent. I could not help respecting him for the way he had coped with the intolerable situation he had been in since he was twelve years old, when the accusations were first made. Johnny expressed over and over again both his delight and his astonishment that a nationalist Jew like me was willing to hitch himself to the defence wagon. It was only natural that we also speak of O'Connor. Johnny said that what he had told me in the dining room had been with Nishnic's full understanding and consent. When we returned to the hotel, we felt a strong sense of co-operation, mutual trust, admiration, even closeness. Johnny returned to the US the next day, and I went back to my home in Tel Aviv.

On Sunday 17 May I went to see Demjanjuk at the Ayalon Prison for the first time since the trial had commenced. He received me joyfully. I was correct and polite, but no more than that. Before my arrival, I had made a decision not to talk with him at all about O'Connor. If he tried to initiate a conversation on the subject, I would avoid the matter. I told him that I intended to meet with him three or four times a week until the trial resumed, so that we could plan his upcoming testimony together. I told him that, while I would prepare him to testify, it would be Gill who would examine him in court. Demjanjuk agreed to everything. I brought a large number of documents in English, containing all of Demjanjuk's statements and testimonies from 1978, when he had first been questioned about the suspicions raised against him, to 1986, when he had been interrogated by the special investigation team in Israel. I explained at length why he had to be well-acquainted with each of these documents, and urged him to devote all his time to studying them. I divided the material into several batches for him, so that he could prepare for each meeting during the first two weeks by studying at least the documents I wished to discuss with him. He consented willingly.

The examination of Helmut Leonard, the German SS man, was to begin on 18 May in the magistrate's court in Köln, Germany. This Leonard, a retired German police sergeant, already seventy-one when he gave his testimony, was stationed as a clerk at Travniki during the years 1942–44. The prosecution hoped his testimony would bolster their claim that the Travniki document was original and authentic and that it belonged to Demjanjuk.

What happened during Leonard's testimony was what English jurists drily refer to as 'the witness not coming up to proof'. Not only did he fail to say what Michael Horowitz, who conducted the proceedings for the prosecution, expected him to say, but also that 'Document T/149 [the Travniki document's exhibit number] should have contained an assignment to the Treblinka SS camp if its owner was indeed stationed at Treblinka, even for a period of two or three weeks. I would have updated the card file personally.' Leonard added that 'Each certificate contains a date of issue. A service certificate [as the Travniki document was defined] without a date of issue is no more than a crude forgery.' As if this were not enough, the witness took the trouble to explain: 'A guard caught at Treblinka with document T/149 would have been arrested, because Treblinka was outside the area permitted him according to what is written on document T/149. According to document T/149, the bearer of the certificate was never in Treblinka, but rather in Sobibor and Uksau. The bearer of T/149 would have been arrested, for the same reason, had he stayed in one of the villages close to Treblinka.'

With these words Leonard unequivocally confirmed my claim that the Travniki document, even if not a forgery, had not belonged to Ivan the Terrible. It must have belonged to a guard who had never been in Treblinka and could not, therefore, have been Ivan the Terrible. Leonard's testimony was so bad for the prosecution that it decided of its own volition to forgo the questioning of the other German SS man from Travniki, Heinrich Schaeffer, lest he make matters even worse. In the mean time it was learned that the questioning of the ex-guard Amanavitsious would not take place either, because the witness had died. Since Otto Horn's examination in Berlin was not to begin until June, O'Connor returned to Israel straight after Leonard's testimony, on 21 May.

On Tuesday the 26th I visited Demjanjuk. We were busy preparing his testimony when O'Connor entered. He greeted Demjanjuk and immediately said: 'I succeeded in destroying Leonard's testimony to such an extent that the entire case has now been destroyed. That is why Judges Levin and Tal have left secretly for Germany, in order to speak with the judge who heard Leonard's testimony, and with the judge who will hear Otto Horn's examination. They will try to find a way to save the case from collapsing completely and from ending in acquittal. Even Sheftel knows nothing about this.'

I could not believe my ears. Even at that stage I had not expected O'Connor to make such an insane declaration. But Demjanjuk, who did not understand how crazy O'Connor's contention was, turned to me and asked, 'Do you know anything about that?' O'Connor did not know that that very week the media had widely reported the resumption of the trial of Mordecai Vanunu, and that Judge Tal was on the bench in that case. O'Connor's lie had illustrated so well how he deceived and misled Demjanjuk, and promoted his emotional dependence on O'Connor. After a moment's hesitation I decided to take advantage of Demjanjuk's question to destroy the bond between them once and for all. So I said, 'You should know that at this very moment Judge Tal is sitting and hearing the Vanunu trial. You can read the report of it tomorrow in the *Jerusalem Post*. Judge Levin is also, of course, in Israel, and has not gone on the mad journey that O'Connor is so brazenly describing. You should know that most, if not all, of what O'Connor tells you is absolutely false, just like this most recent story. O'Connor himself doesn't believe for a moment that Levin and Tal have really gone to Germany, and certainly not for the reason he said. He is simply taking advantage of your naïvety to deceive you disgracefully. Now he'll tell you, even in my presence, that he has alibi witnesses, and I'm telling you, in his presence, that he's lying, that he doesn't have and never has had any alibi witnesses, and that he barely understands what an alibi witness is.'

Demjanjuk's face reddened. He was flustered, and it was evident that he had not understood most of what was said. I realized that what bothered him more than anything else was the huge rift between me and O'Connor. When he finally opened his mouth, he said weakly: 'I don't know if the judges went to Germany or not, that's not so important. But I want you not to argue with each other and for you to work together.' My response was unambiguous: 'So long as O'Connor occupies himself with nonsense and lies, working together is inconceivable.' I rose and said as I arranged my papers, 'I came here to help prepare for your testimony. O'Connor's presence makes it impossible to continue. I am going now and will return the day after tomorrow to continue our work.' Demjanjuk asked that I wait, but I made it clear there was no point.

That evening, Nishnic called me at home: 'What's this new nonsense of O'Connor's about Levin and Tal going to Germany?' It turned out that O'Connor had also tried to sell this crazy story to Nishnic and Johnny. I told him about the incident in Demjanjuk's cell, and how Judge Tal was taking part in the Vanunu trial. Nishnic said: 'He's totally out of his mind. It's good that you said what you did in front of my father-in-law. Maybe it will finally open his eyes.' I returned to Demjanjuk's cell later that week, to continue my work with him. I intentionally refrained from talking about O'Connor, and I silenced Demjanjuk when he wanted to say something about the matter.

We were getting closer to the date on which Otto Horn, the SS sergeant from Treblinka's Camp 2, would be questioned. O'Connor departed for the magistrate's court in Berlin; the three Israeli judges also left. Horn was the only identification witness who was a storm trooper rather than a Holocaust survivor. He was also meant to contradict the version of the story that claimed Ivan the Terrible had been killed during the uprising.

His identification of Demjanjuk had been made before American investigators in November 1979. As with Reichman, the identification procedure was carried out by OSI investigators. (The defence did not possess, at the time Horn testified, any information about a record of the interview (a 'memorandum') written at the time this interview took place. Such records were later discovered by the defence, in very mysterious circumstances.)

Like his predecessor Leonard, Horn also failed to 'come up to proof'. Among other things, he told the court: 'The photograph only resembles Ivan, and that's what I said before.' Also: 'There is a similarity, and the similarity is in the round face.' And later: 'That's about the way Ivan looked, it could be him. It's similar.' Finally: 'The resemblance between the photograph and Ivan comes down to the round, full face.' In a proper criminal proceeding such doubtful testimony has no value at all, especially not as identification evidence. Even non-lawyers easily understand that. But in Demjanjuk's case Horn's worthless testimony could be admitted. This court, indeed, attached particular weight to it in the verdict.

There was clearly no need for a cross-examination. All that was necessary was to rise and say, 'In light of Horn's testimony, it is clear that we do not have a real identification witness before us, so I waive my cross-examination.' O'Connor thought otherwise and spent two entire days in superfluous cross-examination. One of his most embarrassing questions was: 'Are you one hundred per cent certain that this photograph is a photograph of Ivan from Treblinka?' After all, even a negative answer to this question would help the prosecution.

In the mean time I met with Shaked regarding the twenty documents that would be submitted by mutual consent. During the course of this meeting I intimated that O'Connor was about to be dismissed from the case. Shaked chose not to react. When O'Connor returned to Israel I told him about the agreement, and emphasized that it had been concluded with Gill's approval. As expected, O'Connor rejected it absolutely and said he would object to the submission of the documents. I reminded him that according to our new procedures he had to accept the decision, and that he had an obligation to prevent the public disgrace that would result from the defence speaking with two voices. But he was adamant: 'I am the lead counsel and I will make the decisions.'

'That's no longer true,' I reminded him again.

O'Connor was furious. 'I called attorney Matti Atzmon. He will replace you soon. You and Gill won't decide anything.'

During the days that followed I began to think that the time had come to make another move towards getting O'Connor dismissed: a public declaration that he was no longer chief of the defence. The announcement would be preceded by one to the judges a day before the trial was to resume, at a chamber session previously set by them. On Sunday night, 21 June, Nishnic called. He asked: 'Who is this Atzmon O'Connor says is the best criminal lawyer in Israel?' I did not know Matti Atzmon at all, and had never heard his name until O'Connor mentioned it. I was, however, pretty sure he was not 'the best criminal lawyer in Israel'. I added that O'Connor's idiocies were not worth another thought. Then I told him about O'Connor's refusal to abide by the decision Gill and I had reached over the documents, and his intention of sabotaging our agreement with the prosecution. Nishnic was enraged. This seemed the right moment to tell him about my plan to announce O'Connor's new status. He seemed hesitant, but agreed in the end. His consent sealed O'Connor's fate. O'Connor's reaction to the move would be to attack and slander me in the media. I would not respond, his frenzy would continue, and a few days later there would be no choice but to fire him.

The in-chambers meeting was set for six o'clock at Binyanei Ha'uma. At five I met with Gill and we agreed that he would notify the judges of the change in O'Connor's status. We entered the chambers at the assigned hour, and after an explanation from Shaked of the testimony to be presented up to the end of the prosecution case, I indicated to Gill that the time had come to make his statement. Now *he* was hesitant.

I prompted him again, but he still could not make the statement. So I took the floor myself. 'I would like to notify the honourable court, as well as the lawyers for the prosecution, that from this moment onward O'Connor is no longer serving as chief defence counsel in the case, and that the status of all the defence attorneys is equal. If the court requests, the defendant will confirm this publicly.' There was a tense silence. After a few seconds Judge Levin responded: 'For us, O'Connor was and remains chief defence counsel.' I was amazed. Such a thing was unheard-of – a judge deciding the status of the defence attorneys. I replied: 'With all due respect, in a matter such as this the defendant, and not the court, decides.' Judge Levin answered: 'I have said what I have said and will not say anything further.' At this point O'Connor interrupted in a puerile voice, as if someone was about to take his favourite toy away: 'Everything Sheftel said is wrong. I am the lead counsel.' I decided not to react, and the discussion went on to other matters. But a look of dissatisfaction was apparent on Judge Levin's face.

Back at the hotel I explained to Johnny that O'Connor would now start acting up for the media and slandering all of us, me in particular. We had no intention of getting into a debate with him, but it would be best if Johnny did all he could to restrain him, even if there was no chance of success. Johnny answered as expected: 'If that's what happens, we'll throw him off the case immediately.' I decided for the first time to hint at my intentions: 'And will your father agree?'

'I'm sure he will.'

'I'm not so sure,' I said, closing the matter.

The next day the trial resumed with the testimony of Dr Shmuel Spector of Yad Vashem, who was presented as an expert on the subject of the 'Galician division'. This was a combat division of the SS made up of Ukrainian volunteers. Demjanjuk had always claimed that in the spring of 1944 he was sent from Chełm to an area near the city of Graz, to join this unit. There he was tattooed on his left arm, and turned from a prisoner into a collaborator. By his account, however, it was finally decided to attach him to the Vlasov army instead of to this division. Spector was supposed to demonstrate that Demjanjuk's story was impossible from a historic point of view, because the Galician division was nowhere near Graz in the spring of 1944; it arrived there only close to the beginning of 1945. The entire subject was marginal. O'Connor's cross-examination in the afternoon was surprisingly brief and finished the same day, in the evening, with no results.

The next day's witness was Dr Shmuel Krakovski, presented as an expert on the Germans' POW camps. He was also meant to show that

Demjanjuk's account of his doings in the years 1942–44, and especially the time he claimed to have spent in the Chełm camp, was historically flawed.

Now I rose and asked the court, in accordance with the arrangement with Shaked, that the prosecution submit a series of documents and define their nature. Permission was granted, and Shaked began. O'Connor let out angry growls and interrupted the proceedings from time to time. At several points he whispered to me, 'You're killing Demjanjuk,' in such a way that Demjanjuk would hear him. Then suddenly something went wrong with the microphones. O'Connor rose and said: 'Your Honours, because of the technical problem, my client requests, if possible, a five-minute recess. He wants explanations. He is somewhat bewildered and confused by these proceedings, and if it is possible, we ask to meet with him in his cell.' The recess was granted.

As soon as we entered Demjanjuk's cell I assailed O'Connor. 'You are embarrassing the defence. These documents will be submitted no matter what you do, and if you interfere, you'll pay dearly.' Gill also protested: 'Everything that is going on is acceptable to me and I have given my consent, and you have to accept that.' Demjanjuk looked lost and did not get a word out. The 'consultation' ended and we returned to the courtroom. This time O'Connor remained silent until Shaked finished.

In the mean time, O'Connor's removal from the position of chief defence counsel had leaked out to the press. As soon as the recess began, the journalists pounced on Gill, Johnny and me. As we had agreed in advance, each of us offered only a single, brief comment: 'I have nothing to say except to confirm that it is correct. O'Connor is no longer chief defence counsel.'

O'Connor did not disappoint me. After denying the report and insisting that he was still leading the defence, he launched a wild attack against Gill and me. Among other things, he told the reporters that 'I would never buy a used car from Sheftel.' Under that headline the next day's papers were filled with many stories and details, all totally imaginary, about what was going on in the defence team. The articles quoted many O'Connor gems, most of them unrestrained attacks on me. He went way too far, his foolish talk paving his way out of the defence. The reporters were much less interested in Krakovski's testimony than what was going on within the defence team.

I will note only one element from Krakovski's testimony, because of its marginal nature. At Demjanjuk's denaturalization trial in Cleveland in 1981, a historian testifying for the prosecution said that Chełm ceased functioning as a POW camp no later than January 1944. Since Demjanjuk had always insisted that he had been held at the Chełm camp until the spring of 1944, such testimony could impeach the truthfulness of his account. Yet here came Krakovski and stated unequivocally that the Chełm camp was evacuated only in April 1944, and that there were POWs there until then. This bolstered Demjanjuk's claim, if indirectly. Despite the minor importance of Krakovski's testimony, O'Connor questioned him for a day and a half. The result of this interrogation was, as usual, infinitesimal. This concluded the 'historical section' of the prosecution evidence. They had only one more witness, Dr Antonio Cantu, an expert on paper and ink. Shaked and Gill completed their examinations quickly, and this marginal testimony was concluded within a day. The trial's fourteenth week was coming to a close, and the prosecution had finished putting their case. The record now filled five thousand pages.

In the mean time, with the media's active assistance, people were absorbed by what was happening with the defence. The trial itself interested no one. O'Connor fanned the flames in dozens of interviews in which he threw caution to the winds. Even though I had imposed silence on myself, I felt I had to take one more small step to force O'Connor to lose control completely, without getting drawn into an exchange of insults with him. In response to repeated requests from the media that I respond to O'Connor's charges, I gave one more sentence: 'Do not rejoice when thine enemy falls.' When this reached O'Connor's ears, he went berserk, and his comments to the media became hysterical.

Suspecting that his fate was sealed, he grasped at the last and lowest means of saving himself – anti-Semitism. He called Nishnic and explained that I could not be trusted because when it came down to it I considered Demjanjuk and his family no more than a bunch of goyim. Nishnic reacted angrily and slammed the phone down. But O'Connor would not give up. He went to Demjanjuk and Johnny and told each of them separately that Mossad had planted me in the case in order to get rid of him and pave Demjanjuk's way to the gallows. This desperate stratagem also worked as a boomerang, providing final proof to Demjanjuk and his son that there was no choice but to dismiss him immediately from the case. Johnny and Nishnic told me about these conversations two weeks later, in Cleveland, but I was past surprising.

O'Connor's media uproar now peaked, and this meant I could finally express my views openly. On Thursday evening I asked Gill and Johnny to a meeting. 'At first I thought that removing O'Connor from the position of chief defence counsel was sufficient to create a situation in which Gill and I could run the defence in practice. O'Connor has not agreed to this and has even disgraced the defence in the most sordid way, by hysterically attacking his colleagues in the press. He did this without Gill or myself saying one word critical of him in public. We have firmly refused to react against his public attacks on us. Even direct requests from both Johnny and Demjanjuk that he hold his tongue have been no use. As a result, from this Monday I no longer intend to sit on the same bench as O'Connor.' Johnny's response was immediate. 'You will no longer sit on the same bench with O'Connor because Monday will be the last time O'Connor sits on that bench.' Gill said, 'O'Connor has clearly shown during the past week that he is impossible to work with, and that his interest in the case is what is good for O'Connor and not what is good for his client.' Johnny concluded with an announcement: 'Ed and I have decided that on Monday I will have my father sign some blank sheets of paper and that we will all sit together in Cleveland and draft O'Connor's dismissal letter and our notification of this to the court. You,' Johnny said, turning to me, 'will deliver the letter to my father and he will hand it to O'Connor.' My account with O'Connor is closed, I thought to myself.

We also agreed that, a day or two after next Monday's session, I would go to Cleveland, where we would all meet to plan the defence presentation. Attorney John Broadly, of the Washington branch of the firm of Jenner & Block, would also be there, as the family wanted him to replace O'Connor. I agreed to go, but emphasized that I would have to return to Israel quickly in order to continue the preparations for Demjanjuk's testimony. Then I headed for Brifer's room to update him. He received me genially; he appeared to sense the purpose of my visit at once. When I finished speaking he gave me his warm congratulations and said that it had been obvious to him that O'Connor would be dismissed during this week.

That night I told Doron about the recent events. He commented on the damage I had suffered as a result of all the nonsense O'Connor had had printed about me. I explained that it was actually this behaviour and the coverage it had received that had been the last straw for the family. We both judged that O'Connor would not surrender his position easily, and that the court would raise every possible impediment, even though it was required by the rules of procedure to confirm O'Connor's release. The judges, Levin in particular, would do this because the sacking would be seen as 'my victory' in the public confrontation with O'Connor.

The next night Nishnic called me at home and thanked me warmly for my help in getting rid of O'Connor. 'We would never have reached this moment without you,' he said. I thanked him, saying: 'You would have reached the conclusion that you had to throw O'Connor out, but it would have taken more time.'

The defendant in a criminal trial in Israel has the right to request, at the end of the prosecution case, that he be acquitted without being required to respond to the charges. This is known in English law as 'pleading no case to answer'. For this to be successful, the defendant must persuade the court that, even if all the evidence presented by the prosecution were truthful, it would be insufficient to convict him. In making such a plea, the defence may not disparage the reliability of the evidence; they may only try to convince the judges that it carries insufficient weight to convict. If, for instance, it were to be clear that a photo spread was the only evidence that could prove the defendant's guilt, and if the photo spread was manifestly lacking in any evidential value, then there would be no need to ask for the defendant's response and he should be acquitted forthwith. The Demjanjuk case cried out for the defence to make this move. Hundreds of Supreme Court rulings invalidated photo spreads that had only a fraction of the faults found in every one of the spreads the prosecution was basing itself on.

There was, of course, one other piece of evidence that related to Demjanjuk by name: the Travniki document. Yet this document did not link Demjanjuk to Treblinka in any way. The document not only failed to support the identification testimonies, it actually contradicted them. At the time that the identification witnesses claimed to have seen Ivan the Terrible at Treblinka, the bearer of this certificate was elsewhere. Identification witness Boraks, for instance, claimed that Ivan the Terrible had beaten him and thrown him off the train on Yom Kippur, the day he arrived in Treblinka. In 1942, Yom Kippur was on 22 September, and the Travniki document showed that its bearer was stationed on that day at the Uksau farm, a hundred kilometres from Treblinka. Even if the document was authentic, therefore, it did not belong to Ivan the Terrible but to some other guard who was nowhere near Treblinka. For this reason, in the words of mine that so infuriated the court: 'The Travniki document wanders through the survivors' testimony like a bull in a china shop.'

I prepared my arguments for the coming Monday along these general lines. It was obvious that there was not the slightest chance that they would be accepted. I guessed that the court would reject them without even asking for a reply from the prosecution. I said all this to Johnny, Gill and Demjanjuk, but explained that we had to adopt this procedure for two reasons. First, the court's hostility could not be allowed to keep us from using every means available under the law. Second, making such an argument would give the defence its first opportunity to lay out, in a methodical way, all its arguments against the quality and weight of the prosecution evidence. Even if this were not to bear immediate fruit, its effect would be felt later on.

O'Connor was currently telling the media that I had promised the Demjanjuk family my anticipated petition would bring about Demjanjuk's immediate release, that the Demjanjuk family would be disappointed and I would have to pay the price. Several reporters called me for my response, but I disappointed them. All I was willing to say was that I had no intention of responding to anything that O'Connor had said or might say.

The session of Monday 29 June opened with a hearing on various procedural issues, and I began my argument about an hour later. The bench did not hide their dissatisfaction – to put it mildly – with my decision to ask for Demjanjuk's immediate acquittal. But they could not prevent me from doing so. Instead, Levin poured his scorn on me for having the impudence to make such a claim. I was used to Judge Levin interrupting me, but this time he just would not let me speak. At times he himself felt that he had gone too far. Then he would say, 'OK, I won't obstruct you any more'; but a few minutes later he would interrupt again. In the short gaps between interruptions he made a show of not listening, chatting with his colleagues. This session was one of the low points of the entire trial. As I had anticipated, Shaked was not even asked to respond to my arguments. As soon as I finished, Levin dictated a decision denying my motion. The court then decided to postpone the continuation of the trial for less than a month; so the defence would have insufficient time to prepare for its presentation. It would resume on 27 July.

After the session, when I entered Demjanjuk's cell to say goodbye, he told me that during the break Johnny had made him sign blank pieces of paper, and that he knew that these would be used to write O'Connor's dismissal letter. I told him, 'You can be sure that it is the right thing to do. Even if you have doubts now, you will in time be convinced that it was the right step.' Demjanjuk responded: 'I do what my family says. I am inside and they are outside. I hope they know what they're doing.'

On the Friday, I left early in the morning for the US, and after a stopover in New York I arrived in Cleveland. Johnny and Nishnic were waiting for me at the airport and drove me to the Holiday Inn.

The following day I met Demjanjuk's wife Vera for the first time. She was a pleasant woman, a little less limited than her husband. But she was a fascinating example of the ridiculous preconceptions about Jews common among the goyim. I was astounded to discover that she believed Adolf Eichmann had been a Jew. All my efforts to explain her error were in vain. On Friday I had also met with Demjanjuk's daughters, who were very pleased to see me, though Lydia again expressed her doubts about my ability to hold up. The family were very happy at O'Connor's dismissal and thanked me for assisting them.

Over the weekend we gathered in the large basement of a travel agency which had been made available to us. (Later, when I discovered that the agency belonged to a foul anti-Semite named Jerry Berntar, I severed all contacts with him and brought his involvement in the defence to an end.) It was here that I met John Broadly, who was occupied at the time with legal procedures in the US relating to Demjanjuk's case. These procedures had reaped successful results for him, but were still not completed after seven years. They were aimed at making public all the documents that had been maliciously concealed from Demjanjuk for more than ten years by the American Department of Justice. (Most of these documents originated in the Soviet Union, and when they were released it was found that some of them proved the American authorities knew very well, while conducting their proceedings against Demjanjuk, that he was not Ivan the Terrible. Other documents showed that the Americans had fabricated the results of the photo spreads they had conducted for Reichman and Horn.) Broadly impressed me as an excellent attorney who knew his work well. He expressed serious doubts about whether he could join the case, however, because he did not believe the Demjanjuk family could raise the high advance payment that his firm had made a condition of his joining the case. After speaking with Broadly I was sure that my apprehensions in the opening session about responsibility for the case falling on my shoulders were about to be realized. Now, however, that possibility was not frightening; on the contrary, I felt satisfied and challenged.

The lawyers and the Demjanjuk family spent the weekend in lengthy discussions about the defence's preparation for its impending presentation. We also typed O'Connor's dismissal letter and the announcement to the court. I was given the task of drafting the letter, and I emphasized with no small pleasure that his dismissal was 'the result of his unbefitting and embarrassing performance in and out of court'. I spent the remainder of my time working hard, but I also spent some time with Johnny and Nishnic. On Wednesday the two of them drove me to the airport and I set out for Israel. I landed on Thursday afternoon, and the next morning I was in Demjanjuk's cell with several copies of the letter and announcement.

Demjanjuk greeted me tepidly, and he looked tense and unsure of what to do. I handed him the papers, two copies of each, and asked him to give O'Connor the letter if and when he came to visit. Demjanjuk held out an uncertain hand and asked me: 'Do we know what we're doing? I don't feel right about O'Connor, he's been on the case for five years.' I answered, 'He's been on the case for five years, and there has not been a single day that he has not done you harm. Furthermore, over the course of those five years he has deceived you and your family.'

Demjanjuk asked: 'Can you promise me that if O'Connor is dismissed and you are the chief defence attorney in the case, I will be acquitted?'

I responded without hesitation. 'Absolutely not. That is exactly the kind of dishonest promise that O'Connor made to you for years. You should know that a lawyer who promises you any such thing is dishonest and unprofessional and you should keep your distance from him. What I can promise is that I will represent you to the best of my abilities.' I can't say this made him feel more secure. We talked for another half an hour. I had little time because I wanted to submit the announcement to the court that same day. Before leaving I told Demjanjuk: 'A few days from now the court will convene to confirm O'Connor's dismissal. Judge Levin will do everything he can, directly and indirectly, to induce you to change your mind. You have to be strong and stand fast in the face of this.' I could tell from Demjanjuk's expression that he could not handle this assignment. I decided that very minute to call Nishnic and tell him to come to Israel immediately, to help his father-in-law in court.

I set out for Jerusalem and the court secretariat, where I left the announcement of O'Connor's dismissal and a copy of his dismissal letter. I then went to the American Colony in order to give O'Connor the letter, in case he hadn't yet seen Demjanjuk. He was not in his room. I pushed one copy under his door, and left another with the receptionist. Then I went to the office of the hotel manager and told him that from that day forward the Demjanjuk family would no longer be responsible for O'Connor's hotel bill.

When I got home to Tel Aviv I called Nishnic, and as soon as he picked up the receiver I said: 'Ed, I've submitted the dismissal letter. But I have the distinct impression that Demjanjuk is hesitating. He isn't sure of himself. O'Connor is putting heavy pressure on him. Demjanjuk sees me as an outsider, someone he cannot trust unconditionally. I ask that you take the first plane to Israel, so you can meet Demjanjuk before the court session, reassure him and support him when the court convenes. Otherwise, Judge Levin will sabotage the whole thing.' After a short conversation, Nishnic agreed to set out at once. I felt better.

On Friday, at midnight, the news of O'Connor's dismissal was broadcast as the lead story. From that moment my telephone did not stop ringing. In the end, at two a.m., I had to disconnect it. The reporters, who did not hesitate to call me at home at this late hour, got nothing out of me except confirmation that the report was accurate. On Saturday morning the media renewed its efforts to squeeze information out of me, and they did not stop until the next day.

O'Connor called a press conference in Jerusalem on Sunday. At his side was his 'personal adviser', attorney Matti Atzmon. O'Connor accused me of conspiring with the prosecution to bring about his dismissal from the case, and promised to reveal the particulars of the conspiracy when the court reconvened. He said he did not recognize Demjanjuk's dismissal letter and considered himself Demjanjuk's lead counsel. The media, of course, gave the conference huge coverage. The headlines were almost identical in all the papers: O'CONNOR: 'I WILL REVEAL SHEFTEL'S LINKS WITH THE PROSECUTION.'

I spent several hours in Demjanjuk's cell that morning. We continued our work of preparing him for his testimony. Of course I told him that his son-in-law would be arriving the next day and would meet him in court. Demjanjuk gave a sigh of relief. In the afternoon I went to collect Nishnic at Ben-Gurion Airport, and he cursed O'Connor all the way to his hotel, partly for forcing him to make this journey.

I set out for court the next day with Doron, picking Nishnic up on the way. When we arrived, we went straight into the packed courtroom. Most of the audience was made up of journalists. The air was full of tense anticipation. My mind was on the meeting between Nishnic and Demjanjuk. When Nishnic emerged from Demjanjuk's cell, he told me, 'Everything's fine,' and took his place in the front row.

Demjanjuk was brought into the courtroom. O'Connor took his regular place to my left. The judges entered, and Judge Levin launched into a long discourse about the documents before the court. He began with O'Connor's dismissal letter, which stated that attorney John Broadly would replace him. It also made Demjanjuk's request that the trial be postponed so as to enable his new defence team to make proper preparations. Without mincing words or making any pretence at objectivity, Levin stated: 'This announcement is unacceptable to us for two reasons. First, it links the release of the defence attorney to a postponement of the proceedings; and second, the announcement includes the appointment of another attorney in place of Mr O'Connor.' The letter did not link these things at all; Levin was the one who linked them. He intimidated Demjanjuk, telling him repeatedly that there was no chance of O'Connor's dismissal inducing the court to grant any kind of delay. Levin added that he had a document before him from O'Connor, stating that the dismissal notice signed by Demjanjuk did not reflect the defendant's true wishes. It was obvious that Demjanjuk's self-confidence was being shaken.

Demjanjuk, who at the court's order had been standing the whole time, was now asked, 'Is Mr Sheftel your defence attorney? Do you, sir, want Mr Sheftel to serve as your defence attorney in this trial, without any connection to O'Connor?' Demjanjuk's confusion grew. He did not know what to do. I addressed him in Russian: 'Ask for a ten-minute recess to consult privately with Nishnic.' I wanted not only to involve Nishnic again, but also to neutralize O'Connor's presence in Demjanjuk's cell. Demjanjuk's reply was: 'I request a recess to speak with my son-in-law.'

'You request to consult with whom?' Judge Levin asked.

'With my son-in-law, who has arrived from the US,' Demjanjuk said.

'You wish to consult with your son-in-law without the presence of your defence attorneys?' Levin queried.

'Yes,' Demjanjuk replied.

Judge Levin continued to explain at length why the trial would not be delayed under any circumstances, and then declared a recess. When the judges exited, the commotion in the courtroom increased. Nishnic came up on to the stage. I told him: 'Ed, it's all in your hands. You've got to reassure him and give him the confidence to face up to Levin's pressure, and explain to him that his family, not Judge Levin, has his interests at heart.' Nishnic left, and returned a few minutes later to tell me again, 'Everything's fine.' I was unconvinced. Demjanjuk returned and seemed more collected and sure of himself. I told him in Russian: 'Don't be afraid of Judge Levin, stand up for yourself.' He also told me, in Russian, 'Everything's fine.'

The judges entered the courtroom and Demjanjuk rose to his feet. The hum of the video cameras and the photographers' flashes increased the tension. Judge Levin spoke. 'Do you, sir, stand by your letter that you wish to release O'Connor from being your defence attorney? Do you wish to see Mr Sheftel as your defence attorney, without any connection to Mr O'Connor but independently, and does the same hold true for Mr Gill?' Demjanjuk responded quietly and confidently: 'Yes.' The matter should have ended there, but Judge Levin went on. 'And what is your position with regard to Mark O'Connor?' Demjanjuk surprised me again by responding: 'As everyone knows, since the trial began my lawyer has not performed his duties properly . . .'

Levin cut him off: 'That's a different question. That is open to debate. I am waiting for an answer to my question.'

Demjanjuk answered: 'My family has decided to discharge O'Connor because his continued work would be to my detriment . . .'

Judge Levin again interrupted him. 'And what is your decision? What is *your* decision, sir?'

'I have decided to accept my family's decision. I am in a cage, I am in jail. So I am forced to accept my family's decision. I will accept any decision my family makes.'

Judge Levin did not give up. 'I can accept that answer except for the word "forced". No one is forcing you. The decision has to be yours.'

This time Demjanjuk answered firmly and with a tone of anger in his voice: 'I told you that my family's decision is my decision.'

But Judge Levin still would not concede and repeated the question that Demjanjuk had answered positively and unreservedly just two minutes before. 'What is your answer to the question of the appointment of Mr Sheftel as your defence attorney?' He had finally succeeded in confusing Demjanjuk, who answered:

'As far as I know, Mr Sheftel is a lawyer who knows Israeli law.' Levin repeated his question twice. 'I don't understand your question, Your Honour,' Demjanjuk replied. 'As far as I can tell, if Mr O'Connor leaves, then Mr Sheftel replaces him.'

Levin did not accept this very clear answer and said: 'If he did not understand, I will try to explain to him. For a defendant to be represented in this court by a defence counsel, he must grant him power of attorney.' After further explanations Levin added: 'With regard to Mr Sheftel, up until now he has worked under the power of attorney given to Mr O'Connor.' Finally, Levin summed up what he wanted from Demjanjuk: 'You, sir, must give or submit to the court a written power-of-attorney, signed by you, or you must notify us here that Mr Sheftel has been appointed by you to be your attorney before us.' Levin was simply ignoring Demjanjuk's previous two clear announcements of this. This time, however, Demjanjuk gave an unclear answer: 'In my opinion, that decision will be up to Mr Broadly.' Judge Levin quickly latched on to this and said: 'In other words, you do not consider Mr Sheftel your attorney in this trial.'

I had in my possession a power-of-attorney signed by Demjanjuk appointing Gill and me to represent him as defence attorneys in the trial. I had had him sign it on Sunday and had intended to submit it only at the end of the session, after the formal decision about O'Connor's discharge. Now I understood that I had to submit it immediately before it was too late. Levin took the document and asked Demjanjuk: 'Mr Sheftel has presented me with a signed power-of-attorney. Is this your signature?' Then he immediately added: 'I previously asked the defendant if he would like to notify us that he considers Mr Sheftel his defence counsel in the trial before us. The defendant did not give us a positive answer. Now Mr Sheftel has notified us that he has in his possession a document signed by the defendant that constitutes a power-of-attorney, according to which the defendant appoints him to be his defence counsel. I would like to receive from you, sir, a clear and definitive answer – does the defendant request that Mr Sheftel be his defence attorney in the trial before us?' Demjanjuk now replied clearly and without hesitation, 'Yes.' Judge Levin simply would not accept such an answer. 'Did you sign the document that Mr Sheftel is holding in his hands?' Did Judge Levin think I would submit a forged power-of-attorney to the court? Demjanjuk again answered unambiguously: 'Yes.' Levin stuck to his guns. 'Henceforward, do I understand correctly, or do my colleagues and I understand correctly, that the defendant intends to tell us that from this moment on he will be represented by attorneys John Gill and Yoram Sheftel, yes or no?' Again Demjanjuk responded succinctly and clearly: 'Yes.'

The entire courtroom was wondering what Judge Levin would do next. He launched into a long lecture, in which he explained again to Demjanjuk that the trial would not be postponed. Demjanjuk, with all his limitations, understood the gist of Levin's questions. He said with a peasant's simple courage: 'Your Honour, from everything that has been said here now it seems to me that you are trying to scare me.' He was not the only one who thought that – it was obviously the feeling held by everyone in the room. Levin pounced indignantly on Demjanjuk. 'So the defendant's claim, that when we present him with facts and explain the situation and the law to him so that he will not be surprised, that we are frightening him, what kind of language is that?' Demjanjuk had no choice but to retract his words under this onslaught, and he said: 'Your Honour, I apologize for having used a word that wasn't so appropriate, but I've only got four years of education.' Judge Levin went into another long monologue, which was nothing more than a continuation of the attempt to scare Demjanjuk. At the end he again asked: 'Does the defendant stand by his decision even if there is no postponement of the trial? Is that the defendant's position?' Demjanjuk, exhausted, replied: 'My decision is what I've already said, but if the court decides otherwise, I agree with what the court decides.' Judge Levin's efforts were finally bearing fruit. He repeated his question and emphasized again that the trial would not be postponed. Demjanjuk, who had completely lost his powers of concentration by this time, got mixed up and suddenly burst out with something foolish: 'My decision was that instead of Mr O'Connor would be Mr Broadly. But you have decided that instead of him will be Mr Sheftel and Mr Gill . . .'

'We are not the ones who decide,' Levin interrupted him, and again launched into a monologue on 'needing things to be absolutely clear'. In the end, Levin decided to declare another recess for consultation, and I called on Nishnic. But in the mean time O'Connor had succeeded in getting into Demjanjuk's cell in a last desperate attempt to reverse the decision. I told Nishnic: 'Demjanjuk isn't decisive enough. Judge Levin is harassing him. It looks like we'll have to bring Mrs Demjanjuk and Johnny here, because you're not a blood relation.' The two of us entered Demjanjuk's cell, and managed to catch the end of O'Connor's new plan: 'Each of the defence attorneys will bring his own witnesses and will work without any connection or contact with the others.' No ludicrous plot was beneath his consideration so long as he retained his position as defence attorney. It looked as if Demjanjuk agreed. He turned to me and asked that we nevertheless make an effort to work together. 'For me,' he said. Nishnic was apparently also confused, and instead of rejecting the idea categorically astounded me by asking: 'What do you think?' I responded without hesitation: 'Gill and I will not work with O'Connor under any circumstances. You have to choose between us and O'Connor.'

O'Connor intervened: 'Sheftel is just blustering. Neither he nor Gill will leave the case.'

I responded sharply: 'I, and Gill too, am not the miserable type of lawyer who tries to remain on the case when his client doesn't want him. We will not remain one minute longer if you are not dismissed.' Then I addressed Demjanjuk. 'It would be best that, before you make a final decision, you speak with your wife and son. They will be here in another day or two. You should make a decision after you speak to your blood relations. We'll have to request a few days' delay.'

O'Connor understood that time was against him and that any delay would be to his disadvantage. He tried to object: 'We have to finish this matter now.'

This time it was Nishnic who cut him off. 'You will not decide when and how to finish. My father-in-law will ask for a delay of a few days.'

We all returned to the courtroom. Demjanjuk was again asked to rise. Judge Levin asked him what his decision was. Demjanjuk responded as we had agreed: 'It is very hard for me to make a decision today. I would ask to postpone this session for at least two days, so that I could at least consult with my family. I am not able to give my decision right now.' The court granted Demjanjuk's request and set another session on this matter for Monday 20 July.

I was disappointed and very angry. I had not expected everything to be sweetness and light at this session, but I had believed that O'Connor would be dismissed. Judge Levin had succeeded in temporarily thwarting my plans, but this only made me more determined to be rid of O'Connor. Levin's conduct had been so biased that even the press, despite its hostility to me and its desire that I suffer a humiliating failure, defined his behaviour as an attempt 'to delay O'Connor's dismissal by Demjanjuk', and stated that 'the court has saved defence attorney O'Connor for the time being'.

Doron, Nishnic and I slipped quickly out to my car and headed for Tel Aviv. Along the way I told Nishnic off for the weak knees he had suddenly suffered when we were in Demjanjuk's cell. He agreed that he had been out of line. We decided to bring Johnny and his mother to Israel immediately. I likewise demanded that Nishnic ask Demjanjuk to instruct that O'Connor was no longer allowed to enter his cell. He promised he would bring his full influence to bear. That same evening it was settled that Johnny and Vera would arrive in Israel on Friday.

I reported the next day to Demjanjuk's cell to continue the preparations for his testimony. When I arrived, he informed me that Ed had been to see him the previous day. During their talk he had been persuaded to stop seeing O'Connor and had even notified the prison authorities of this. I confirmed this over the telephone in the guardroom. Then I devoted myself to my work with Demjanjuk, as if everything was going smoothly.

Johnny and his mother landed at Ben-Gurion on Friday afternoon. I reached Nishnic's room towards evening; he was deep in conversation with Johnny about the recent events. After shaking hands emotionally, Johnny told me that Broadly had finally notified them that he would not be able to join the defence. Both of them seemed very disappointed by this, and doubted whether Demjanjuk would now agree to fire O'Connor. 'But that's exactly why you've come here, to persuade him to accept your position,' I said.

I was surprised to hear Johnny ask: 'Maybe it's worth keeping O'Connor nevertheless, now that it's clear Broadly will not come?'

'I don't think the two things are connected at all. O'Connor has to be dismissed no matter what, because of the damage he does every minute he is on the case, as you know better than I. There is no point in having begun this move if you yourselves are not certain it is correct.'

'Ed and I don't have a shadow of doubt,' Johnny said. 'The problem is with my father and mother. They are just plain scared, because O'Connor has been making them crazy for five years.'

I then told them about Demjanjuk's decision not to allow O'Connor to visit him in his cell any more. I added that it looked to me as if he were finally starting to break free of O'Connor once and for all. Both of them were very encouraged by this. I asked them simply: 'If Vera tells him, in clear and forceful language, that it is the family's firm decision to dismiss O'Connor from the case, will he do it?'

They answered in unison: 'Of course, no doubt about it.'

'If that's the case,' I said, 'convince Vera and make it clear that there is no possibility of O'Connor, Gill and I working together. If O'Connor remains, Gill and I will resign. We will not agree under any circumstances to sit on the same bench as him, after what he did during the trial last week.'

On Saturday, Demjanjuk saw the three members of his family. Nishnic later told me that Vera had been very insistent and lucid. She left her husband in no doubt that he had to accept the opinion of his son and son-in-law, because they were well acquainted with all the facts that required O'Connor's discharge. She herself supported this unreservedly. Demjanjuk promised that he would tell the judges in the clearest possible way that this was what he wanted and would not allow them to confuse him. I met the Demjanjuk family for dinner, and they gave me a further report of their talk with Demjanjuk. O'Connor had arrived at the prison gate shortly before them but had not been allowed to enter, in accordance with Demjanjuk's instructions.

Vera's and Johnny's arrival in Israel, the media reports about their desire to see O'Connor dismissed immediately, Demjanjuk's refusal to see O'Connor any more – all these led Matti Atzmon to recommend to O'Connor that he deposit a letter of resignation with the court. Atzmon believed, as he later told me, that this would minimize the humiliation awaiting O'Connor in court the next day. O'Connor, who apparently understood finally that even Judge Levin would not prevent his dismissal, took Atzmon's advice. His letter of resignation had been tendered on Sunday, but we did not know this when we arrived at court.

The courtroom was even more crowded than at the last session, and the local and foreign media were fully represented. However, in stark contrast to the previous session, there was no tension in the hall. Seconds later we learned the reason: O'Connor had deposited his letter of resignation. I acted indifferent, but inside I was exultant. O'Connor, who I noticed out of the corner of my eye had already taken his place on the defence bench, had reached the end of his road in the case. Even Judge Levin would not prevent that. Seconds later we found ourselves surrounded by reporters asking our reactions to the resignation. I responded concisely. 'I have not seen the letter. I have just heard about it for the first time. I have nothing to say.'

Then O'Connor and I were summoned to the judges' chambers. The judges wished to conduct the hearing on my motion to postpone the trial's resumption behind closed doors. Only afterwards would they enter the courtroom and complete the process of O'Connor's dismissal. I realized that even at this stage, when O'Connor's resignation was before them, the judges had still not despaired of preventing his discharge. During the hearing, which lasted for about half an hour, they barely allowed me to get a sentence out without interrupting. This time Levin had continuous help from his two colleagues, Judge Dorner especially. All we were requesting was a postponement of a few weeks. Of course, we really needed more than three months, and under the circumstances any other court would have acceded willingly to our request, at once. This was especially valid given its granting of all the prosecution's many motions for delays, from the time of Demjanjuk's extradition to Israel up until the filing of charges against him seven months later. But, given the behaviour of this court so far, I understood that I could ask for no more than a few weeks.

Instead of granting my request, Judge Levin said: 'We will soon be legendary for our patience – in the rest of the world such trials take two months.' Levin was referring to the trial of Klaus Barbie, the notorious Gestapo commander from Lyons, whose trial had begun in France around the same time as Demjanjuk's trial in Israel, but which had been completed within three months. Judge Dorner showed her hand when she said: '*O'Connor* is ready for the trial.' The insinuation was transparent, but Dorner took care to gloss it: 'If you aren't ready, tell us now, and we will not release O'Connor from the trial.' Levin, for his part, remarked unambiguously: 'There is no connection between O'Connor's leaving and the postponement of the trial.' I thought to myself, What has really happened here? The case's chief defence counsel for the last five years has been dismissed from the case, in part because he has not prepared any line of defence. That was 'really' no reason for a postponement and there was 'no connection' between the two? By law, a court may refuse to confirm a defence attorney's resignation, and I knew that the judges would invoke this power if I insisted on the postponement.

O'Connor was sitting motionless in the chambers this whole time, but his face was puce with anger. When I was finally persuaded that there was no chance of postponing the trial, I wanted to receive a clear mandate from the family to agree to the judges' order that I present myself within the week with the defence arguments, even though it was clear to everyone that we were completely unprepared. I therefore asked for a few minutes' recess for consultation. I explained the situation to Demjanjuk and his family. Their response was unequivocal – I was given the green light. I returned to the chambers and told the judges that Demjanjuk and his family were resolute in their desire to see O'Connor dismissed from the case. If the only way to accomplish this was for me to agree to appear without any postponement, I would agree.

The hearing was now transferred to the courtroom. Judge Levin addressed Demjanjuk without much in the way of preamble: 'Does the defendant accept Mr O'Connor's request to be excused from representing him, even on the understanding that the trial will not be postponed?' Demjanjuk rose and responded self-assuredly and without hesitation: 'Your Honours, you have given me four days to think, and I want to notify you that I am interested in replacing Mr O'Connor, without any connection to the trial's continuation.' I looked at O'Connor. His face was still as red as a tomato, and he hissed something between his teeth that I could not make out. The scene in the judges' chambers when I was forced to apologize passed before my eyes and I said to myself contentedly: 'You've got what you deserve, you scoundrel.'

This time Judge Levin understood that there was no point in trying to confuse Demjanjuk with dozens of questions, and he instructed drily: 'The defendant may be seated.' Then, without delay, he began dictating a fairly long decision into the record. The key sentence was: 'We grant the petition and discharge attorney Mark G. O'Connor from continuing to represent the defendant in this trial.' The end of the decision stated that the court would begin hearing the defence presentation on 27 July 1987, and would sit continuously until 25 August.

When the judges rose, there was uproar in the courtroom. The reporters broke up into groups and pounced on the members of the Demjanjuk family and on me. I did not hide my delight at what had happened, but I made certain to express myself with restraint. Nevertheless, I stressed that 'Because of O'Connor's failure to perform his duties adequately on the one hand, and the court's refusal to postpone the trial on the other, the defence presentation will begin with the hands of Demjanjuk and the defence tied.' After the commotion died down we went up to the defence offices. There I told the Demjanjuk family: 'I cannot promise you, or Demjanjuk himself, anything more than that I will devote all my talents and energies to this case. I doubt whether it will do any good in this court. But I am certain that from this point onward Demjanjuk will receive much better legal representation than he has in the past.' The family thanked me and expressed their unreserved trust in me. I parted from them and headed back to Tel Aviv.

Any number of thoughts skipped through my mind along the way. First and foremost, I felt a huge measure of satisfaction at having gained the full trust of the family. This gave a big boost to my self-confidence, and I was no longer at all afraid because the case had fallen on my shoulders. On the contrary, I felt that I would bear the burden honourably.

O'Connor began immediately to disseminate his version of the circumstances that had led up to this decision. According to him, he resigned because he was unwilling to enter into a confrontation with the court, as I was willing to do and as the Demjanjuk family demanded of him. He argued that, because of his great respect and admiration for Demjanjuk's judges, he preferred to resign rather than come into conflict with them. This, then, was the reason for the resignation of the very same man who had shamelessly told Johnny and Demjanjuk, over the course of months, that every Thursday, after the end of the week's sessions, Judge Levin met Minister of Justice Avraham Sharir for a briefing on what to do the following week and how to bring Demjanjuk quickly to the gallows.

So it happened that I not only joined Demjanjuk's defence team in a fit of madness, but also, within a fairly short time and in absolute contradiction of my original intention, became the chief defence counsel. The facts were so astonishing that I had trouble convincing myself that they weren't just a figment of my imagination. I knew that the public's hostility to me would grow once I began playing first fiddle. But I was now completely immune to it and no longer gave it a thought. I was focused on the future, about which I had absolutely no apprehensions.

6 · The Collapse of the Defence Case

O'Connor's dismissal removed a major obstacle for the defence. Yet, obviously, the move did not help in the central task I now faced – obtaining the necessary evidence to construct an effective defence for Demjanjuk.

It was a much weightier responsibility than the one I faced when, five months previously, I had joined the defence team as O'Connor's assistant. Even a few weeks before O'Connor's dismissal, I considered such an undertaking beyond me, and thought I had neither the strength nor the ability to carry it out successfully. And it was absolutely clear, given O'Connor's blunders and the short time available to me, that, for all practical purposes, the mission was impossible. Against all logic, I actually felt very sure of myself. I was even serene, at ease with the huge challenge. To this day, when I think back and relive those feelings, I cannot understand where they came from.

It was again that wonderful combination of a lack of *seichel* and plenty of *mazel* that helped me out of the tight spot I had walked into, with my eyes wide open. The lack of brains made me take up the task in such impossible circumstances. A heavy dose of luck produced an entirely unexpected event that granted me precious time to put together an effective defence.

According to Israeli law, in contradistinction to Anglo-American law, the defendant in a criminal trial does not, in practice, have the right to remain silent. He need not testify, but should he choose not to take the stand the court may consider this as corroboration of the prosecution's case. It is not *required* to do so, but it may. Knowing the attitude of the court before which Demjanjuk was being tried, it was clear to me that if he chose not to testify the court would hold it against him in every possible way. Furthermore, Israeli law states, again in contrast with Anglo-American law, that if the defendant chooses to testify his testimony must be heard first; only after it is completed may the rest of the defence witnesses testify.

Demjanjuk would therefore have to testify, and also he would be the first defence witness. The preparation of his testimony was therefore the most urgent matter to attend to. As I have noted, O'Connor had never spoken to Demjanjuk seriously and thoroughly about the range of complex problems his testimony involved. As a result I had begun even then, in mid-May, holding three or four meetings each week, of five hours each, with Demjanjuk. On the day O'Connor was finally dismissed from the case, just a week before Demjanjuk's testimony was to begin, his was the only testimony that was ready. (Whilst testimony from two additional expert witnesses on the Travniki document also seemed to be ready, as Gill had maintained at our meeting in Cleveland, it would soon turn out to be worthless.)

In the years 1978–84, Demjanjuk had given more than ten statements and testimonies in connection with the legal proceedings conducted against him in the US. In addition, over thirty statements made by him had been recorded during his interrogation in Israel, which began immediately after his extradition in March 1986. Demjanjuk had not confirmed most of them with his signature; they had been recorded in summaries made by his interrogators. When a man gives more than forty versions of events that took place decades before, it is only natural that there will be contradictions between them. Demjanjuk's personality only complicated things: he was unable to explain the contradictions between his various statements and assertions. Moreover, he was not even capable of remembering them all, or even most of them, or getting to a reasonable level of familiarity with the details. He surprised me again and again with his poor memory. Sometimes the name of Cleveland, the city where he had lived for more than thirty years, escaped him. Even though for two and a half months he had made no small effort to read, understand and memorize the material, and despite our many talks about every aspect of this material, his mastery of the facts was fairly shaky. This was still the case just before he took the witness stand. As explained above, however, there was no escaping that he had to testify.

Before this series of meetings began I had not really had a chance to get acquainted with Demjanjuk. Unlike the rest of his family, he never asked me why I had joined his defence. From our very first meeting, in January 1987, he took it as read. He did, however, exhibit curiosity about my parents' Ukrainian origins. He repeatedly asked me about their childhood and was disappointed to hear that they did not know the language. He also referred frequently to my single status. He was very interested in my mother's feelings about my jealously guarded bachelorhood, especially since I was an only child.

Demjanjuk revealed himself to be a committed anti-Communist who despised the Soviet regime with his entire soul. He considered it an occupation force in his homeland, and saw the Ukrainian Communists as quisling collaborators. Like many Ukrainian goyim, Demjanjuk identified the Soviet regime with the Jews. In his view, they were the dominant element in this regime, and it could not exist without them. (The Ukrainian people's worst enemy was, in his eyes, Lazar Kaganovitch, the last Jew in the Politburo. During the 1930s, Kaganovitch was appointed by the Communist Party to oversee the bloody collectivization programme that led to the deliberate starvation of some ten million farmers throughout the Soviet Union, the great majority in the Ukraine. He also played a role in the policy of cruelly suppressing Jewish culture and nationalism in the Soviet Union.) Demjanjuk repeatedly expressed his hope that his children would be privileged to see the destruction of the Soviet Union and the emergence of an independent Ukrainian state from its ashes. He never dreamed, however, that he himself would live to see this. He certainly never imagined that he would, in April 1993, be visited by the Ukrainian Ambassador to Israel.

During our conversations a thought would sometimes pass through my head: Suppose I am wrong, and this goy really is Ivan the Terrible? What a horrible thing I would be doing by sitting with him for hours and hours, preparing the testimony aimed at persuading the court that he is not. At that time my feeling that he was innocent was no more than intuitive, and privately I did not entirely reject the possibility that I might be wrong. These thoughts weighed heavily on me; I would cheer myself up by reminding myself: Even if in the end you are wrong, you know it is a sincere and real error and not deliberate blindness meant to ease your conscience.

I made another attempt to take the measure of the man. From time to time I would let the well-known Yiddish word *gevald* hang in the air. The survivors, both in their testimony and in their written statements, frequently mentioned the horrible screams of '*Gevald!*' that came out of the Treblinka gas chambers after the Jews had been packed into them by the gang of German and Ukrainian murderers led by Ivan the Terrible. I had no doubt that the memory and echo of this word would follow Ivan the Terrible wherever he went until the day he died. Letting the word out from time to time, as if I did not notice, and pretending not to look at Demjanjuk, I would carefully examine his expression. Time and again he gave no sign that the word and its meaning were familiar. One might argue that he dissembled because he knew I was watching him, and I also considered this possibility. But from my acquaintance with him it was clear that this goy did not have the ability to stage such a deliberate charade.

Even though I had taken responsibility for preparing Demjanjuk for his testimony, Gill would be the one to perform the examination in chief. I have often been asked why. I knew that the moment Demjanjuk rose to testify in his own defence was likely to be one of the trial's most dramatic moments. All eyes would be on him and the lawyer questioning him. It was precisely for this reason that I insisted on Gill presenting the defence's questions to Demjanjuk. If I were to rise to question him, the gossip would be that I had joined the case only for this moment, and that I had had O'Connor dismissed simply to secure the starring role in the case. As the date of the testimony approached, I prepared more than seventy questions in English for Gill to base his interrogation on. I gave a copy to Demjanjuk as well. We rehearsed the questions, and especially his answers, over and over again.

Gill returned to Israel on 23 July 1987, four days before the trial was to resume. On each of the next three days we sat with Demjanjuk in order to put Gill in the picture. This, of course, was much easier than preparing Demjanjuk. When we left the cell on Sunday afternoon, 26 July, Gill was completely prepared; Demjanjuk, on the other hand, was much less so. Our sense was, however, that he would be able to get through the examination in chief acceptably. As the trial's resumption approached, the tension within the Demjanjuk family grew, and some of its members arrived in Israel, including Lydia. On the Sunday evening before the trial was to reopen, we all ate supper together in the hotel. I was happy to discover that they felt comfortable about O'Connor's dismissal. I was especially gratified when Lydia told me during the meal that 'We do not expect you to get our father acquitted. It looks like that is impossible in this court. We hope that you will work hard and professionally and make every effort, and the most important thing is that you do not crack.' Such low expectations in a client's family in a capital case are all a defence attorney needs to be able to work with a clear head. When working on a criminal case I always explain the case's weak points to my clients. I do not hesitate to give a gloomy forecast if that is the reality. So I took advantage of this meal to express my opinion that Demjanjuk's testimony would be very difficult. Given that there were no few contradictions between the dozens of statements he had made, Gill and I explained, he would find himself in an unpleasant predicament, to put it mildly. It was again Lydia who pleased us by telling us that this was the first time in the past five years that they had been given a realistic appraisal by their lawyer, and they appreciated it very much. Today I can see that it was only because of the family's ability to take reasoned and intelligent positions under the most difficult circumstances that made it possible for them to endure even more difficult moments and to get through the whole process relatively unscathed.

Gill and I wanted to have time for a short talk with Demjanjuk before the next session. After a brief visit to the defence offices we went down to the courtroom. It was still half-empty, yet the atmosphere hinted at the commotion to come. At eight precisely Demjanjuk was brought to his cell next door. We entered at once; Gill went over some of the important questions he was about to ask, in order to refresh his memory. Then I told Demjanjuk: 'You should be aware that the judges will disturb you, and ask you questions, all with the object of confusing you and tripping you up. I know how hard it is for you to keep your balance and to be able to give good answers in such a situation.' Demjanjuk nodded to signify that he had understood.

Anticipation of Demjanjuk's testimony had again focused public attention on the court, like the survivors' testimony during the first weeks. The hall was crammed with visitors and representatives of the national and foreign media. I discovered that there was even a crew from Panamanian television. The usual protesters also took their places. As ever they were not silent, but they attracted much less attention than before. I no longer even raised an eyebrow at their outbursts, but the inaction of the police and the Ministry of Justice officials continued to infuriate me. There was no small number of public figures in the courtroom; Shevah Weiss, who has recently been elected Speaker of the Knesset, was in his usual seat. From the day the trial opened he had not missed an opportunity to express his strident opinions about it.

I was excited, but it was easy to hide it. The atmosphere in court did not remind one at all of the trial of a man accused of murdering nine hundred thousand Jews. It was more like the ambience surrounding a film star's entry into the Oscars ceremony. Everyone was waiting for Demjanjuk, the leading man, to appear. I noticed O'Connor in the sixth row. I looked him over well. His expression said it all.

Demjanjuk was brought in and the hubbub increased. A minute later the clerk gave his call and the three judges slowly took their places. No attempt was made to silence the audience. After his usual opening, Judge Levin turned his gaze to the defence bench and asked: 'Is there an opening speech?' I nodded. Levin knew from our meeting on the day O'Connor was dismissed that the defence intended to exercise its right to make an opening speech before beginning to present its evidence. Levin relaxed in his chair and said, 'Please, Mr Sheftel, proceed.'

I had appeared in hundreds of criminal trials before this one, but I had never made an opening speech, because the prosecution had never done so either. I had decided to do so here both to balance the prosecution's speech and to take advantage of the opportunity to outline, for the first time, in a systematic way, the evidence that we intended to present. At the time, the great majority of this evidence existed only in theory.

I rose and began my speech with an apology. 'To begin with, I find it only proper to apologize most sincerely to the survivors who have testified in this trial, for having had to endure whole days of cross-examination that dealt with questions that the defence declared were not in dispute, for having had to answer questions about, among other things, the colour of the flames that came out of the pit in which the bodies were burned, the distance from the gas chambers to the pit, et cetera.'

Next I gave a detailed survey of the evidence we intended to present. When I reached the section on the Travniki document, I said, 'We will bring experts of the first order who will blast this document to bits, leaving nothing behind – not the signatures . . . nor the photograph . . . nor the stamps nor anything relating to the document in this case.' Carried away, I continued: 'Nothing will remain of it. We will destroy this document, shredding it till nothing is left.' Here Judge Levin interrupted me, the one time during the entire trial that he made a comment with a touch of humour: 'But Mr Sheftel will, of course, leave us the original.' I responded with a smile: 'Of course. Only the original will remain.'

The other comments made by Levin and his colleagues during my opening statement were less amusing. One of the many interruptions from Levin while I was discussing the Travniki document was: 'Mr Sheftel, you need to prove that the specific document before us is a forgery.' In other words, in Demjanjuk's case it was not enough for the defence to create a reasonable doubt. This slip of the tongue, like so many others, showed again that in Demjanjuk's show-trial a man was guilty until proved innocent; it also contained a strong implication that the defendant's fate was already sealed.

My opening speech lasted for about an hour and a half. Immediately thereafter, Levin said, 'I understand that the defendant will testify for the defence.'

'Absolutely.'

'The defendant is requested to rise. Please state your name. What is your name?'

Demjanjuk responded: 'Your Honours, my name is John Demjanjuk. I am John Demjanjuk.' The commotion in the courtroom began again, and there were catcalls from all sides. Levin finally decided to take action to calm the audience, then continued.

'Just one minute. You have been called to testify for the defence. I must warn you, sir, that you must tell the truth and the whole truth, because if you do not do so, you will be liable to the penalties prescribed by law. Who is performing the examination for the defence?' I pointed to Gill, and Levin went on. 'The defendant is now asked to listen to the questions he will be asked, and to respond to them. The choice is the defendant's, as he chooses, to testify standing or seated, whatever is convenient for you.' Demjanjuk sat down, and his testimony began.

In response to Gill's questions, he related the story of his life up until his conscription into the Red Army. He was born in 1920 to a peasant family in a small village named Dub-Makarenzi in the Vinitsa district of the Ukraine. He attended elementary school for nine years, but completed only four grades. At the age of seventeen he became an assistant tractor driver in the *kolkhoz* to which his village belonged. He described the horrible famine in the Ukraine in which millions of people starved to death. Because of the famine, his family sold their house for ten loaves of bread and set out to join relatives in Moscow. At the age of eighteen he joined the Komsomol.

Levin displayed impatience from the very start of the testimony. This was especially obvious in comparison to the free hand he had given the prosecution in bringing long testimonies even about undisputed facts. Now, after about half an hour of the testimony, for the first time in five months Levin began rushing the examination, with remarks like 'If the defence counsel wishes, he may relate that, but be brief'; 'Mr Gill may speed up the questioning quite a bit.'

Before the break was declared, Levin said, 'We request of the audience, based on past experience, that there be no catcalls directed at the defendant, the defence counsels or the prosecution when we leave the courtroom. We will reconvene after the recess.' Levin again tried to distort the true picture with his remarks into the record. Given the great tension in the courtroom during Demjanjuk's testimony, the judges estimated that this time the disturbances would peak, and this was liable to make it difficult to reconvene. So for the first time since the trial began Levin warned about disturbances by the audience during the break. To keep the record from reflecting the daily reality in the courtroom – that is, insults and threats against Demjanjuk and his Israeli defender – he cynically added to his warning the words 'or the prosecution', as if there had been any instance when someone had screamed at the prosecution.

Levin knew very well what he was saying. Even before the judges reached their chambers, the 'regulars' broke out in loud shouts, and were joined by many others. From every corner of the hall came the nastiest curses yet. The reporters besieged us, but we could not hear their questions above the racket. I decided to leave the hall with the

Demjanjuk family, but succeeded only with great difficulty. The shouts increased, and now the curses and threats were directed largely at me.

When we returned, the police and Ministry of Justice officials were for once trying to silence the people, but even now they would not eject the offenders from the courtroom. Finally, a few minutes late, the trial resumed.

Demjanjuk now related that his conscription into the Red Army had been deferred from 1940 to the following year, since he was so poor that he did not even have any of the basic personal effects then required. A short time after that the German Army invaded the Soviet Union, and Demjanjuk was stationed at the front as an artilleryman. During the retreat, near the Dnieper River, he was wounded in the back. He was treated in several hospitals, and after recovering was attached to a different artillery unit, near the city of Kutaisi. From there he was transferred to the vicinity of Baku. During the winter, at the beginning of 1942, his unit was transported by sea to Kerch in the Crimean peninsula, part of which had already been taken by the Germans. From there he was sent to the front. In the spring of 1942 he was captured by the German Army after a massive offensive (the famous battle of Kerch, in which an entire Russian army numbering a quarter of a million soldiers was destroyed; half the soldiers were killed and the rest captured). At first he was in a group of about seventy who worked for several weeks in the Crimea reconstructing railway tracks damaged by the fighting. Afterwards he was transported, along with many other prisoners, to a POW camp near the city of Rovno, where my mother lived until coming to what was then Palestine in 1935. He spent about a month there in frightful conditions. Afterwards he was transferred to another camp, near Chełm. Demjanjuk categorically denied the prosecution's claims that at Rovno he enlisted in the SS auxiliary forces.

At this point a lunch recess was declared. The judges' exit gave the cue for another uproar, smaller this time. Gill and I went to express our satisfaction with the progress of Demjanjuk's testimony. We sat with him for about an hour in order to refresh his memory about the matters still to come. When we emerged it was already two p.m. and we all went to have something to eat. The members of the Demjanjuk family commented again and again on the crowded and hostile atmosphere in the courtroom. They were shocked to hear that the hostility towards me was no less than that directed at their father. I wanted to tell them, 'Just wait and see what happens when I open my mouth,' but I remained silent.

Demjanjuk's testimony now reached a decisive point, since everything he said about his actions up to the end of the war was disputed by the prosecution. He testified that he had been transferred from the Rovno to the Chełm POW camp in the autumn of 1942. The prosecution's version had him at the Rovno camp in the summer of 1942, volunteering for the SS auxiliary forces, and sent to that body's training camp at Travniki. Demjanjuk denied absolutely that he had ever been in Travniki, Treblinka or Sobibor.

Demjanjuk said that at the beginning of his stay in the Chełm camp he worked in digging trenches fortified by pieces of old railway track, and in constructing barracks, both of which served as accommodation for the prisoners. From the spring of 1943 until the winter of 1943/44, he worked at digging peat in a mine near the camp. He also engaged sporadically in other labour, such as loading train trucks. He spent a year and a half at Chełm, until the spring of 1944. This section of Demjanjuk's testimony was of the utmost importance, because it set out the details of his alibi for 1942–43. According to the charge sheet, Demjanjuk was one of two gas-chamber operators at Treblinka from summer 1942 until autumn 1943.

Demjanjuk recounted that in the spring of 1944 he and a few hundred other Ukrainian POWs were sent by train to the vicinity of Graz in Austria. There they were told they would soon be attached to a Ukrainian combat division affiliated to the Waffen-SS. Demjanjuk remained near Graz for several weeks, at which time his blood type was tattooed on his arm. In the end he was transferred, with some of the other prisoners who had come from Chełm, to the Vlasov army rather than to the Ukrainian division. He was stationed at a base close to Hoiberg in southern Germany.

He remained at this base from the summer of 1944 until about three weeks before the war ended. He admitted that in Hoiberg he became, if not by choice, a part of the German war machine, serving as a bodyguard for senior officers in the Vlasov army. Just before the end of the war, Demjanjuk set out with a group of soldiers to the city of Bischofshofen, where they surrendered to the US Army. At the end of the war they were transferred in the direction of Munich, and then to a displaced-persons camp in Landshut. He was there until 1947. Here he met his wife and began to work as a driver for the American Army. From Landshut he went to the DP camp in Regensburg, where he stayed for about two and a half years. After this he moved to the city of Ulm for about half a year, and after short stays in several other places he emigrated, at the beginning of 1952, to the United States. After working for a short while as a farm labourer he settled in Cleveland, Ohio. He trained as a mechanic, and worked balancing engines at one of the Ford factories in the city for thirty years, until his retirement.

Demjanjuk explained that he made many false entries on the form he filled out in Germany in 1948 in order to be granted the status of refugee, the first step towards receiving an immigrant visa to the US. He maintained that he did this in order to give the impression that he had left the Soviet Union before the war began, so as to prevent his forced repatriation. The prosecution's version was that he had done so in order to conceal his activities at Treblinka.

On this form he stated, among other things, that from 1937 to 1943 he had worked as a driver near the town of Sobibor. The prosecution argued that he wrote this because around March 1943 he was transferred for a short time from Treblinka to Sobibor. Gill asked Demjanjuk about this specifically, and Demjanjuk replied, 'Even if I have only a fourth-grade education, I am not so stupid as to say "Sobibor" if I was there, and I am telling you that I was never there in my life.' He said that only when the accusations of his being Ivan the Terrible began circulating did he first hear that there had been a death camp of that name near Sobibor town. In 1948, when the form was filled out, he said 'Sobibor' purely by chance. He had heard of it from someone who had been in the DP camp with him. Neither did he discount the possibility that he had actually said 'Sambur', also the name of a town in Poland that he might have recalled while he filled out the form.

Earlier, outlining his life story, he had mentioned a grandchild born to him in America. Levin snapped: 'Just a minute, we heard that he has several grandchildren. So which grandchild? Mr Gill asks where the grandchild was born. We are dealing here with the most important matters in the trial, so we have to be precise.' After Demjanjuk's response, Levin went on with barbed derision: 'Now we come to the critical question you were asked – where were you living when this child was born?' (When the identification witnesses were asked numerous questions that did not deal with 'the most important matters in the trial', such as their doings in the towns of their birth and their lives after escaping from Treblinka, and when they gave lengthy responses to these questions, Levin of course had listened with great interest and never thought of interrupting them.)

Gill asked Demjanjuk several questions to conclude the evidence in chief. In his answers, Demjanjuk forcefully denied that the Travniki document and the signature thereon belonged to him, and at the end of his testimony he said, in his inept way, 'I answer that I never have been and am not now Ivan the Terrible.'

* * *

THE COLLAPSE OF THE DEFENCE CASE 125

On Tuesday Blatman began his cross-examination. After a while he directed a question at Demjanjuk that was based on things he had said in a statement made in the US in 1980. I rose and demanded that Demjanjuk be presented with this statement and the section on which he was being questioned. According to the rules of procedure, a witness has the right to see any document he is asked about. Levin decided, 'When the witness requests it in order to give his answer – whether he does not remember or whether he is not sure or whether he thinks his words are being imprecisely quoted – if he asks to see it, it will be given to him.' A short time later Demjanjuk was again asked about things he had said in a statement he had made in the States. I rose and said: 'Again, in the name of the defendant, I request that if he is asked about things that have been recorded, just as the prosecution witnesses were treated – being allowed to see documents about which they were questioned – this same treatment be accorded the defendant.' Levin took a different tack. 'We do not accept that as a general rule. When the witness asks to examine a document, we will allow him to do so, if it is really necessary to the examination. So long as the witness does not request this ... it is not mandatory.' I began to respond, 'If I may be allowed, I –' But he cut me off at once: 'We have decided!' I tried again: 'Yes, but I represent the defendant and I ask on his behalf that he be allowed to examine it.' Levin got cross. 'No, no, no, you are not testifying in his name. He knows. He is a witness. He will ask for it.' So Demjanjuk, whose limitations were so obvious, would not be treated as every other defendant in the country's courts was treated, and he would not be permitted the aid of his attorney.

During the break, I instructed Demjanjuk to say, whenever there was mention of a document relating to statements of his, that he did not remember precisely what was written in the document and to demand the document be given to him immediately. In order to ensure he did this, I told him that in every such instance I would turn towards him, and he would thus know that he was to make this demand. This arrangement worked. After a few such occurrences Blatman reacted. 'I am very sorry about this method, which sabotages the cross-examination. This is not how a cross-examination is conducted, when the witness's attention is directed to the need to demand and examine documents.' But of course this is precisely how cross-examinations *are* conducted. Even more astounding were Levin's words. 'Mr Blatman, this has been noted in the record and is being taken into account and will be taken into account when the testimony is evaluated ... it is being taken into account. So there is no reason to be upset.' So, when Demjanjuk demanded what Levin himself said he had the right to demand, he apparently damaged his own testimony. I thought to myself that Demjanjuk really could do nothing but sit and wait patiently to be sent to the gallows.

As the cross-examination continued and I carried on turning to face Demjanjuk, and Demjanjuk continued to exercise his right to examine the documents he was being asked about, Levin commented: 'We are trying to go above and beyond the call of duty for you, and I am not asking for thanks because that is our job. We are acting with great patience, allowing you to examine material, something that is not allowed in every case . . .' This was Levin at his best. First he acted in contradiction of procedural practice, and then he tried to create an impression in the record that he was going out of his way to help Demjanjuk by reverting to practice. Now, Levin could have been expected to do what he always did at his best – return to his original position. And indeed, later in the cross-examination, when I again rose and requested that statements on which he was being questioned be placed before him, Levin said: 'There is no such procedure. Once and for all . . . first he has to answer, and in this matter we have acted towards the defendant with great patience.' The term 'kangaroo court' leaped to mind.

Blatman cross-examined Demjanjuk for two whole days. Two main points emerged: Demjanjuk was questioned by the American authorities about the suspicion that he was Ivan the Terrible in 1978, two years after he had been so identified by some of the Treblinka survivors. At that interrogation, he claimed that he had been in two POW camps in Poland. One was Rovno, but he simply could not remember the name of the second. While this first interrogation took place thirty-five years after he was captured, Blatman continued to point out (with good reason) that he had paradoxically forgotten the name of the second camp (Chełm), where he claimed he had been for a year and a half. Yet he remembered the name of the first, where he had been for no more than a month. This showed, Blatman berated Demjanjuk, that if he had been in Chełm camp at all it had only been for a few days. In any case, he claimed, it was clear that this alibi of Demjanjuk's was a total fabrication: from the summer of 1942 to the autumn of 1943 he had been in Treblinka, not in Chełm, and there he had earned the name 'Ivan the Terrible', because of his horrible cruelty and crimes. Blatman continued to question Demjanjuk about this – but he was not the only one.

According to Israeli procedural law, a judge may ask a witness only questions of clarification, questions that are 'so essential that if they are not asked all or most of the testimony will remain unintelligible', as defined in Israeli legal precedents. Levin and his colleagues ignored this rule, enthusiastically taking part in Blatman's cross-examination whenever they saw fit. Their questions bore no resemblance to 'questions of clarification'. Levin in particular took over the cross-examination completely at times, and functioned as head of the prosecution team. At these moments I kept my composure only with great difficulty. Paul Brifer told me that he could not bear to watch this farce, and at one point simply walked out of the courtroom.

To the barrage of questions fired at him by Blatman and the judges about his inability to remember the name of the Chełm camp, Demjanjuk responded: 'Yes, I forgot, I couldn't say at that time. I can't forget after forty years? I keep explaining and I'll explain again, more than forty years had passed, and when I had to answer quickly, in a hurry, I could not remember everything. But no one wants to understand that.' He repeated this in various ways and emphasized: 'I said that I was in two camps. I only forgot the name of the second one. But not that I was in two camps. That I always remembered.'

The second matter about which Blatman interrogated Demjanjuk at length was the date of his arrival in the Graz area and his later enlistment in the Vlasov army at the military base next to Hoiberg. According to Blatman, if Demjanjuk joined the Vlasov army at all it was only at the beginning of 1945, after the end of his 'service' in the extermination camps. This, Blatman argued, struck at the veracity of Demjanjuk's alibi. Demjanjuk forcefully denied Blatman's version. He had arrived in Graz in the spring of 1944, after Chełm, and shortly thereafter, in the summer, had been transferred to Hoiberg. Blatman again argued that the Vlasov army had been founded only in November 1944, so Demjanjuk could not have been at this army's base in the summer of that year. The defence later proved that this argument lacked foundation. Demjanjuk stuck to his story.

On 30 July Blatman concluded his part of the cross-examination, and handed over to Shaked. The media, going out of their way to trumpet Demjanjuk's guilt, launched an unbridled attack on his testimony, blatantly and repeatedly violating the principle of *sub judice*. At first, the headlines declared UNDER DEFENCE'S GUIDANCE, IVAN IS A MARTYR BEARING A CROSS ON HIS BACK. During the cross-examination conducted by Blatman and the judges, they went even further: THE CRACK IN THE ALIBI WIDENS; MORE CONTRADICTIONS IN DEMJANJUK'S TESTIMONY; DEMJANJUK CONTRADICTED HIMSELF ALMOST THE ENTIRE TIME; JOHN 'JUSTIFIES' IVAN; DEMJANJUK IN TROUBLE AGAIN; NO CHANCE – HE WON'T BREAK DOWN CRYING AND CONFESS; HE SAYS MUCH AND EXPLAINS NOTHING. Such headlines always accompany show-trials, such as the lynch-trials of blacks in the first half of this century in the southern United States. This was the style of the anti-Semitic press in France and Russia during the Dreyfus and Beyliss trials.

I must admit that Demjanjuk's testimony was not especially persuasive at this stage. On Saturday night, 1 August, I had to go to Britain and leave Gill alone on the defence bench against the prosecutors and a hostile court. I went to meet several potential defence witnesses whose testimony was essential, and I had no other time to see them. They were Professors Elizabeth Loftus and Willem Wagenaar and Count Nikolai Tolstoy. Gill understood the vital nature of the trip and even helped me persuade Nishnic, who was concerned that Gill would not be aggressive enough in the face of the hostility.

Shaked's cross-examination focused on three issues. The first was the form Demjanjuk had filled out in 1948. The second was when he had begun working as a driver – had it been in 1947, as he claimed, and as indicated by the driving licence he had taken out in Germany in 1947 and which was also an exhibit in the case, or was it before the war? The third was the way Demjanjuk signed his name, and the similarities with the signature on the Travniki document.

Discussing the form, Shaked tried to show that Demjanjuk had said he had worked as a driver in the vicinity of Sobibor in the years 1937–43, both because he had been a guard in this camp for a short period and mostly because he wanted to hide the fact of his being Ivan the Terrible from Treblinka. Shaked maintained that Demjanjuk had to put down a place where he had really been so as to be able to provide details about its environs and persuade any interrogator of the truthfulness of his story. Shaked also claimed that Demjanjuk prolonged the period he had been in Sobibor in order to cover the time he was at Treblinka. But Sobibor was a horrific extermination camp, just like Treblinka. Why then would Demjanjuk have chosen to refer to it of his own volition? After all, he could have chosen to mention some other place he had been, somewhere that was not a death camp. Shaked's solution was preposterous. He argued – not bothering with proof – that in 1948 Sobibor was less well-known than Treblinka and that Demjanjuk therefore was not afraid to mention it by name.

Demjanjuk replied that he stated he had worked in the vicinity of Sobibor during those years because he wanted to show he had left the borders of the Soviet Union before 1 September 1939. The Yalta Declaration stated that anyone who had left the Soviet Union before that date would not be returned against his wishes; anyone who had left thereafter would be. Demjanjuk had wanted to conceal his service in the Red Army because this fact could also have been a justification for his repatriation. Shaked suggested that at the beginning of 1948, when he had filled out the form, there had been no reason to fear his forced repatriation to Russia because this process had been concluded at least a year and a half previously. Demjanjuk answered that he did not know how long the process continued, but he and many others like him were very frightened that they would be sent back to Russia. In 1948 there were still many rumours about Russian officers circulating in the DP camps with precisely this intention.

Shaked pelted Demjanjuk with numerous detailed questions about the name 'Sobibor': where and how he had heard of it in 1948; from whom he had heard of it; why he decided to include it, of all names, in the form; and so on. Demjanjuk, of limited intellect and slow memory, responded as best he could, even though he was expected to remember the smallest details of a form that a translator had filled out for him forty years ago. It was clear that he did not remember anything, but he tried to use his limited logic to explain what he had done all those years ago. The attempt was doomed of course. This line of examination did however raise doubts about the significance of these questions and answers. They were pointless, like the questions O'Connor had asked the survivors about the distance between their barracks and the gas chambers. But Levin not only allowed Shaked to go into as much detail as he wished, but also joined in with the cross-examination, alone or with the help of his two colleagues. Sometimes the bench and the prosecutor kept up this barrage of questions for as long as an hour.

The second main point in Shaked's cross-examination was the attempt to show that Demjanjuk had been a driver even before the war. The motor that injected the gas into the chambers in Treblinka was a tank engine with a pipe attached to convey the exhaust fumes. These fumes killed nine hundred thousand Jews at Treblinka. Shaked wanted to convince the court that Demjanjuk was insisting he could not drive a car before the war in order to bolster his claim that he had not operated the gas chambers, since someone who did not know how to drive could not have operated a tank engine. This was a ridiculous argument, but Levin gave it full weight in the verdict.

Almost daily during my stay in Britain I could read extensive reports on events in Jerusalem; I also spoke about it with Tzvia. She was not impressed by Demjanjuk's testimony. 'They are simply killing him,' she kept telling me. This deplorable picture did not change when Shaked's cross-examination focused on the way Demjanjuk signed his name. On 5 August the prosecution's and judges' cross-examination finally reached an end, and Gill's re-examination began.

The purpose of a re-examination is to clarify matters that remain unclear after the cross-examination. Sometimes it may serve to repair some of the damage done to the testimony in the cross-examination. The court was not content with the crossfire-examination it had just conducted, and as soon as the re-examination began the judges began ruling out many of the questions that Gill posed. They did this both by sustaining the prosecution's objections and on their own initiative. To cap it all, Levin also interfered during Gill's questions and asked Demjanjuk yet more questions of a manifestly antagonistic nature. He castrated the re-examination. Yet the bench could not leave it at that. As soon as Gill finished questioning Demjanjuk, the judges addressed themselves to asking some 'questions of clarification'. Levin and his colleagues launched into a long interrogation, ignoring the definition of the term 'questions of clarification'. The three judges fired their hostile questions one after the other, and every one of them found its target.

After some two weeks of questioning, Demjanjuk finally finished his testimony – drained, exhausted and battered. The serious travesty of justice displayed for these two weeks made no impression on the media. They praised the prosecutors and judges to the skies and gave their blessing to the placing of the rope around Demjanjuk's neck. No member of the Israeli legal community raised his voice in protest; there was not a single honourable man among the professors in the country's three law schools.

On Thursday 6 August Edna Robertson took the stand. I was in a small town called Abingdon, just outside Oxford, that day. This was the home of Nikolai Tolstoy. Gill had told me that Ms Robertson was a document examiner, an expert of the first order with an excellent reputation in the States. He said she had made many successful appearances in American courts. Three months before her testimony she had been in Israel with another document examiner, Fabian Tusson, and they had spent three days at the Israel Police laboratories examining the original Travniki camp exhibits, including the 'Travniki document' itself. Gill was solely responsible for forensic aspects of this document, and was supposed to introduce expert testimony to refute the points made by the prosecution experts, especially their conclusions that the document was authentic and belonged to Demjanjuk.

Gill had performed competently during his cross-examinations of the two prosecution experts, and before the trial resumed he had told me that with Robertson and Tusson he would be able to prove that the Travniki document was a total forgery. I trusted him unconditionally and at that time was up to my ears in other matters. So I did not take the trouble to ask him for more details about Robertson's testimony, and took his confidence at face value. It was based on this that in my opening statement I had said we expected to 'blow the Travniki document to bits'.

It quickly became clear that Gill's confidence was misplaced. To the defence's embarrassment, Robertson was shown to be worthless. During the evidence in chief she claimed that it was impossible to determine whether or not one of the signatures belonged to Toyfel, the quartermaster. She claimed that the signature of Streibel, the Commandant, was a forgery. This determination was based on the ostensible difference between the slant lines of the signature on the document and the slant lines in other undisputed Streibel signatures. Robertson put special emphasis on the forgery of Demjanjuk's signature, based on the great variation in appearance of the Cyrillic letters M, D, K and 'ya' on the Travniki signature and in undisputed signatures of Demjanjuk's. The most sensational finding in her testimony was that the stamp contained two different types of ink; one in the section that was printed over the photograph and another in the section on the document itself. This indicated that what we had before us was a crude transplant of the photograph from some other document. Such a clear forgery of such an important component of the document was sufficient to rule out the authenticity of the document as a whole.

Robertson had reached this conclusion by using a video spectrum scanner (VSS), and said she frequently used this device in her work to determine the difference between two samples of ink. The Israel Police laboratory is equipped with such an instrument, and she had used it for the tests she had run. She said that when one inserted the Travniki document into the machine the luminescence from the part of the stamp on the photograph was different from that of the stamp on the document, and this proved that two kinds of ink were used.

After returning to Israel I went to Jerusalem, and at the hotel I went directly to Gill's room. After telling him about my successful meetings with Loftus, Wagenaar and Tolstoy, I was given a progress report on the examination of Robertson. I was very enthusiastic about what I heard, especially the wonders of the VSS and Robertson's astounding discoveries. Later that day I went over the record of Robertson's Thursday testimony, and it seemed to reinforce what Gill had said. The evidence in chief continued on Monday the 10th, and the witness made an excellent impression on everyone.

Shaked opened his cross-examination with an offensive question. 'What do they call you, Doctor Robertson or Professor Robertson?' This was said in a condescending tone; furthermore, Robertson had never presented herself as either doctor or professor. I therefore rose and said: 'I think that the question is insulting. It is absolutely clear to my colleagues that Ms Robertson is neither a doctor nor a professor. The purpose of the question is to insult her and I do not think such questions have any place here.' I wanted to say a few more words, but the interpreter interjected, 'The microphone.' She meant that the tiny microphone attached to my shirt had not been turned on. Levin attacked immediately: 'Better that there be no microphone, the comment is not fit for the microphone. Please sit down. We *had* a few days of quiet. Please, sit down!' The court is required to defend the honour of the witnesses appearing before it, and disallow questions intended only to hurt them. Levin's behaviour was so shameful that he was even criticized by the retinue of media sycophants.

Levin, however, could not content himself with that insult. A few minutes later Shaked attacked Robertson for failing to submit the album she had prepared for her testimony to the prosecution in June. This took some nerve on his part; after all, contrary to accepted practice, Shaked had given the defence the album prepared by Bezaleli, the prosecution's expert witness on the document, only on the day of his testimony, in the courtroom itself. But when I objected to the line of questioning, Levin did not wait for Shaked's response. 'So, Mr Sheftel. First of all you have apparently come here today in a very aggressive mood, and it would be worth your while to cool down a bit. Second, I am surprised by the comment itself. I have seldom encountered a prosecution that supplies the defence with such extensive and competent services.' Then he added: 'From this point forward, objections, if there are any objections, may be made only by Mr Gill, as the person conducting the examination in chief. There's no point in making a muddle here. Mr Sheftel will sit quietly and not interfere. Please, Mr Sheftel. Mr Shaked, you may proceed.'

Shaked had already succeeded early on in showing that Robertson was not a member of the American Society of Document Examiners, nor of the American Academy of Forensic Science, the two bodies for senior document examiners in the United States. Judges Levin and Dorner joined Shaked's cross-examination at this early stage, indicating that they intended to continue hostilely and illegitimately interrogating the witness. On one of these occasions Gill tried to raise an objection about the way the bench was intervening in the cross-examination. Levin responded: 'Does Mr Gill want this to be a court in which the witnesses testify what they want, relate what they want, and the court does not try to clarify matters for itself, does not try to get into the logic of the matter, and then has to rack its brains afterwards when it has to hand down a verdict? ... That is not our approach and that is not our attitude.' But the attempt to 'clarify matters' was so pugnacious that on the first day of the cross-examination Judges Levin and Dorner shot such a barrage of questions that they exhausted Robertson and brought on an asthma attack. It was clear that she physically could not continue to answer further questions. The scene was so embarrassing that Levin had to ask her, 'Would Ms Robertson like to request a fifteen-minute recess?' Robertson gasped, 'I would,' and the recess was granted.

The final blow to her testimony came at the end of Tuesday's afternoon session. The prosecution brought the VSS machine to court and inserted several of the Travniki camp records that had pictures on them, documents whose authenticity was not in dispute. Demjanjuk's driving licence, which included a picture, was also inserted. The result of inserting the Travniki document for testing – the visible difference in luminescence between the two parts of the stamp – was also obtained when all the other documents were put into the machine. On every document, one type of luminescence was seen on the part of the stamp that was on the picture and a different type on the rest of the stamp. Thus the difference in luminescence could not demonstrate that the stamp was forged. Robertson's conclusion now looked like the bad joke of an amateur who had found herself in a courtroom during the proceedings of an important trial by mistake. I was deeply embarrassed and frustrated, especially after the boast I had made in my opening speech. Shaked dragged the scene out as long as he could. With obvious enjoyment he shoved one document after another into the wretched machine, showing up Robertson's blunder again and again.

We returned to the hotel defeated and humiliated. I ate alone and went straight to my room. A few minutes later Johnny knocked on the door. His face was as angry as mine was despairing. I invited him in, and he said: 'I want to make it clear that I have no complaints about you, and I know that you weren't involved in this embarrassment. It was horrible to sit in the courtroom and watch how they carved Robertson up. She's just not the right calibre. She did amateur work and Gill too made a fool of himself.'

I tried to cover for Gill. 'Look, Johnny, Gill is not a document examiner by training, he's a lawyer. If his expert tells him something that seems logical on the face of it, and if it can discredit the document, what reason does he have to doubt it?'

Johnny was not convinced and continued to ask difficult questions. 'Would you bring an American expert who was not a member of the associations they mentioned?'

'Yes, because before Shaked's cross-examination I did not know there were such associations in America.'

This response did not convince Johnny either. 'Yes, but you aren't an American lawyer, and Gill is. He should have known that. I'm sure that the second witness Gill intends to call about the Travniki picture, and who is supposed to refute Smith's and Altmann's testimonies, won't look any better.' I had run out of arguments.

'The situation is pretty miserable,' I said with a sigh. 'We'll have to pull high-quality expert testimony on this document out of a hat, and this time I'll be in the picture. During my visit to Britain I took steps to get good, appropriate expert witnesses for the identification and on historical matters. The same will happen with the Travniki document.' I don't know where I found the audacity to say that, but I meant it seriously and believed that I would do it. There was only one problem: I had not the slightest idea how. But Johnny was encouraged. We exchanged more stories about Robertson's testimony, joking and laughing to overcome our anger and frustration.

Next morning Shaked and the judges continued to expose Robertson. Her testimony finally ended after a week. The court record stood at 6,300 pages. The headlines celebrated the prosecution's success. PROSECUTOR SHAKED CRUSHES THE AMERICAN EXPERT IN CROSS-EXAMINATION; GOD HELP YOU PLEASE, MRS ROBERTSON; YOU CAN GO NOW, MRS ROBERTSON. This time, at least, they had a point. In an interview Ms Robertson said: 'They have humiliated me in front of the whole world. My career has been destroyed. From now on they will laugh at me in every court. Had I known what to expect, I would have stayed at home.' She also went around saying that they would give Anita Pritchard, the next defence witness, a breakdown just like her. For some reason she forgot to mention that she had recommended Pritchard to Gill. She was right: it was too bad she hadn't stayed at home. Back at the hotel, Ms Robertson came up to me, shook my hand and said, 'It was a pleasure working with you.' I did not try to hide my anger: 'I wish I could say the same.' I pulled my hand away and left.

I was surprised to discover that Gill was not disheartened. He tried to persuade me that Fabian Tusson would plug the hole left by Robertson's testimony. But I was sure Tusson suffered from all Robertson's shortcomings, possibly many more. So I told him sternly: 'After the first week of Demjanjuk testimony, I learned a lesson and decided, in consultation with you, that there was no point calling his wife as a witness; so I expect you to abandon the idea of calling Fabian to testify. His testimony will be so bad that Robertson will come out looking like a genius. Fabian will not testify.'

As Ms Robertson was packing, Ms Pritchard arrived at the American Colony. The Demjanjuk family was in despair; Vera kept muttering, 'They'll hang him, they'll hang him.' At the moment, that seemed certain. Instead of going home for the weekend as usual I decided to remain in the hotel and get an idea of Pritchard and her testimony.

The three of us met in Gill's room. The crux of Pritchard's testimony was that, because of the brain's structure, people make identifications with the left eye, and the data is processed on the right side of the brain. Therefore, the actual identification is of the right side of the identified person's face. Altmann's photomontages of half of Demjanjuk's face with half of the Travniki photograph were therefore of no value, among other reasons because when there is contrast in the picture the clearer side is absorbed better by the observer. In Altmann's photomontages there was always a contrast between the two half-faces he had joined.

Pritchard's position on Professor Smith's testimony was that when we interpret the superimposition of one picture on another through a transparency or through the imposition of one face on another on video tape, we are more affected by our expectations than by what we actually see. Smith's conclusions about the apparent match between the Travniki photograph and known pictures of Demjanjuk could not, therefore, be accepted. Pritchard's third point was the most important. She said that there was no literature or theory known and accepted by the international scientific community that adopted or even related to the theories and assumptions expressed in Altmann's and Smith's testimonies.

Finally, Pritchard tore pictures at random out of magazines, cut them in two and connected each half-face to another half-face. The results showed in ten out of twelve examples that the two half-faces were no less correlated than Demjanjuk's half-face and the half of the Travniki photograph. The pictures she prepared did indeed create such an illusion.

There was one thing I did not like, however. Ms Pritchard said when I asked her that she had appeared as an expert witness of this particular type only once. I also discovered that she had not completed her PhD. When we all left the room I took Gill aside. 'Gill, how can you bring, in this case, an expert witness without experience in court in the subject she is to testify on?' I asked him in annoyance. 'That's all there is,' Gill answered quietly. 'I couldn't find anyone else.' I didn't want to cloud the atmosphere between us any more, so I chose not to respond.

I spent the entire weekend racking my brains over what to do about the fact that the defence, for all practical purposes, had no answer to the prosecution experts' testimony on the Travniki document. Even though I knew it was impossible – at least given the time available and the zero probability that Levin would grant me the time I needed to prepare such testimony – I was feverishly preoccupied with it. On Saturday night I reached the conclusion that we should contact the expert who had revealed the truth about the 'Hitler diaries'. These diaries, published as authentic by the German weekly magazine *Stern*, were soon proved to be a fairly amateur forgery. If an expert of this stature found defects in the Travniki document, we might correct the poor impression left by Robertson's testimony and refute that of the prosecution experts. Of course even this would not really help Demjanjuk, because of the court's hostility, but we could not base our work on this assumption. I called Nishnic and assigned him the task of tracking down the expert.

On Monday, Pritchard took the stand, and presented her arguments as at our meeting. When the evidence in chief was concluded, the prosecution requested a consultation in chambers; Shaked asked for a day's delay in order better to prepare for the cross-examination. I took advantage of the opportunity to tell the judges that we had decided to forgo Vera Demjanjuk's testimony, as well as that of Fabian Tusson, so the defence would have no witnesses the following week. As a result there was no option but to advance the recess to immediately after Pritchard's cross-examination. The judges were not pleased, but they had no choice. They returned to the courtroom and announced that the next day's session had been postponed to the day after and the recess in the trial would be advanced. We would reconvene on 7 September 1987.

Shaked had no difficulty in showing that Pritchard was not an expert at all. It came to light later that she had prepared her testimony on Altmann's album of photomontages using photocopies rather than the originals. Gill had received the original album in March in order to give it to an expert for the defence, but for some reason he had not given it to Pritchard. Her desperate plight on the witness stand was cut short only by a break.

Pritchard went up to the defence office to rest a bit, sat down heavily on a chair, stared at the ceiling and said she would never return. Gill and I did all we could to encourage her, and after drinking a glass of cold water and resting for a few minutes she began to pull herself together. Meanwhile I called my office and told Doron what was happening. He was astonished at the bungled testimonies and at the ease with which Shaked was knocking them down. Finally we succeeded in persuading Pritchard to return to the courtroom, but she did so with a total lack of motivation. Apparently she knew that the rest of her testimony would be entirely destroyed.

The cross-examination then revealed that Pritchard's course of study was rather dubious: large parts of it were not recognized by the American educational authorities. It also turned out that she had never published a research report in a recognized scientific journal. In short, it looked as if Pritchard was anything but an expert. Some of her theories were

THE COLLAPSE OF THE DEFENCE CASE 137

also called into question, and even the re-examination could not save her. When she came down from the witness stand, at six in the evening, drained and discouraged, her testimony seemed like an even worse joke than Robertson's.

The only comfort was that this phase of the defence case was over. The record stood at 6,500 pages. With the advancement of the recess, I now had another week to prepare for the next stage. As soon as we got back to the hotel Johnny approached me: 'Now Gill can't avoid responsibility. There is no reasonable explanation for him not having supplied Pritchard with Altmann's original album.'

'That doesn't matter,' I responded. 'Even if he had, the situation would be no better.'

'That's true,' Johnny said, 'but a lawyer who doesn't make sure his expert witness is supplied with the original material needed for their testimony is such a dolt that he is also capable of using a witness like Pritchard in an important trial like this. Gill will call no more witnesses in this trial. He can't be depended on.' I saw no point in trying to defend Gill further. Johnny was absolutely right.

In the mean time Paul Chumak, an experienced lawyer who had previously spent seventeen years as a crown prosecutor in Canada, received a permit from the Minister of Justice to appear as an additional foreign defence counsel for Demjanjuk. Chumak was Ukrainian by origin and British in his habits and manners. He knew nothing about the case when he joined the defence, but from the moment he arrived in Israel (on the last day of Demjanjuk's testimony) he devoted days and nights to studying the case. He came to court every day to observe the proceedings.

After Pritchard's testimony, I ate supper with Chumak. We both agreed that after this stage of the trial the defence was in a catastrophic state. Chumak did not hide his astonishment at the low quality of the witnesses Gill had produced, but he was not hurtful. The situation looked hopeless to him. He stressed repeatedly that no way could an adequate defence be prepared in three weeks.

Before I fell asleep I rang Nishnic and told him about Pritchard. He had succeeded in finding the name of the expert who had uncovered the forgery of the 'Hitler diaries': Dr Julius Grant, a British expert whose office and laboratory were in London. Nishnic said he would locate the precise address within a few days, and then make initial telephone contact with him. I was very encouraged by this, but reminded him of the urgent time factor. The next day I spoke at length with Johnny. We analysed the situation present and future. I was surprised, and no less happy, to find out how much he trusted me in spite of the terrible state the defence was in, especially since I had not tried to paint a rosy picture of what was to come. At no stage did I try to create any such false confidence. Johnny would later tell me that it was precisely because I never gave any illusions during that difficult time that he trusted and believed in me.

Just after five in the afternoon I went to Pritchard's room to make a short courtesy visit before returning to Tel Aviv. I knew she had shut herself up in her room right after completing her testimony and that she was leaving Israel the next day. I knocked on her door. There was no answer. I asked at the reception desk if they knew where she was, and was told that she was apparently in her room, because her key was not at the desk, and that she had not been seen since her return from court the previous day. I began to worry that something was wrong. I returned to her room and knocked again. Again there was no answer. I peeked through the keyhole; I could not see the bed, but the room looked as if it had not been cleaned; it was very disordered. I went straight back to the reception desk and told them what I had seen. I demanded that they open the door immediately. One of the hotel employees opened the door with the master key. Pritchard was spread-eagled on her bed, dressed in pyjamas. She was breathing heavily, and she had obviously lost consciousness. I asked that an ambulance be called immediately. No sooner had the paramedics begun carrying Pritchard out than reporters and television crews began arriving at the hotel. Gill and I rode in the ambulance with Pritchard, who was still unconscious, to the Bikur Holim Hospital. An army of reporters and photographers was waiting there.

At the hospital we found out that Pritchard had decided to kill herself. About two hours before I knocked on her door she had swallowed several dozen sleeping pills. Pumping her stomach and other treatments quickly got her out of danger. She was discharged the next day and even caught her flight home. A death sentence was hanging over my client's head, I thought to myself, but at least I had managed to save the life of one of the witnesses!

After all this I returned to Tel Aviv and tried to evaluate the situation. Since time was so short, Count Tolstoy would not be able to prepare thoroughly for his testimony on the historical issues; neither would Professor Wagenaar for the identification issue. With regard to the Travniki document the situation was infinitely worse, and the fact that we had finally found the name of the expert who had revealed the Hitler diary forgeries did not mean he would be willing and able to testify in the trial. It all seemed hopeless.

7 · Out of Thin Air

I had met Nikolai Tolstoy on Thursday 6 August 1987, arriving at his home in Abingdon in the afternoon. It was a medium-sized country house, surrounded by a large garden. Tolstoy received me with great warmth and led me to his study. Along the walls, from floor to ceiling, were bookcases containing thousands of volumes. Tolstoy, who was a little over fifty, looked fifteen years younger. His hair was fair, he was clean-shaven, and he radiated nobility of a mixed Russian-British sort.

We began with courtesies, and I was surprised to discover that the Russian of this respected member of the Tolstoy family was less fluent than mine. I then told him about the trial and about the warped way it was being conducted, focusing on its historical aspects. Tolstoy said he had followed the trial's progress through the British media and expressed his absolute revulsion at the way the judges were running it. He was especially disgusted by the trappings that had made it into a classic show-trial. I enumerated the historical issues raised by the prosecution, and laid out my expectations of his testimony.

As we talked I realized that Tolstoy was a historian of the first order, an expert on Soviet history and the KGB. He had even devoted himself to the subject of the forced repatriation of Soviet soldiers and citizens during the years after the war, and written two of his books on this subject. While he was not an expert on German POW camps, the Galician division or the Vlasov army, he said he could read the relevant literature, consult fellow historians and prepare thorough testimony on the subject. On exactly the dates his testimony was expected, he was supposed to be visiting Mozambique as a guest of the government. However, since a man's life was at stake, he would postpone his trip. I warned that he could not expect to have an easy time of it in court. The prosecution would try to wound him, on a personal as well as professional level, and the bench would not only not prevent this, but would actively participate. Tolstoy did not seem at all alarmed. He was not afraid of the hostility, but repeated his concern that, because of the minimal amount of time available to him (less than a month), and his many other obligations, his ability to prepare properly would be reduced.

Tolstoy displayed great curiosity about what had led me to join the defence of Demjanjuk. I satisfied his curiosity and also told him all about the hostility to me from the courtroom audience, the Israeli general public, the media and, worst of all, the judges. Tolstoy commented that these were obligatory components of any show-trial. I sensed Tolstoy's great disgust for the Soviet regime. He considered it had destroyed traditional Russian nationalism, and as a Russian patriot and scion of a family that symbolized that nationalism he considered its destruction a catastrophe with far-reaching consequences in his own life. Neither of us could imagine, of course, that in the space of five years the Soviet Union would cease to exist. We parted very affably at eleven at night and agreed to stay in touch by phone. I left a copy of the English translation of the historical testimonies, and promised to send the various exhibits he requested as soon as I returned. He in turn promised that he would do his best to ensure that his testimony would benefit the defence as much as possible.

I returned to my hotel in Oxford, and along the way I mused that I would never have met such a charming Russian-British nobleman had I not been Demjanjuk's defence attorney – so the case was not causing me only trouble and strife. Tolstoy had the abilities to be a witness of the first order, but I was afraid his testimony would nevertheless not go well, because of the lack of time to prepare.

Towards the end of August, Nishnic finally made contact with Dr Grant, who had expressed his willingness, in principle, to come to Israel and examine the Travniki document and other documentary exhibits. Dr Grant told Nishnic that if these examinations revealed defects in the Travniki document he would be happy to appear in court as an expert witness for the defence. But he would not be able to come to Israel before 3 September 1987. It was therefore clear that there was no real chance that he would be able to prepare his testimony properly. Nevertheless, lacking any alternative, I urged Nishnic to send Dr Grant to Israel as soon as possible. I had made enquiries about Grant through several friends of Meyer Lansky's, so as to prevent any surprises of the Robertson and Pritchard type. I learned that he had for decades been considered the number-one forensic expert in the world, with an unassailable reputation.

September arrived and the defence case still seemed hopeless. On Thursday morning, the 3rd, prosecution and defence attorneys were suddenly summoned to Judge Dorner's chambers at the Jerusalem District court, where we were informed that Judge Tal had suffered a heart attack the previous night. As a result, Dorner explained, the trial would not resume as planned. It would be postponed 'indefinitely', by several weeks at least. I have to confess I was happy. As we left the chambers I was thinking, I really do have the luck of a goy. I turned to Shaked and said, 'Dovele's [that was how I referred to Judge Dov Levin] hard, bad heart would not postpone the trial for even two days, but Judge Tal's weak, good heart has arranged a two-month delay for Sheftel. Now, whether Dovele likes it or not, we will have a proper defence.'

Tolstoy was arriving in Israel that afternoon, and there was no way of telling him to cancel his trip. I left for the airport to receive him; as soon as he emerged from the terminal I told him about the postponement of the trial. I thought he would be disappointed at having come to Israel needlessly, but quite the opposite. 'Shefy, I have to tell you that despite all my efforts I was unable to prepare the testimony well. I'm just as happy as you that the trial has been postponed. Now that I have a few more weeks, you will be able to get the maximum benefit from my testimony.'

A quick glance at his notes was enough to show that they needed to be filled out and improved; and I was glad that he did not have to take the witness stand on Monday: he was not ready. Based on the material he had prepared and additions arising from this conversation, I would compose a series of questions in English, divided into topics and subtopics, which would define the evidence in chief. My guess was that the trial would not resume before the end of October, so we decided to meet again in late September or early October in England, to work on his material.

I told Tolstoy that Dr Grant was scheduled to arrive in the country that night, and he intended to conduct a series of examinations of the Travniki and other documents. A decision on whether he would testify would be made on the results. I explained to Tolstoy that Grant would testify, if at all, immediately after him. Tolstoy had of course heard of Dr Grant and valued his talents. He thought that his testimony on the historical aspects of the Travniki document combined with the forensic aspects in Dr Grant's testimony would make such a great impression as to bring about a result for the defence. I agreed with him about the impression, but disputed the outcome; since, after all, we were talking about a show-trial.

On 16 September there was another meeting in Judge Levin's chambers, to set a date for the trial's resumption. Levin commented that 'We can't blame Sheftel for Judge Tal's heart attack.' I interrupted: 'Who knows, Sheftel is benefiting so much from this heart attack, he won't be surprised if they accuse him of that too. As unfortunate as it is, I can say with assurance that, because of the court's refusal to postpone the trial as requested, it is only Judge Tal's heart attack that makes it possible to be prepared.' Levin's face expressed his repugnance at what I had said, but he did not speak. It was agreed that the trial would resume on Monday 26 October. I left the chambers feeling relaxed; convinced that I would accomplish my mission. Now, with a timetable in hand, I spoke to Nishnic. We agreed that I would set out on another trip during the first week of October: first to Holland, to see Professor Wagenaar of Leiden University again, and thence to England to see Nikolai Tolstoy and Julius Grant, who had in the mean time completed his examinations in Jerusalem. In light of the results he had agreed to appear as a defence witness.

On 7 October I met Tolstoy in the lobby of the Ritz Hotel in London. He was in London on business and had chosen the hotel as a place to meet. He informed me that he had almost completed his work. His testimony would begin on Monday 2 November, and would probably continue for the entire week. I handed him the 110 questions that I had prepared for him. Tolstoy studied them at length, and said that they all seemed fine: he would arrange his notes accordingly. We decided that he should arrive in Israel on the 29th. I was in such a good mood that even the bill for our two cups of coffee and two pieces of cake, which came to more than $40, could not spoil it. I was certain Tolstoy's testimony would go well.

On 2 November I began the examination in chief with questions aimed at displaying Tolstoy's expertise and talents. He had an MA from the prestigious Trinity College, Dublin. He listed the books he had written, among them *Night of the Long Knives*, *Victims of Yalta*, *Stalin's Secret War*, *The Minister and the Massacres* – all touching directly on the subjects in his testimony. He emphasized that all the books were based on meticulous historical research, and that the amount of research needed for any one of them was much more than that required for the average doctorate. He also submitted several superb reviews of his books by well-known professors of history.

The first subject of his testimony was the forced repatriation of soldiers and civilians to the Soviet Union during the first years after the war. We hoped to prove that at the time Demjanjuk applied for refugee status, in March 1948, he had many objective and rational reasons to fear that he was still liable to be sent back to the land of Stalin. Tolstoy explained, basing himself on a large bibliography, that during the years after the war more than half a million people were forcibly returned to the Soviet Union. He had studied this subject for fifteen years and written two books about it. Referring to historical sources he showed that officials of the UN refugee agency in the displaced-persons camps tended to accept, and even to encourage, the false declarations of Soviet citizens, to help them evade repatriation. The most important point in his testimony on this subject was that forced repatriation continued at least until the summer of 1947, with Soviet officers methodically combing the DP camps. Tolstoy also quoted a debate in the House of Lords in 1948 over whether or not to continue this policy. There was a Soviet delegation in Frankfurt until 1949 whose sole task was forced repatriation. Finally, Tolstoy explained that it was quite reasonable for Demjanjuk to have written that he had worked as a labourer close to the town of Sobibor from 1937, because this put him outside the Soviet Union before 1 September 1939. (As I have noted, the Yalta accords stated that anyone who had left Russia before this date would not be forcibly returned.) Tolstoy's testimony thus refuted the prosecution's contention that forced repatriation came to a complete halt in May 1946, and that it was unreasonable for Demjanjuk to have feared it in March 1948. Indeed, it strengthened his claim that he entered false information on the application because he feared forced repatriation, and not because he was Ivan the Terrible.

After this, I asked Tolstoy questions on the Vlasov army. Tolstoy confirmed Professor Meizel's testimony that this army had been officially established in November 1944. But he also said that hundreds of thousands of Red Army soldiers who had fallen into the German Army's hands and volunteered to fight in its ranks were referred to as the 'Vlasov army' as early as the beginning of 1943. He said that Hitler, while unwilling to give these soldiers an independent command under General Vlasov, instructed that as much propaganda benefit as possible be gained from them. For this reason the soldiers were provided with insignia carrying the initials ROA, standing in Russian for the 'Russian Liberation Army', better known as 'Vlasov army'. Hundreds of thousands of soldiers bore these insignia in 1943, and Tolstoy had photographs from 1943 to back up this claim.

As for the Heuberg camp, where Demjanjuk claimed to have been from the summer of 1944 until almost the end of the war, Tolstoy testified that this was a gigantic camp where many ethnic groups had served (even Indians). It was certainly possible from a historical standpoint that, as Demjanjuk claimed, there were soldiers wearing the ROA tag at this camp in 1944. This too was an incontrovertible response, grounded in solid historical fact, to the prosecution's claim that Demjanjuk could not possibly have been in Heuberg in the summer of 1944 as part of the so-called Vlasov army.

During the afternoon session I asked Tolstoy about the Ukrainian division, also known as the Galician division. Tolstoy explained that in 1944 there was chaos in the German Army, especially in the units made up of captured Red Army soldiers. There were constant disputes between the different branches of the German Army and the command of the Waffen-SS (the SS combat divisions); these disputes more than once led to groups and units of Soviet soldiers being transferred from place to place and from command to command. Most likely this chaos made it impossible to keep orderly records, or any records at all, of the movements of some of these units. As a result, it was definitely possible that Demjanjuk was part of a group of former POWs in the neighbourhood of Graz in the spring of 1944, meant to be attached later to the Galician division. Likewise, it was certainly possible that several weeks later he was sent to another unit entirely, at Heuberg. Tolstoy illustrated all this with several concrete examples. This was a response to the prosecution's claim that Demjanjuk could not have been in Graz in spring 1944 because army records showed that the Ukrainian division reached this area only ten months later.

I moved on to the last major subject of his testimony: the Travniki document. Tolstoy remarked that document forgery of all kinds had been an important element of KGB activity from the moment it was founded. He gave as an example the forgery of reports to show that the Germans and not the Soviets had murdered fifteen thousand Polish officers in the forest near Katyn in 1941. (He also noted that, to his shame, a member of his family was a signatory to the false Soviet report on this incident.) An entire division of the KGB, known as 'Division 14', dealt solely with the forgery of documents. Tolstoy related that in his book *Stalin's Secret War* he had dwelt at length on document forgery by the KGB, and had therefore studied the subject in depth. Towards the end of this session, an authentic report was submitted that demonstrated the sophistication of the KGB's forgers. According to Tolstoy, no document should be ruled authentic simply because certain details, such as seals or words, are correct. This assumption is especially invalid in relation to a document suspected of being forged by the KGB, because the historical details were well known to the KGB forgers.

With regard to the Travniki document, Tolstoy explained that the fact that nothing was known about its archival background was in itself enough to raise grave misgivings about its authenticity. The archival background of a document, and the reliability of the certifications recording the background, are important factors in its verification. But even such verification would be insufficient to prove it was not a forgery. Only access to archives whose proper and honest management is widely accepted could aid in determining the authenticity of a document.

Precisely the opposite was true of archives in the Soviet Union. Tolstoy also presented concrete examples on this subject.

He maintained that because something like the Travniki document was transferred via a private messenger like Armand Hammer, known for his dubious connections with the Kremlin, after the Soviets had refused categorically to provide it through normal channels, was enough to raise suspicions, especially from the historical standpoint, that it was a forgery. The fact that the document had also been given to the Americans in 1981 by Rudenko, the Soviet States Attorney, raised even more suspicions. This man, according to Tolstoy, was one of the twentieth century's greatest forgers. His deceptions were at the base of the infamous Moscow trials (mostly of leading Jewish Bolsheviks) in the late 1930s, at which he had served as deputy chief prosecutor. Rudenko had also tried to present forgeries as evidence in the Nuremburg trials; but the Americans and British prevented this.

The conclusions Tolstoy drew were, first of all, that Demjanjuk's story about his movements from the time he was taken prisoner by the Germans in May 1942 until the end of the war – including his alibi that he had been a POW at the Chełm camp from autumn 1942 till spring 1944 – were certainly reasonable from a historical point of view. Second, if any conclusion at all could be reached about the Travniki document, it was a presumption that it was forged.

The judges could not restrain themselves during my questioning of Tolstoy. They interrupted over and over again and disallowed questions. Among other things they prevented him testifying that in the hundreds of interviews he had conducted during his research, in cases where the time-lapse was identical to that between the war and the date when Demjanjuk was first investigated in the US, the interviewees made mistakes, were confused or did not remember details, very much like Demjanjuk at the time he was questioned.

Blatman's cross-examination concentrated on Tolstoy's anti-Soviet views. He responded to Blatman's grilling without any special effort, even seasoning his answers with his delightful British humour. Nevertheless I was forced to intervene: 'I would like the record to reflect the fact that the witness was questioned on his personal and political views. The court has ruled on various occasions that it would not allow this.'

Levin responded: 'Then why have you risen, sir? To object or to ask him to continue?'

'I have risen to draw attention to the fact that the examination is being conducted in the context of personal political views.'

'But an entirely legitimate line of questioning is being conducted.' This was the same Levin who intervened during the testimony of prosecution witness Dr Karkovski, when O'Connor asked a question touching on his political views, with: 'That is not relevant to our trial. So Mr O'Connor will not ask such questions, and if he does, the witness will not be required to respond on his political views.'

The afternoon session was largely devoted to further interrogation on Tolstoy's politics, especially his opinion that Soviet officials who committed crimes against humanity at the behest of their government should be brought to justice just like Nazi war criminals. Tolstoy kept on responding brightly and serenely and had no trouble deflecting Blatman's nuisance-value questions.

During supper at the hotel Tolstoy remarked on the court's biased attitude. Since the judges had rejected my comment for the record, the next morning, before beginning his testimony, he would demand to declare that he would not continue if he were not treated as the prosecution witnesses had been. I tried to explain that Levin would be quite pleased by this announcement, since he could then remove Tolstoy's entire testimony from the record. But Tolstoy was not convinced. After supper I went up to Gill's room and told him about the conversation. We estimated that Levin would refuse to let Tolstoy open his mouth. Gill asked to be the defence's 'bad boy' this time, rising to voice a sharp protest if Levin did not allow Tolstoy to make his declaration. Perhaps such a step would satisfy Nikolai. But at breakfast Tolstoy was even more upset and would not budge from his position. I was pretty tense, worried that all the effort I had put into Tolstoy's testimony would be lost in one fell swoop.

As soon as the morning session was called to order, Tolstoy addressed Levin. 'Your Honour, before continuing, I wish to make a declaration. A brief announcement.'

'There is no such thing,' Levin objected. 'You will respond to the State Attorney's questions.'

Gill rose to make his protest. 'The witness wishes to make a declaration because he feels he is being personally attacked by the prosecutor. The court has previously stated that it is forbidden to raise any personal point, anything about the witnesses' political views. But Mr Blatman has spent most of his time asking about the witness's political views and private life. The court's behaviour is thus unacceptable to us.'

Levin was somewhat surprised at Gill's statement. 'We have heard what Mr Gill has to say. We do not agree with what has been said. We believe that this is a misinterpretation of our decision. In any case, we will not enter into a debate with Mr Gill regarding the declaration he has made before us.'

After a few more exchanges, in which Blatman was also involved,

Tolstoy finally succeeded in saying his piece. 'I am sorry, but if I am not guaranteed fair treatment, customary in the free courts of the Western world, I will not be able to continue.'

Levin responded as expected: 'I must protest at the form of that answer. It is an attack on and contempt of this court. We will ignore the comment and demand that Mr Tolstoy respond to the questions put to him. If the witness does not wish to respond to the questions, we will have to draw the necessary conclusions with regard to his testimony.' He turned to me. 'If Mr Sheftel wants a five-minute break, we will grant him one.'

'Fine, thank you, I request a recess,' I responded.

I explained to Tolstoy that the practical way to achieve his goal was to rise and object to every question of a political nature. If the bench overruled the objection, there would then be real reason for us to consider terminating his testimony. Tolstoy was not convinced. Gill's and Johnny's attempts were also unsuccessful. We returned and Gill argued again that the court was not balanced in its treatment of the witnesses. Levin interrupted to rebuke him. He emphasized, as usual, how fair the court had been with the witness. Tolstoy repeated his statement, in a blunter way, and Levin rebuked him. The exchange went on for several minutes without resolution, and another recess was declared.

It was Blatman who suggested a way out of the predicament, agreeing that Gill could declare that he would no longer question Tolstoy on his political views. Nikolai consented to this agreement. We all returned to the courtroom and Gill rose: 'During the break we spoke with Mr Blatman and Mr Tolstoy, and we were informed by Mr Blatman that he had no intention of going into the witness's personal character. Mr Blatman said that the questions to be posed henceforth will be directed solely to the historic side of his expertise.' The knot was untangled. Blatman cross-examined Tolstoy for two whole days, but was unable to make any real dent in his testimony on any of the four central points. At times, Blatman's questions were reminiscent of O'Connor. For instance he tried to demonstrate that, because of the Russians' opposition to the Marshall Plan in June 1947, Demjanjuk had no reason to fear, in March 1948, inter-bloc co-operation on forced repatriation. Imagine: Demjanjuk, a refugee with a fourth-grade education, was supposed to be a sophisticated political commentator, familiar with the range of problems between the Eastern and Western Blocs. Although Blatman succeeded in getting Tolstoy to admit that he was not an expert on the Vlasov army or the Ukrainian division, Tolstoy nevertheless stressed that his testimony on these subjects was based on prolific research into the literature, and was therefore well-founded historical fact.

The judges interfered little during the re-examination, and it seemed that Tolstoy's statement about the quality of the proceedings they were running had made some impression on them. To my surprise, his demand for fair treatment found a supportive audience in the Israeli public, in spite of the propaganda campaign being conducted by the media against the defence in general, and at present against Tolstoy and the substance of his testimony in particular. More than a hundred phone calls expressing empathy for him reached his room and mine at the hotel. He was moved by this outpouring of sympathy and thanked the callers with all his heart. The media were full of venomous distortions and lies. The headlines shouted: FOUR AREAS OF EXPERTISE, ONE EXPERT; TOLSTOY FINISHED AND SPRINTED TO HIS PLANE WITH A SIGH OF RELIEF; TOLSTOY QUOTES A NAZI MAGAZINE; IT'S HARD TO BE AN EXPERT ON SO MANY THINGS. Apart from the lies, articles explicitly expressed their opinion about Tolstoy's testimony, something the law forbids. Yet no one protested.

When Tolstoy left the witness stand I felt a great sense of satisfaction, but I did not delude myself or him for a moment that his testimony would be followed by the court. Yet the balanced and objective reporting in the foreign press brought home to me that a significant turning point in the trial had been reached. The pressure I was under at that time was unreasonable. In addition to everything involved in preparing and examining witnesses, I continued each night to summarize the record of every session. I never went to sleep before three in the morning, sometimes later. This continued for many long weeks.

The trial had resumed on 26 October, before Tolstoy's testimony. On that day Avraham Shifrin took the witness stand, the only Israeli who was not intimidated by the atmosphere surrounding the defence and who agreed to appear as an expert witness for us. Shifrin, a sixty-five-year-old from Zikhron Ya'akov who had emigrated from the Soviet Union in the early 1970s, was a well-known anti-Soviet activist. He had written a book on Soviet concentration camps and published many studies of KGB crimes; he had been invited several times to testify before committees of both houses of the American Congress about KGB activity. In the early 1950s he had worked as a Soviet prosecuting attorney, and in this context became closely acquainted with the KGB's *modus operandi*. Shifrin was later accused of spying for the US and jailed for some ten years, spent in the notorious gulags.

Precisely because of the public campaign against the defence, I was determined that at least one of our expert witnesses be Israeli. I had contacted several Israeli professors of history, directly and indirectly, but all rejected the idea out of hand. There can be no doubt they feared that the media would attack them, and one of them told me frankly, 'If I agree to appear as a defence witness, I will no longer be invited to be interviewed as a historian on television.'

I got Shifrin's name from a well-known doctor who had also immigrated from Russia at the beginning of the 1970s and who knew Shifrin well. I first met him in early June and he agreed to appear as a defence witness immediately and without hesitation. He would testify on the KGB and its methods of forgery, to show that the Travniki document should be treated with great suspicion – since even the prosecution did not deny that it had been in the KGB's possession.

After my meetings with Tolstoy it was clear that there was no longer much point in having Shifrin testify. Tolstoy was going to address the subject of KGB forgery at length, and I was convinced he would have a much greater impact than Shifrin. Nevertheless I did decide to get Shifrin to testify, both because it gave the defence and its witnesses extra preparation time, and also because of my strong desire to show that in spite of the vindictive media campaign against Demjanjuk and the prejudice of the court I had succeeded in bringing an Israeli witness who was not deterred by all this.

The most important result of Shifrin's testimony was the exposure of the true nature of the prosecutor, Michael Shaked. Judge Levin had ruled that the defence had to submit to the prosecution the expert opinion on which each expert witness's testimony was based. So I sent Shifrin's written statement to Shaked three months before his testimony began. Indeed, I reported in advance to Shaked on every measure I took to prepare the defence, even though I was not required to do so. So I was greatly surprised when, as soon as Shifrin took the stand, the prosecution requested that his testimony be disqualified, on the grounds that it was no more than anti-Soviet propaganda. Even Levin had to reject this unjustified request. Shaked's behaviour was shameful both ethically and as a colleague; he could, after all, have notified me of his intentions, as is generally done. Under normal circumstances I would have severed all contact with him for the duration of the trial. I did not do this, only because the friendly working relations between me and Shaked thoroughly annoyed Levin, who did his best to sabotage them.

As expected, Shifrin immediately became a target for the media, but this did not discourage him. A man who has been a political prisoner in the gulags can stand up to media insults. When he had finished his testimony I thanked him sincerely for the courage he had displayed and for having done all he could to aid the defence.

* * *

When Shifrin and Tolstoy had finished testifying, it was Dr Grant's turn.

I had first met Grant on 3 September. He arrived in Israel at midnight, and I waited for him without having any inkling what he looked like. After all the travellers had dispersed, I could not see anyone who seemed to be waiting for me. A few moments later my eye fell on a short, skinny old man who could barely stand upright. He was leaning on a trolley that held two suitcases. I decided to approach him, even though I did not think he was Dr Grant. 'Excuse me, are you Dr Grant?' I asked hesitantly.

'Yes, that's me,' the old man answered, extending a small, bony hand. I was in total shock. Still, I managed to shake his hand, noticing how weak it was. Oh what a mess, I said to myself. The defence is in so much trouble it can't even trust Lansky's friends. This helpless old man will make such a miserable appearance in court, Edna Robertson will look like a star in comparison. I've never been so badly let down in my life.

As we walked to my car, we had a brief, polite conversation. It was enough to encourage me a little. 'At least the man isn't senile,' I muttered ungraciously to myself. In the car Dr Grant suddenly said, 'I drive a sports car too.' I was surprised that such a fragile old man could drive at all, but it was too much to imagine him in a sports car. 'I've got two questions for you, Dr Grant. How old are you and what kind of sports car do you have?' I asked. 'I'm eighty-six and I drive a Jaguar,' he responded contentedly. All my fears about his court appearance evaporated at that moment. He must be fun to work with, I said to myself. Along the way I gave him an outline of the mission the defence had assigned him, and the timetable for accomplishing it. His comments and questions showed unambiguously that Julius Grant had a razor-sharp mind; he radiated professionalism of the highest order. I also discerned at once the man's great modesty.

A few minutes after I entered my room, Nishnic called to hear my opinion of Grant. I told him briefly about the huge difference between my first impression and the excellent estimation I held him in only minutes later. I could feel Nishnic's relief. It was a big gamble bringing Grant to Israel, since it could not be kept secret from the prosecution and the court. If after completing his tests he did not appear as an expert witness, it would indicate that he had found no flaw in the Travniki document. Clearly Dr Grant would never agree to appear as a witness in court in order to point out irrelevant flaws in the Travniki document. I could not be absolutely sure that he *would* find flaws, and of course I could not know what his overall conclusion about the document would be. But I had no other option, so I took the risk.

At breakfast I put my thoughts on the Travniki document to Dr Grant. After the disintegration of Robertson's and Pritchard's testimonies, I realized it was best not to attack the entire document, but rather to concentrate on its most obvious weak points, the *Demjanjuk* signature and the photograph. In the case of the signature, even the prosecution could find no expert witness willing to rule without doubt that it was the defendant's. As for the picture, the prosecution witnesses agreed that it had been separated from the document at some point; there was a suspicion that it had been taken from some other Soviet document and planted by the KGB on the Travniki card. If an eminent expert were to point out these two flaws, or even one of them, the inevitable conclusion would be that the document was forged. I was happy that Grant agreed unreservedly with my assumptions, and before we left for the police documents laboratory he said, 'I am sure that our working relationship will be fruitful.'

By prior agreement with the prosecution, a room where we could talk privately was made available for us at police headquarters. The original documents Grant was to test were brought in, with the exception of the Travniki document, of which we had a good photocopy. Only later, during the tests themselves, was Grant allowed to examine the original. We spent about an hour and a half going over some forty documents, with me explaining the nature of each particular paper and its place in the general picture. Grant took notes in a little black book, from time to time gazing at the documents with a magnifying glass. After this he said he could begin his examinations immediately, and estimated that he would need two more days to complete his work. One of the police officers led him to the laboratory, and I returned to the hotel.

After his second day of work, I collected Dr Grant from the police headquarters, and enquired into the progress of his examinations. Grant said with assurance that there was no possibility that the man who had signed the Travniki document with the name 'Demjanjuk' was the same man who had made all the undisputed signatures of Demjanjuk the defendant. I was overjoyed. 'Would you be prepared to give detailed testimony in court?' I asked immediately. 'Certainly,' Grant answered. When we reached the hotel I went up to my room to call Nishnic and tell him what I had just heard. 'That's the best news I've heard about Demjanjuk in the last ten years,' he said excitedly. He was right; the fact that the world's most respected forensic scientist believed the signature on the Travniki document was not Demjanjuk's, and was willing to testify to this under oath, was the most important development in Demjanjuk's favour since suspicions were first raised against him in 1976.

Dr Grant completed his examinations; but emphasized that he had much more work to do in his English laboratory and that with the aid of his notes and the high-quality enlarged photocopies he had been given he could continue his work without needing the originals. We parted and established that we would meet again in London at the beginning of October. I never ceased to marvel at this wonderful old man – at his integrity, his alertness, his professionalism. He told me all about his work, and how he slept eight hours every night. Despite his gauntness, he turned out to be no small gourmand; each day he went through three full meals. As well as driving his Jaguar, Dr Grant liked to pilot his yacht from the island in the Thames he owned, several dozen miles from London.

On 8 October, the day after I met Tolstoy at the Ritz, I set out for Dr Grant's office, located on the famous Regent Street. I arrived at the appointed time, but his secretary told me he was testifying at the Old Bailey and would be back in the office at any moment. Within a few minutes he arrived, out of breath, apologizing profusely for not being on time. Grant told me that his additional examinations had made him even more positive that the signature on the document could not possibly be Demjanjuk's; it was not even similar. As for the picture, he was coming to the conclusion that it had been attached to the document at some later date in the Soviet Union, though he was less definite about this. He had found no flaws in the signatures attributed to Toyfel and Streibel, nor did his findings raise any questions about the document's paper or ink.

I asked Dr Grant to attack head-on several general conclusions at the basis of the testimonies of prosecution experts Bezaleli the Israeli and Epstein the American. He consented without hesitation. I also asked him to prepare an album to illustrate his findings. This request was firmly rejected. 'I have been appearing as a witness in courts in Britain and seventy other countries around the world for more than sixty years,' he said firmly, 'and I have never needed albums to explain myself to the judges. This trial will not be the first in which I make one.' He apparently noticed my look of disappointment, for he smiled and added: 'You can be sure I will succeed in explaining the substance of my findings and conclusions to the judges in the clearest possible way.'

He had carefully studied the English record I had provided of the testimony by the prosecution's forensic experts, and commented that these experts had at times put their client's (the prosecution's) wishes above their professional integrity and conscience; he wondered how they could act this way in a capital case. We agreed that once I returned I would summarize our conversation in writing, and that this document would be the basis of his expert opinion and his testimony. On 6 November Dr Grant landed once again at Ben-Gurion Airport. I met him and took him to the hotel. We devoted the entire weekend to final preparation for his testimony; I also prepared a list of some fifty questions that I would present to him during the examination in chief.

On Monday he took the witness stand. Unlike all the other witnesses before and after him, he gave his entire testimony, lasting three long days, standing. 'I prefer to stand, because I am accustomed to it,' was his response to Judge Levin's suggestion that he remain seated. As is customary in the examination of an expert witness, I opened with questions relating to his expertise. Dr Grant had graduated in chemical sciences at London University in 1925. While a student, he had been on the panel of experts that examined the Tutankhamun mummy and established its authenticity. From the end of the 1920s he was a senior chemist for a paper production company, where he devoted himself to the development of security paper, such as that used for printing currency, and specialized in examining counterfeit banknotes. He invented a paper from which it was impossible to erase a signature without leaving traces, and another kind on which it was impossible to write in invisible ink. He developed a special process for copying fingerprints from paper and developed the use of ultra-violet radiation in forensic examinations. He had written twenty-eight books, some of them fundamental forensic-science texts that had gone into many editions. At the same time he had begun appearing in court as an expert witness, something he had done more than fifteen thousand times, in Britain and over seventy other countries around the world. No court had ever ruled his expert opinion incorrect. In 1951 he began working as an independent forensic scientist in the Hehner and Cox laboratories, which he bought that same year. His unique method was the combination of testing handwriting and the chemical structure of the ink and the quality of the paper or cloth. As a result he had developed a special expertise in dating documents. Dr Grant was the founder and President of the Forensic Science Society of Document Examination in Britain. Since 1947 he had been the only honorary member of the world's most prestigious organization in the field, the American Society of Document Examiners, and was the only man to have served as President of the British Society of Legal Medicine without being either a doctor or a jurist. At the end of this section of his testimony, he recounted some of his impressive professional successes, such as revealing the forgeries of the 'Mussolini diaries' and the 'Hitler diaries', aiding in finding the would-be assassins of

Cyprus's President Archbishop Makarios, and other such high-profile stories. After two hours it was clear to everyone that the world's foremost forensic expert was on the witness stand.

Grant proceeded to discuss general matters relating to making decisions on signatures. He presented the scale for ranking his findings: two positive levels of 'Highly Probable' and 'Probable', an intermediate rank of 'Maybe' and a single negative level: 'Unlikely'. He mentioned that this ranking was known in England as the 'Grant scale', and was used in all English and Welsh courts. Grant explained that signature analysis is not an exact science, and that there were certainly cases in which the forger fooled the expert. Then he analysed each of the signatures on the Travniki document. He stated immediately that the signature of Streibel, the Commandant, contained nothing to raise suspicion. The same was true of Toyfel's signature, although in this case there had not been enough original signatures available to make an unambiguous finding.

As for the signature attributed to Demjanjuk, he stated: 'It is unreasonable to assume that this signature is his. I am referring to the comparison I made between the signature on the document and the other undisputed signatures I have examined.' He then explained how he had reached this conclusion. The letter D on the document was very different from the Ds in all other known signatures of Demjanjuk's in the years 1947–86. The same was true of the letter M. Also in Demjanjuk's known signatures the writing was not continuous, the pen being lifted several times. The signature on the document was written continuously, with only one raising of the pen, after the letter D.

Dr Grant's testimony made a great impression on all those who heard it, and the frequent, unnecessary interruptions by the judges, especially Levin, did nothing to impair it. When the session resumed, Grant presented the implications of his findings on the signature. In his opinion, there was no connection between the authenticity of the Streibel and Toyfel signatures and the authenticity of the whole document. Of course, the prosecution said the document was not forged merely because of the authenticity of the Streibel and Toyfel signatures. Grant explained: 'If we have a Mr A and a Mr B, and both are honest men, there is no reason to conclude from this that Mr C is also honest just because his name appears on the same document as those of the others.'

Grant moved on to the picture. First he pointed out that there were two holes in the right side, whilst on the paper under the holes in the photograph, there were no holes. The perforations were of the diameter of a staple, and the distance between them was also appropriate for a staple. Grant had found purple ink inside the holes; this ink was identical in type and colour to that used by the KGB for translating the German words on the Travniki document, which were written on the paper itself. This led to the conclusion that it was more logical to assume that this photograph had been unstapled from some other Soviet document and attached to the Travniki document in the Soviet Union than to assume that this was the picture originally attached to the document at Travniki in 1942.

On the basis of his conclusions about the photograph and signature, Dr Grant determined: 'The Travniki document cannot be an authentic document belonging to the defendant Demjanjuk.' He added another important comment: 'If the photograph is removed from the document, it will be possible to ascertain unquestionably whether or not its origin is another document.' He explained that if there were no purple ink spot on the part of the document hidden by the photograph, then the ink in the perforations on the right of the photograph must come from another document, and the photograph itself was therefore taken from another document originating in the Soviet Union.

Levin had often excused his intervention in the examination of witnesses as the result of the court's desire to discover the truth. Yet this desire became very weak when faced with the Travniki document, despite the explicit determination of the most distinguished forensic scientist in the world that the riddle could be simply resolved. His efforts to reveal the truth did not extend so far as ordering that the photograph be removed.

Shaked's cross-examination began on Tuesday morning; he intended to question Grant at least until Thursday evening, and perhaps even into the following week. At least, that's what he told me after Monday's session. Yet he quickly discovered that the longer he took the more he lost: Grant rebuffed all his attempts to discredit his testimony, easily and elegantly.

Shaked began by trying to make an issue of two bands of rust on the document that Grant described as parallel. Shaked argued that they did not fit the geometric definition of parallel lines, and Dr Grant had to refer him to his precise statement that the lines were parallel like the sides of a paper-clip. Then Shaked launched into a lengthy round of questions on the matter of what type of paper-clip had been in use at Travniki. Dr Grant had no knowledge of this, of course, and did not hesitate to say so. Shaked submitted a Gem paper-clip as a prosecution exhibit. This brought me great satisfaction, precisely because it was so banal. The defence's testimony had finally succeeded in diverting the trial – or at least one aspect of it – from the track of a show-trial on to a track where the prosecution submitted evidence of accepted legal validity. The media immediately understood that the submission of a paper-clip as a prosecution exhibit heralded a significant turning point in the trial's character. The next day's headlines gave expression to their disappointment: A PORTRAIT OF THE HOLOCAUST AS A PAPER-CLIP; THE BIG BLUNDER; A PAPER-CLIP DETECTIVE STORY.

Giving up on the paper-clip, Shaked tried to challenge Dr Grant's conclusions another way. He began questioning him about one of the famous trials he had been involved in as an expert witness, a case based on a signature that the defendant said was his. There was no dispute over the extreme variation between this signature and all the defendant's other known signatures. The prosecution had argued that the difference showed the signature could not be the defendant's. Grant had invited the man to his laboratory, where he re-created the position the man claimed to have been in when he signed, and asked him to sign again. It turned out that the signature from the re-enactment was amazingly similar to the exceptional signature that the prosecution had said could not be his. On the basis of his findings in this case Dr Grant had written an article setting out his thesis regarding a person's position during signing. The object of Shaked's questions was clear to the judges, and their expectations increased as he pursued this point, their faces revealing their satisfaction. Now came Shaked's decisive question: 'Could it be that the person who signed the name "Demjanjuk" on the Travniki document did so while standing with gear on his back, in a very uncomfortable position, and that this is therefore an exceptional signature by this person?' He meant, of course, to say that Demjanjuk had signed the Travniki document under awkward conditions, when registering at the camp, and that this was why the signature was different from his other signatures. The judges leaned straining over their desk to be sure of hearing the response. Dr Grant answered without hesitation: 'The signature on the Travniki document was definitely not recorded under the conditions you have presented. We see here good penmanship that follows the line; the signature on the Travniki document is notably clean.' The judges reacted as if they had been punched in the face. Dorner's and Levin's heads snapped back, and an expression of deep disappointment and frustration spread over their faces. Few people noticed, but I think there was no other moment in the trial that demonstrated so bluntly which side the judges were on. Nor could Shaked conceal his great disappointment. When the judges recovered from the blow, they announced a recess.

After the break, Shaked asked Dr Grant, with the judges' assistance, whether he would stand by his opinion that the signature on the document was not Demjanjuk's even if Demjanjuk himself were to acknowledge that it was. Grant replied: 'I have never yet encountered a situation in which I have determined that a given signature was not signed by a certain person and he said that it was.' Shaked again seemed lost, and the session ended within a few minutes. The next morning he questioned Grant, again with the judges' active assistance, about the photograph. Here also he was unable to elicit anything in his favour, so his cross-examination ended. My re-examination was brief, aimed at showing that, contrary to one of Shaked's assertions, Grant had examined dozens of original documents in the police laboratory.

After a witness finishes answering the questions of both sides, the bench may ask questions of clarification, but only if all or most of the testimony would remain unintelligible without these questions. This time it was Judge Tal who asked: 'When a handwriting expert determines that a signature is forged or not forged, he does not allow the court to make this distinction, he does not actually let the court decide the question, but rather decides the question *for* the court. Is that not correct?' The very asking of this question showed an intolerable bias: when the prosecution experts had ruled the Toyfel and Streibel signatures authentic (and that therefore the entire document was authentic) the judges had accepted without raising an eyebrow. In other words, the extent to which a witness 'invaded this court's jurisdiction' was open to interpretation. Only if the determination was not to the prosecution's liking was it 'deciding for the court'.

On Wednesday afternoon Dr Grant concluded his impressive testimony. I reminded Shaked of his promise to examine Grant at least until the following evening. He answered drily: 'From my point of view there was no point in continuing to examine him, I wouldn't have been able to get anything out of him.' The opinion of the 'independent' press was just the opposite, and the headlines of their biased articles said, CREDIBILITY DAMAGED; WITNESS IN TROUBLE CONTRADICTS HIS TESTIMONY; TWO RUST STAINS ON GRANT'S GOOD NAME; EXPERT WHO REVEALED THE FORGERY OF THE HITLER DIARIES STOOD HELPLESS.

Dr Grant was happy to have completed his testimony sooner than expected, and suggested we go to the Israel Museum to see the Dead Sea scrolls. 'I hope you won't try to argue that they're forgeries too,' I laughed, and the old man smiled playfully. The next day I took him to the airport. Before we parted he told me, 'It was a pleasure to work with you, you were entirely professional.' I had never received a greater compliment. The privilege of meeting and co-operating with this extraordinary man is enough to justify the decision to serve as defence attorney in this trial, I said to myself. I made a habit of visiting him each time I went to Britain, and each time it was a moving experience. I last saw him in January 1991; he was still working, but his ninety years were clearly weighing on him. About two months later he died.

Now came the defence's most important witness, the Dutch professor of experimental psychology Willem Wagenaar.

Back in the first week in July, when we had gathered in Cleveland, everyone had agreed that the defence must present as an expert witness an experimental psychologist specializing in visual memory. The witness would have to be of international stature and reputation and to have specialized in photo-spread recognition. The best candidate was Professor Elizabeth Loftus of Seattle University's Psychology Department. Professor Loftus had appeared as an expert witness at hundreds of trials in the US to analyse from a psychological point of view the merit of photo spreads as evidence. She had written a book called *Eye-Witness Identification*, considered the experimental psychologists' bible on the subject.

On 29 June 1987, about a week before the meeting in Cleveland, Professor Loftus had published an article in *Newsweek* explaining why she could not accede to requests to appear as an expert witness for the defence in the Demjanjuk case. Loftus was Jewish, and her family and friends firmly opposed her appearing in this case. This opposition was, of course, based on the assumption that Demjanjuk was Ivan the Terrible. During my stay in Cleveland I tried to persuade the professor to reconsider. After repeated and lengthy efforts, she proposed that I go directly to her Uncle Joe and try to get him to withdraw his opposition. If I succeeded, this would pave the way for her to consent. She gave me his number in Petersburg, Pennsylvania. I called him and when I explained the purpose of my call he agreed to meet me at his home. I flew to Petersburg and knocked on Uncle Joe's door. His wife greeted me pleasantly and led me to the garden, where her husband sat waiting. We introduced ourselves but before I had a chance to sit down Uncle Joe launched his attack: 'How do you, a Jew and an Israeli, have the nerve to defend that loathsome goy, that Ukrainian murderer, who with his own hands murdered almost a million Jews?' I was a bit taken aback by Uncle Joe's energy, since he looked more than eighty. I responded with the same words I had used so many times in recent months, and showed him the page of eight pictures from which Demjanjuk had been identified, on the basis of a photograph from 1951, as Ivan the Terrible. I pointed out that Demjanjuk's picture jumped off the page compared to the others, and it therefore immediately drew the viewer's attention.

'Elizabeth Loftus, your niece, is the world's most important scientific authority for showing why Demjanjuk's identification from these pictures is without value,' I concluded.

Uncle Joe looked impressed. But in a somewhat hesitant tone of voice he asked, 'And what if he is really Ivan?' I answered in the Jewish tradition – with another question. 'And what if he really *isn't* Ivan?' And I added: 'And what if they hang him for being Ivan and we later find solid evidence that he wasn't Ivan? What a disgrace that would be!' Uncle Joe fell silent. Then we talked for another hour, and when we parted it was apparent that he was less determined than when we began, but he would not put aside his opposition to Professor Loftus's appearance in the trial.

To prevent me going away entirely empty-handed, Professor Loftus told me about a colleague, Professor Wagenaar, a well-known experimental psychologist from Leiden University. She had already spoken to him by phone and he had seemed willing to appear as an expert witness on the subject of photo spreads. She emphasized that he would accept reimbursement only for his actual expenses; Professor Wagenaar did not feel it morally correct to accept money for work in a case where the defendant would be liable for the death penalty if convicted. I asked Loftus if he was really an expert of the first order, and she confirmed that he was. At the end of our conversation she said that on 3 August there was to be a conference of experimental psychologists at Swansea University in Wales. She would be there, as would Professor Wagenaar, and it would be best if I could meet him then and discuss his testimony.

Meeting the two of them in August, I was struck during our initial greetings by Wagenaar's face and by the intellectual power he radiated. I came to our meeting supplied with the English translations of the reports from Radivker and Kolar on all their identification procedures. I also had the set of photographs from which Demjanjuk had been identified, as well as the English record of the testimonies of the identification witnesses, of Ish-Shalom and of Radivker and Kolar. In addition, I had all the identification reports on Federenko. This made a large, heavy pile of three thousand pages. So as not to alarm them with the huge amount of material, I stressed that O'Connor's cross-examinations, which took up about half the material, need not be read, because there was no connection between them and the identification issue. For three days, about two and a half hours each day, I sat with Wagenaar and Loftus and discussed the whole range of facts touching on the process by which Demjanjuk had been identified as Ivan the Terrible.

On 5 August, towards the end of our third meeting, Professor Wagenaar gave me his opinion. 'The photo spreads in which Demjanjuk was identified are all worthless, and may not be trusted.' I breathed a sigh of relief – another row of bricks laid in the defence case. We decided that Wagenaar would present the experimental psychologist's view of photo spreads, addressing specifically the spreads conducted in Demjanjuk's case. He added that he intended to conduct several experiments with his students, to provide concrete examples of the photo spreads' unreliability. Professor Loftus pleased me enormously by saying she would help Wagenaar prepare his testimony, and even expressed her willingness to be present in court when he testified. Wagenaar stressed that he needed at least two months to prepare properly for his testimony – that is, until the beginning of October.

Some two weeks later, on the day Anita Pritchard concluded her botched testimony, I called Wagenaar's office at Leiden in low spirits. I asked him how he was getting on with his preparations. 'If I have to testify before mid-October, it would definitely be better for me not to testify at all,' he said. 'I am now convinced that I will not be able to be ready before then.' I promised to do all I could to postpone the day of his testimony.

When I called him again on Friday 4 September, my mood was entirely different. I told him about the indefinite postponement of the trial's resumption, estimating that his testimony would not be heard before November. 'In that case,' he said, 'you'll have expert testimony on the photo spreads.' After it was decided to resume the trial on 26 October, I suggested to Wagenaar that he begin his testimony on 16 November. He agreed, and we made an appointment to meet in Holland during the first week of October.

On 2 October I met the professor in his office at Leiden University, and two days later in his home in Zeist. His testimony was more or less finished, and he presented it to me in detail. He had already drafted most of his expert opinion. I suggested, as I had to the other witnesses, that to make his preparations easier I would send him a set of questions in English that I would ask during the evidence in chief. Wagenaar assented willingly. At the end of the month I sent him a list of forty questions, and on 12 November he landed at Ben-Gurion with his wife. Professor Loftus arrived three days later with Nishnic, who felt he should be present when the defence presented its most important expert testimony.

As soon as Wagenaar took the witness stand, Shaked again revealed his true colours. He objected to hearing the witness, on the grounds that it was inappropriate to hear the opinion of an expert witness on the value of the photo spreads, that this was a subject the judges alone should deal with. Once again he had not felt it necessary to inform me of his intentions, despite the daily contact between us and despite the fact that I had given him information on the nature of Wagenaar's testimony long before I was required to do so. I rose and requested half an hour's recess, emphasizing that I had not received any warning from the prosecution on its objection. Because of the complexity of the subject, I said, I could not respond to such an argument immediately. Levin assented to my request only after yet another sharp exchange.

After the recess I explained what could be expected from Wagenaar's testimony, and argued that such testimony is routine in courts in most of the Anglo-Saxon world. Judge Dorner asked, or better suggested, 'Can't we hear his testimony without touching directly on the evidence before us, but only in a general way, using examples not from this trial?' In other words, the court would be willing, in its great benevolence, to hear the witness only if he did not refer to the facts in the case in which he was testifying. It was obvious that the court simply wanted to prevent Wagenaar from pointing out the zero evidential weight of the photo spreads in which Demjanjuk had been identified. I responded that there was no point in hearing a lecture on the theory of memory and photo spreads, since the place for such a lecture was a university, not a courtroom. To assist in solving the questions in dispute, I insisted, the court needed testimony that would directly address those questions. In the end Levin decided: 'We will begin to hear him and we will hear him up to the point that there is a specific objection to a specific question and then we will have to decide.'

To open, I presented Wagenaar with the usual series of questions on his qualifications. He was the Dean of the Faculty of Social Sciences at the famous Leiden University, and a professor of experimental psychology with more than twenty years of research behind him. Memory was his special area of expertise. He was a member of the American Society of Psychology, Section 41, the division that deals with legal psychology. This was the most prestigious organization of its kind in the world dealing with law and psychology. He had testified as an expert witness on the subject of memory in more than forty trials, always specifically addressing the facts of the case. He had published many scientific articles in important and well-known journals.

Professor Wagenaar explained that it was first necessary to see whether there was a memory problem in the case. In his opinion it was sufficient that some of the Treblinka survivors had identified Demjanjuk's picture as that of Ivan the Terrible and others had not, to establish that there was indeed such a problem. He emphasized that most psychological research is based on a brief contact between the identifier and the identified, with the identification happening a short time thereafter

– conditions completely different from the identification process in Demjanjuk's case. The confrontation between the survivor-witnesses and Ivan the Terrible had been very lengthy, lasting about a year. But the identification of Demjanjuk had been made a long time later, about thirty-five years. Therefore, in Wagenaar's firm opinion, psychological research on the merit of photo spreads could be very helpful in Demjanjuk's case.

Psychology sees the photo spread as a memory test. People not blessed with a good memory for faces will fail. A photo spread must be conducted in such a way that people who saw the suspect committing the crime will point to him if his picture appears, but if his picture does not appear they will not point to anyone. The test must therefore be difficult, to prevent the witness pointing by mistake at someone who is not the criminal. Wagenaar stressed that the goal of his testimony was to demonstrate the difficulties involved in identifications by eye witnesses, and that he was doing so in direct reference to the facts of the case. He added that it was not his intention, nor was it within his capability, to express an opinion about the memory of any of the survivors. He summed up: 'It is not the identification witnesses but rather the identification process in which they took part that is the subject of my testimony.'

Wagenaar used pictures to demonstrate how and why identification witnesses had in the past erred in identifying a given person as a criminal. The errors almost always occurred when there was great or even some similarity between the person they falsely identified and the real criminal. Wagenaar emphasized that these witnesses were certain they were right and as sure of themselves as witnesses who were not in error. For this reason, it is very difficult for a court to discover the error in their testimony. He believed that in criminal cases of this type efforts should be concentrated on conducting a proper and non-suggestive photo spread that would prevent identification errors as far as possible.

Psychological research recognizes two kinds of factor – 'bias', in Wagenaar's words – that can influence witnesses to misidentify a photograph or person. The first kind are called 'positive-response bias' and are general in nature; the second are called 'specific-response bias', and are specific to the identification process in question. Wagenaar enumerated five positive-response biases: 1) the identifier's belief that a picture of the person he has been asked to identify appears among the photographs; 2) the importance the identifier attaches to seeing the criminal punished; 3) the identifier's knowledge that none of the figures depicted is innocent of crimes; 4) the identifier's conviction that he will never forget the criminal's face; 5) the identifier's knowledge that other people have previously identified the suspect from among the same pictures. These biases all applied conspicuously to Demjanjuk's identification by each of the survivor-witnesses. This, of course, meant that the photo spreads would have had to be impeccable; otherwise there could be no certainty that the identifications were correct and reliable. Wagenaar then enumerated seven specific-response biases. These occur when the identifier, as a result of one or more of the previous irregularities, makes a decision to identify a figure in the photo spread as the criminal, and then has to decide whom to choose. The first is when the 'target picture' in the spread is the only one that fits the criminal's general description; the second is when the target picture is very different from the rest of the pictures; the third is when the pool of pictures is small; the fourth is when the target picture looks more like a 'criminal face' than the others; the fifth is when the interrogator unconsciously indicates to the identifier (for instance, by an instinctive nod) which is the target picture; the sixth is when there is an explicit insinuation; and the seventh is when the target picture was seen by the identifier in a previous photo spread. Wagenaar said that five of these seven irregularities (numbers one to three, five and seven) clearly applied to all the photo spreads in which Demjanjuk had been identified as Ivan the Terrible. His picture was the only photograph of a bald man with a round face and a short, fat neck; it was twice as big as the other pictures, and clearer and sharper than the rest.

Wagenaar emphasized in particular that biases of both types could easily lead to a mistaken identification in a photo spread. Later he pointed out the existence of each of these irregularities in the specific circumstances of the photo spreads conducted in Demjanjuk's case. Then he gave his conclusion: 'Given the presence of all the positive-response biases, the presence of most of the specific-response biases makes it almost certain that every survivor who pointed to one of the pictures would point to Demjanjuk's picture.' This concluded the first day of his testimony.

Just before nine p.m. Nishnic knocked on my door. I could see straight away that he was excited. 'Shefy, I've gone over the entire record of Dr Grant's and Tolstoy's testimonies, and of course I was in court all day today, and I want to tell you that we have an overwhelming reply to all the prosecution evidence.'

I had to calm him down and explain how things really were. 'Wagenaar has not even got through the evidence in chief,' I said, 'and in any case I don't think it's a good idea to come to any conclusion about a testimony until the cross-examination is over.' But Nishnic would not let up. 'There is no reason to assume that Shaked will have any more success with Wagenaar than he and Blatman had with Tolstoy and Grant. They were only smart when it came to Robertson and Pritchard.'

'Ed, listen to me, get this into your head,' I said in as dramatic a voice as I could muster. 'All my work has but one goal – that when we appeal the conviction to the Supreme Court, the case file will contain a foundation of evidence that we can use in our arguments to show that the conviction was in error. When the appeal is heard I want to be in such a position that the Supreme Court justices will not be able to say, "Then why didn't you present evidence about that?" Ed, just forget any hope that the testimonies of Tolstoy, Grant and Wagenaar will lead to Demjanjuk's acquittal. That's just not on the agenda of this court.'

Nishnic looked disappointed. 'OK,' he muttered. 'I realize you want to be very cautious, but it's clear that the picture has changed completely.'

'It's changed completely as far as the testimony goes,' I agreed, 'but Levin has not changed, and in this trial he and not the evidence is what counts; you of all people, knowing the record as well as you do, should know very well what he will decide.'

The next day, Professor Wagenaar testified on the experiment he had conducted with his students, to demonstrate that the photo spreads lacked any value as a reliable test of the survivor-witnesses' memories. He had chosen twenty-five students at random and shown them the page of eight pictures. He asked the students to select the picture of the bald criminal with the round face and short, thick neck. They chose Demjanjuk without exception. Taking another twenty-five students, he showed them Demjanjuk's picture along with seven pictures of other men with round faces, balding heads and short, fat necks. This time only two out of the twenty-five selected Demjanjuk. The simple conclusion was that when one picture stands out as unique even people without the relevant memory will choose it. Certainly many more people will choose it than when it does not stand out. Professor Wagenaar's conclusion, then, was that the photo spreads conducted in Demjanjuk's case lacked any evidential value. It would never be possible to know if the survivors singled out Demjanjuk's photograph because he was Ivan the Terrible or simply because he resembled Ivan the Terrible.

Shaked opened his cross-examination by trying to challenge Professor Wagenaar's expertise, but this came across as simple pettiness. Then he claimed that even experimental psychologists were divided on the question of whether there was any point in psychologists appearing as expert witnesses on the subject of photo-spread identification. Wagenaar responded that the minority of experimental psychologists with reservations about such testimony believed it was not appropriate in every single case, but not one of them claimed that an experimental psychologist should never testify on identification. Shaked asked if it were nevertheless not true that there were profound disagreements between psychologists with regard to the factors that influence an identification witness to point out a given person. Wagenaar replied that the situation was precisely the opposite – the theoretical approach he had just presented was accepted by the entire psychological community in this field. Shaked tried a different angle and asked whether or not it was true that most professionals believed nothing could be inferred from identification experiments conducted under laboratory conditions, with reference to 'real' identification processes done by the police. Wagenaar rejected this categorically and referred Shaked to the copious professional literature showing the opposite. Shaked then presented a different assumption, according to which there is a certain period after an event when an eye witness's memory of a face does not fade. Wagenaar responded that after eight weeks there is a drastic decline in an eye witness's ability to remember a criminal's face; again he cited the literature to support this.

The only time it looked as if Shaked had succeeded in dealing a fairly serious blow to Wagenaar's testimony was when he referred to a study conducted by Professor Bahrick. Bahrick's research had shown that members of a given American high-school class had succeeded, with an accuracy rate of ninety per cent, in correctly identifying pictures of their classmates some forty years after graduation. The conclusion was clear – when people are in contact for a long time (like Ivan the Terrible and the survivor-witnesses), their identifications are reliable even decades later. This seemed to have weakened Wagenaar's learned testimony – but we were well-prepared on this point, and in my re-examination Wagenaar revealed the reason for the high percentage of identifications Bahrick had found. All the participants in the study had brought class pictures from home and conducted their identifications from these. The survivor-witnesses did not, of course, bring Ivan the Terrible's picture from home with them. Nor had they seen him even once, in person or in a photograph, during the thirty-five years after their escape from Treblinka. So there was absolutely no similarity between Bahrick's study and the identification process in this case. The judges also took part in the cross-examination, and at many points the witness was subject to a barrage of questions. But Wagenaar held his ground and his testimony was not dented. The media behaved as usual though, and the headlines for the stories about Wagenaar's testimony were: IT'S NOT AN EXACT SCIENCE; EPISODIC EXPERT; THE PROFESSOR FORCED TO DEFEND HIS PROFESSIONAL INTEGRITY, and the like.

Professor Wagenaar's four long and exhausting days of testimony came to an end on 19 November. The court record now filled eight thousand pages. I felt wonderful, and Nishnic, Johnny and I decided to go out for a celebratory dinner at the Notre Dame Hotel with Wagenaar, his wife and Professor Loftus. When we sat down Nishnic recalled his previous visit and the despondent mood we had been in then. Now the mood was bright, and I praised Professor Wagenaar profusely for his courage and honesty. I had two reasons for being in such good spirits. First, Wagenaar's testimony had been scientific confirmation of the claim I had been making from the start, that the photo spread from which Demjanjuk had been identified had no value as evidence. The second reason was even more important: even though the defence case was not over, it was already clear that we had been able to raise serious questions, and create much more than the reasonable doubt needed in a criminal case, on the three major issues that the prosecution evidence had dealt with – the identification (through Professor Wagenaar), the Travniki document (through Dr Grant), and the issue of the alibi and the historical evidence (through Count Tolstoy). So, after the defence case's ruinous and pathetic beginning, under almost impossible conditions, I had succeeded in bringing a group of experts of a superior calibre to those of the prosecution, and their testimony had challenged the prosecution's case. Even at this juncture I did not delude myself that this would receive any practical expression in the verdict. Nishnic, on the other hand, several times repeated his opinion that 'Even a hostile court like this one cannot ignore the doubt created by the defence evidence.' Each time, I interrupted him, 'You'd better believe it can.'

Our next witness was William Flynn, a forensic expert from the US. The idea of inviting Flynn to testify began to run through my head immediately we won the oh-so-precious reprieve as a result of Judge Tal's heart attack, and when it was clear that Dr Grant would appear as defence witness. My idea was to find a top-flight forensic expert who was an expert not only in examining documents but also in their forgery. Through such a witness the defence would submit forgeries of each element in the Travniki document. The quality of the forgery would be so high that any forensic expert who examined these pieces would be forced to declare that forensic science could not determine they were forgeries. This expert would forge Streibel and Toyfel's signatures – not just their handwriting but also the ink and paper, which would contain only chemical components that existed in 1942. The conclusion to be drawn from the forgery would be clear: the fact that there were elements of the Travniki document that contained nothing to indicate they were forged did not mean that they were genuine. This conclusion would join Dr Grant's testimony, and it would deal with the finding that the *Demjanjuk* signature on the document was forged and that even the photograph was not authentic. All this would demonstrate that there was much greater than a reasonable doubt about the document's authenticity.

Careful enquiries revealed that Flynn was one of the five most prominent forensic experts in America. On Sunday 20 September, a week before Rosh Hashanah, Flynn landed in Israel. It was just a few days since we had learned that the trial would resume only on 26 October. Flynn would testify at the end of November, and would be able to prepare properly. When we reached his hotel Flynn looked refreshed and alert despite his long trip, and asked that we meet again within half an hour to discuss the tasks he was to accomplish during his time in Israel. He radiated professionalism and was blessed with an abundant sense of humour. I expressed the view that it would be best for him to concentrate his examinations on the document's weak points. I explained that from the defence's point of view the point of his testimony was not to render an expert opinion like Dr Grant's. Here I was careful with my wording: 'The defence's expectations of you focus first and foremost on your demonstrating to the court why the inability to prove that certain components of the document were forged does not mean that they are *not* forged. This must be made clear both with a theoretical-scientific explanation and especially by showing examples of forgeries of different elements of the Travniki document, which you will prepare and submit during the course of your testimony.' Flynn expressed his full consent.

Next morning we went to the document laboratory at the national police headquarters in Jerusalem, and spent about two hours together going over all the original documents that we wanted him to examine. Then Flynn said he was prepared to begin working immediately and that he would devote himself first to examining Demjanjuk's known signatures and comparing them with the signature on the Travniki document. When I returned in the afternoon to take him back to the hotel, Flynn came up to me and said, 'Mr Sheftel, I just don't understand how the Israeli police's number-one expert on document examination reached the conclusion that the document is authentic. Any novice document examiner would immediately see that Demjanjuk did not sign it.'

Two days later during our summing-up meeting he said he would have no trouble preparing the forgeries I was interested in by the beginning of his testimony. He also suggested preparing an additional counterfeit: a photomontage of his own face superimposed on the body of a German Army officer. This would show that the Travniki photograph was not only under heavy suspicion of having been affixed to the document for the first time in the Soviet Union, but also that it was possibly a photomontage, not an authentic photograph. He said that he had carried out, for American intelligence agencies, forgeries much more difficult and complex than those he would accomplish now.

Two months later Flynn arrived in Israel to take the witness stand. Talking to Nishnic about his testimony, I was surprised to hear him say, 'Shefy, Gill told me he would like very much to conduct Flynn's examination. He wants to correct the bad impression he made with Robertson and Pritchard.'

'I don't think a case in which the death penalty is a possibility is a fitting arena for a move meant to restore someone's lost honour,' I responded. 'Still, I don't want to stand in Gill's way. If you, as the defendant's son-in-law, believe it would be proper to do so, there is no problem as far as I am concerned.' Gill, Flynn and I sat together on Saturday night and the entire next day, reviewing the substance of his testimony. I was again impressed with Flynn's high professional calibre and with the extraordinary forgeries he had prepared.

Flynn was a member of the American Society of Document Examiners and the American Academy of Forensic Sciences. He served as Vice-President of the former organization and as a chief examiner in its entrance exams. Flynn had examined tens of thousands of documents for the FBI, the American Treasury Department and more than forty different police forces throughout the United States. As well as passing various courses given by American intelligence services, he had successfully completed the most advanced FBI courses. He had testified as an expert witness more than a thousand times, in almost every state of America, and at Arizona's public document-examination laboratories, which he headed, he had carried out and supervised the examination of more than 1,500,000 documents. He had published articles in the most important professional journals in his field, and had taught the most advanced courses of documentary forensics in the United States. In addition, he had inspected a large quantity of documents forged by the KGB. His most notable professional achievement, which gave him a world-wide reputation, was his work on the 'White Salamander' case. This involved a group of some 140 documents allegedly dating from the early days of the Mormon Church in the 1830s. All of them had been forged by Mark Hoffman, one of the best forgers in history, and many qualified experts were taken in. Among these was Dr Antonio Cantu, who had stated that even after Hoffman's forgery had been revealed a forensic expert performing a standard examination of them would declare them authentic. Flynn had exposed the forgery by conducting comparative examinations of the type of ink used in other Mormon Church documents written on the same days that Hoffman's forged documents had allegedly been written. He discovered chemical components different from those in Hoffman's forgery, even though all the elements in the ink and paper used by Hoffman had been in use during the 1830s.

Flynn outlined his position on the limitations of forensic science in revealing forgeries. He explained that the White Salamander affair had changed forensic scientists' own perception of their ability to uncover the forgery of historical documents. Forensic science, he said, did not at this point have the means to determine beyond the shadow of a doubt whether a paper such as the Travniki document was authentic. This was especially applicable to decisions in criminal cases, so it was necessary to add a third category to professional opinions on such documents: 'indeterminate'.

Flynn went on to analyse his findings on the Travniki document. He could find no indication that Streibel's signature was forged; as he had noted, however, this was not sufficient to prove it authentic. The same was true of Toyfel's signature and of the paper and ink. With regard to the Demjanjuk signature, he had not the shadow of a doubt that it had not been signed by the defendant. Likewise he explained why it was more reasonable to assume that the photograph had been attached to the document for the first time in the Soviet Union and not at the Travniki camp. His examination led him to conclude that the forged signature was sufficient to determine categorically that the entire document was forged. Flynn commented that, had the prosecution witnesses Bezaleli and Epstein written in the American Society of Document Examiners' test that they judged the Travniki document authentic solely on the grounds that the Toyfel and Streibel signatures were authentic (i.e., as they had stated in their testimony), he would have failed them. He likewise stressed that he was unable to examine archival documents like the one in question, and thus compare it with documents issued the same day or at least during the same week. It would never be possible to make a reliable comparison between the Travniki document and real original documents of the same type. There was thus no sure way to determine, especially for the purposes of a criminal trial, that the Travniki document was authentic. Flynn's forensic conclusion on this point was the same as Tolstoy's historical conclusion.

Now Flynn came to his own forgeries. Shaked objected, and Levin briskly ruled: 'Objection sustained, because the questions are not relevant. The entire matter is irrelevant to this trial. Additional justification, if needed, will be given in the verdict. We rule out questions on this subject.' The court once again proved that the relevance of a piece of evidence was sometimes determined by the prosecution's convenience. From the defence's point of view there was no more need for Flynn's testimony, so I asked for a fifteen-minute recess. Within minutes we decided unanimously that I would inform the court we wished to terminate Flynn's testimony and have it struck from the record in full, as if it had not been given. 'Your Honours, in the wake of the court's decision forbidding the submission as evidence of the signatures that the witness has forged, as well as the photomontage he has composed, on the grounds of irrelevance, and since the court of course has the prerogative to make this decision, and since we do believe that these items are relevant, we see no point in this testimony. We did not bring it simply to repeat Dr Grant's testimony. We have a high estimation of the witness, of his professionalism and his proficiency, but we did not call him only to repeat parts of Dr Grant's testimony. Under these circumstances, we waive his testimony and request that it be struck in its entirety from the record.'

The judges were very surprised by this strong reaction, which contained an element of protest at its arbitrary decision. It was clear they did not know what to do. Levin asked for Shaked's position, and he said: 'Your Honours, I am very sorry about the decision the defence has announced. I do not consider myself an adviser for the defence on this point.' Levin, who had apparently reached a decision in the mean time, grew impatient. He interrupted Shaked and asked him aggressively, 'So what is your position? I don't understand.' Shaked's position was perfectly clear already: the development was none of his concern. Levin was not satisfied with this, so he played dumb. Shaked had not yet grasped Levin's intention, so he responded: 'I have no position on the subject. The decision is the defence's. The defence has decided to forgo the witness's testimony.' The matter should have ended there, but it would have left a strong impression of the defence's protest at being wrongfully blocked by Levin. Levin was not the type to give up; he turned to Shaked and explained what he was supposed to do. 'That's not exactly the case, that's not exactly the case. If I have asked Mr Shaked, it is because it would be legitimate for you to say that the testimony should stand and that you should be allowed to cross-examine.' But suddenly he realized he had gone too far, turning himself so obviously into a legal consultant for the prosecution in front of the TV cameras. So he softened his words: 'Not that I suggest that this be the prosecution's position, I just want to explain to Mr Shaked that he is not forbidden to insist that the testimony stand. Just so that there are no legal misunderstandings on this point.' To cap it all he added cynically: 'The witness would feel very disappointed, because he has come and taken the trouble to speak to the best of his knowledge, and his knowledge is great, and to the best of his ability, and his ability is great, but the representatives are of course the ones who will decide.'

Shaked finally saw what Levin was getting at. 'Since I am also surprised by my colleague's decision, I would perhaps request some sort of recess to consider the matter.' At this point Judge Tal, who was apparently uncomfortable with what was going on, intervened in an effort to save the situation. 'Perhaps before Mr Shaked gets his recess, he will consider – and I am speaking for myself, without having consulted my colleagues – perhaps Mr Shaked will consider whether to retroactively withdraw his objection to the submission of the signatures and the photomontage.' Levin was alarmed by this possibility, and had no qualms about saying, 'Fine, but here I have to comment that the minute we accept the evidence, the defence may assume that the matter is relevant and argue it in its summations, and then Mr Shaked will be in trouble.' So Levin brought the show-trial to another of its lowest points: not only had the presiding judge become legal adviser to the prosecution; he had also gone out of his way to frustrate his judicial colleague's attempt to find an honourable way out of this embarrassing position.

The recess lasted for three hours, during which there were also consultations with the defence (and with the participation of State Attorney Blatman, who had been summoned to the courtroom) in the judges' chambers. Shaked had no choice but to take a position consistent with Levin's guidance, and when the court reconvened he said, 'Your Honours, the situation presented by the defence is intolerable both for the court and for the prosecution . . . The witness has said many things and we definitely have much to question him about in cross-examination, and we insist on our right to do so.' Levin settled back in his chair and asked pleasantly, 'Then do I understand that you wish to cross-examine the witness?'

'Yes, Your Honours,' Shaked replied, like an obedient pupil. A recess was again called. During it many people, even some from the press, told me that the court had again gone too far in its intervention. But nobody wrote about it.

During the afternoon session, the prosecution and the judges tried to force Flynn to testify against his will, and rebuffed all my attempts to lend support to his refusal. The next morning Flynn was much more determined, and categorically refused to proceed with the farce. He used some clever reasoning. Since he had been invited to testify by the Demjanjuk defence fund, he said, he would be liable to a civil suit being filed against him by the fund if he were to continue testifying against the will of the defendant and his representatives. Only when Levin understood that he would be unable to get another word out of Flynn did he order a halt to the forced testimony.

Now the court was about to start another recess, to last until 14 December 1987 – this time because the theatre was about to host another show, the deliberations of the Zionist Congress.

At this point it was obvious that, witness by witness, the defence evidence was becoming more impressive and more significant. It looked as if Levin wanted to cut off this dangerous development at the root. There is no other way to explain why he decided arbitrarily that 18 January 1988 would be the date for the prosecution and defence summation arguments to take place. Without batting an eye he dictated the following into the record: 'The earlier the testimonies are concluded, the more time there will be for the preparation of final arguments; if the testimonies drag on, it will of course be at the expense of the time available for the preparation of final arguments.' In other words, the court threatened that if the defence continued to bring relevant testimony it would hurt its own chances of preparing properly for the summations. Levin knew very well that no one but I would prepare the defence's final arguments; the state prosecution, by contrast, could make use of a large team of lawyers, aides, clerks, policemen and support staff. All I had was Tzvia. It was another contemptible decision by Levin, designed to create a huge problem for the defence of insufficient time and to put it at a disadvantage.

Next I called Professor Yassar Iskan, a forensic anthropologist from the University of Florida, to fill the gap left by Pritchard's deplorable performance and to provide the defence's answer to the testimonies of Smith and Altmann. As agreed between me and Nishnic in September, Chumak was to prepare Iskan's testimony, which he did capably and proficiently. Iskan's evidence in chief was to last for two days; but because of a death in his family Shaked would be unable to begin his cross-examination on time. We came to the prosecution's assistance by saying that, if the court were to hold only morning sessions that week, we would be prepared to 'stretch' the evidence in chief over a week. That way, Shaked would be able to conduct his cross-examination after his seven days of mourning were over.

Professor Iskan's testimony began with a presentation of his impressive abilities, especially compared to the meagre ones of Sergeant Altmann from the German police and professor of dentistry Smith. Iskan was an expert on the human skeleton, human biology and physical and forensic anthropology. Since 1981 he had been a senior member of the Forensic Anthropology Department of the American Academy of Forensic Sciences, which had only thirty-four members. He was responsible for assessing articles for publication in the most prestigious American journals in this field; had himself written many books, articles and reviews; and had worked on some forty cases for various police forces in the US. Likewise, he often lectured on courses and seminars for senior police officers, legal-medicine associations, and the like.

Iskan's testimony was boring, because it dealt with innumerable dry technical details. The major conclusion was that a positive scientific identification of a person is valid only when it can show absolutely that a specific person, not someone else, has been identified. Fingerprints or the condition of the teeth are classic examples of such absolute identification. Comparisons between various *facial* features has not yet been studied sufficiently thoroughly. Therefore, Iskan maintained, even when there are two photographs, and both were taken under ideal conditions to produce total clarity, all that can be determined is that the two photographs are 'possibly' of the same person. If none of these ideal conditions exists, even this cannot be said. According to Iskan, the photographs used by Altmann and Smith in their comparisons to show that the Travniki photograph was of Demjanjuk were in no way ideal. Therefore, he stated categorically, it was not only *im*possible to find that the Travniki photograph was of Demjanjuk; such a finding could not even be deemed 'possible'.

Iskan had never encountered, in any scientific publication, the view that morphological measurements of the face could be a basis for determining identity. As for Altmann's testimony, in the absence of statistics on the interdependence of morphological features (such as broad noses and thick lips among black-skinned people), a determination that two faces are identical on the basis of one or another identical morphological features cannot be made. He noted that there was not a single scientific publication in the world about the morphological features which Altmann had based his testimony on. Given the state of research in forensic anthropology, it was utterly impossible to determine that the Travniki photograph was of Demjanjuk. As for Professor Smith's testimony, Iskan said there was no scientific research dealing with comparisons of the faces of identical twins. Smith's mathematical exercises on identical twins had no scientific relevance to determining a person's identity.

He did not leave it at that. He had prepared a video tape containing photographs of the kind appearing in Smith's tape. He used photographs of his assistant, and showed, with the help of photographic games, that there was a better fit between his assistant's picture and the Travniki photograph than between the latter and the known pictures of Demjanjuk. Iskan also took measurements of the type Smith had made, and here too he showed that his assistant resembled the Travniki photograph more closely than known photographs of Demjanjuk did. This, of course, made Smith's testimony look ridiculous.

Shaked attempted to show that Professor Iskan was not as great an expert as he claimed to be, but to no avail. Amiably, sometimes with humour and displaying an expertise that demanded respect, Iskan responded comprehensively to all Shaked's queries. As usual the judges, led by Levin, joined in firing a barrage of questions at the witness. Levin especially tried to refute Iskan's declaration that there was no scientific basis for Smith's and Altmann's theories, because he knew that this statement alone could invalidate their testimonies. When I tried to protest, Levin did not allow it: 'Mr Sheftel will explain to Mr Chumak what he wishes to say, and he will make the objection.' He thus repeated his absurd and arbitrary ruling that only the attorney who had undertaken the examination in chief was allowed to object to questions in the ensuing cross-examination. The reason for this was that at my side were two foreign lawyers not acquainted with Israeli procedure, who could thus almost never object to any cross-examination question.

An exchange that took place later in the session illustrates very well the absurdity of Levin's ruling. I directed the court's attention to the fact that Chumak wanted to voice an objection. 'Mr Chumak would like to raise an objection on the matter of the court's intervention in the cross-examination, and not on a specific question of the prosecution's.'

Levin responded: 'And I said that there is no question at this stage, so there are no grounds for an objection.'

I stood my ground. 'There was a question before.'

Levin stood his: 'What was before was before.' The court continued to pressure Professor Iskan, and Chumak rose and said:

'In cross-examination, in my opinion, the prosecutor must conduct the cross-examination, and if there is excess intervention by the court it can cause problems. Mr Sheftel will cite the precedent set by Israeli courts.'

Levin did not give in. 'If the court's intervention is not to the defence's liking, it may raise that point on appeal, if the verdict is appealed.'

But I would not give in either. 'Your Honour, with all due respect, the precedent has not been put before you and I think that I may raise it before Your Honours.'

Levin raised his voice. 'Please, Mr Sheftel, you have not been given the floor. If Mr Sheftel nevertheless wishes to draw our attention to the precedent, he will cite us the precedent and only the precedent, without additional explanations. Mr Chumak will explain what he wishes.'

I began to cite the precedent: 'I refer to criminal appeal –' but I was interrupted:

'Give it to us. We will read it.'

'Why shouldn't I read it out loud?' I asked naïvely.

'Because we said so,' Levin responded impatiently. 'Please, if Mr Sheftel wishes, then Mr Chumak may convey it to us.'

'Mr Chumak cannot read Hebrew,' I insisted.

Levin got angry. 'So, Mr Sheftel, we have ruled. If that is not to your liking, so be it. That is the way we work.'

'Is there a precedent for a lawyer not being able to read a precedent out loud?'

But Levin brought the matter to an end. 'Sir, we have ruled on procedure here, and the procedure will be as we have ruled.' The trial was being televised live, and he did not want me to read the following section from a well-known Supreme Court ruling: 'We see as unacceptable the method practised by some judges, according to which the judge wanders through the length and breadth of the field of battle. He questions here, explains there, supervises, guides and in practice takes the legal process into his own hands.' This is exactly what Levin and his colleagues did, almost every day of the trial. Furthermore, they 'wandered' in such a way that they always helped the prosecution. None of this, however, was able to damage Iskan's testimony, because he knew how to hold out against the pressure from Shaked, Levin, Tal and Dorner.

Another very important point came up in Iskan's testimony, and determined the identity of the next witness. He related that during his preparations he had by chance met an anthropologist, Dr Donald Ortner, a senior scholar at the prestigious Smithsonian Institution in Washington DC. Iskan mentioned that he was soon to appear as a witness for the defence in the Demjanjuk case, focusing on the scientific and evidential invalidity of identifying faces by comparing photographs. To his astonishment, Ortner said that Professor Smith had contacted him before testifying for the prosecution, asking whether it was possible through a comparison of known photographs of Demjanjuk and the Travniki photograph to determine their identity or disparity. She had even sent him the photographs used in her work. Ortner told Smith unequivocally that it was not possible unless the face had some obvious unique identifying mark, such as a scar or birthmark. He did not leave it at that: he sent all the material he had received from Smith to the FBI and asked for its opinion. The FBI experts reached the same conclusion as Ortner. He sent Smith his opinion and that of the FBI experts, and warned her that this method had led to many errors of identification in the past.

In the wake of Iskan's testimony, we asked to be supplied with the opinions of Dr Ortner and the FBI experts, so that we could submit them as defence evidence. We also asked that Professor Smith be recalled to testify, on the grounds that she had deliberately concealed the existence of these documents from the court. At first the prosecution objected, and withdrew only when the judges, hostile as they were to the defence, recommended it. The documents were given to the defence, a year late, and were immediately submitted as defence exhibits.

At the beginning of the following week, on 28 December 1987, Professor Smith took the witness stand with great reluctance for a continuation of her cross-examination. In response to Chumak's questions she admitted to all the details of Professor Iskan's version of events. But she argued, with great temerity, that these opinions were irrelevant, and this was why she had not told the defence of their existence. She even went so far as to explain why they were not relevant: they did not contradict her testimony because they did not state that the Travniki photograph was not of Demjanjuk. This answer was extremely misleading, since the FBI experts and Dr Ortner had concluded unequivocally that identity could not in general be determined by photographic comparisons, and specifically not with the photographs in question. Smith's preposterous statement was embarrassing. Chumak continued to press her. 'Don't you think that it is the court's job to decide what is relevant?' Levin came gallantly to Smith's assistance: 'When an expert is asked to render an opinion, he must present the court with his own opinion, as he understands it, as it is formulated by him. He need do nothing beyond that.' Levin himself did not believe this. After all, in the verdict, he and his colleagues wrote: 'An objective expert witness must place the entire picture before the court, presenting the entire range of contrary opinions.' But instead of censuring Smith for behaving as she had and ordering a criminal investigation against her for obstruction of justice, Levin lent her his support. Before leaving the stand, Smith mistakenly blurted out the truth about the quality of her work: she said the subject of her testimony was 'an as yet unploughed field'. This alone was sufficient to invalidate her testimony. For an expert witness's testimony to be considered, it has to be 'accepted by the international scientific community'; 'an unploughed field' does not meet that requirement. Yet this was not enough to prevent the bench from granting full weight to Professor Smith's testimony in its verdict. No objective court would ever behave in such a way.

Professor Iskan's testimony and Smith's reappearance made a strong

The page of photographs including Demjanjuk (bottom left) and Federenko (bottom right) from which Demjanjuk was identified

The Travniki document

Above: Judges Dov Levin (centre), Zvi Tal (left) and Dalia Dorner

Mark O'Connor (top), the author (left) and Michael Shaked

Demjanjuk (far left) in the dock during Professor Smith's testimony

Ivan Marchenko on his wedding day

Ivan Marchenko on the day of his arrival at the Travniki camp

Ivan Marchenko (the taller figure) with Ivan Takchuk, at Travniki

Dov Eitan

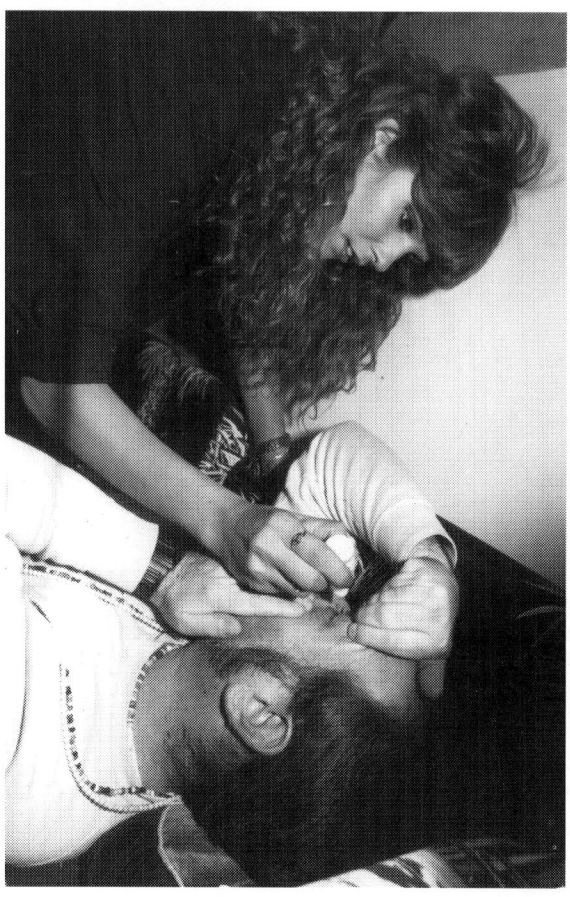

Eti Yisrael
nursing the author's eye

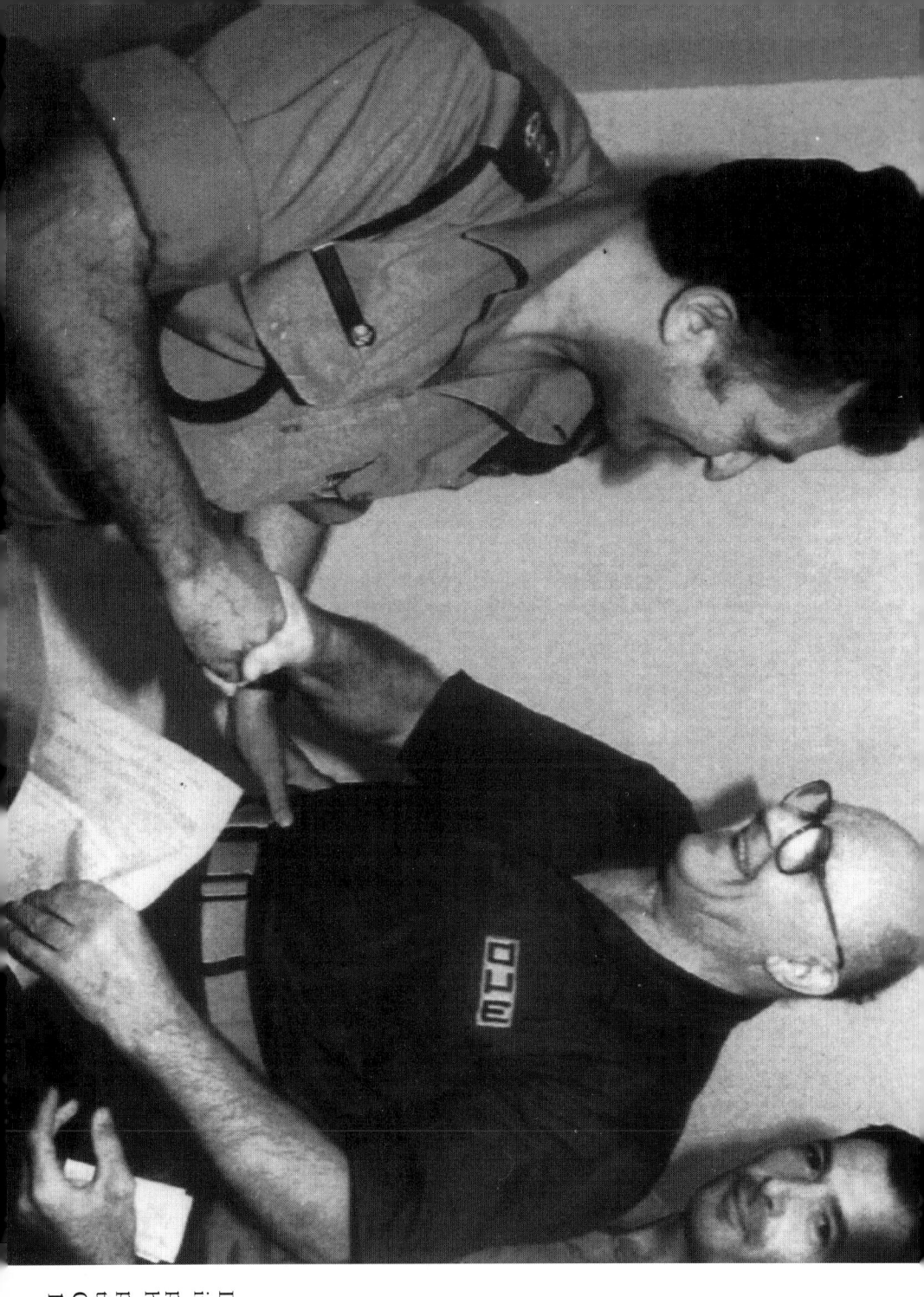

Demjanjuk, holding his release papers, shakes hands with a prison guard at the Supreme Court on 29 July 1993

impact. Chumak was very skilful, and when the questioning ended I felt relieved. The media continued to feed the public 'truths' like BLOOD-STAINS ON ISKAN'S SUIT; ISKAN'S OPINION DOES NOT ACCORD WITH RESEARCH; THE SELF-ASSURED WITNESS BEGAN TO WAVER; ISKAN'S ANSWERS EVASIVE. The level of truth in these foolish headlines was reflected in another that appeared at the same time: 800,000 PEOPLE HAVE VISITED DEMJANJUK TRIAL. The theatre hall contained no more than four hundred seats. At the time the headline appeared there had been ninety-four sessions, and during most of them the hall had been nearly empty. The Israeli media's computations were about as accurate as their news reports.

During the recess, Gill and Chumak went to Germany, to Hamburg. On 9–10 December they were to question a German SS man called Rudolf Reiss, who had been a sergeant at Travniki. I strongly objected to using his testimony, for two reasons, the first being that it was unnecessary. Leonard, the prosecution's SS witness from Travniki, had already eroded the prosecution's claim that the Travniki document had been issued by the SS to Ivan Demjanjuk at the camp in 1942. The second reason was a matter of conscience. I was not prepared under any circumstances to use the testimony of Nazi thugs. I thought that something so offensive was more the prosecution's style, in keeping with the morality of people who were maliciously conducting a show-trial.

In the end I agreed, but only as a compromise. Gill, Nishnic and many people close to the Demjanjuk family, especially the anti-Semite Jerry Berntar, had incessantly pressed for the defence to take evidence from the Deputy Commandant of Treblinka, the fiend Kurt Franz. He had been sentenced to life imprisonment in 1964 in Germany, and was incarcerated until July 1993. I opposed this categorically, because using the testimony of Treblinka's Deputy Commandant would look very bad and could be interpreted as meaning that Demjanjuk had asked for his ex-commander's assistance. I emphasized also that in any case no court would believe Franz's claim that Ivan Demjanjuk was not Ivan the Terrible, since he had lied flagrantly at his own trial and denied all the atrocities he committed at Treblinka. Then there was my moral opposition, and at one point I even threatened to resign from the case. Our compromise was that Kurt Franz would not be called to testify for the defence; the defence would question Reiss, but I would not take part, nor would I refer to it in my summation. I was glad when Reiss's testimony turned out to be a complete failure; his comments showed him to be the same Nazi scum, the same crude liar he had been at Travniki.

Gill and Chumak stopped off in Poland on their way, in an effort to discover archival material for the defence. Their search led them to the Jewish Historical Museum in Warsaw. The museum's Director, Vladislav Horn (who had been following the trial in the Polish and international media), received them warmly, and when they told him the purpose of their visit he revealed that the Jewish Museum possessed a long statement in Yiddish in Eliahu Rosenberg's handwriting. He commented that this testimony had not appeared among Rosenberg's statements in the court file in Jerusalem. Gill and Chumak asked to be allowed to photocopy the statement. Horn invited them to return for it in the afternoon. He apparently wished to consult an official of the Communist Party, which was still in power in Poland. When the two of them returned, Horn notified them that he could not allow them to photocopy Rosenberg's statement. All their efforts to persuade him were to no avail, and they left Warsaw empty-handed.

When the two of them told me about what had happened in Warsaw, I understood immediately. 'It's no coincidence that, of all of Rosenberg's statements, this one in particular has disappeared. The prosecutors went to the Warsaw Jewish Museum in 1986, and Horn must have told them about the statement as well. But, of course, he allowed them to read it. They realized it contained a precise description of the killing of Ivan the Terrible on the day of the Treblinka rebellion, 2 August 1943. Rosenberg claimed to have seen the deed with his own eyes, and to have taken part in it. That's why his statement does not appear in the court file.'

'How do you know?' they asked in astonishment. 'Simple logic,' I responded. 'And no power in the world will prevent me obtaining that statement in full.' During Iskan's testimony I was in constant touch with Nishnic on this matter. I would submit a visa application to the Polish diplomatic legation in Israel, and go to Warsaw with Johnny to obtain the evidence. My visa application was flatly rejected. The Polish Information Agency issued a vile statement that my request was denied because 'Demjanjuk's son wishes to retrace his father's deadly steps, and that would cause the victims much anguish.'

That very evening we decided that I would call the Jewish Museum in Warsaw and speak to Horn, in Yiddish. I would try to persuade him to give me the statement personally, in exchange for a *kleine matune* ('a small gift'). I would tell him that, when I arrived in Poland, I would play him a recording of our conversation, and after receiving his *kleine matune* he would give me the evidence. In fact I would send the recording of my conversation with Horn to Cleveland, and Nishnic would travel to Warsaw with it, pretending to be me. He would play the recording, hand over the *kleine matune*, and receive a photocopy of Rosenberg's statement. Nishnic reported to me directly from Warsaw that the move had succeeded.

By 22 January I had in my possession a photocopy of Rosenberg's statement. It included the following:

> Fifteen minutes before four a grenade explosion was heard in the first camp and a few shots from both sides. Everyone knew the rebellion had begun. Shmuel Zhelo emerged from the barracks first and shouted in Russian, '*Revolutsia Vberlina*' [revolution in Berlin]. We came out of the barracks and turned towards the Ukrainians who guarded us. Mendel and Chaim, who pumped water, jumped on the sentry who stood by the barracks gate, took his rifle, and whoever else was free came to help throttle him and throw him into the pit. Zhelo took the rifle, and Moshe the tailor, who also knew how to use a rifle, took another. They lay down on the ground and shot in the direction of the first camp's gate, so that no help could come through there. Then we broke into Ivan's machine room. He was sleeping. Gustav, the first one, gave him a blow on the head with a *shpatzle* [pitchfork], so that he remained lying there for ever. Then we ran to the barbed wire. It had already been cut through in a few places, but the gate had not yet been broken down and it was hard to get through. Then panic broke out, everyone jumped and held on to the wires with their hands. Many fell in and could not get out. I don't know what happened to them, because then the shooting started.

I notified Shaked of my success, and told him what the statement contained. He vigorously denied any knowledge of the statement, adding that when he'd learned of it the prosecution had contacted the Jewish Museum to get the statement handed over to me. Only a fool would believe such a story. In any case, I submitted an immediate request that the statement be accepted as evidence for the defence, and that Rosenberg be recalled to the witness stand to explain the contradiction between his testimony and his statement.

On the third day of Shaked's summing-up, 27 January 1988, Rosenberg returned to the witness stand. This was the second instance of a prosecution witness being caught 'red-handed' in a lie and being forced to testify again. Before the trial began, I had vowed to question the survivor-witnesses on one subject only: the identification process they had taken part in with Israel Police during the years 1976–79. I was especially resolved not to question them on any matter touching on Treblinka itself. Therefore I would not examine Rosenberg myself; we agreed that Chumak would do so.

Rosenberg confirmed that the statement, which covered sixty-six pages, was his, written in his hand on the date that appeared on the document – 20 December 1945. He said the document had been written to record accurately the horrible tragedy of Treblinka. When Chumak reached the section dealing with the rebellion and the killing of Ivan the Terrible, he confirmed the accuracy of the section describing the explosion at three-forty-five (the signal that the rebellion was to begin), and that he had seen and heard Shmuel shouting when he came out of the barracks. But he said he had not seen Mendel and Chaim jump on the sentry with his own eyes; he had only heard about it later. Rosenberg confirmed that when he wrote 'We came out of the barracks' he meant himself and others who were there, and this had really happened. He maintained that in fact he had not seen anything. His mission was to run immediately with five others from the barracks to the barbed-wire fences and spread blankets over them, to make it easier for others to climb over when they fled. He claimed that he had mentioned Mendel's and Chaim's actions only because this is how they were related to him afterwards. Feigning innocence, he said this might have been a mistake, and perhaps he should have mentioned that he had not seen Mendel and Chaim nor the killing of Ivan, but had only heard about them from his comrades in the forest later. Chumak pressed him, and drew his attention to the fact that anyone reading this section would be completely unable to distinguish between what Rosenberg had seen and what he had heard. Rosenberg agreed. And he confirmed that when he wrote that 'Ivan' had been killed in the rebellion he meant 'Ivan Grozhny' (Russian for 'Ivan the Terrible'), the operator of the gas chambers.

Then Chumak asked: 'So how, sir, can you appear here and identify this man as Ivan when you said in 1945 that Ivan was dead and that Gustav had killed him? Has he returned from the dead?'

'I would have liked to see him dead, Mr Chumak,' Rosenberg responded, 'but I did not see him. People told me, and that was my heartfelt wish. I was in paradise when I heard that.' Just as Rosenberg had described Ivan the Terrible's death because it was his heartfelt wish, he identified Demjanjuk as Ivan the Terrible because it was his heartfelt wish. Dr Arad of Yad Vashem had emphasized in his testimony that Holocaust survivors often tend to recount incidents they had not personally witnessed as if they were facts. The sole reason was their desire to make reality conform to their dreams.

Chumak continued: 'You don't just say he was killed. You go into detail. How do you explain that?'

'In the forest, all of us wanted to take the credit for having done it. But now he's sitting here.'

Hearing this, Demjanjuk started shouting, in Hebrew: 'Liar. Mr Rosenberg, you're a liar!'

Then Rosenberg was asked: 'When you wrote what you wrote, you first recounted the killing of Ivan and afterwards you said, "Then we ran to the barbed wire" and so on. In other words, according to the order that you wrote it, first they killed Ivan and then afterwards ran to the fences.'

Rosenberg's answer was pathetic and unconvincing. 'Yes, Your Honours. I repeat that I am not a writer, I didn't write in chronological order.' This answer made it pointless to question him any more.

Rosenberg was very tense, and looked like someone who has been caught out in a lie. Throughout his testimony he had stood with his arms crossed, his body leaning on the stand; from time to time he swayed agitatedly. He was obviously lying. There was also an element of arrogance in his expression, as if he were saying to Chumak: 'I might be lying, but the judge is on my side and nothing can help you.' Despite his pathetic and false testimony, the court accepted all of Rosenberg's ridiculous explanations without reservation, and gave a 'high level of certainty' to his 'identification' of Demjanjuk as Ivan the Terrible.

It looked as if this was the end of the defence case. The prosecution's final arguments were already under way, and I delivered our own final arguments over the course of two weeks that ended on 18 February 1988, one year and two days after the trial opened. Four days later I left for a skiing holiday in Poiana.

Before I left, Johnny brought to my office a bundle of documents that had just arrived from Cleveland. These were documents that John Broadly had managed, after great effort, to extract from the Office of Special Investigations with the help of an order from the Federal District Court in Washington. I took the documents, as well as the court record of the summing-up sessions, with me to Poiana.

The new evidence included documents from the Soviet Union and the United States. They had been deliberately withheld from Demjanjuk and his attorneys by the OSI for over ten years, because of their decisive importance for the defence. As I delved deeper into the evidence I found it increasingly hard to believe my eyes. While it was not evidence of the type that reached me three and a half years later – proving decisively that Demjanjuk was *not* Ivan the Terrible – it showed quite clearly that the evidence purporting to prove that Demjanjuk was Ivan the Terrible, and the prosecution's interpretation of that evidence, were no more than a house of cards on which nothing could rest. The new material included fifteen statements by Treblinka survivors, recorded in the US at the end of the 1970s by the OSI. The American authorities had blanked out the name and other identifying details of the survivors, to prevent them being called as witnesses. Each survivor had been presented with a series of photographs that included one of Demjanjuk. Not one of them had picked out his photograph as that of Ivan the Terrible. Some of them had identified Demjanjuk as holding sundry 'jobs' at Treblinka, but these had nothing to do with Ivan the Terrible. For instance, one pointed to Demjanjuk and claimed that this man had been the engineer of the train that brought the victims to Treblinka; another maintained that Demjanjuk was a camp guard whose height was five foot five (Demjanjuk is five foot eleven), who did duty in the watch towers. Yet another pointed to a different man's picture as the operator of the gas chambers. In short, it was a mess of incompatible and contradictory testimony, showing that at Treblinka there had been at least ten men who looked fairly like Demjanjuk, and that none of them had been either Demjanjuk or Ivan the Terrible. This confirmed my claim that an identification procedure based on a photo spread must take all the necessary precautions, otherwise it may give false results. Because of these faulty photo spreads, we could never know if the survivor-witnesses selected Demjanjuk because he was Ivan the Terrible or simply because he looked like him. The survivors who 'identified' Demjanjuk as ten entirely different people at Treblinka were just as mistaken as the trial witnesses.

Furthermore, these fifteen statements, together with other evidence already in the court file, raised to forty the number of statements or memoranda from Treblinka survivors who had *not* identified Demjanjuk as Ivan the Terrible. This stood against the five survivor-witnesses and the testimony of SS member Otto Horn, who did not identify Demjanjuk anyway. The memoranda summarizing these fifteen interviews showed that some of the survivors had forgotten the names of the camps they had been in, even when they had been held there for many months. It will be recalled that Demjanjuk had forgotten to note the name of the prison camp at Chełm when he was first interrogated in 1978, and the prosecution maintained that this was proof he had never been there. The survivors' forgetting the names of their concentration camps proved that Demjanjuk's forgetfulness could not mandate a conclusion that he had not been held at Chełm.

But by far the most important document in the package was a statement taken in 1979 by the Soviet states prosecution and sent that same year to the OSI. The statement was made by Ignat Danilchenko, a guard at Sobibor. He claimed that he had arrived at Sobibor in March 1943, and that a blond guard named Ivan Demjanjuk had been there for some time already. This guard, according to the statement, was about an inch higher than Danilchenko himself (Danilchenko was six foot tall, Demjanjuk only five foot eleven). He added that even before his arrival at Sobibor this guard had earned himself a reputation as an experienced 'hunter' of Jews in the ghettoes around Sobibor. Danilchenko had been shown pictures of Demjanjuk and of other men. He had pointed to Demjanjuk's picture as being of the guard who had been with him at Sobibor. All the survivor-witnesses kept insisting that they had seen Ivan the Terrible over the course of a year, from the summer of 1942 to the day of the uprising on 2 August 1943, and they pointed to Demjanjuk's photograph as being of Ivan; yet Danilchenko claimed that this very picture was of a guard who had not only been in his platoon in Sobibor from March 1943 but had also been in Sobibor before that. Danilchenko's challenge to the prosecution's identification evidence was so decisive that the thought flashed through my mind, for the first time, that perhaps it was still possible to get Demjanjuk acquitted in the district court. But as scenes from the show-trial began passing before my eyes I was forced to admit to myself that even this new evidence would not be enough to save my client from the gallows.

Danilchenko had initially been quoted in the small, pro-Soviet Ukrainian newspaper, the *Ukrainian Weekly*, published in New York. This was in 1976, in an issue that contained a photograph of the Travniki document. Alongside was a quote from Danilchenko, saying that he had been with a guard named Demjanjuk at Travniki, Sobibor, Regensburg and Flossenbürg. This was a Soviet plot against Demjanjuk. (See Chapter 1.) Yet I should emphasize, to the Soviets' credit, that they never claimed (why will become clear in Chapter 15) – not even on the basis of the ludicrous identifications made of Demjanjuk in Israel – that he was Ivan the Terrible from Treblinka. The Soviets based themselves on the Travniki document, which they had forged, and on Danilchenko's statement, which they recorded later on. Danilchenko's statement and the document ostensibly corroborated one another with regard to Sobibor.

As soon as I returned to Israel I submitted a petition that the court accept all these documents as defence evidence; and that Professor Wagenaar be recalled to testify on the new material and explain why it could provide absolute proof of the substance of his testimony, especially regarding the poor quality of the photo spreads. The court convened on 15 March to hear my petition. This time the session was held in a normal courtroom, in the Jerusalem District Court building. Shaked understood the fatal significance of this new evidence, and tried with all his might to prevent the documents being accepted. He claimed that since the documents had been given to John Broadly at the beginning of February 1988, they could have been submitted during the summations. He used various procedural arguments, but his claims were so feeble that he was forced to retract them and to agree with Levin that his objection to the new material was 'only for the record'. The court decided to accept the documents as evidence and acceded to a joint request from me and the prosecution to hear additional summations the following week. But my petition to recall Professor Wagenaar was denied.

On 21 March 1988, more than a month after the trial appeared to have ended, the additional summations began. The judges were in the process of writing their verdict; they had already found Demjanjuk guilty, and were now setting out reasons for the decision. Even a completely objective court would find it hard to make an about-turn at such a late stage; it was especially unlikely given that the unexpected new evidence did not prove the defendant's innocence but only indicated that the evidence for his guilt was not solid. Now, as in the past, the judges would not allow themselves to be confused by the facts.

This was very apparent from the irritated comments they made during the two sessions of additional summations. The climax came, unusually, from Judge Tal, who proposed an original 'solution': 'I have been thinking about how Danilchenko's statement can be reconciled with the rest of the prosecution evidence. If God grants me thirty more years and I am then asked about this trial, I will no doubt say that I saw the prosecution and the defence daily for an entire year, even though there were actually long recesses, two months that we did not sit and weeks that we did not sit. So a man can say I saw him each day, even though there were breaks.' In other words, even though the survivors all said that they had seen Ivan the Terrible every day from the summer of 1942 until 2 August 1943, this did not mean that they really had. It might have been that Ivan the Terrible had earlier left Treblinka for Sobibor. Any court that would send a defendant to the gallows on the basis of such a pathetic 'explanation' should be ashamed of itself.

This was not the end of their machinations. Shaked asked the bench to grant all this evidence zero weight, Danilchenko's statement in particular. He referred to it repeatedly as 'a piece of paper we know nothing about'. This is a logical argument if it stands alone. But it is duplicitous for the same prosecutor in the same case to base himself on statements by people who were not examined in court because they had died before the trial began.

Shaked made one more request, much fairer and more comprehensible: 'If there is an intention of making use of these documents against the evidence the prosecution has presented, then we would like to halt the trial and be allowed to investigate this question in a serious way. Because the possibility that my colleague has raised ... is not a very simple one.' Of course I seconded Shaked's request, but Levin said to me: 'You can rest assured that we will not, nor is it possible to, investigate the Danilchenko matter. We will end with this document. What it contains is what there is. What it does not contain, it does not ... If it speaks for itself, it speaks for itself. What is to be concluded from that *we* will consider, so don't go all the way to the Soviet Union.'

The judges, Levin especially, were so keen to convict Demjanjuk as soon as possible that even a joint request from the prosecution and the defence could not halt the race to the gallows even for a moment. Shaked did not give up and repeated his request the next day. 'I have said what I have said,' Levin responded. 'What I ask for is a short argument, without repeating things that have already been said.' I chuckled bitterly to myself. How could Levin again be unwilling to find the truth? Could there be *any* piece of evidence calling the conviction into question that he would be prepared to consider? Summarizing the record of these two sessions, I wrote, 'The end of the road: the noose is ready.'

8 · Dovele

'Dovele' (pronounced *Dov*-eh-leh) is a nickname in Hebrew and Yiddish for anyone called Dov. This was my name for Supreme Court Justice Dov Levin, who presided over the special panel of three judges sitting in judgement on Demjanjuk. None of the others left so deep an imprint on the process as Levin; and more than any other judge he is responsible for the verdict and the death penalty that the court imposed on Demjanjuk.

As soon as the trial began I saw, as did most others who observed him, the great malice displayed by Levin towards me. Throughout the trial he never stopped snarling at me, harassing, insulting and humiliating me – blatantly, spitefully and without restraint. I have no doubt that he did this purely to disgrace me before everyone and ruin my legal career.

As soon as I realized this, I stopped calling him anything but Dovele, to tell myself and those around me that not only would he not get what he wanted, but that his behaviour would not affect my performance in the slightest, nor would it darken my mood by a shade. It said that even when Levin was frothing with anger, threatening me, insulting me, trying to trip me up, none of this would bother me. The only reaction he would get from me would be a laugh and a refusal to take him seriously.

I used this nickname even in my frequent contacts with Shaked and the rest of the prosecution team. When I told Shaked that I intended someday to write a book about my experiences and adventures during the trial, he asked me to send him the chapter on Dovele before the book's publication. Six years ago it was already clear to both of us that this would be a fitting title for the chapter about Levin's conduct. While some of these events have been related in previous chapters, it seems only proper to explain how they were part of a calculated policy pursued by the court, and by Levin in particular.

My first appearance in Levin's courtroom was in March 1976, when he was still a judge in the Tel Aviv District Court. I was then a lawyer with less than a month's experience, and the hearing was on a petition to detain for the duration of the trial Sarah Elkanovitch, who was at the centre of Israel's most dramatic and sensational criminal case of that year. The subsequent dismissal of the charges against her by a three-judge panel of the district court, about a week after my appearance before Levin, and the rejection of the state's appeal against this decision to the Supreme Court a few weeks later, were an excellent start for a novice attorney. The hearing before Levin was brief. His justifiable decision to detain my client was expected. I was so excited about my first appearance that I paid no attention to the judge's character and his attitude towards me. Between that day and the beginning of my involvement in the Demjanjuk case, I appeared before Judge Levin on many occasions. In 1981 he was appointed to the Supreme Court, and I appeared before him in this new position no small number of times. In 1986 itself I appeared to appeal the conviction of a client for sale of heroin. Levin headed the panel of judges, and he wrote the acquittal verdict.

Like most of my fellow attorneys in Tel Aviv, I loathed appearing before him. His irritability, his short temper and his rude way of addressing us in court all won him the reputation of being the judge to avoid at all costs. Many professional colleagues suggested to me that an incident that had occurred several years previously was the reason for Levin's appalling behaviour during the lower-court trial and thereafter. In 1979 I represented one of several people accused of laying an explosive at the door of a police superintendent. The charge completely destroyed the man's apartment, but luckily none of the residents was hurt. Since this crime was defined as a serious felony, the trial was held in the Tel Aviv District Court before a panel of three judges, headed by Judge Levin. After a month, Levin suddenly announced that the rest of the trial would be postponed to 1 September 1979, after the court system's summer recess. Enquiring at the clerk of the court's office, I discovered the reason for the postponement was that Levin was making a trip overseas. The defendants, who had been detained throughout the trial, thus had to remain in prison for a considerable extra period.

Around this time the Supreme Court handed down a series of opinions (mostly written by the Chief Justice of the time, the late Judge Yoel Zussman) according to which the continuous hearing of a criminal trial should not be delayed, even for a short time, especially when some or all of the defendants are being detained. In any trial not so conducted, the decisions said, the defendant was to be released on the spot. When I found out the reason for the postponement, I petitioned the district court to release my client on bail forthwith. This enraged the judges, Levin in particular; the court rejected my petition unanimously. I then decided to appeal this decision to the Supreme Court. As luck would have it, the hearing was set to be heard by Chief Justice Zussman. I referred him to the series of precedents that he himself had established on this issue, emphasizing that the reason for the delay was Levin's trip; I concluded by saying that in light of the Supreme Court's rulings it was inconceivable that my client remain in jail under these circumstances for three and a half months. Justice Zussman was ambivalent. In the end he handed down the worst possible decision from my point of view: he criticized Levin for making a trip that meant my client would sit in jail unnecessarily for three and a half months, but nevertheless decided to reject the appeal (because of the highly serious nature of the crime with which he was charged). The situation was aggravated further when the decision was published in the press. To the best of my memory, the headline was: PRESIDENT OF SUPREME COURT SHARPLY CRITICIZES JUDGE LEVIN OF THE TEL AVIV DISTRICT COURT. At that time Levin's appointment to the Supreme Court was under serious consideration, and such criticism was certainly not beneficial. After the newspaper report, all my fellow lawyers, especially those who were appearing with me for the other defendants (and who, afraid of Levin, had not joined me in my appeal to the Supreme Court), told me, 'You're finished with Levin. He'll make you regret it every time you appear before him.'

When that trial had finally resumed, it was clear from the moment the judges entered the courtroom that Levin could barely restrain his anger and loathing. He held back for a few seconds while he disconnected the microphones. Then, his words unrecorded on tape or on paper, he launched into a wild attack. 'That was a horrible thing you did. Its goal was to harm the judges. That takes a lot of nerve! A self-respecting lawyer does not act that way. The proof is that only you submitted an appeal to the Supreme Court.' I was in shock and did not respond. Never before nor after, until the Demjanjuk trial, did a judge assail me in such a way. Levin continued to pummel me for the remainder of the trial.

A short time later I appeared before the same panel in a rape case. Levin missed no opportunity to insult and lash out at me. As in the bombing of the policeman's home, it ended in a conviction that was overturned on appeal.

As I have noted, from then on until the Demjanjuk affair I appeared many times before Levin, and as time passed his harassment and his negative attitude to me seemed to abate. Most of my friends were convinced that the Demjanjuk case opened an old wound of Levin's that I thought completely healed. The trappings of the theatre and the live radio and TV broadcasts were a fitting arena for Levin to destroy me as a lawyer once and for all.

Apparently, the show-trial and the media uproar surrounding it led Levin to lose all notion of impartiality. On 25 March 1987, two days after I asked the judges to disqualify themselves from hearing the case further, I was on my way to see the clerk of the court, whose office was next to the judges' chambers in Binyanei Ha'uma. This section of the building had been remodelled specifically for the trial. The chambers and the clerk's office branched off a long corridor, and a person walking down the hall could peek into the rooms. When I reached the office I noticed that Nira Aslan, one of the clerk's staff, was holding a large sheaf of pages on to which press cuttings were photocopied. Curious, I asked her what they were. Nira, who was a friend to me throughout the trial and who greatly assisted and encouraged me during unpleasant moments, responded, 'What, don't you know? Every morning the judges receive a collection of clippings on the trial from all the daily papers, and I prepare a full set for each of them.' I was flabbergasted, and could barely control myself.

'What do they do with all the clippings?'

'They file them in a binder that each of them has in their chambers,' Nira replied. 'Those binders long since turned into albums. They read the reports of the trial almost every morning when they arrive, and often during the breaks as well.'

'How do you know?'

'It's very simple. Almost every time I enter their chambers when they are there alone, I find them studying the albums.'

'And who sends them the material?'

'There's a contract with a cuttings agency called Yifat.'

'And when did they start receiving the cuttings?'

'They began arriving a few days before the trial started. They're supposed to arrive each day until it is over.' Then she added: 'When you go down the hall, you'll see them looking through the albums.'

I was so upset that right then and there, almost at a run, I set out past the judges' chambers. Their doors were open, and I could easily make out Levin and Dorner immersed in their albums of clippings. Judge Tal was studying a different book. I returned to Nira and told her: 'You're absolutely right. They're sitting there unashamedly reading press cuttings about the trial.'

Israel does not have a jury system, so its judges determine the guilt or innocence of a defendant. They must therefore, like a jury, isolate themselves from all outside influences. To read press reports about a trial they are judging is unthinkable. The Israeli Supreme Court has ruled in the most explicit way that 'A judge must build a wall between himself and the media in the cases he judges.' Even if by chance he encounters a headline relating to a case he is judging, he is expected to skip over the article and not read it. In the entire legal history of the State of Israel there is no record of a judge – certainly not a Supreme Court justice – methodically collecting and reading, on a daily basis, press reports of a trial in which he is involved. The sense of disgust for Levin and his colleagues I felt at that moment was one of the factors that made it easier for me to withstand the deluge of bile they directed at me during the trial.

My first impulse was to submit another petition for the judges to disqualify themselves. On second thoughts, I rejected the idea. A petition for the disqualification of a judge is not the kind of procedure that should be pursued more than once in a trial. The best way to highlight the improprieties of a judge who has not disqualified himself, and who continues his misconduct, is on appeal. In addition, I thought to myself, let's let Dovele and his colleagues get thoroughly buried under those press clippings, until the end of the trial. After all, that alone is solid enough grounds to argue that the entire trial should be made null and void.

Every day during the weeks that followed I checked that the judges were still reading press cuttings that came in to them. I decided to ask one of the staff to throw the following sentence casually into a conversation with Levin: 'Sheftel knows about all the press clippings from Yifat.' I wanted to know what his response would be. It was not long in coming. The next day an order was issued forbidding entry into the court clerk's office from the door near the judges' chambers. Likewise, walking down the corridor adjacent to the chambers was forbidden. 'I don't want anyone walking around in these corridors, especially not Sheftel,' Levin said, so it was reported to me.

During the course of the trial I consulted several times with Justice Haim Cohen, retired Vice-President of the Supreme Court. I got up the nerve to approach him because in a pre-trial interview he had warned against the possibility that there would be a travesty of justice in the Demjanjuk case. (This convinced me that he would agree to receive me and give me advice.) When the defence case was approaching its conclusion, I went to Justice Cohen's home to ask his advice about the swelling albums of press clippings. By that time I had photocopies of all the cuttings and I brought some of them along. I informed him briefly of the facts of the matter, and he was astonished. 'Mr Sheftel, do you know what you're saying? That just can't be. I refuse to believe it. You're imagining it.' I drew out the cuttings and explained that they have been photocopied from a complete album of press cuttings like that found in the judges' chambers. Justice Cohen mumbled, 'I can't believe it, I can't believe it. How can they do such a thing? It invalidates the entire proceeding.'

I then told him about my intention of calling the head of Yifat to testify as a defence witness. I could submit through him copies of all the cuttings on the trial that his company had collected for the judges, as well as the contract for this service. Justice Cohen disliked the impudence this implied, but he agreed that the situation required it. He suggested that I should announce my intention in advance, in chambers, so as not to embarrass the judges more than necessary. I accepted this advice – as I did all the other guidance he gave me during the trial.

Towards the end of Professor Iskan's testimony, during a routine meeting in chambers and in the presence of Gill, Shaked and Daphna Bainwall, one of the prosecution team, I announced to Levin and his colleagues that I intended to ask for Mr Carlos, Managing Director of Yifat, Inc., to be called as a witness. Levin played dumb and asked what I needed him for. 'I wish to submit through him, as an exhibit, the album of press clippings lying on Your Honour's desk. The album contains all the Israeli cuttings on the trial that Your Honours read so diligently each day. I also wish to submit the contract signed with Yifat through which the album on Your Honour's desk was compiled.'

The faces of Levin, his fellow judges and all the prosecutors went green. 'Why is that relevant?' Levin asked ingenuously.

'It is very relevant,' I responded. 'Justice Haim Cohen, whom I consulted and who advised me to raise this matter first in chambers before raising it in the courtroom, believes that this alone is sufficient to invalidate the entire proceedings.'

Levin interrupted. 'I inform Mr Sheftel this very moment that we will not allow this Carlos to testify.'

'I have here a request to call him as a witness. I will submit it to the clerk's office immediately. The court will, of course, make its decision about the request as it sees fit.' Whatever Levin's decision, I thought, the scandal would become public the following week.

Five days later, Levin decided to cut short Professor Smith's additional testimony and hold a hearing on my request to call Carlos as a defence witness. I rose. 'The testimony of Mr Carlos, Managing Director of the Yifat company, is most vital. We wish, through this witness, to present as evidence all the press cuttings that this witness has sent to the court for Yifat. The vast majority of these cuttings constitute incitement against the defendant. According to advice the defence has received from one of the country's greatest jurists, they utterly undermine the defendant's right to a fair trial.'

Here Levin interrupted me. 'I understand that you are referring to, as you told us in our chambers, the former Vice-President of the Supreme Court.' This comment was gratuitous. It is unacceptable to refer in the courtroom to things said in chambers, all the more so if they have to do with a retired senior judge. Then he added: 'Yes, what are you asking for?'

'According to the legal advice the defence received, the fact that this material was under the honourable court's continuous scrutiny from the start of the trial, and in fact a few days before it began, is sufficient, in the case of a conviction, to reverse the verdict on appeal.'

Judge Tal intervened: 'Maybe we can save the time his testimony would take. It is clear that the court knows that press clippings were indeed sent to the court and that they lay in our chambers, so there is no need to waste time on this question of fact. As for the legal implications of the fact, Mr Sheftel can of course argue before us on this issue, and if there is an appeal, and if he finds it necessary to argue this on appeal, he will do so.' Levin intervened, adding among other things that:

'The judges are well-acquainted with the press clippings.'

In response, I said: 'The reason for calling this witness is manifold. First, we wish to use the witness to submit a copy of the press album that he prepared for each of the honourable judges. We want –'

I was again cut off by Levin. 'That is not relevant for the purposes of this trial. For the appeal, if there is an appeal, and if Mr Sheftel wishes, the material lies in the Clerk of the Court's office. There is no need to submit the material through a witness because it is already here.'

In light of this I said, 'If the album is available and use may be made of it, we wish to make the matter formal and turn the album into an exhibit in the case.'

Levin asked with characteristic sarcasm: 'What, isn't the court's announcement better than a piece of evidence?'

I responded, 'Not at all, but . . .'

Again Levin interrupted. 'The court has confirmed and declared that this material that Mr Carlos gave the court is in the court, and that this material is transferred to the judges' chambers. Nothing more is necessary, so we will not call the witness.'

I tried again. 'We wish to submit it, and I will explain the relevance forthwith.'

Levin stuck to his guns. 'The material is not relevant.'

I continued to insist. 'The material is relevant because it is in its entirety a violation of the rule of *sub judice*, which is a part of our legal system.'

Levin responded in a furious tone of voice: 'I'm very sorry, this entire argument is irrelevant. We will not call the witness and Mr Sheftel may be seated.'

I tried again: 'We wish to call the witness for a number of reasons, including to present the contract for the supply of the newspaper articles.'

This time Levin completely lost his composure: 'That doesn't interest me. The contract does not interest me and is not relevant to the trial, and if Mr Sheftel wishes to ask for it in the appeals stage, he may submit it as evidence in the appeal. Neither the cuttings nor the contract is relevant to the trial.' He concluded by turning to Chumak: 'Mr Chumak will continue the examination of Professor Smith.'

So, whilst the court admitted all the facts the defence raised with regard to the album, with characteristic imperiousness it prevented Carlos's testimony from being heard. Not because this testimony, which was meant to show how far the court had degenerated, was irrelevant, as Levin tried to make out (inappropriate behaviour by the court is always relevant); but solely in order to prevent the attention of the public being focused on the court's misconduct. Here was another example of the cowardice and hypocrisy of the thousands of members of the Israeli legal community. There was not a single jurist with the courage to write an article condemning this business now that it had been made public.

During my final arguments I tried to refer to the album. 'At the time of our request to submit the album of press clippings as an exhibit, Judge Tal said explicitly that it would be possible to refer to it in the final arguments.' Levin's response was: 'Why is Mr Sheftel getting off the track?'

I responded that 'Sometimes, worthwhile things may be found off the track. In every article of law, for instance, the title of the article is in the margin.'

Levin was undeterred. 'When someone drives up on the hard shoulder then tries to return to the highway, he generally turns over or causes an accident. So it's not a good idea to leave the road.' He was trying to present my argument on the album as inadmissible, and added: 'So don't get off the road. We want you to get out of here safely.'

I tried to insist: 'A good driver can sometimes get off the road but return to the highway safely.'

Levin brought the matter to a close. 'Fine. But why take risks? Please pass that over and finish your final arguments.' He was determined never to let me speak of the album on live television.

But it wasn't just press cuttings. Not only did the judges collect and diligently read reports of the trial; briefings were also given to the sycophant reporters responsible for those reports. I learned of this from one of the journalists. These briefings were given by Levin alone; his colleagues did not take part. So here you have a Supreme Court justice, serving as presiding judge in a special court trying a capital case, reading press reports of the trial for an entire year. These reports prejudge the defendant, denounce his witnesses and vent their spleen on his defence attorney. Instead of filing a criminal complaint against the perpetrators of this violation of a defendant's right to a fair trial, as Israeli judges have done in the past, the judge invites the offending journalists to his chambers for 'guidance and clarification' while the trial is in progress. It is no wonder, then, that some of these sycophants told me more than once that they were sure that no action would be taken against them, despite their illegal reporting.

Public confirmation that journalists were being invited to Levin's chambers was given in an article published by Tom Segev in the distinguished daily *Ha'aretz* on 22 July 1988. Segev spoke to Levin by phone, and the latter confirmed that he did indeed meet every so often in his chambers with some of the Israeli journalists who were covering the trial. 'Sometimes the reporters want to clarify things,' Levin explained to Segev. What Levin 'forgot' to mention was that, for this trial, a special press spokesman delegated by the Ministry of Justice and the court was also available to 'clarify things'.

If anyone believed that, after the conviction was handed down and the death penalty imposed, the court would finally call a halt to this behaviour, they were wrong. The ink was barely dry on the verdict when Levin set off on a lecture tour of the United States. In lectures before Jewish audiences, he justified the verdict time and again. The Israeli media contacted a large number of retired Supreme Court judges to ask for their opinions, but without exception they refused to answer, on the grounds that this would be illegal because the verdict had, by law, to undergo the scrutiny of a court of appeal. Until the appeal was concluded, they could not talk. Levin, an active Supreme Court justice, was somehow unfettered by restrictions that every retired judge felt to be binding. He repeatedly addressed disputed questions about the trial, and the verdict to which his signature was affixed. So, for instance, at a lecture at the Jewish Community Center in Norfolk, Virginia, he said – in 'broken English', as reported by Ohio's largest newspaper, the *Plain Dealer* – 'We cannot be impressed by someone claiming "I am innocent." Innocence is not what you say in your testimony, innocence must be proven.' Of course, every first-year law student knows that the iron rule of Israeli, as of American, criminal law is that the prosecution must prove the defendant's *guilt* beyond a reasonable doubt. Demjanjuk, however, had to prove his innocence, and since he was unable to do so his fate was sealed. Later in the same lecture Levin said that Demjanjuk 'was given an especially fair trial by his judges. I promise you that that is how it was, not because I say so, but . . . because the judgement says so . . . it was a very, very fair trial.' The question that was not asked in response to this self-righteous drivel was, of course: Who then wrote the judgement?

A fortnight before, on 1 May 1988, less than a week after sentencing Demjanjuk to hang, Levin had given a lecture at the Beth El Synagogue in West Hartford, Connecticut. One of the listeners recorded the lecture and sent it to the Demjanjuk family. Levin gave a profound 'psychological' explanation for accepting the identification testimony of the survivors as a basis for conviction. 'People who have lost almost everything they had, in such a deliberate process of destruction, are unable to forget. It may be that their memories are pushed into a corner for a time, but when they give testimony at the trial of one of the horrible perpetrators, it reawakens everything.' The Supreme Court justice thus explained to his audience the considerations that led to his conviction of a defendant whose verdict was up for review on appeal. This is unheard-of. Moreover, Levin knew very well that only one in five Treblinka survivors had identified Demjanjuk as Ivan the Terrible. Later in his lecture, Levin justified the death penalty he had signed, knowing that this too was under discussion in the appeal.

After the verdict was handed down I gave many lectures, took part in many press conferences in North America and appeared in countless radio and television interviews. At almost every opportunity I re-presented the glaring misconduct of the court that had sentenced Demjanjuk to death. I always mentioned the album of press cuttings and Levin's lecture tour. Again and again I was met with utter disbelief and was asked to prove what I was saying. Only by reading out the trial's English court record where the judges themselves confirmed the facts about the album, and by quoting from press reports of Levin's American lecture tour, could I persuade my interviewers and their audiences that it was all true. This disbelief did not surprise me. Any audience in an enlightened country would have trouble believing that in a democratic state like Israel judges, and especially Supreme Court justices, could act as Demjanjuk's judges did.

Then there were the in-chambers sessions called from time to time, the majority of them conducted without minutes being recorded. It was only natural that in such a long and complicated trial as Demjanjuk's it was necessary to hold meetings in chambers from time to time, to conduct free and informal discussions of various technical matters. There is nothing wrong with this and it does not contradict the principle of a public trial. But the meetings held in Judge Levin's chambers during this trial soon became a tool with which he tried to impose various things on the defence that he was not willing or able to force on us in open court, before the television cameras.

So, for instance, the hearing on the prosecution's request to hear some evidence in Germany was conducted in chambers. The judges thereby saved the prosecution, and apparently themselves as well, much embarrassment, given my reasons for objecting to the request. This was not the only time that a hearing might have been embarrassing for the prosecution and the bench was transferred to chambers over the defence's objections, circumventing the requirements of a public trial.

Meetings in chambers were employed for other improper purposes. On 23 March 1987, I asked the judges to disqualify themselves from continuing to hear Demjanjuk's case. The petition was rejected, and the next day I appealed the decision to the Supreme Court, and it was scheduled to be heard a week later. In the mean time a meeting in chambers was called, the meeting where Levin succeeded in making me cave in and promise to make a public apology for my hapless statement about 'why this hall has been rented'. Seeing that things were going his way, Levin tried to go one step further, and demanded that we withdraw the appeal pending before the Supreme Court. Exploiting this situation to put pressure on the defence was so sordid that Judge Tal interjected: 'What my colleague Judge Levin has said is his own opinion. I disassociate myself from it. You have every right to appeal our decision not to disqualify ourselves, and there should be no intervention in your considerations.' I looked at Judge Dorner. She wore an expression of neutrality, as if the entire matter was no concern of hers. Levin apparently sensed that he had gone too far and began fidgeting nervously. He soon recovered, however. 'Of course it is your right to do as you see fit.' Broken and drained as I was at that moment, I did not retaliate. There can be no doubt that in an open court, in front of the cameras, Levin would not have dared to do this.

A basic rule of in-chambers meetings is that, like the formal sessions in the courtroom, they are conducted only when both sides are present. Levin broke this rule three times, always in connection with the same matter. Count Tolstoy, it will be recalled, was cross-examined by State Attorney Blatman about his political views during most of the afternoon session of 3 November 1987. The next day Gill voiced a firm and fully justified protest against this, since the court was operating a double standard whereby the defence could not question the prosecution's experts on *their* political views. Gill's criticism troubled Levin, precisely because it was justified and correct, and because it was on the record. Levin would have liked Gill to apologize and retract, as I had done previously. He knew very well that he could not threaten Gill with contempt of court charges, as he did to me, since such a move against a guest attorney would look very bad. He therefore tried to achieve his goal by summoning me to his chambers alone. He did this once with his fellow judges present, and twice without them; at these meetings he demanded that I make Gill issue a public apology and retract his protest.

At the first of these meetings, when Tal and Dorner were there, I responded: 'I do not think it fitting that I serve as a courier for the court. In such a matter as this, if the court so desires, it may address Mr Gill directly.' The next time, a week later, the two of us were alone in his chambers. Levin again demanded vehemently that I make Gill apologize and retract. I continued to insist that Levin should address Gill directly. I added: 'In any case, I do not believe Gill would even consider apologizing. He thinks the defence has already apologized once too often in this case, and I have no intention of ruining my relations with him over this issue.' Levin was angry: 'Instead of helping the court, you are, as usual, being a smart alec.' Exasperated, he told me to leave.

He did not give up, however, and called me alone into his chambers again. This time he threw down the gauntlet. 'You should know that in a case like this the judgement will address and evaluate the work of the attorneys, both prosecution and defence. Tell your friend Gill that if he does not withdraw what he said and make a public apology in the courtroom, we will not hesitate to give him the most negative possible evaluation in the judgement, and that will be very unpleasant for him.' This happened at the end of December, when the trial was in its final stages. Levin's behaviour was already at a nadir, and I thought there was nothing he could do to surprise me now. But this last threat proved me wrong. Levin would not dare say such things in any other situation, not even in a meeting in chambers in the presence of his fellow judges. One to one, however, he felt no shame. I responded: 'It's only because the defence has already asked once during this trial that the judges disqualify themselves, and because a self-respecting defence does not take such a step twice in one trial, that we will not resubmit our disqualification motion in the wake of what Your Honour has just said. In fact, better you should summon my colleague Gill and tell him the same thing directly.' In a rage I turned round, excused myself and left before Levin had a chance to say another word.

I told Gill about this exchange, of course. He said angrily that he would not apologize under any circumstances, and that if he were called alone to Levin's chambers he would know the reason and would not even bother to go in.

The trial's schedule was another of Levin's tools for obstructing the defence and helping the prosecution. During the prosecution's presentation of its case, the court had all the time in the world, and displayed unbounded patience. The prosecution was given a free hand to bring whatever witnesses it wanted, and was not asked to submit a schedule to show when each witness would testify and how long the testimony would take. At the opening session the prosecution was given sole discretion to present any evidence it saw fit, even to support facts that the defence was not disputing. As soon as the defence began to present its case however the judges, Levin especially, lost patience. Suddenly, nothing was more important than the time factor. The need to conclude the trial as quickly as possible became an endless refrain in the meetings in chambers. Levin intoned over and over again: 'Soon we will be the laughing stock of the world. Klaus Barbie's trial, which began about the same time as this one, ended long ago, but we continue to tread water with no end in sight.'

For some reason, the bench considered itself to be in some sort of crazy race with Klaus Barbie's judges. When Barbie's trial ended and Levin realized to his chagrin that he had lost the race, he hoped to 'lose' by the smallest possible margin, so as not to become a 'laughing stock'. So he forced the defence to submit in advance a list of all its witnesses and to give the precise dates on which they would give evidence; and to commit itself to completing the testimony of two of its expert witnesses per week. He was unimpressed to be told that the length of the prosecution's cross-examination was not under the defence's control and it was thus unlikely that the schedule could be followed. When we explained that if the defence was bringing expert witnesses to Israel from overseas, and the schedule was being upset because of the prosecution's cross-examination, the defence was likely to incur heavy and unnecessary expenses that it would not be able to bear, Levin ruled: 'Mr Sheftel will leave such matters to the court.'

'Will the court also pay the expenses?' I asked.

'The court is concerned with saving public expenditure for funding the trial,' Levin said angrily.

'And the defence is concerned with saving private expenditure for funding the defendant's defence,' I replied. In the end I was able to get agreement for only one expert witness to be heard each week, even if the testimony ended before the week was over. Levin did not hesitate to exploit the closed meetings in chambers in his efforts to lock the defence into a timetable that would make it impossible to function.

As the defence case progressed and one after another expert witness of international stature punched holes in the prosecution evidence, the court began to serve as the prosecution's legal counsel. A sterling example of this was Levin's repeated advice to Shaked not to forgo cross-examination of Flynn after we had asked for the testimony to be struck from the record. During the final arguments this provision of legal advice to the prosecution became even more obvious, and touched on the most important issues in the case.

Since it was obvious that all the photo spreads conducted in Demjanjuk's case were completely invalid, one way of getting around this was by arguing that, according to Israeli precedent, there was no need to conduct a photo spread in such cases, because of the extended contact, over the course of a year, between the identification witness and Ivan the Terrible. Photo spreads are in fact reserved for cases of momentary, chance contact between the identifier and the identified, at the time the crime was committed. This exceptional rule applies if the extended contact or acquaintance between the identifier and the identified took place a few months before the trial, or even a year or two prior to it; it does not, of course, apply in cases of extended contact or acquaintance that occurred decades previously. In such a case a photo spread *is* required. Thirty-five years passed between Ivan the Terrible's extended contact with the survivors and their identification of Demjanjuk as Ivan the Terrible.

During Shaked's arguments about the photo spreads, Judge Dorner considered herself obligated to advise him to point his arguments in this direction. 'To the best of my understanding, Radivker did not conduct photo spreads of the type used after a robbery. She assumed that there had been extended acquaintance and that [the survivors] would point the man out to her.' 'Correct, correct,' Shaked quickly agreed, taking the advice. Dorner, like a conscientious teacher with a pupil who has corrected himself after having a little trouble getting started, added: 'It's important to mention that.' The verdict made it clear that this advice had not been given for nothing. It was one of the central excuses the judges made for ignoring the many fundamental flaws in the photo spreads. In stating that there had not been any need for photo spreads, the court ignored not only Israeli precedent but also its own obligation to ensure proper identification procedures were followed.

Sometimes, the court 'forgot' to advise the prosecution on a particular point. This 'forgetfulness', and the occasional spark of fairness that Shaked still showed, meant that in his summing-up he could not reach a conclusion against Demjanjuk on certain points. In my final arguments, I used the prosecution's arguments to strengthen my own arguments. So, for instance, Shaked concurred in his summing-up that Yehiel Reichman had not succeeded, in New York in 1980, in identifying the Travniki photograph (in a photo spread) as that of Ivan the Terrible. Every novice jurist knows that the only possible consequence of this can be the rejection of Reichman's identification of Demjanjuk as Ivan the Terrible, made on the same occasion on the basis of a photograph taken nine years later. When in my summation I touched on the subject of Demjanjuk's 'identification' by Reichman, I said: 'My learned colleague Mr Shaked said in his final arguments that he cannot deny those parts of the identification report on Reichman that do not favour his case, including Reichman's non-identification of the Travniki photograph.' Levin lost no time in interrupting me. 'Of what importance is it what the prosecutor denies or does not deny? . . . Must we be bound by the prosecutor's argument?' Later he added: 'As far as I am concerned, it neither helps nor hurts if the prosecution argues that.' The court thus preferred in its interpretation of the evidence to go *beyond* the prosecution's declared position.

There is only one explanation for such behaviour. The judges, like the media, had to all intents and purposes convicted Demjanjuk in advance, long before they did so officially in their verdict; so they did everything in their power to ensure his conviction. Judge Dorner gave this clear expression in an unfortunate slip of the tongue. Shaked's final arguments were addressing the question of Ivan the Terrible's age. Shaked wished to show that according to the testimony of the identification witnesses this corresponded with Demjanjuk's age. Dorner asked Shaked: 'Are there other, objective sources, not witnesses, for the age of Ivan the Terrible, and not necessarily of the defendant?' The 'not necessarily' says it all, implying that Dorner identified Ivan the Terrible with the defendant. Immediately thereafter this position was made explicit. 'I would like to rephrase the question, and for you to check if there is a source from Treblinka that describes . . . the defendant's age without any connection to . . .' Of course she had been going to say 'without connection to the survivors' testimonies', but she suddenly understood that she was giving away her conviction that Demjanjuk had been at Treblinka and that he was Ivan the Terrible. She corrected herself quickly: 'Ivan the Terrible's age, not the defendant's age.' This correction simply re-emphasized unambiguously that Judge Dorner had convicted Demjanjuk even before the case had been decided. This makes it clear why the judges were unwilling, under any circumstances, to be 'confused with the facts'.

The strong and deep-rooted anti-Semitism that was a common fact of life for generations among Ukrainians is well known. In many cases, waves of hatred led to horrible pogroms, murders and robbery. This is all familiar, but the court obviously had to disregard this and decide the case on its merits. Judge Tal apparently did not agree.

When Dr Krakovski, the prosecution's historian-witness, completed his testimony, Judge Tal decided to ask him 'questions of clarification'. It will be remembered that the court may ask such questions only if most or all of the testimony would remain incomprehensible were the questions not answered. Tal said, 'Were there not additional reasons for the Germans to expect co-operation from the Ukrainians, for instance a long tradition of hatred of and hostility towards the Jewish population, from the days of Chemilnitzki in the mid-seventeenth century, wasn't that one of the reasons?' Tal's pathetic question would later be exploited by the North American Ukrainian community, its spokesmen claiming that, because he was Ukrainian, Demjanjuk did not receive, and could not have received, a fair trial in Israel. Krakovski himself refrained from repeating Tal's error and dodged the question elegantly. 'I am not able to enter into all the details of their history, national character and various aspirations.'

The most upsetting aspect of the judges' conduct, Levin's especially, was their favouritism, the double standard they operated almost all the time. Whenever one of the defence attorneys voiced a criticism of one of the prosecution's many blunders, Levin was enraged, quickly censuring and insulting him. During the testimony of Superintendent Bezaleli I objected to the prosecution's attempt to let him testify on a subject that was not addressed in his written opinion. I called this attempt a 'scheme'. Levin was not satisfied with merely overruling my objection; he had to tell me off. 'Mr Sheftel speaks here of scheming. Don't use that expression.' Half an hour later Shaked attacked one of the defence arguments: 'For the defence to argue now why it doesn't have the original exhibit that the court has, that's a deception.' Levin was not upset by *this* expression. In a long decision handed down after Shaked's arguments, there was not one word criticizing his use of the term 'deception', a much stronger pejorative than 'scheme'. The court concluded its decision, as usual, by complimenting itself. 'Throughout the trial this court has gone out of its way to aid the defence, on every matter, all in the framework of the law and often beyond the requirements of the law.' This self-praising by the judges was an integral part of the record from the first stages of the trial. The intention hidden behind these compliments was obviously to obscure the true nature of the proceedings by creating a false impression in the record.

Gill did not get much sympathy either. On one occasion he dared to comment, with good cause, that Shaked's objection to a question he had asked Professor Smith during cross-examination was suggestive, that it indicated to the witness what answer she was to give. Levin assailed him wrathfully, shouting: 'Such talk is a matter of a lawyer's manners and education.' Only a month previously, when Levin had excoriated me for using the words 'That's not why this hall has been rented', he had only praise for Gill's education and good manners: 'I have a very high estimation of attorneys O'Connor and Gill who, with their good manners, apparently bestowed by the education they received, do not dare make such charges,' he said then. Shaked, though, could refer to the defence attorneys and their conduct however he chose without Levin demanding that he be polite.

During the final arguments, Levin made repeated comments to the effect that I was not basing myself on the evidence. There was no truth to this claim. He was referring to my mention of facts and incidental matters that were part of any average general education. Analysing Epstein's testimony, I cited the fact that 'In Poland, on 25 September, it is not very hot.' Levin interrupted: 'You are again getting into speculation that is not part of the evidence.' Later I referred to the well-known fact that, even as late as April 1945, millions of soldiers were still fighting in the ranks of the German Army. Levin did not hesitate for a moment. 'That has not been proved, we have no evidence of that before us' – he even censured me for referring to a fact contained in every book on the Second World War.

In contrast, Shaked was able to say whatever he wished in his final arguments, and to refer again and again to facts that had not been mentioned in the evidence. He was not censured, nor was even polite exception taken. As soon as he began his final arguments, Shaked gave a detailed description of various experiments the members of the prosecution team had performed among themselves on 'suggestive recall'. None of these experiments had been brought to the court's attention in the framework of the evidence. Levin and his colleagues not only failed to rebuke Shaked; they listened with great interest. Shaked concluded that he had a licence to mention any fact not shown in the framework of the evidence. He referred to 'eight hundred studies' on the memory of Holocaust survivors demonstrating that Professor Wagenaar's testimony was without foundation. This was truly despicable. Not only was there no mention of these 'eight hundred studies' in the evidence, but Professor Wagenaar, who had spent an entire week in the witness stand, had not been asked a thing about them by Shaked. Levin did not react to this; Shaked, seeing that all was well, used the same stratagem in another attempt to damage Professor Wagenaar's testimony. He quoted an article by a psychologist who stated that 'Nothing important has happened in the lives of the camp survivors since their liberation from the Nazis.' This article was not found in the evidence; again it was met with thunderous silence from Levin. Throughout his final arguments Shaked referred continually to facts that were absent from the evidence, and Levin listened attentively; not a single word of criticism was directed at Shaked. I could only imagine how he would have exploded at me, in the most violent terms, if I had behaved like Shaked.

Did Levin, then, ever reproach the prosecutor? On one occasion: one of those few times that Shaked displayed fairness to the defence. Gill was examining Bezaleli, and Shaked remarked that the English translation of a certain document that Gill had before him was not precise, and was therefore impairing his examination. Levin was quick to scold him: 'Why should you be coming to the defence of the defence?' As far as he was concerned, it was undesirable for the prosecutor to behave fairly towards Demjanjuk's defence attorneys – so very undesirable that Shaked was, exceptionally, reprimanded.

During this phase of the trial, Levin made unbridled attempts to prevent the defence stating its arguments on critical issues. He disrupted the defence methodically, with interruptions, pointless queries and the presentation of illegitimate questions – and, of course, constant rebukes and insults. Between these attempts he was demonstrably and derisively inattentive, doing his best to appear supremely uninterested in the defence's arguments. This behaviour reached its nadir over the matter of the Walus trial.

During my summing-up I asked to be allowed to cite a very famous judgement given by a federal court in Chicago in 1978 in the case of Frank Walus. The background facts were amazingly like those in the Demjanjuk case. Walus was identified by twelve Holocaust survivors from the Czestochowa and Kilsen ghettoes as a fiendish Gestapo agent who had worked there in the years 1940–43. All the witnesses were able to tell of horrible atrocities he had committed, which they had seen with their own eyes. The identification was made in 1976, the year that Demjanjuk was identified. Just as in Demjanjuk's case, a picture of Walus had stood out against other pictures presented to the survivors. The detail that made Walus's picture exceptional was the checked jacket he wore in the photograph. Walus was brought up on proceedings to revoke his American citizenship; the lower court denaturalized him, basing itself on the identification by the twelve survivors. The judge rejected all the arguments of Walus's defence attorney about the poor quality and invalidity of the identification procedures. The attorney's arguments were fundamentally similar to the ones I raised about the photo spreads through which Demjanjuk had been 'identified'. Walus protested his innocence the entire time, saying that in 1940–43 he had been an agricultural labourer in Germany. He even summoned German farmers he had worked for to testify to his alibi. The judge preferred to believe the survivor-witnesses. A short time after the verdict was handed down, during the appeals proceedings, Walus produced documents from the German social security department, confirming his claim that he had worked in Germany at the time he was alleged to have been a Gestapo murderer in the Polish ghettoes. The prosecution did not dispute the authenticity of the documents, the verdict was rescinded and Walus's citizenship restored.

This verdict was a compelling example of the possibility that as a result of suggestive photo spreads Holocaust survivors might err when it came to identifying a man who had wronged them. Levin was aware of its importance and relevance, and feared the far-reaching implications for the trial in general, and for the reliability of Demjanjuk's identification by the survivors in particular. He was therefore determined to prevent the defence citing this judgement in its final arguments.

When I was about to refer to the Walus trial, to point out the great similarity between it and the Demjanjuk case, Levin attacked me with determination. 'That is of no interest to us. If Mr Sheftel wishes to draw our attention to a reference, he may do so, but we will not go into the facts of the case.'

'The legal reference is, Your Honours, like any other reference, any other judgement, based on the facts of the case,' I responded.

Levin blushed and got very angry. 'We have told Mr Sheftel once and we will not repeat it. Only the reference and no more.'

'But the legal reference relates to the facts,' I insisted. So did Levin.

'We are interested only in general rulings. If it is only for specific facts then the entire matter is not worth anything. Please continue your final argument, and if you wish to draw our attention to the facts in the judgement, we will not allow you. Don't argue with us!'

This time I was unwilling to give in to such injustice. I decided that if Levin would not let me present the facts of the Walus case and demonstrate the similarity with the Demjanjuk case, I would halt the presentation of my arguments. So, when this latest outburst was over, I said: 'The court forbids me to refer to these facts, so I wish to present arguments on why I should be allowed to do so.'

'We have already given an interim decision on this matter.'

I stood my ground. 'I would like to explain my position, Your Honours.'

'Then, please, continue your summation, and after you finish the other parts and wish to argue this matter, we will discuss it,' Levin responded.

Here Judge Tal intervened, apparently uncomfortable with Levin's position, as he had been several times during the trial. 'If Mr Sheftel could tell us in one or two sentences what rule of law derives from the Walus precedent . . . then we'll see what the factual basis is.' Levin perhaps understood that he had gone too far, and kept silent.

I therefore decided to quote case law, as Judge Tal had requested, and then went into a long, detailed argument of the facts. Levin suddenly intervened, in total contradiction of his position: 'After you address the case law, you may certainly say that this rule reflects such and such a factual background.' And he added self-righteously: 'No one is preventing you from saying that the rule of law was determined against such and such a factual background, no one is preventing you.' Really? Just fifteen minutes ago he had declared that the court would not go into the facts. This exchange took place about a year after the trial began, when the record already stood at more than ten thousand pages. Levin's behaviour up to that point had broken all records, yet I was once again taken by surprise. This was not because of his refusal to allow me to refer to the facts in the Walus case, but because in such a brief span of time, with cameras and microphones broadcasting his words live, he did not hesitate to take two contradictory positions on the same issue.

Anyone following the case could only conclude that Levin simply enjoyed abusing Demjanjuk's defence attorneys at every opportunity. At times it seemed as if he lay in ambush, searching for such an opportunity, and sometimes he made himself ridiculous with his zeal for attacking the defence. For example, during his cross-examination of Radivker, O'Connor asked her how many children she had. The question was obviously superfluous and irrelevant. But Levin, instead of ruling the question out, launched a venomous attack on O'Connor. 'Imagine, Mr O'Connor, if she has no children. Imagine that she has no children. Would the question be a pleasant one? Perhaps Mr O'Connor can understand. You are asking a woman who has been through what happened in Europe during the Holocaust whether she has children. Perhaps she wanted children and has none. And Mr O'Connor knows very well how good it is to have children, since you have children who make you happy. And if she was God forbid in a situation that she could no longer have children, then such a question is an embarrassing question, an unfair question.' Levin was having so much fun publicly insulting O'Connor that he ignored Radivker's statement in answer to a question from O'Connor just a minute before, that she had immigrated to Israel in 1964 with her husband and daughter.

The court record is strewn with hostile remarks and insults against the defence, such as: 'The public is also beginning to be bored by the argument'; 'Go on. What, are you staring at me? I'm listening. When I address my colleague the judge, my ear is pointed in your direction'; 'completely unethical defence attorneys'; 'This is an unfit and unseemly defence team ... but that's all there is'; 'the consequence of the defence's scheming'; 'The defence is throwing sand in our eyes'; 'whining defence attorneys'; 'You're giving us a headache,' and many more. One can scan the record without finding a single real complaint against anyone from the prosecution (and not because there was any lack of reasons to rebuke them).

Truth to tell, it was not just Levin who was aggravating; I didn't pull any punches, and made efforts to annoy him. The difference was that Levin did it in full view, with the goal of hammering away at me until he had irreversibly damaged my legal career. I did my part without him realizing I was doing it. He never imagined that, for the benefit of our eventual appeal to the Supreme Court, I was baiting him into filling the record with outbursts that no judge should allow past his lips, however angry.

Three months into the trial, I had a good grasp of Levin's behaviour patterns and reactions. I knew what gestures and phrases were likely to upset him. So, for instance, when I stood at my desk, questioning or arguing, with my body leaning forward and waving my left arm in a particular way that annoyed him, taking care to draw out an accented syllable, as in 'Ukraaaaainian', Levin would grow more and more irate until, almost always, he erupted at me. There was a sentence I constantly repeated – 'The weight of the photo spreads is double zero' – which Levin loathed, precisely because it was so true, and he would lose his temper almost every time I said it. The same was true of the word 'unambiguously'. The more appropriate the context in which I used this word, the more angry Levin would get. These outbursts, beginning about half-way through the trial, gave me much pleasure and satisfaction, because most of them came at my own invitation.

In the final stages of the trial this talent of mine had become so sophisticated that I would tell my fellow defence attorneys, on our way to the theatre, 'Today at nine-forty-five, ten-thirty and twelve-fifteen Dovele will go crazy.'

At first they would ask, 'How do you know?'

'I'm going to make little provocations at those times, and he will lose his composure completely,' I would answer. Later they stopped asking, because all my predictions were correct.

During the final arguments this reached perfection. Eyal Megged, a childhood friend, came to court during all the defence's summations. Just before they began we drove from my home to Jerusalem, and I took two books with me: Menachem Begin's *White Nights*, which deals with Begin's detainment as a political prisoner by the KGB, and Berl Katznelson's *Writings*, Volume V. Surprised, Eyal asked, 'Why do you need those books for your final arguments?' 'To annoy Dovele,' I responded, 'when I quote from them.' Eyal sat in the first row and burst out laughing at Levin's reaction when I made use of the two books. He did this each time Levin lost his composure, as if I had ordered it in advance, whether it was my use of the name 'Miroslaaaaaavski', or when I said that 'The Travniki document wanders through the identification testimonies like a bull in a chiiiiina shop.'

All lawyers who appear frequently in court have catalogues of instances and circumstances in which the judges did not treat them fairly. I doubt, however, whether these catalogues include any such important trial in which the judges behaved in such an unacceptable way as these three, Levin in particular, behaved in the Demjanjuk trial. Levin's hostility to me and his partiality were so blatant that, despite the public malice towards me and the media's sycophantic propaganda exalting the judges, it happened at times that passers-by or taxi drivers would turn to me and say, 'That Demjanjuk should definitely be hanged, that's clear. But all the same, Judge Levin is acting as if he is the chief prosecutor and not the presiding judge.'

During the appeal, as I finished my arguments about the improper conduct of Levin and his colleagues, I said: 'As a result, the defendant's trial in the lower court was a travesty, not a fair trial.' Two years after that, Judge Haim Cohen gave an interview to the local newspaper *Al Hasharon*, and expressed the same idea in a much sharper way. 'It was a spectacular for the people. Any resemblance to justice was purely coincidental.' This travesty of a trial will always be, justifiably, a stain on the Israeli system of justice.

In retrospect I must say that even though the court's attitude towards me – and Levin's in particular – was unpleasant from time to time, and once even brought me to the point of collapse, I would never have evinced the fighting spirit, devotion and determination that I showed in this case had the judges not behaved as they did. I believe that this, more than anything else, led to my being able to present the Supreme Court with more than eighty pieces of evidence that turned the judgement of the special district court into a laughing stock for the entire world. It was my sweet revenge on Dovele and his colleagues for all they had done to me.

9 · To the Gallows

In most trials, I wait for the verdict in suspense. This time, however, there was no suspense or tension, because I knew precisely what the result would be. I had no doubt at all that Demjanjuk would be found guilty and that he would be sentenced to death.

This had been my feeling from the trial's very first day, and it only increased during the weeks that followed. A month into the show-trial I was already certain that, no matter what facts were brought before the court, at the end of the process Demjanjuk would be convicted and sent to the gallows. The day before the decision was handed down I voiced my opinion in a newspaper interview: 'Personally, I feel fine. I am not in suspense because I have no illusions about the verdict. I have been predicting the bottom line, and the reasons for it, for more than a year, and I've conveyed it to my client and his family. They value my frankness. It is the first time in years that they have not been humoured, that they have not been given false promises.'

The final session took place on 22 March 1988. It was convened to hear final arguments on the new evidence submitted by the defence. Judge Levin adjourned it with the following words: 'You will receive notification of the reading of the verdict. You will be informed – I hope – within two or three weeks. We will let you know sufficiently in advance.' I called Nishnic; I estimated, from what Levin had said, that the verdict would be handed down sometime in mid-April, and the family should make travel arrangements accordingly.

I gave him a detailed report on the last three sessions, which had all dealt with the new evidence, and he was disappointingly optimistic about its bearing on the verdict. He was convinced it would bring about Demjanjuk's acquittal. 'The new evidence, especially Danilchenko's statement, clearly shows, as you explained in court, that the prosecution's identification evidence is unreliable. It is so clear that Shaked himself asked to halt the trial so he could find out what was going on,' Nishnic told me more than once during that conversation. My response was unambiguous: 'Levin will write the judgement, and you know very well that he refused Shaked's suggestion that the trial be postponed. If any other indication of the imminent conviction were needed, Levin's refusal is it.' I finished by saying, for the umpteenth time, 'Ed, this trial would end in conviction even if we were to bring the real Ivan the Terrible to the theatre in Binyanei Ha'uma and he even confessed to being Ivan the Terrible.' Nishnic was not persuaded.

Surprisingly, the new evidence and the hearings at which it was presented attracted a great deal of attention. During the four weeks until the verdict was announced, several lawyers told me that they considered the new material very impressive, and that it was adequate to establish a reasonable doubt about the quality and weight of the identification evidence. Ironically, I found myself arguing heatedly with them. Even Doron's position had changed. Now he believed that, in light of the implications of the new evidence, a miracle acquittal could not be ruled out; if there were no acquittal, there might at least be a minority opinion from Judge Tal. Even this seemed wildly improbable to me.

On Saturday 16 April, a few days after my office was notified of the date on which the verdict would be handed down, the Demjanjuk family arrived in Israel, this time in full force. I met them that evening at the American Colony Hotel. Nishnic was practically certain that two days hence he would be leaving Israel with his father-in-law. Johnny was much more realistic, but he also had a spark of hope that a miracle might happen. The same was true of Vera. Irene and Lydia were very pessimistic.

On Sunday Gill and Chumak also arrived in the country, and that evening Nishnic called what turned out to be a pathetic meeting between himself, Johnny and the three defence attorneys. The subject was ensuring Demjanjuk's safety from the moment his acquittal was announced until he left Israel. All my protests against even holding such a discussion were swept aside. As the only Israeli lawyer in the group, I was supposed to outline various plans of action in case of Demjanjuk's acquittal. This I did, repeatedly pointing out the folly of even raising each of the alternatives.

Gill and Chumak agreed without reservation that Demjanjuk would be convicted. Since the new material contained no positive proof that Demjanjuk was not Ivan the Terrible it could not save him. For the whole day I repeated many times, especially to Nishnic, that all the labour and effort I had invested had but one goal – to prepare a strong factual basis for the legal arguments in the appeal.

On the Friday morning I had visited Demjanjuk in his cell. He was agitated, and so was I. It was the first (and the last) time in my life that I had to tell a client of mine that within a few days he would be sentenced to death. It was only natural that I did not know how to put this. In recent months I had told him over and over again that, despite the impressive evidence the defence had presented, nothing would help; in the end he would be found guilty and sent to the gallows. Now, however, it was three days before the verdict, and the gallows had become almost tangible.

At the beginning of our meeting I told him about his family's imminent arrival. At the end I told him: 'We will be seeing each other in court again three days from now. As I have been telling you for a while, all the evidence we have brought will not help you. This court will convict you and sentence you to death.' Demjanjuk was tense, but his face remained placid and he did not respond. I added: 'I hope very sincerely that you and your family think that I did everything I could to represent you in the best possible way.'

'I am sure of that and I want to tell you that I was not sure whether my family was right about O'Connor. But now I see that they were right, and I am certain that we did the right thing when we got rid of him and brought you in his place,' he responded. He said this with evident emotion. I decided to touch on an additional point that disturbed me.

'Precisely because the court is going to find you guilty and sentence you to death, I fervently request that, primarily for your own sake, you behave respectfully and politely, as you have during the entire trial. Don't burst out shouting and don't behave discourteously.' Demjanjuk gave his word.

On the day of the verdict, I ate breakfast with the Demjanjuk family and lawyers. The atmosphere was gloomy. Nishnic, as usual, asked me whether I still held to my pessimistic view. 'I'm ninety-nine-point-nine per cent sure that the sentence will be death,' I said unhesitatingly. 'I'm not saying one hundred per cent only because nothing has actually happened yet.'

At close to eight-fifteen the hall was already packed. Most of those present were media people and Holocaust survivors, with a few politicians thrown in. To my great surprise, the audience was in suspense: not all of them were as sure of the result as I. During breakfast I had explained to my fellow lawyers and the family that even though the court would apparently take hours to read the judgement it would be possible to know the result at once. According to Israeli law, when the verdict is 'not guilty' it is announced at once, and only afterwards are the reasons for the acquittal read, if at all. If the court did not immediately declare Demjanjuk not guilty, it meant that it had decided to convict him.

When we entered the hall, the prosecution team were already in their places. To my surprise, they too seemed tense. Whilst they were well aware that the evidence they had presented in court was flimsy, especially in light of the counter-evidence presented by the defence, they must also have been aware of the court's bias. There was no reason for them to be in suspense.

The courtroom had never been so full of reporters. As befits a show-trial, the government press office did all it could to make sure that every reporter and every TV and radio station in the country relayed the verdict to every corner of the world; their efforts, of course, were crowned with success. The din made by the various instruments of the various media – clicks, whirrs etc. – created the familiar atmosphere, utterly unlike that which is supposed to prevail in court.

In the mean time we were urgently summoned to Demjanjuk's cell. There we discovered that, as on several other occasions during the trial, Demjanjuk had severe back pain. He was stretched out on the bed in his cell. Despite the injection of muscle relaxant he received, he did not look as if he could sit in the courtroom. Perhaps the awareness that he was going to be found guilty did not give him much motivation to overcome his pain and be present in court. Demjanjuk was absent from the entire session, lying in his cell, wearing earphones to hear the verdict, translated simultaneously into Ukrainian.

The judges took their places. All three wore serious and slightly worried expressions. Levin opened: 'Good-morning, please be seated, criminal case 373/86, State of Israel versus Ivan John Demjanjuk, court session of 1 Iyar 5748, 18 April 1988.' Gill rose. 'Your Honours, there are some unexpected difficulties this morning. Mr Demjanjuk has back pains. I request that the court open the session without the defendant's presence.' There had been other instances in which there had not been silence when the judges entered the courtroom, but this time Gill's words were completely drowned by the commotion among the press and audience, and the reporters barely reacted to the judges' presence in the hall. The prosecution did not object to the session being held without Demjanjuk. Levin decided: 'We accede to the defence's request and we will begin reading the verdict in his absence.'

He then explained that part of the judgement would be read in full, part in summary, and part would be skipped. He also stressed that the parts would not necessarily be read in order of their appearance in the written judgement. After a few introductory words on the shocking magnitude of the deeds described in the charge sheet, Levin proceeded to read the judgement itself. After five minutes it was clear that it was a conviction. I could easily see Shaked sighing with relief. The audience, however, did not know. The tension began to subside only in the afternoon, when most of the audience and the press realized, after hearing the commentary on the radio, what it all meant.

Once I was convinced that Demjanjuk had been convicted, I told Gill and Chumak and then made a sign to Nishnic, who passed the word on to the rest of the family in the front row. An hour later, with Levin still reading details about Treblinka, entirely divorced from the specific charges against Demjanjuk, I decided to step out of the courtroom for a while. I was surprised to find how undisturbed I was by the conviction. Perhaps Demjanjuk's absence contributed to this. When Nishnic noticed me leaving he left as well, and less than a minute later Johnny joined us. Nishnic was very upset, having been so disappointed. Both of them asked me what to expect next. I explained that after the reading of the judgement, which would take a few more hours, there would probably be arguments on the sentence. The prosecution would doubtless ask for the death penalty, and it was equally certain that the court would grant this request. My opinion was that it would be best to finish the whole business that day. 'In any case, the moment it is decided that Demjanjuk is Ivan the Terrible, he will be sent to the gallows,' I explained. 'If he isn't, everyone will think the court actually has some doubts about his guilt.'

Members of the foreign and national press approached us. I agreed to make the following brief statement: 'I am so unsurprised that I am not even disappointed. Disappointment is a matter of expectations. I expected conviction from the end of the trial's first month. However, I am one hundred per cent certain that, given the evidence that has been presented, Demjanjuk should have been acquitted. The verdict is fundamentally in error and there can be no doubt that we will appeal.' Johnny was much more outspoken: 'Justice has not been done in this trial. The court did all it could to provide a foundation for the prosecution arguments and to challenge the defence arguments. The decision is based solely on the emotions of the Holocaust survivors. It is a real disgrace. When the world looks at this trial, people will say that Demjanjuk was the victim of Israeli justice.'

During the morning break, the members of Demjanjuk's family decided not to return to the courtroom. The main reason was that it became clear that Demjanjuk would not participate in the rest of that day's session. His wife and daughters were not really surprised by what had happened; still, they wiped tears from their eyes. Gill, Chumak and I held a consultation. A decision had been taking form, and was now agreed, to ask that the sentencing hearing be held immediately after the reading of the judgement. Gill would sum up for the defence, while I would argue the legal point that the death penalty prescribed by the

Law for the Punishment of Nazis and their Collaborators, 1950, was not mandatory. The court had discretion over whether or not to impose the death sentence.

After the break, the noise in the courtroom was intolerable. The audience was bored, and many people chatted amongst themselves to pass the time. Even though I sat in the courtroom straight through to the noon break, I did not listen. I did not want to get angry. In any case, I would have to spend long days analysing every paragraph in the verdict. All kinds of odd thoughts passed through my head; I especially recall the moments when I reflected that from this point on I was no longer the defence attorney of a man accused of being Ivan the Terrible, but of a man that a court of law had already determined *was* Ivan the Terrible. Such a thought would have made me shiver fifteen months previously, but not now. This was but a formal, unjustified conviction, so I was not especially upset about this change in my status.

During this recess I gave a short interview to Israel Television. Like the other local media, this TV station had been a constant mouthpiece for the prosecution. I repeated my unequivocal position that the court should have acquitted Demjanjuk, but because of the improper way in which the trial had been conducted Demjanjuk had been convicted, as I had predicted from the start. When this was broadcast on the news, an attorney who was also a former Member of the Knesset filed a complaint against me with the Ethics Committee of the Israel Bar Association, claiming that my statement was tantamount to contempt of court. It was a lovely surprise to find that the complaint was rejected outright, without my having to respond to it.

We returned to the American Colony in the afternoon. The entire Demjanjuk family was there. I could not give them any news, nor could I even tell them what Levin had said, since I had not listened.

As seven p.m. approached, the noise in the courtroom grew. The judges were approaching the paragraph that would state explicitly that Demjanjuk was Ivan the Terrible from the Treblinka extermination camp. Fifteen minutes later, the bench declared: 'We determine, unequivocally and without any ambivalence or doubt, that the defendant Ivan John Demjanjuk, on trial before us, is Ivan, called Ivan Grozhny, Ivan the Terrible, operator of the gas chambers at Treblinka and perpetrator of the acts of cruelty and abuse described above.' There was a huge eruption of applause throughout the courtroom. It did not stop even when Levin had finished reading the paragraph. I could see the expression of contentment and satisfaction on his face. As soon as he finished reading, he directed a long look at me, as if to say, 'Did you really think there would be any other result?' I tried to return him a look that said: 'You should know very well, Dovele, that I never even dreamed there could be any other result with you as presiding judge.'

Finally the applause died down, but the buzz of the crowd did not end until the session was adjourned. Many of the people there seemed to have expected that Levin would soon say, 'And we therefore sentence the defendant to death.' I again found myself wondering at the impassivity that pervaded me, despite what I had just witnessed. I glanced at the courtroom and thought to myself that the applause heard in the theatre at the end of the show-trial's last act was a fitting finale for the outrageous legal spectacle that had played here for the last fourteen months.

The reading of the judgement went on for another fifteen minutes or so. When it ended, with a list of the specific articles of law under which Demjanjuk had been convicted, Levin said, 'Since we have convicted the defendant of the crimes attributed to him, the time has come to hold a hearing on his punishment. It is late, and I assume you will wish to read the material and formulate a position. So I suggest that the sentencing arguments be heard next Monday, 25 April 1988, at eight-thirty.' The noise from the audience was so bad that he could not continue. 'Silence, please,' he said, and then added, 'We have given notification and that is the date, unless there is a comment or request.'

It would obviously not be possible to conduct a hearing on the sentencing that same day, as we had wished. Gill therefore asked that the hearing be held the next morning. Levin agreed: 'If that is the defendant's wish, we are willing to schedule it for tomorrow morning.' But Blatman rose and objected strenuously, even when Gill suggested holding the session the next afternoon. In the end, Levin decided to return to the first date – 25 April.

The judgement took up 444 pages and was divided into 118 chapters. Thirty-six of them contained a detailed description of Treblinka and the horrifying extermination process that was pursued there from the summer of 1942 to the autumn of 1943. The rest of the judgement was packed with discredited factual findings and baseless, untenable legal conclusions. Not only was it fundamentally in error; it also suffered from an amazing arrogance. The judges explained over and over again not only why Demjanjuk was Ivan the Terrible, but also why there could be no error in this determination.

The foundation of the error in the verdict, as in all the factual findings that led to it, was the court's view of its mission: chapter 19 of the judgement bears the title 'Memorial'. What is a memorial doing in the judgement of a criminal trial? The final paragraph of this chapter explains:

We will, in our judgement, make, according to the entirety of the evidence before us, a memorial to the souls of the holy communities that have been lost and which are no more, to those who were annihilated and who were not brought to a Jewish grave, because no remnant nor survivor of them remains. To those who were thrown to the flames and whose children are dust and ashes fertilizing the fields of Poland, from which they brought forth food in their lives and on which they found their terrible deaths.

Erecting a memorial to the millions of Jews killed in that unparalleled holocaust is indeed a sacred and noble task. But when the judgement in a criminal trial pretends to this, the result is a shameful legal process that defiles the memory of the Jewish people slaughtered at Treblinka.

This paragraph proved that the trial was practically decided in advance. The court had allowed the prosecution to bring testimonies about the horrors of the Holocaust in general and about Treblinka in particular, even though the defence did not contest these facts. It did so in order to base its judgement on the 'entirety of the evidence', to make it a 'memorial'. The trappings of a theatre hall, and direct radio and TV broadcasts, were all meant to glorify the show-trial and present it to the public as a memorial-building project. From a legal point of view, of course, it was a mockery of justice. In a criminal trial such as this one the accused had no chance of acquittal.

In a show-trial in which the possibility of the defendant being found innocent is excluded, any legal criterion that makes it difficult to convict must be ignored. The following paragraph from the judgement gives an example of this: 'The more the court is deeply persuaded of the witnesses' reliability, and the more it is clearly impressed by the identifying witness's memory, by his sharp eyes and his power of discrimination, it is the court's duty to decide the case on the basis of the factual truth deriving from the entirety of the evidence, even if the guidelines were not precisely and fully applied.' In other words, if the court believes that the survivors' testimonies as heard in the courtroom may be trusted, then it may ignore the fact that the photo spreads preceding the testimonies were not conducted in accordance with the guidelines. This position is diametrically opposed to the establishments of Israeli precedent. Dozens of Supreme Court decisions have ruled that the court's impression of an identification witness during his testimony is not sufficient: it must receive confirmation that the photo spreads preceding the testimony were correctly administered. Only then may it decide to base a conviction on the testimony. For example, one of those rulings states: 'Because of the great risk that the witness's identification might be mistaken, and that this will sweep the court along with it, rules have been developed concerning the way to conduct a photo spread – rules that are meant to ensure that the witness's identification of the suspect is the outcome of his best perception and memory, and not the result of influences that divert the witness's perception, consciously or unconsciously, turning the merely possible into the certain.'

In the trial's central issue, the identification, the court (discussing the weight to be given to Rosenberg's identification) established the following criterion: 'It is the initial reaction that tells first and foremost about the visual impression, analytic ability and the precision and reliability of the identification.' Accordingly, the court could determine that Rosenberg's identification had a 'high level of certainty'. Anyone reading Levin and co. on the criterion for granting such a high grade to Rosenberg's identification would assume that Reichman's 'identification' would not be given any weight at all by the court – after all, it had taken him three hours. But here the judges reached the opposite conclusions: 'Reichman examined all the photographs over and over again – for three hours, he said – and when he reached a conclusion that he could stand by, he pointed to the picture of the defendant and said, "I believe that this is the picture of Ivan from Treblinka."' From here it is only a small step to grant Reichman's identification of Demjanjuk the same 'high level of certainty' as Rosenberg's. So, if the criterion of 'initial reaction' is not appropriate to the identifying witness, the judges have no problem casting it aside and replacing it with an opposite criterion: as they wrote in their misleading language, 'It is very important to mention that the identification ... was not rushed, but came after a serious, responsible and lengthy examination of each picture.'

These passages from the judgement are but the tip of the iceberg. Dozens more gems of this type are strewn throughout its length. I have no doubt that Israeli legal history will name this as the most shameful legal document ever written in the Hebrew language. Retired judge Dov Eitan, who was to appear with me in the appeal to the Supreme Court, drew my attention to these two passages, as well as to many others, as we prepared for the appeal. 'Sheftel, my young friend,' he told me then, 'take it from me, as someone who spent seventeen years on the bench, we are dealing here not with an error, but with something much more serious.' He meant deliberate deceit.

As expected, the Israeli media's opinion of the quality and significance of the judgement did not chime with mine. Having prejudged Demjanjuk while the trial was in progress, the press could only praise the court for walking the furrow they had ploughed. On the day after the judgement was read, the Israeli newspapers carried huge headlines: DEMJANJUK GUILTY ON ALL COUNTS; ALL OVER; DEFENDANT IS IVAN THE TERRIBLE; NO DOUBT, THE MAN BEFORE US IS IVAN THE TERRIBLE; DEMJANJUK CONVICTED OF CAPITAL CRIMES; JUDGES: 'YOU ARE IVAN THE TERRIBLE.' Articles cited the court's fairness and said the judges performed their assignment honestly, diligently and disinterestedly. So, for instance, an editorial in *Ha'aretz*: 'The court carefully observed every letter of accepted criminal procedure; the defence enjoyed absolute freedom, and exploited it to the limit. It cannot complain that it was not allowed to bring witnesses and documents it considered vital . . . It was an exemplary criminal trial and the State of Israel may be proud of it.' Journalist Yosef Lapid of *Ma'ariv* published a long article under the headline DEMJANJUK, YOU ARE THE KILLER, recounting the crimes Demjanjuk supposedly committed at Treblinka. These, of course, are only two amongst dozens of pieces. More than three years later, when the fact that Ivan Marchenko, and not Demjanjuk, was Ivan the Terrible began to sink into the press's consciousness, both Lapid and a *Ha'aretz* editorial demanded that the prosecution not wait for the Supreme Court's decision but announce its willingness to accept Demjanjuk's appeal. In their opinions it was impossible to defend the lower court's conviction in the light of the facts that had been revealed. For some reason they forgot to explain to their readers how this 'exemplary criminal trial' that Israel 'could be proud of' had turned into a trial in which the prosecution should accept the defence's appeal. I need hardly say that they also forgot to apologize to Demjanjuk for what they had written three years previously.

The Demjanjuk family decided to remain in Israel until the sentencing. I felt obliged to be with them the evening after the verdict was handed down, since it had been such a horrible day for them. No one blamed me, even during these difficult hours; quite the opposite – they repeatedly stressed that their finger of accusation was pointed at the court. 'You did all you could. My family and I do not hold it against you. In fact, I want to thank you for everything you have done for us under such difficult conditions. I very much hope that you will continue to represent us in the appeal,' Nishnic told me as we sat with the whole family in the American Colony's well-tended garden. Of course I immediately expressed my willingness to continue as their attorney during the appeals process.

Before I fell asleep that night, the thought again passed through my mind that according to the verdict, which everyone would praise and commend, I had become 'Satan's' lawyer. I could imagine the reactions of friends, acquaintances, and strangers who might recognize me in the street. Yet this would not diminish my determination to prove that Demjanjuk's conviction was based on a horrible error.

Two days later I visited Demjanjuk in his cell. His backache had subsided; he looked better and was in a good mood. He even joked with me, asking if I would still speak to him now that he had been officially declared Ivan the Terrible. To my surprise, he then began a tirade against O'Connor. 'He should be ashamed of himself. I read in the *Jerusalem Post* that O'Connor said the trial was fair. He himself used to tell me all the time that the judges would do everything the government told them to do.' Then he said something he would repeat many times in the years to come: 'How can a court do such a thing in a democratic country like Israel? Shaked and Blatman, they're not so good, but maybe you can understand them. They're prosecutors and they're doing their job. That's why I'm not angry at them. But that's why there's a court, after all.'

The media fanfare for the verdict did not in the least change the friendly relations between the prison guards and Demjanjuk, which was a gratifying surprise. On this visit they were joking, laughing and exchanging banter. Nor was there any tightening of the security regulations, and his family were allowed to visit him every day.

Our conversation dealt largely with what could be expected from the next session, for the sentencing pleadings; and from the sentence, which would be pronounced at the end. I gave Demjanjuk the facts, in unambiguous language. 'Just as I told you in the clearest possible way before the previous session that they would find you guilty, I am telling you with the same certainty that Levin and his colleagues will send you to the gallows.'

'I know, I know,' Demjanjuk responded. His indifference surprised me. Suddenly he pointed to a picture hanging on the wall. It was of his grandson, Eddie. 'I still hope the truth will come out and I'll be able to see Eddie at home in Cleveland some day.' He said this with great emotion and I noticed that his eyes were moist. I had never seen him so worked up.

I felt uncomfortable for a few seconds then said, 'I hope for your sake that you will.'

Then, as before the verdict session, I entreated him to act respectfully and not be tempted into improper behaviour. Before the sentence was passed and after Gill had completed his pleading, Demjanjuk would have the right to the last word. 'It is most desirable that you take advantage of this to declare your innocence once again, but in a well-mannered and courteous way. This will, more than anything else, preserve your honour.'

'What should I say?' he asked.

'Gill will say everything that needs to be said from a legal point of view. What you need to do is to speak from your heart, your own truth, and you must prepare it alone. It's the kind of thing that is best done without a lawyer's advice and guidance.' Demjanjuk promised that he would do as I asked and be on good behaviour. I left after about an hour and a half, promising to visit once more before the hearing.

By now the media had launched a spirited debate on whether Demjanjuk should receive the death penalty or not. The majority of journalists and commentators supported sentencing him to death. Minister of Justice Avraham Sharir outdid them all by demanding the death penalty in an interview he gave to the Israeli defence forces' radio station. Such blatant public intervention by a government minister in a matter under the court's sole discretion was both unprecedented and, on several counts, illegal. This appalling action demonstrated that Sharir had no conception of the principles by which a democratic country functions; of how a person of his standing, in his position, should behave. Furthermore, the statement by the Minister of Justice could only be interpreted as clear instructions to the court on what sentence it should impose. But imposing the death penalty in such circumstances would be seen as the court's accession to the demands of the executive. Once again no one from the media or the Israeli legal community denounced this flagrant and disgraceful violation of judicial independence.

Because I was absolutely certain about what would happen, I was not nervous about the sentencing. It was enough to realize that the judgement had not instigated a new wave of attacks on me, as I had feared, though there was a distinct note of *Schadenfreude* in the press. My mother, however, took Demjanjuk's conviction very badly, and saw it as the inevitable beginning of a troubled period for me. For her, even though Levin had been unfair and unscrupulous, the fact remained that Demjanjuk was Ivan the Terrible. She felt that, even if I was right to say there was no real evidence proving this, it had still been clear in advance that Demjanjuk would not be acquitted, and so I had made a dreadful mistake in deciding to be his defence attorney.

The prosecution, taking no chances with the sentence, leaked to the press that it intended to demand the death penalty. It did not do this in an official press release – which was tantamount to beginning its arguments in the newspapers. On the Monday morning, then, the entire population knew what Blatman and Shaked were going to demand. So the court convened in just the right atmosphere.

The day before the session I went to the prison to see Demjanjuk. I arrived shortly after his family had left, and he was very emotional. He understood what sentence he would receive the next day, but still he asked what was going to happen, as if he were trying to preserve some spark of hope. 'I'm sorry to say that I have nothing new to tell you since our previous meeting, and our many other conversations. Levin will send you to the gallows.' Once again, but this time with even more emotion, Demjanjuk expressed his shock and protest against the court that had found him guilty. I wanted to encourage him, but did not know how. Under no circumstances would I voice optimistic predictions about the appeal. It was the worst conversation I had had with Demjanjuk, every second was a nightmare. After swearing him again to behave respectably in court, and checking that he would take advantage of his right to have the last word, we turned to part. Demjanjuk shook my hand warmly, saying: 'I know you have done everything for me, and I thank you.' It was satisfying to hear this on precisely this occasion, the evening before my efforts were to be rewarded with total failure.

I spent the night at the American Colony. Gill, Chumak and I concluded that the sentencing pleading should be a purely legal one; Gill would not cite 'personal circumstances'. This is an important component of every sentencing pleading, analysing the defendant's character, lifestyle and occupation to justify a lesser punishment. In Demjanjuk's case, any such argument would sound ridiculous, and might even be interpreted as an implicit acknowledgement of his guilt. Furthermore, we were aware that Levin might try to draw us into such an argument, in an effort to make the defence look bad.

So Gill would argue that even though the court had convicted Demjanjuk and determined beyond all doubt that he was Ivan the Terrible, legal history includes many mistaken judgements in which a man who had been executed was discovered to be innocent. Such mistakes are especially common in cases where the trial and conviction centred on the issue of identification. This was the focus of Demjanjuk's trial, and for this reason alone the penalty should be something less than death. I would present arguments only if the prosecution were to argue that the death penalty was mandatory in law and that the court had no discretion in the matter.

I retired to my room early. As I lay on my bed, scenes that I would imagine again and again during the next two years passed before my eyes. They were of Demjanjuk's execution. I saw myself wondering whether to exercise my right, as an attorney, to be present at the execution. It seemed to me that my absence would be an act of cowardice, a flight from reality. I imagined Demjanjuk passing me in the dim corridor of an undefined prison. It was not clear where the corridor began or where it led. Demjanjuk, wearing shorts and a vest, slippers on his feet, held out his hand to me. I was confused and did not know what to do or say. All I could do was shake the extended hand in silence. Suddenly, Demjanjuk's wife appeared in the corridor and my bewilderment grew. Afterwards there was a muffled thud, and a few minutes later a man in prison guard's uniform appeared and notified me that Demjanjuk had been executed. I sank into a deep despair at having been unable to prevent it.

I wallowed in such imaginings until finally, after an hour, I got up and chided myself: You're showing weakness again, getting yourself depressed by a difficult situation. Within minutes I was recovering; the apparitions vanished. I slept soundly, despite the unpleasantness that awaited me the next day.

A few minutes before eight-thirty in the morning, Gill, Chumak and I entered the courtroom and took our places. The hall was noisy, churning, overflowing, people filling the side aisles, and there were again dozens of cameras avidly flashing and clicking. There was so much din that we had to raise our voices to hear each other. Gill was a bit tense, but Chumak and I were calm. About two minutes later Demjanjuk was brought in in a wheelchair. He had hurt his back on the way, and he was clearly in pain. This time, however, he made an effort to endure it. He remained in the wheelchair throughout the session. His tension and anxiety were obvious, and his face was flushed. As soon as he was in his place, I reminded him of his promise to behave respectfully, and he repeated it.

As we were speaking, the judges entered the courtroom. 'Good-morning, please be seated, criminal case 373/86, State of Israel versus John Ivan Demjanjuk, court session of 8 Iyar 5748, 25 April 1988,' Levin announced, but he could barely be heard over the uproar. The judges looked very nervous. They knew that within a few minutes they would be sending Demjanjuk to the gallows. Only after Levin called the court to order was it possible to continue.

Blatman was given the floor. The State Attorney spent a whole hour trying to persuade the court that it had no discretion. According to his interpretation of the law, the court was required to sentence Demjanjuk to death. Knowing Levin, I realized he would take advantage of Blatman's argument to make a show of being benevolent, but would nevertheless send Demjanjuk to be hanged. In fact the judges indicated, during the course of Blatman's arguments, that they rejected his interpretation unequivocally, basing themselves on the language of the law.

I rose to respond. Levin, however, in keeping with his comments on

Blatman's arguments, ruled: 'We release the defence from responding [to the argument that the death sentence was mandatory].' So Gill said his piece on the possibility of hanging an innocent man. During his speech the audience played an active part – there were catcalls, shouts and groans. When this became absolutely intolerable, Levin deigned to intervene. 'I previously requested, and I request again, we will not tolerate any interference from the audience, neither vocal nor whispered. The defence attorney has a right to say what he is saying, and we must consider what he says and decide. The audience will listen and not decide.' Gill concluded: 'Even if the evidence is sufficient for conviction, it is inadequate for the death penalty, and I therefore request that the death penalty not be imposed on the defendant.' He then submitted a long and comprehensive paper to the court, referring to dozens of cases in the current century alone in which defendants executed by American courts had later been found to be innocent.

Before sitting down, Gill asked that Demjanjuk be given the privilege of having the last word. Levin responded: 'It is not a matter of privilege, it is his right to be the person to have the last word and we will certainly grant him that right.' Yet again Levin was trying to sabotage the defence and make it look ridiculous. Just as I had expected, he asked: 'Have you no further arguments that you wish to make with regard to the defendant's circumstances?' I rose and said: 'In light of our intention of appealing the verdict, we see no point in going into those subjects that courts generally consider with regard to punishment. We believe that, given the circumstances of this case, any argument based on the defendant's personal circumstances is liable to be taken to imply a certain admission of the facts of his conviction. There will therefore be no defence argument beyond that presented by Mr Gill.' Levin then addressed Demjanjuk. 'The defendant has the right to have the final word. If the defendant wishes to say something, he will please do so.'

Demjanjuk spoke for about five minutes in a fairly sure voice, with just the slightest tremor. 'I believe that there was an executioner named Ivan Grozhny at Treblinka, and that he tormented the Jewish people, and that the prisoners at Treblinka called him Ivan the Terrible. But I, Ivan Demjanjuk, was never that executioner. Last week, Your Honours recognized me as Ivan the Terrible. That is a great error, a very great one, because I am not Ivan the Terrible, as God is my witness. He knows that I am innocent ... You must sentence Ivan the Terrible, but your sentence will not be for Ivan the Terrible but for someone else, because you have not judged him. You judged another man entirely, Ivan Demjanjuk, an innocent man. I am innocent and it is too bad, too bad.' He closed by saying, 'I am very surprised that in the Holy Land, in a democratic country like Israel, in the twentieth century, such an injustice can happen. I am innocent, as God is my witness. Thank you very much.'

I was pleasantly surprised. Even a simple and uneducated man like Demjanjuk, when facing a court about to send him to the gallows for a crime he did not commit, may rise above himself and make an orderly speech. His cry of protest was impressive, well-mannered and intelligent. 'I really appreciate your keeping your promise,' I told him as soon as he finished. 'What you said was very impressive; too bad it won't have any effect on the court.' I observed the faces of Levin and his colleagues as Demjanjuk spoke. I could see that they rejected, even disdained his words. He who laughs last laughs longest, I thought. Future generations, their scholars and jurists, will have contempt not for Demjanjuk, but for the sentence his judges imposed on him.

'We will go out for consultations. We will give notice when we are ready with the sentence. The sides will wait,' Levin said. He was not heard because of the clamour in the courtroom, which had begun to look like a football pitch surrounded by terraces packed with unruly fans. As we made our way out there were again shouts of the type that had accompanied us throughout the trial. We were kept waiting, and the delay kindled a spark of hope in Johnny. 'Maybe they'll surprise us despite everything, maybe they don't fully agree.'

'I wish you were right,' I answered, 'but I'm afraid you're not.' Gill and Chumak too were certain that the long break did not indicate any kind of surprise. We were recalled to the courtroom at about two in the afternoon.

The hall was seething like a cauldron. The show-trial's climax had arrived, the moment Demjanjuk would be sent to the gallows. I was greeted with curses and insults. When the judges entered, the courtroom fell relatively quiet. Levin turned to Gill and asked: 'Does the defendant still wish to remain seated, Mr Gill?' Gill responded: 'Yes, Your Honours, he has a bad back.' Then Levin said: 'My colleague, Judge Tal, will read the sentence.'

It took about fifteen minutes, and contained the following language: 'We are indeed aware of the danger of imposing an irreversible punishment ... But we ruled in our judgement, without any hesitation and without a shadow of doubt, that the defendant before us is Ivan the Terrible from Treblinka ... What punishment should be imposed on this Ivan the Terrible? A man who murdered tens of thousands and who murdered individuals, torturing and abusing them in their final moments before being sent to their deaths, what sentence should be passed on him? Even a thousand deaths will not atone for his deeds;

hands of flesh and blood cannot reach far enough to give him his deserts ... True, the defendant is not Eichmann. He did not initiate the extermination, nor did he organize death camps for millions, but he served as chief executioner, and eagerly killed myriads with his own hands, and tortured and humiliated and abused and persecuted the miserable. We therefore sentence him, for the crimes of which he has been convicted, to death, in accordance with Section 1 of the Law for the Punishment of Nazis and their Collaborators, 1950.'

Hearing these harsh words, Demjanjuk crossed himself and shook his head. Levin closed the show by saying: 'We have concluded the session. The defendant has the right to appeal the verdict and the sentence, and in fact, in the case of the death penalty, it is obligatory to appeal the verdict. We have concluded the hearing before us and we thank all those who have worked on it.'

An ignoble backdrop befits such an ignoble sentence. The minute the word 'death' escaped Judge Tal's lips, a terrible commotion began in the courtroom. All the disorder there had been up to then was merely naughtiness compared to the chaos that erupted now. The unruly crowd began cursing, shouting and screaming insults. 'Death, death,' 'Death to Ivan,' 'Death to the defence attorney,' 'Death to all Ukrainians,' 'Death, death, death!' The people were dancing, stamping their feet, waving fists in the air. There had been so many disturbances and displays of violence, but this time my heart skipped a beat. The mob was ready to lynch anyone who got in its way. I stayed in my seat and watched. Here, I thought, this is the disgraceful, but apt, finale to Ivan Demjanjuk's show-trial. Whenever I remember that grotesque sight I think that, as the mob shouted, 'Death to the defence attorney,' it could just as easily have shouted, 'Death to the judges,' had the trial not ended in the death penalty. After watching this uproar for several long minutes, I was fed up. My colleagues, shocked by what was happening around them, left the hall with me.

Vera Demjanjuk was waiting impatiently for us at the hotel. We told her about the sentence, and she received the bitter news with a rigid, terrified face. Johnny arrived about an hour later, furious and upset. We all went to the bar to calm down. I gave Johnny some encouragement, and a few minutes later he asked me if I would be willing to stay on for the appeal. I agreed without hesitation. As far as I was concerned, the Demjanjuk affair was not over. It had only just begun.

The media celebration began that same day, and the morning headlines continued to shout: VICTORY-CRIES, FISTS AND SCREAMS; A THOUSAND DEATHS WILL NOT ATONE FOR HIS DEEDS; HE MUST DIE; SENTENCE: DEATH; THERE IS JUSTICE AND THERE IS VENGEANCE; DEATH

SENTENCE FOR IVAN THE TERRIBLE OF TREBLINKA; CHIEF EXECUTIONER TO BE EXECUTED – all plastered in huge letters on the front pages. Not one word of criticism was heard. The shadow of the gallows obliterated the light of reason. The only voice of protest was Johnny's, but no one attributed any importance to him. He was quoted as saying: 'This is not a death penalty, but murder under the protection of the law ... Three judges have murdered an innocent man. Their actions disgrace the victims of the Holocaust.'

If it had been discovered that Ivan Marchenko was Ivan the Terrible only after Demjanjuk had been put to death, then any anti-Semitic idiot would have been able to quote Johnny's words as a manifest example of the ignominy of Israeli justice. Only a set of astounding coincidences that led to the revelation of the truth and prevented the execution saved the Israeli legal system from total disgrace and anti-Semitic attacks of the worst type. But the verdict of the special district court will remain a disgrace for ever.

10 · Judge Dov Eitan Joins the Defence

I met Judge Dov Eitan at the end of the first week of September 1987, at the American Colony Hotel, at the time Count Tolstoy and Dr Grant were staying there. It was a few days after Judge Tal's heart attack.

The poet Eyal Megged, my childhood friend, was also staying at the hotel that weekend with his wife and new-born daughter. Eyal was fascinated by my involvement in the trial, and was particularly enthralled by the struggle between me and Levin. At the height of the media's campaign against me, after my miserable public apology, Eyal wrote an extremely entertaining essay entitled 'Yoram Versus the Teachers', comparing my confrontation with Levin to those I had had with our elementary-school teachers.

Eyal was a close friend of Miriam and Dov Eitan, and that Saturday they came to visit him at the hotel. Going down to the hotel garden, I saw Eyal and his wife in lively conversation with another couple. I approached their table, and Eyal introduced me to Miriam and Dov Eitan. I knew the name Dov Eitan very well. Four years previously, following a storm of public protest about him, Eitan had had to resign from the Bench. During the Lebanon War he had signed a petition calling for an immediate halt to the offensive and an Israeli withdrawal from the Lebanon. He did not use his judicial title when he signed, but people realized that the signature was his and he was strongly criticized. This led to his resignation, in 1983, after which he became a partner in a Jerusalem law firm.

The trial soon became the focus of conversation. Eitan expressed himself most emphatically. He declared his repugnance for the bizarre idea of holding a trial in a theatre and even having it broadcast live on radio and television. Most of his barbs were directed at Judge Levin however; Eitan used the strongest possible language to describe his behaviour. 'Levin is disgracing Israeli justice on live television,' he said. 'I can't bear to watch for more than five minutes when I see what's going on. I'm unbearably angry, it makes me sick. I can't understand how you can have sat there for so many months, for hours and hours, every single day, and not have a nervous breakdown.'

'I know Levin would very much like to see me collapse,' I responded to his flood of words. 'But I will not give him the pleasure.'

Eitan's criticism was very valuable to me, I thought, and gave me much satisfaction. First, he had been a judge for seventeen years, five of them in the Jerusalem District Court. Second, despite his harsh vocabulary, it was obvious that he was not a short-tempered person who frequently expressed himself in such extreme terms. He was a senior, experienced lawyer, in his fifties, and this experience, especially as a judge, was the basis for his criticism. I attached special importance to hearing that an Israeli judge, even if no longer sitting, agreed with me about Levin's intolerable conduct. As we parted Eitan told me not to get discouraged. I did not meet him again until after the lower-court trial was over, but his words stayed with me.

During the week between the verdict and the sentencing I began to consider how to prepare for the appeal. It was clear that there was no point in having a foreign attorney involved in this stage, because appeal hearings focus on legal arguments that demand full familiarity with the fine points of Israeli law and procedure. Yet I did not want to bear the burden of the appeal alone. The obvious conclusion was to find an Israeli attorney – one of stature – to join me. There was, however, only the slimmest of chances that any such attorney could be recruited.

Another notion that started taking shape in my mind was the need to add some 'respectability' to the defence. I now had great confidence in my knowledge of the case, and no doubt of my professional ability to manage it alone on appeal. I was aware of something Judge Haim Cohen had said publicly back in November 1986, three months before the trial opened: 'I would have been prepared to take on the defence in the Demjanjuk trial in order to prevent a situation in which the judges' emotion led to his conviction.' I was apprehensive that the Supreme Court justices' feelings about the Holocaust *would* lead them to reject the appeal; and I thought this could only be prevented by bringing a well-respected attorney on to the defence team. In combination with my memory of the conversation with Dov Eitan six months previously, this thought led me to the realization that Eitan was the man I needed. I did not, however, rush to share this conclusion with others, even the Demjanjuk family.

On the day the sentence was handed down, Gill announced that he would not participate in the appeal. Johnny indicated that Chumak would not continue either. Nishnic told me he intended to approach a well-known lawyer, the Ukrainian-Canadian John Sapinka, and ask him to join me for the appeal. Sapinka was one of Canada's best-known attorneys, and was later appointed to that country's Supreme Court.

Nishnic had mentioned his name several times in the past, but I knew nothing would come of it. Precisely because he was a lawyer of such stature, Sapinka would not want to participate in such an important appeal in a foreign country with whose laws he was completely unacquainted. I was not at all enthusiastic about the idea, but I chose not to tell Nishnic.

On 28 April 1988, just a few days after the sentencing, I was called to meet with Yoel Tsur, the Supreme Court Registrar, to discuss the technical aspects of the appeal. I was shocked to learn, at the very beginning of our meeting, that the Supreme Court intended to hold and complete the appeal hearing during the upcoming summer recess, which ran from 15 July to 31 August. The implication was obvious – they wished to conduct the appeal on a 'fast track' and reject it more or less on the spot, so as to go forward with the execution immediately.

When Tsur finished speaking and I recovered from my shock, I said with determination: 'Tell His Honour Chief Justice Shamgar that if he seriously intends to hold the appeal hearing during July or August this year, then it will be heard without defence attorneys. Whilst I need the Supreme Court's formal permission not to appear, I'm telling you now that even if such permission is not granted I will not appear at the appeal under any circumstances if it is held in July or August. My colleagues Gill and Chumak will not show up either. His Honour the Chief Justice may, of course, set a date as he sees fit, but it would be best for him to know the implications of his decision before making it. An appeal during the break means an appeal without a defence.'

The Registrar looked surprised at my forcefulness. In a conciliatory tone he asked me what dates I suggested. I estimated that I needed six months to prepare properly, so any date after 1 January 1989 seemed reasonable to me. But I was afraid that if I mentioned such a distant date my proposal would be rejected out of hand and might create conflict. I said, therefore, that the end of October was the earliest possible date for the defence. But I decided to myself that once this request was approved I would ask for a further delay until 1 January.

Tsur promised to bring this to the attention of the Chief Justice and notify me of the answer within a few days. I updated Nishnic that evening. We reached an understanding that if the appeal hearing were scheduled for any date before mid-October the defence would not attend. He sounded very worried and expressed his fear that the Supreme Court hearing would be a replay of the lower-court trial. My opinion was precisely the opposite, and I did my best to persuade him of this.

On 1 May 1988 I was requested, together with representatives of the prosecution, to report next day to the office of the registrar. Daphna Bainwall and I were there on Monday morning. I was happy to hear Tsur announce, without any preliminaries, that Chief Justice Shamgar had accepted my request that the hearing begin at the end of October, and that a formal decision would be rendered within a few days.

When I reached Tel Aviv I called Nishnic. He let out a sigh of relief. I told him I intended to ask for an additional postponement until the beginning of January 1989, on the grounds that the family was planning to retain a new foreign attorney who would appear beside me in the appeal, and that this demanded a further delay.

Chief Justice Shamgar again received Bainwall and me in his chambers. I stressed that the appellant's family had decided to retain a new foreign attorney who would appear beside me during the appeal, and that the defence therefore could not prepare itself properly if the hearing began before 1 January 1989. I added that 'There is nothing exceptional about my request, since criminal appeals brought before the Supreme Court are generally heard a year or more after the verdict is given, especially in the case of verdicts in which heavy penalties were imposed by the lower court.' Bainwall said that she would leave the date to the court's sole discretion. Shamgar said he was inclined to agree with me, but added, 'It will not look good to the public if the appeal of a verdict given at the beginning of this year begins to be heard only in 1989. Likewise, it is most desirable from the point of view of the appellant himself that the hearing be concluded as soon as possible, so that he will know where he stands.' This lit a red warning light. It reminded me, both in content and tone, of Judge Levin's refusal to postpone the trial so that the defence could prepare itself properly. Before I could respond, Shamgar brought the discussion to an end. 'The appeal hearing will therefore begin on 5 December 1988. The defence will receive two weeks to present its arguments, and the same period will be made available to the prosecution. At the end the defence will receive two further days.' The formal decision was rendered on 8 May 1988; I therefore had seven months to complete my preparations, definitely a reasonable period of time.

On 10 May I paid a visit to the Tel Aviv court building in order to see my fellow lawyers. When I entered the foyer I spotted Ronny Bar-On, Dov Eitan's law partner. I had meant to ask my friend Eyal to put out feelers and find out whether it was worth approaching Eitan about joining me in the appeal. I decided to grab this opportunity. I knew Bar-On well from the Hebrew University; he had finished law school a year before me. He was happy to see me and asked about my plans for the appeal. I took advantage of his question: 'You may be surprised to hear that my plans have something to do with your firm. I met Eitan during the trial and we had a long conversation about it. I was extremely impressed by his criticisms of the trial as a whole, and of Levin specifically, and I would very much like to ask him to join me for the appeal.' Bar-On, a very practical man, answered as if we were discussing a totally routine case. 'How much can the Demjanjuk family pay?' he asked. I did not hesitate and named the maximum I thought the family could afford. Bar-On responded seriously and to the point: 'Then we can talk.'

I was very excited by this unexpected development and went straight home to call Eyal. I told him about my meeting with Bar-On. He was surprised by the idea of having Eitan join me in the appeal, but he agreed to test the waters with Eitan and to encourage him to respond positively. Eyal called me at home the next evening to say that Eitan was expecting a phone call from me; I dialled the number right away, and when he picked up the receiver I went right to the point. 'Mr Eitan, I understand that Eyal spoke with you about my wish that you join me in arguing Demjanjuk's appeal, and I understand that you did not rule the idea out entirely.' Eitan confirmed this, and I added: 'I see no point in going further into this on the phone. If you think the idea is worth exploring, it would be best for us to set up a time, soon, to talk it over.' We agreed to meet two days later, at eight in the evening, where we'd first met. Eitan's tone of voice hinted that he was fairly interested.

I was most concerned about Nishnic's position. He very much wanted to bring in a well-known North American attorney. Nor was I sure that the figure I had quoted to Bar-On at the court building would be acceptable to the Demjanjuk family. I thought these things over for half an hour then called Nishnic to update him. As soon as he picked up, I told him with great excitement, 'It looks as if the problem of the additional attorney will be solved within the next few days.' Nishnic had, of course, given me a green light to make enquiries about getting an eminent Israeli attorney to agree to join the case. But I had told him I thought the chances of finding someone were slim, so he was very surprised.

'Who are you talking about?' he asked.

'I hope to reach an agreement on bringing in a lawyer who served as a judge for seventeen years. Five of those years he sat in the Jerusalem District Court, where Judges Tal and Dorner also serve.'

Nishnic let out an exclamation of amazement and asked for details. I told him about my contacts with Eitan, and gave special emphasis to his background, including the circumstances that led to his resignation from the bench.

Nishnic chuckled: 'That's the best news I've heard for a long time.'

I realized this was the time to ask for a favour. 'I hope that, if the negotiations with Eitan reach a positive conclusion, the matter of the foreign attorney will be off the agenda once and for all?' Then I asked whether I had the authority officially to offer the sum I had quoted to Bar-On, and if the family could afford it.

'There's not one cent in the defence fund right now,' Nishnic said, 'but even if I have to plough up and down North America ten times, I'll raise the full amount.'

I explained that it would be necessary to pay a third of the sum quite soon, and Nishnic promised he would see to it. 'It would be a disaster if I were to reach an agreement with Eitan on Thursday, and then discover you can't keep your end of the bargain,' I warned him.

'Up till now I've kept all my promises and obligations, and the same will be true in future,' he responded.

In the mean time I was adjusting to the change in my status since the verdict was handed down. I was no longer attorney for the 'phoney Satan', but rather for Satan himself. I was pleased to see that the subject disappeared from the headlines two or three days after the sentencing; a few days later it was also pushed out of the newspapers' inside pages. True, when I walked down the street I still felt the malevolent glares from all sides, but I had got used to that long ago.

On Thursday 13 May I arrived at the American Colony Hotel; Bar-On and Eitan were already there. I went straight to the point. 'Dov, the conversation we had in this very spot a little more than eight months ago has not left my mind for a moment. The idea has been going round and round in my head to ask you to join me at the appeal stage. After we spoke on the phone I told the members of the Demjanjuk family what needs to be done to make this a reality. I therefore propose, with their consent, that you join the defence. If we reach an agreement in principle today, the two of us will travel to Cleveland in the near future. The family will, of course, cover all the expenses. We will close the deal there.'

'How exactly do you see my involvement in the case? What exactly do you expect of me?' he asked.

First and foremost, I expected him to deal with a very important part of the appeal, the judges' misconduct. I reminded him of his words eight months ago about Levin's disgraceful behaviour. I also repeatedly stressed the legal invalidity of all the photo spreads in which Demjanjuk's picture had been identified as that of Ivan the Terrible; and showed them the sheet of photographs that had been used. Eitan examined the pictures at length. 'I agree,' he said.

'With such weak evidence and after such a disgraceful show-trial, your conscience should be easy with the idea of joining the defence,' I added.

He responded: 'In principle, I agree with your approach entirely.' I explained that these were initial thoughts, open to revision.

Then we spoke about his fee, and reached an understanding on this subject as well, after I convinced them that Nishnic could make the payments. We also agreed that it would be worthwhile going to Cleveland to discuss the details with the family. Even though the family had not told me this explicitly, one of the purposes of the trip would be to allow some of the major North American defence-fund donors to form a direct impression of Eitan, before his involvement in the case was sealed. The trip would not be able to take place before June: I wanted to study the 444-page judgement in depth, so that I could give the family a precise and detailed evaluation of it and of the possibility of challenging the factual findings and legal conclusions on appeal.

I now applied myself energetically to continuing that study. This was not an easy task: almost every finding in it was biased and invalid. Reading it outraged me, particularly because of my familiarity with the smallest details. I was overcome by an intense feeling of frustration. Each time I waded through this legal morass I grew anxious that, precisely because almost every word in it was unfounded, I would not be able to persuade the Supreme Court to admit to such a travesty. After a few days of delving deep into the document, I reached the conclusion that it was not only written in an arrogant tone, but that it was also argued unintelligently. I slowly gained confidence that I could make a strong and persuasive argument to the Supreme Court, and strip the judgement bare. Eitan, a friend of Judge Tal's who had served with him on the bench, said, 'I'm not remotely surprised that Levin and Dorner signed this verdict, but I will never understand how Tal agreed to put his name to such a terrible document,' he told me several times.

Our trip to Cleveland would take place on 5 June. We decided that we would arrive at Ben-Gurion Airport separately, so that no one would suspect that Eitan had joined the defence. We wanted this to remain secret until we were ready to reveal it. We arrived in New York in the evening, and the next afternoon Johnny and Nishnic met us at Hopkins Airport. Nishnic, so easily sparked into enthusiasm, was already whispering to me as we went to get our luggage, 'Eitan is making a tremendous impression on me.' During our trip from the airport to the Holiday Inn Nishnic was euphoric.

That evening, around six, Nishnic collected us from the hotel and took us to the Demjanjuk home. Eitan's stately and handsome appearance only magnified the excellent impression he made on everyone who met him. After refreshments were served, the family inundated him with questions. In his replies he cited in particular the improper conduct of the judges, led by Levin. Eitan had also studied the judgement thoroughly for the occasion, and expressed his full agreement with my evaluation of the central legal issues, especially the legal invalidity of the photo spreads. He explained that there were two elements that made him consider favourably the offer to join the defence: first, Demjanjuk had not had a fair trial; second, the judgement seemed to be in error on the identification issue.

He was asked if there was any real chance of winning the appeal, given what had happened in the district court. 'It is very difficult to evaluate the chances,' Eitan responded. 'One thing is clear, however. The appeal to the Supreme Court cannot possibly make Demjanjuk's situation worse, nor is there any alternative course of action that can help him. I believe the appeal is not hopeless. I must however make it clear that, as in any criminal appeal, the odds are that it will be rejected.' This brought the Demjanjuk family back to the bitter reality, and gloom filled the house. I intervened: 'If a jurist of Eitan's stature is willing to join the defence, that is sufficient to make it possible to present a respectable and serious argument against the conviction. There is therefore a chance that must be pursued.'

Eitan, understanding that I wished to emphasize the positive, immediately said, 'I agree unreservedly with Sheftel.' The mood improved again, but Nishnic brought the conversation back to the chances of the appeal:

'The Ukrainian community has reacted to the conduct of the trial in the worst possible way. The majority do not believe that the scenario will be any different in the Supreme Court, and everyone is aware that Levin himself is a Supreme Court justice. Our supporters and potential donors believe there is not much point in continuing to pay the costs of the defence, because there is no chance that Demjanjuk will get a fair hearing in the Supreme Court.'

'What do you suggest instead?' Eitan asked.

'Mass demonstrations against the injustice done to Demjanjuk,' Nishnic replied.

Eitan said without hesitation: 'Such demonstrations will help Demjanjuk as much as aspirin helps a cancer patient.' The conversation went on for more than three hours, and the longer it continued the more I could feel the family's satisfaction with Eitan growing.

When we returned to the hotel, we sat at the bar and discussed the evening. Eitan expressed his surprise that the Demjanjuk family was so nice, and not full of resentment towards Israel and Jews, as he had feared, because of the disgraceful treatment of Demjanjuk. 'I would expect such Ukrainian goyim to be much more anti-Semitic than they are, after what Levin did to them.' I especially remember Eitan saying, 'When I was sitting on the bench I always tried to see beyond what was going on in the courtroom. I always tried to see the tragedy awaiting the defendant who was on trial before me, and even more his family, which certainly had done no wrong, were I to commit an injustice and convict someone I should not convict. What we saw today in the Demjanjuk home is the kind of scene I used to imagine.'

During our meeting we had learned that three visitors from Canada were expected on Sunday: Paul Chumak; Peter Yatzik, the leading contributor and fund raiser for the family in Canada; and his assistant, Igor Kloufutz. I told Eitan that this would be a decisive meeting, and we began to brainstorm about our next move. We agreed that even if Eitan's involvement in the case was finalized we would not publicize the fact, at least not until the end of August. He should be exposed for as short a time as possible to the media's hostility and the other threats that were my daily fare. But the publication of Eitan's involvement in the defence could help to raise money for the defence fund, so we decided not to delay publicizing it for too long.

On Saturday we met Johnny and Nishnic again, and in the evening went out together to catch some of Cleveland's nightlife. Nishnic indicated continually how pleased he was with Eitan. I took advantage of his good mood to get a definite statement from him that he had abandoned the idea of bringing in a foreign attorney. Eitan found himself liking the Demjanjuks more the longer he spent with them.

On Sunday a shiny new silver Mercedes entered the driveway. Chumak, Igor Kloufutz and Peter Yatzik emerged. After being introduced to each other by Nishnic and Johnny, we all got to work. Yatzik, whose brash, nouveau attitude bordered on the uncouth, addressed me in fairly good English, with a heavy Ukrainian accent. 'Convince me, all of you, that there is any point to this appeal. In my opinion, it's a waste of time and money.' I did not like his tone at all, but I could understand the sentiment behind it.

'If Demjanjuk and his defence attorneys don't show up for the appeal, everyone will interpret it as an acknowledgement that he is really Ivan the Terrible, that he knows this and is therefore convinced that he has no chance on appeal. Furthermore, there is no other alternative that can get Demjanjuk out alive,' I maintained.

Yatzik interrupted: 'And what if we organize demonstrations and make an international scandal out of it?'

This awakened my patriotic instincts. 'No sovereign state, and certainly not Israel, will be deterred from carrying out a sentence on someone its courts have found guilty. The Jews who founded the State of Israel don't actually have a ghetto mentality: no one, especially not the Supreme Court, will be bothered by a few thousand Ukrainians demonstrating. No one will get excited about it because your average Israeli, rightly or wrongly, considers the average Ukrainian to be a common anti-Semite.' This made an impression. Yatzik decided to change tack:

'OK, let's talk law, not politics.'

Eitan intervened and explained how he perceived the injustice done to Demjanjuk in the lower court, and the more than negligible chance that the conviction might be reversed. This, he said, certainly justified a determined fight in the appeal. He concluded on a humorous note: 'Even judgements that *I* rendered at times were reversed on appeal to the Supreme Court.'

The Canadian delegation wanted to know everything about Eitan. As a result, a large part of our conversation was about him, his years as a judge, the circumstances of his resignation, and so on. Yatzik explained that if and when Eitan's involvement was decided, he would make every possible effort to see that the necessary funding was found. We then discussed the ideal date for making Eitan's involvement public. We explained our reasoning and stressed that plenty of time would still remain for the defence fund to take advantage of the publicity in its fund-raising efforts. Four hours later Yatzik told Nishnic that as far as he was concerned there was nothing to prevent Nishnic agreeing terms for Eitan to join the defence.

After the Canadians had left, Nishnic suggested we all go down to the basement, the headquarters of the Demjanjuk defence fund. The basement, about ten by forty feet in size, contained a fax, a telephone, a photocopier, a computer, various other office machines, and tens of thousands of documents. Nishnic said that, from all he knew of Yatzik and his commitment, he was convinced that they could bear the financial burden. It was determined that, on his return to Israel, Eitan would send a draft agreement setting out his terms. Nishnic drove us to our hotel and, before we parted, turned to Eitan: 'I am very happy that such a brave and wonderful person as you is joining the defence of my father-in-law.'

The next morning we began formulating a work plan. Eitan would spend six weeks making a careful study of the court record and the exhibits, and we would meet a few times a week to exchange initial opinions. Only after this would we decide which subjects each of us would argue.

In June I went to see Demjanjuk. My last visit had been two days after the sentencing, and I wanted to update him on recent developments. He was tense with anticipation, having learned from telephone conversations with his family that I had just returned from the US, where we had agreed to take on another lawyer for the appeal. The prison authorities listened in on his calls as a matter of course, so he had got no additional details. I spent about an hour telling him about recent events, and he was delighted to hear that an Israeli attorney who was also a former judge was prepared to join his defence. He was full of praise for Eitan even before he had met him. I explained that he would not be able to meet Eitan before the beginning of September, and I made him pledge to keep the entire matter completely secret, especially from his guards. Before we parted I warned that he should watch his tongue during phone conversations with his family as well, lest he even hint at Eitan's identity. When I rose to go, Demjanjuk said: 'I don't involve myself in such things, these are things my family decides. Even though I'm in a cage, I do think it is very good for me that an Israeli judge will be one of my defence attorneys.'

The time allotted for submitting a notice of appeal was coming to an end. Before leaving for Cleveland I had submitted a petition, which was approved, to receive an extension until the end of June for submitting the notification, but I had not started writing it yet. Looking back, it is hard to comprehend how I managed, in ten days, to prepare the 101 pages that constituted the notice of appeal. Criminal appeals notices in complicated cases usually fill no more than five or six pages. But when I sat down to write I could not stop. I challenged almost all the judgement's factual findings and legal conclusions. I divided the notice into major and secondary topics, and because it was so long I even included a table of contents. I sent it, of course, to Eitan to read before I submitted it, and he approved it, with the exception of a small number of revisions.

At this time signatures on the contract between the defence fund and Dov Eitan were exchanged, as planned, by fax. I sent Eitan the 175 booklets containing the eleven thousand pages of the district-court record, as well as four thick binders containing the 465 exhibits, which themselves took up some five thousand pages.

The appeals notice was filed on 30 June 1988. To my surprise, the media picked it up and quoted it widely; the one-sided commentary of the past was noticeably absent. The very tone of the headlines was different: HARSH CRITICISM OF JUDGES' LINKS WITH MEDIA APPEAR IN

DEMJANJUK APPEAL; DEMJANJUK'S JUDGES EXPOSED THEMSELVES TO INCITEMENT AGAINST HIM; COURT REQUESTED TO ACQUIT DEMJANJUK BECAUSE OF LACK OF EVIDENCE OR BECAUSE OF REASONABLE DOUBT. The appeal notice was translated into English and sent to Cleveland. When Nishnic and Johnny finished reading it, they told me that they were very pleased, especially with its criticism of the judges.

Eitan began a careful study of the record and the exhibits, and we met two or three times each week as agreed, to clarify the huge corpus of legal material. In addition to the other virtues I have cited, Eitan showed himself to be sharp-minded and a quick study. From meeting to meeting I became more convinced that he could make a most significant contribution to the defence's arguments in the appeal, going far beyond simply adding 'respectability'. Towards mid-August, as his familiarity with the material was growing, we agreed that I would make the arguments on the three substantive issues – the identification, the Travniki document and the alibi with its associated historical testimony. Eitan, for his part, would tackle the issue of lack of jurisdiction, the improper conduct of the lower court, and the back-up argument for a different sentence. Despite this division of labour, both of us would be fully involved in the preparation of every subject.

The date for publicizing Eitan's enlistment in Demjanjuk's defence was approaching. We had promised the scoop to our mutual friend Eyal Megged, who had a column in the weekly magazine *Koteret Rashit*. As the day of publication drew closer I began teasing Eitan that 'Thanks to you, I'll be spared half the threats and indignities I've been suffering.' When the day arrived, the amazing news appeared on the magazine's front cover. The caption over the article was *Former District Court Judge Joins Demjanjuk's Defence*. I held the magazine, overcome with delight. I was no longer Demjanjuk's only Israeli attorney. I was part of a team that also included a former judge, a respected jurist of the first order. Even though I had withstood the deluge of wild attacks for more than a year and a half, I nevertheless felt a great sense of relief. No one could execrate me now for being the only Israeli who had stooped to defending Demjanjuk. The item was given prominence on the evening television news, as it was in the hourly radio bulletins. The next day the newspapers gave the story full exposure. All the reports emphasized that Eitan was a former judge, and Eitan himself was quoted as asserting that the verdict did 'not remove the many question marks surrounding the defendant's identity', and as saying that he 'sees eye to eye with Mr Sheftel on the conduct of the court, and of Judge Levin especially'. There was not the tiniest grain of criticism in these articles. We had gained respectability.

Now the time had come for Eitan's first visit to Demjanjuk, which we had set for Sunday 4 September. I wanted to keep up the momentum in the media, so we leaked the date of our visit to ensure that reporters and photographers would be waiting for us when we emerged from the prison. We would then hold a brief press conference.

I had never seen Demjanjuk so worked up. I introduced them and he shook Eitan's hand warmly for a long time. 'I want to thank you very much for agreeing to work with Sheftel and be my defence attorney. You must be a very brave and very honest man.'

After a short silence Eitan responded, somewhat tense and nervous: 'I sometimes followed the trial. Having been a judge for seventeen years, I want to tell you as clearly as possible that you did not receive a fair trial. For that reason, and because, in my opinion, there are many doubts about your identification as Ivan the Terrible, I have agreed to be one of your defence attorneys.'

Tears welled up in Demjanjuk's eyes. Eitan was disconcerted by this emotional reaction, as was I. Demjanjuk recovered and said, 'My family and I will never forget what you are doing for me, and I want to thank you very much once again.'

We talked for two hours. Eitan was the main speaker, and he explained to Demjanjuk that from the legal point of view this was not an open-and-shut case for the prosecution. He expressed his confidence that the Supreme Court would treat the defence completely differently to the district court. The proceedings would be proper, fair and conducted in a quiet atmosphere not hostile to the defence. Towards the end of the meeting Demjanjuk signed a power-of-attorney appointing Dov Eitan to represent him in the appeal. Afterwards we rose to part and Demjanjuk was again very emotional, thanking Eitan repeatedly.

When we emerged from the prison a crowd of reporters was waiting for us; the foreign press was well-represented too. Eitan said that Demjanjuk had officially appointed him as his attorney. He referred to Demjanjuk's good spirits, and emphasized that he continued to profess his innocence and to claim that he had been mistakenly identified as Ivan the Terrible. Two days later Nishnic called me and told me excitedly about the huge impression Eitan's addition to the defence team had made in the American media. He thought it best that I come to Cleveland sometime within the next ten days and set out from there to give fund-raising lectures in Ukrainian community centres in several Canadian and American cities. The proposal caught me by surprise and I asked to be allowed to think it over before giving an answer.

I consulted Eitan and we decided that the case was sufficiently well prepared to allow me to go, so long as the trip did not last more than ten days. We were aware of the financial difficulties the defence fund was facing, and that we had to help. The next day I spoke to Nishnic and we agreed that I would set out on 16 September for Toronto. Igor Kloufutz could meet me there, and Nishnic would arrive from Cleveland the next day. On Friday evening I landed in Canada for the first time. Igor took me straight to a hotel in central Toronto, telling me that a programme of four lectures had been organized. The first was on Sunday in a community centre near Toronto; afterwards would come Detroit, Chicago and Cleveland.

Nishnic was in a boisterous and optimistic mood and tended, as usual, to exaggerate: 'Everyone is anxious to see and hear the only lawyer brave enough to defend Demjanjuk.' I had given much thought to my lectures in the days before my flight. I was well aware that I would be speaking before an audience made up mostly of goyim particularly prone to anti-Semitic prejudice. I felt uncomfortable criticizing even Judge Levin before such an audience. I decided to stress that the improper behaviour of the court that had sentenced Demjanjuk to death was utterly untypical of everyday Israeli trials. I repeated to myself the sentence that I planned to use in my lecture: 'There can be no doubt that if a Jew were put on trial in the US or Canada, charged with murdering nine hundred thousand non-Jewish Americans, with the same evidence available against Demjanjuk, he would not only be convicted but he would probably not even get to court because he would be physically eliminated first, either lynched by an angry mob or killed secretly by those charged with detaining him.' I also intended to explain how and why I had decided to join Demjanjuk's defence team, to review the many flaws in the identification of Demjanjuk as Ivan the Terrible, to say a few words about Dov Eitan and to stress that the Supreme Court would be an entirely different story, at least with regard to the fairness of the proceedings. I would conclude by warning against giving the Ukrainian community's public support of Demjanjuk the slightest anti-Semitic or anti-Israeli tinge. Then I would take questions from the audience.

I outlined this for Nishnic during breakfast, and he gave his wholehearted approval. He told me they had decided to take advantage of my visit by holding a press conference in every city on my itinerary. In addition, appearances had been arranged on radio and TV interview and call-in shows. I was actually pleased with the heavy workload, since this level of activity always spurs me to do my best.

My first press conference was held that very afternoon. I opened with a statement that included an attack on the improper conduct of the court and of Judge Levin in particular. I explained the lack of legal weight of the identification evidence and provided up-to-date information on recent developments in the case. One question that came up at all these press conferences and interviews was whether Demjanjuk could possibly win a fair trial in the Supreme Court after what had happened in the lower court. I always responded that he would get the same fair trial that every other appellant to the Israeli Supreme Court receives, and the reason for the difference between the trial and the appeal was that the former had been a show-trial. The Toronto press conference lasted about forty-five minutes. Immediately thereafter we went to tape a television interview for broadcast on that night's eleven o'clock news. Even though it had been an extremely busy day, when Nishnic took me back to the hotel at about ten p.m. I felt fresh and alert, and instead of going up to my room we sat and chatted into the small hours.

The next afternoon I began my lecture at the Ukrainian community centre, in one of the Toronto suburbs. About three hundred people, most of them elderly, packed the auditorium. I spoke for about an hour, precisely according to the plan I had outlined for myself. Then the questions began. Almost everyone who asked a question began by praising my courage and thanking me for being willing to serve as Demjanjuk's defence attorney. The questions themselves, as at every lecture, expressed scepticism about the possibility that Demjanjuk could get a fair trial in Israel; each person used a different example from the trial to support his position. I responded to each one patiently, but also in stronger terms when that was necessary. I tried to make my answers clear and direct and to avoid beating around the bush; they were received with understanding and sympathy. Afterwards, Nishnic addressed the crowd with an emotional appeal for them to give generously to the defence fund.

The total amount collected during this campaign was $30,000. I later completed four further lecture tours of the US and Canada on the same model. Sometimes the tour included a lecture at a university, and sometimes also at its law school. I gave a total of about forty lectures, reaching almost every large city in North America, and a similar number of press conferences and interviews. I loved every minute of these trips – the public lectures, the crowded schedules, the frequent hops from city to city and hotel to hotel. My mother also liked them (even though she still had many reservations about my involvement in the case): when I returned from such a journey and told her of my adventures, she would joke with me: '*Aleh farbrenteh antisemiten in America, zamlen gelt far Yoram, meiner teireh yiddishe kind*' ('All the staunchest anti-Semites in America are collecting money for Yoram, my dear Jewish son').

Although the media's treatment of Eitan after he announced he was joining the defence was not hostile, he was soon receiving telephone threats. The callers demanded that he end his involvement in the case immediately, or he would be eliminated. I had never stopped receiving such threats, but I had long since learned to ignore them, and I was happy to see that Eitan did not seem concerned either. He categorically rejected my suggestion that he file a complaint with the police. One of his reasons was that they would immediately leak it to the press and the publicity would double the number of threats.

November arrived, and our preparations were nearing completion. We were convinced that the issues of the court's lack of jurisdiction on the charge of genocide, and of identification, were the most persuasive. Making a successful case on just one of these points would be sufficient to bring about Demjanjuk's acquittal. We decided I would open with a brief survey of the structure and contents of our pleadings. Eitan would then make the arguments for lack of jurisdiction and would continue with the subject of the lower court's improper conduct. Afterwards I would discuss the identification, the Travniki document and the alibi and historical evidence. I would summarize the defence argument against the conviction; Eitan would conclude with the alternative argument regarding the sentence.

During the week before the appeal hearing was set to open all the attorneys were called into Tsur's office for a discussion of the arrangements. It was a technical and fairly tedious discussion. The boredom was broken by Oded Me'ushar, the head of the Ministry of Justice's Special Projects Division. Eitan asked that for security reasons the defence be allotted two spaces in the car park reserved for judges and prosecutors, right next to the entrance to the court building. Oded Me'ushar jumped up as if he had been bitten and announced that this was not even to be considered, it was impossible to free up a parking space for us there. I saw this mean reaction as a direct continuation of Me'ushar's failure to keep order in the theatre where the show-trial had been held. In the end the Registrar forced him to provide the spaces. We were about to leave for the Ayalon Prison when we learned that the arrangements for hearing the appeal in Supreme Court Courtroom 1 were in full swing. We wanted to peek into the room before leaving the building. Our hearts sank. In the hall, very close to the entrance, were two small radio studios. In the middle of the room workers were busy installing a television-camera mount. I muttered: 'First there was a show-trial, now there's going to be a show-appeal.' Eitan didn't know how to take it. 'It's unbelievable. Why are they so stupidly repeating the district court's mistake?' That very moment we decided to return to the Registrar's office and find out what it all meant.

He explained that the hearing would indeed be broadcast live on two radio stations and one television station. 'That is totally unacceptable to us, and we will find a way to express our views on the matter before the hearing begins,' I said angrily. Tsur did not respond, and we quickly left his office.

On our way to the Ayalon Prison we decided, as Eitan suggested, to let forty-eight hours go by before discussing the issue, to prevent our anger from leading us astray. It was clear, however, that we would not let the matter drop. When the appeal hearing finally began, a year and a half later, it was conducted without radio and television studios in the courtroom. The five judges apparently understood that they had made a very bad mistake when they decided to conduct the appeal on live television. It should be remembered, however, that that was their original intention, and that all the preparations for it had been made.

By the time we arrived at the jail we had calmed down a bit. Demjanjuk was happy to see us; Eitan seemed a bit perturbed and I was more or less reserved. We sat with Demjanjuk for about an hour and told him about the general state of our preparation. He was encouraged by what he heard, and I thought it best to make it clear again that there was no reason to be over-optimistic. Before we went, Eitan turned to Demjanjuk and said: 'I hope with all my heart that the next time we see each other you will be free.' He then warmly shook Demjanjuk's hand. This was the last time that Demjanjuk and Eitan saw each other, and Demjanjuk later reminded me several times of Eitan's last words to him there.

We drove to my home in Tel Aviv, and spent several hours going through the issue of lack of jurisdiction from every possible viewpoint. At close to six in the evening Eitan got up to leave. 'Be in touch tomorrow,' he said. 'We have lots of other things to settle. We also have to set a meeting for Tuesday morning, most probably in Jerusalem.' I escorted him to his car and we said goodbye. And that was the last time *I* saw him.

The next day, 28 November 1988, I was totally occupied with last-minute corrections and improvements to my arguments on the identification issue. I spoke with Eitan by phone twice, the last time at close to midnight, and we agreed that I would call his office the next morning to agree when and where we would meet. I continued to work into the night, going to bed at three in the morning.

The telephone woke me. Tzvia was on the line, and she said in a frightened voice: 'If you're answering, you must be all right. Get up and get yourself together, because I've got something very bad to tell you.' It was clear something serious had happened. A few seconds later I told her: 'I'm awake. What happened?' Her words hit me like a bolt of lightning. 'Shaked called and said that Eitan apparently committed suicide this morning by jumping from the Jerusalem Tower' (a twenty-storey office block in central Jerusalem). 'He called a minute ago to tell us.' 'I can't believe it, it can't be,' I mumbled. Then Tzvia told me that even before Shaked's call a reporter had rung the office and asked about me, thinking I had been the one who had jumped to his death. Because of this, Tzvia had thought at first that I might have committed suicide. I brought the conversation to an end and called Eitan's home. Miriam answered. 'What happened to Dov?' I asked.

'I don't know myself,' she said in a broken, exhausted voice. 'They say he committed suicide. That can't be, I don't believe it. He left home before eight in the morning. We ate breakfast together. He told me he was going to his office, and we made an appointment to meet at eleven to buy a new suit for the appeal.' I was speechless with shock. I didn't know what to say, I felt so flustered and helpless. After some hesitation I said:

'Miriam, I'm going to get dressed and drive straight to you.' It was almost nine. I quickly dressed, and before leaving I called the office to ask if there was any news. 'No news, except a deluge of phone calls from reporters. Some of them think you're the one who jumped.' I told Tzvia that I was on my way to Eitan's house, and that I would be in touch during the day.

All the way to Jerusalem I mulled over how such a thing could have happened. The suicide could not have anything to do with the appeal. After all, only yesterday we had made an appointment for today. Eitan gave no indication of being in any sort of distress. Quite the opposite – he seemed to be looking forward to the appeal and to be confident in himself. Nor did the possibility that something had happened during the night seem reasonable. After all, Miriam said that this morning he had been in entirely normal spirits and had even made a date to go out with her later to buy a suit. It was baffling. The possibility that it was a murder seemed unreasonable: it was hard to believe that Eitan could have been pushed to his death in broad daylight, in an office building that at eight in the morning is already bustling with workers and visitors. Later, when I learned that Eitan had jumped from a window in the foyer of the Jerusalem Hotel, on the fifteenth floor of the Jerusalem Tower, I was certain he had not been pushed.

As I neared Eitan's home I was overwhelmed by guilt. If I had not suggested that he join the case, perhaps he would not be dead now. Ronny Bar-On and several relatives and friends were already at his house. Miriam was in a state of total shock and was pacing helplessly to and fro. I pressed her hand and tried to express my turbulent feelings. 'I'm totally shocked. I don't believe it. I hadn't noticed a hint of distress with regard to the case. But I still feel guilty.' Miriam responded in a broken, soft voice: 'Don't blame yourself. No one, not even Ronny, noticed any problem with regard to the case.' Afterwards we spoke briefly about how we had heard about the tragedy. As always when I am confronted with loss and sorrow, I felt very awkward and did not know what to do or say.

Bar-On told me that Eitan must have arrived at the office at about eight in the morning. No one was there then. He left his briefcase and went to the Jerusalem Tower, a two-minute walk from the office. He jumped to his death at about quarter-past. His body and face were smashed beyond recognition; he had been identified by the ID card in his wallet.

By midday I was starting to recover. I called the Supreme Court clerk's office and asked for an urgent meeting, to postpone the trial at least until the middle of the following year. Shmaryahu Cohen, the Chief Clerk, had already heard about the tragedy and said he believed that, given the special circumstances, it would be possible to call a meeting for as early as the next day, without written notification. An hour later he told me the meeting had been set for eleven the next morning. I called Shaked, notified him of the substance of my conversation with Shmaryahu and expressed my hope that the prosecution would not put any obstacles in the way of postponing the trial. I explained that if the appeal were not postponed, for whatever reason, I would not even think of reporting to the courtroom on 5 December. Shaked promised that the prosecution would not be an obstacle and said he was confident that the appeal hearing would be postponed for a few months.

I left Miriam Eitan at about three in the afternoon. She thanked me for the swiftness with which I reached her home, and hoped I would be able to manage on my own. When I entered my apartment I heard the phone ring; it was Nishnic. It was nine-thirty a.m. in the States, and the dreadful news had already made its way over the ocean. 'It's not a suicide, it's murder. Now they'll also try to murder you and wipe out the entire defence. It just can't be suicide,' Nishnic shouted hysterically.

'I understand your anxiety,' I said, trying to sound calm, 'but from the information I have now, it doesn't look like murder.' Nishnic sounded in total despair. He repeated that it had happened only because Demjanjuk had a very good chance of being acquitted on appeal. I saw no point in arguing with him. In the end I told him about the meeting scheduled for the next day for my request to postpone the hearing. We agreed that if it were not put off, I would not show up. I told him that it was certain that it would be delayed, so there was no point in anyone from the family coming to Israel, and that the next day I would also visit Demjanjuk so that he would hear about what had happened from me. Nishnic said that his father-in-law must be in total shock from the tragedy, and thanked me for going to see him so quickly. At the end of our conversation he made me promise to be careful. 'You're the next in line,' he insisted. I made no response, and before hanging up I urged him to call Miriam and express the Demjanjuk family's sorrow. Nishnic did this as soon as our conversation was over. The telephone in my apartment did not stop ringing that evening, but I felt I couldn't talk to anyone, and let it ring.

I arrived at Demjanjuk's cell the next morning at half-past eight. He had already heard the news and looked like someone whose whole world has been shattered. He seemed much more disturbed than after he had been sentenced to death. He shook my hand with tears in his eyes and in a trembling voice said: 'Sheftel, what a tragedy, what a catastrophe, what a wonderful man he was. You remember that he said on Sunday, before you went, that he hoped the next time he saw me I would be a free man?' I again felt very awkward and did not know what to say. Demjanjuk was absolutely sure that Eitan had been murdered. 'Now they've murdered Eitan, I'm sure that no matter what happens we won't be able to reverse the death sentence. My fate has also been sealed.' He had never expressed himself so pessimistically. I spent about an hour telling him about the meeting that was to take place at the Supreme Court and expressing my certainty that the appeal would be delayed by several months. Before we parted, Demjanjuk asked that I convey his heartfelt sorrow to Eitan's wife. 'I'm very sorry that she and her children have suffered such a horrible tragedy because of me,' he said. As I left he said: 'Sheftel, take care of yourself.'

The five judges who were to hear the appeal were Chief Justice Meir Shamgar, Deputy Chief Justice Menachem Elon, and Justices Aharon Barak, Eliezer Goldberg and Avraham Halima. Blatman, Shaked and Bainwall were there for the prosecution. The atmosphere was grim. I opened by explaining that Eitan was supposed to have argued a significant part of the appeal, about a third. His tragic death required a postponement of the hearing so that the defence could reorganize and find a lawyer to replace Eitan – a task that would certainly not be easy. Justice Goldberg asked whether it would be possible to divide the argument, to begin by hearing the part that I was supposed to have presented and then, after a delay, to hear the part that Eitan was supposed to have presented. I explained that this would also require dividing the prosecution's response, and the entire proceeding would be disjointed. Furthermore, I added, Eitan was to have advised me on my part. Blatman said that the prosecution also preferred not to split the proceedings up, and agreed that the tragic circumstances required that the appeal be postponed for quite a while. When Chief Justice Shamgar asked how long I needed, I said at least six months. In the end they decided the appeal would be postponed until 5 May 1989. The hearing schedule would be precisely as already determined.

The next day, Thursday 1 December, a sunny, warm winter day, I left my office at around noon to attend the funeral of my dear colleague. I had placed a mourning notice in the newspaper: 'I bow my head before the tragic death of the bravest and dearest of men, Dov Eitan.' I was still tormented by the thought that had I not asked him to join the case I would not now be going to his funeral. While there was no hint that his joining the case had led to his death, that made no difference to my feelings. I knew Eitan had been immersed in the preparation of the appeal. Over the previous months he was enjoying the learning process and the preparations for our arguments. These contradictory thoughts only added to my confusion. Again and again I recalled his last meeting with Demjanjuk and our own final conversation, on Monday night. He was certain then that a week later he would be reporting to the Supreme Court to begin the appeal. I had spoken with Miriam and Bar-On a few times over the last two days, and they too said that they had never noticed even a trace of doubt, or lack of confidence, or any other reservation about the step he had taken. But a heavy sense of guilt continued to weigh on me.

I arrived at the Jerusalem municipal funeral home a little after one. The grounds were filled with people. Dozens of judges, headed by Chief Justice Shamgar, had come to pay their respects. His wife and daughters, Bar-On and many lawyers, relatives and friends were there. Judge Tal, whom Eitan so valued, gave the eulogy for the judicial community: 'I do not understand how our beloved Dov Eitan could allow himself to put an end to his life.' I stood and listened to the eulogies, and from time to time I looked around at the crowd. When the eulogies and the *El maleh rahamim* prayer were concluded I walked towards the exit along with the rest of the crowd to drive to the cemetery.

Beloved, honest, brave Dov Eitan set out on his final journey. A few minutes later I began a deeply painful journey of my own.

11 · Acid Attack

On my way out of the funeral home I met Edna Shabtai, widow of the writer Ya'akov Shabtai. We stopped and began to talk about Eitan and his mysterious death. A few minutes later I suddenly heard a man shouting loudly close by, but didn't understand what it was about. A second later I felt a sharp burning sensation on my face, especially around my eyes.

I went into shock. The voice was still shouting, but I still could not grasp what it meant. A few seconds later I realized that someone had thrown acid on my face. I sprang as fast as I could move towards a sink that stood three yards away, and began rinsing my face, especially my eyes, which were burning fiercely. A kind of foggy barrier began to form before my eyes. My vision was weakening. Frantically I kept washing my eyes. Yoram, son of Jerusalem District Court judge Ezra Hadaia, helped me. The pain in my eyes was growing worse by the moment. My sight was blurring. I went on rinsing my eyes for two or three minutes that seemed like an eternity. I was terrified that I was going blind.

A stranger, a wonderful person named Mr Elbaz, suddenly appeared and volunteered to drive me to hospital in his car. As I left, writhing with pain, some of the Supreme Court justices passed by; I could just make out the frightened looked on Shamgar's face. A minute later I was in Elbaz's car, and in less than ten minutes we arrived at the Bikkur Holim casualty department.

My eyes were washed and a doctor explained that a large quantity of acid had been thrown at me. Most of it had penetrated my left eye, with a tiny amount entering my right as well. My face had not suffered any damage. Washing only made the pain worse. The right eye at least, the doctor said, was nothing to worry about. I felt much better. At most I'll be blind in one eye, I thought to myself. Then I was told that I should get to the eye department of the Hadassah Hospital in Ein Karem as quickly as possible.

Elbaz offered to take me to the Hadassah as well. We went straight up to the ophthalmology ward, and Dr Moshe Ilsar began treating me immediately. He applied various kinds of drops to my eyes, some to help relieve the pain. After examining my sight he determined that my right eye would recover completely. My left eye, he said, was in a critical condition. It was bandaged and I was given a small room containing one bed. I asked Dr Ilsar to do whatever was necessary to prevent reporters and photographers entering the ward, and he promised to do so.

Finally alone in the room, I was very distressed. The thought that I had so nearly been blinded was hounding me constantly. From the moment the trial had begun, almost two years before, I had received all kinds of threats, and openly dismissed them all. I had never expected to be physically hurt, and behaved accordingly. Yet now the threats had gone from the potential to the real. It was alarming, and horrible scenes in which I was blind and helpless began to pass before my mind's eye. I began to shiver along with the sharp pain.

A few minutes later several reporters and photographers managed to get into my room, and they had time to take my picture before being thrown out. In spite of the terror, the pain and the hatred, even at this moment I felt no regrets about my involvement in the Demjanjuk affair, and didn't contemplate bringing it to an end. Even the fact that this attack had taken place only two days after Eitan's death, during his funeral, didn't make me want to leave. It was as if there were now a physical bond uniting me to the case.

That afternoon a telephone was brought into my room and a wave of calls ensued. Most were friends, but some were pushy journalists. I refused to speak to the latter. I learned from my friends that the news reports had defined my injury as mild. When I told them it was more serious, they tried to encourage me, and some even came to visit me that evening. I realized that word of my injury must also have reached my mother, who always listened to the news. I called her at home. She had already heard, but hadn't been able to get through on the phone. When she heard my voice she burst into tears and mumbled in a mixture of Yiddish, Russian and Hebrew, 'My Yoram, *mein teire kind*, my only one.' I tried to calm her, but only after many long minutes did she begin to respond. She was almost seventy-eight at the time, and it was only with difficulty that I was able to talk her out of coming to me that very evening. About an hour later the visitors began arriving. The first ones were Eitan's widow and daughters and Ronny Bar-On. The tables had been turned; Miriam and her daughters now felt guilty about my injury having happened at Dov's funeral.

Meanwhile the pain had dulled, and my treatment entered a kind of routine. Every half-hour a nurse would come in and put drops in both my eyes. My left was bandaged the whole time, and I felt, rather than seeing everything with the one eye, that I were half blind. The physical pain had diminished considerably and the growing flow of visitors raised my spirits. The trauma had almost subsided and I began to return to myself. I understood that I had no choice but to spend at least a week in bed. I responded without hesitation to all my friends who asked how the drama would affect my future plans: I would never consider abandoning the case, I said, since that was exactly what the hooligan who threw the acid at me wanted.

In the mean time I learned that the hooligan's name was Yisrael Yehezkeli. He had been caught, had confessed and was being detained. He had been one of the regular members of the audience during the trial, and not only had he confessed to the deed but he revelled in it. I was not remotely surprised. I told my friends that evening what I would later say several times in a very personal interview that I gave from my hospital bed to the magazine *Ha'olam Hazeh*: 'I have nothing but contempt for anyone capable of such a vile deed, but this man, even though he cannot of course be absolved, is to a certain extent also a victim. He is the victim of a methodical campaign of incitement that has been conducted against me and which, as is now clear, has declared open season on me.' Suddenly I understood that it was a miracle it had taken so long for the media's incitement against me to bring me serious injury.

Nishnic rang around half-past seven, with Johnny at his side. They had learned of my injury from the American media, and had had great difficulty finding out the phone number in my room. Nishnic was, as usual, excitable. 'What's happened to you, Shefy?' he asked as soon as he had identified my voice.

'I thought I'd be blinded, but it looks like I will be blind in only one eye,' I answered in a jolly voice.

'I told you Eitan didn't commit suicide, that he'd been murdered, and I asked you to be careful because you were the next in line. You have to arrange for twenty-four-hour police protection at your room in the hospital. You can be sure that they'll try to finish what they began at Eitan's funeral.'

I had no intention of changing my habits in the slightest, and even if I had asked for police protection it would not have been supplied. So I evaded the question: 'I'm aware of what's going on around me and I take appropriate measures.' I spoke to them for about a quarter of an hour, and they again made me promise to take special care, and to learn my lesson from what had just happened. I promised I would. They, of course, wished me a full recovery, and I ended the conversation with an assurance that the events of the last two days would not make me leave the case. Half an hour later Paul Chumak called from Canada, and we had a friendly chat. John Gill, on the other hand, did not call – not that evening nor any of the other eight days I spent in hospital. I have not spoken to him since, something I am not sorry about.

By now my weariness was overwhelming. Just as I was considering asking to be left alone so that I could sleep, the phone rang again. When I picked up the receiver, I was very surprised. On the other end I heard Demjanjuk's thick, heavy voice, and I was able to make out the sigh of relief he emitted when he recognized me: 'I'm very happy to hear you. I thought all the reports on the radio about your injury were lies. I was sure they had killed you, just like they killed Eitan the day before yesterday. I told the guards who are watching me that I would believe you are alive only if I could talk to you on the telephone and only if I heard and identified your voice. In the end they let me call you.' I told him all about it, and then he said, 'I believe that after you recover we'll see each other once more, and that's all.'

'What do you mean?' I asked. Demjanjuk explained: 'When you recover you'll come to say goodbye, because after what happened to Eitan the other day and to you today, I am sure you will not want to continue and I understand completely.'

'You've known me for almost two years,' I responded jovially, 'and I don't understand why you're insulting me, especially when I'm in such a disagreeable state. From what you know of me, do you really think I would run away now, of all times?'

'Sheftel, you really are a hero,' Demjanjuk mumbled. 'My family and I will always remember that.'

That same eventful day a policeman had come to my room and taken down a detailed statement. He told me about the state of the investigation, and mentioned that Yehezkeli had confessed that he had been at my mother's apartment on the previous Friday, 25 November. He had told her that, if Eitan and I did not stop representing Demjanjuk immediately, we would be eliminated. Yet he denied any involvement whatsoever in Eitan's death. Yehezkeli had introduced himself to my mother as Avraham Berman.

Now I remembered that that Friday I had visited my mother in the evening and she had been very agitated. She said she wanted to tell me something, but made me swear not to do anything about it. I promised. She related that after she lit the Sabbath candles she heard the doorbell ring. When she opened the door she saw a man of about seventy, who presented himself as Avraham Berman. He asked to be allowed in. When he sat down, he said he represented an organization that fought 'against Nazi collaborators of Eitan's and your son's type'. He had come to warn my mother, he said, that if she did not prevent me from continuing my involvement in Demjanjuk's defence I would suffer a bitter and horrible fate, as would Eitan. My mother, upset, told me that she began to plead with this odious person for my life. But he went on, saying that the only way to stop me being killed was to halt my involvement in the case. 'Berman' told my mother that his address was 14 King George Street in Jerusalem. I had understood that Berman was not his real name: the address was that of Eitan's office, a building in which there were no residential apartments. Despite all this, even when the policeman told me about him, I was convinced that old Yehezkeli had not pushed Eitan to his death.

Just before ten the last of my visitors left. I was finally alone. I was exhausted, and fell asleep within minutes.

At six in the morning I was woken by a nurse for the eyedrops. I got up to wash, and removed the bandage from my left eye. My right eye was nearly blinded by the sight in the mirror. Its companion was swollen, and so disfigured it hardly looked like an eye. I closed my right eye and discovered, to my dismay, that I could barely see anything – with difficulty I could make out my outline in the mirror. The barrier that had began to form over my eye following the injury seemed to have got thicker; now it was as if someone had covered my eye with a filthy, opaque piece of glass. Then I came back to realities and realized how seriously I had been hurt, and how hard it would be – if at all – to restore vision to my eye. I immediately began trying to console myself with thoughts such as what might have happened if a few more drops of acid had got into my right eye, or I had not found the tap where I washed my eye straight after the attack. Still standing in front of the mirror, I was relieved that I could at least see myself clearly through my right eye.

My elderly mother arrived, running towards me as if she were a girl of eighteen, and in a second we were embracing. She wailed in her usual mixture of Russian, Yiddish and Hebrew. When she had recovered somewhat she asked, 'What about your eye, will it be possible to save it, what will become of my Yoram, I have no one in the world but you,' and burst into tears again. I tried to comfort her and said it could have been worse, if the other eye had been equally injured. But this thought only made her cry more. A few minutes later, when she had calmed down again, she said, 'This case is a curse. Your partner is already dead, and he'll be the death of both of us, when are you going to put an end to it already?' I said nothing. I couldn't see any point in telling my mother what I had told everyone else, and I didn't want to make a promise I would not keep. She stayed with me all day, talking with my visitors. At close to eight in the evening she returned to her home with one of my friends. That was the only Friday in her entire life, since the age of twelve, that she did not light her Sabbath candles on time.

In the mean time the weekend papers had arrived in my room. All of them termed my injury 'slight', and said in various ways that no serious damage had been done to my eyes. In places, Yehezkeli was presented as a hero. 'I am sure that all Jews are pleased with what I did,' he had said immediately after being arrested. One headline ran: 'ALL BECAUSE OF YOU,' THE HOLOCAUST SURVIVOR SHOUTED AT SHEFTEL. Yehezkeli was not a Holocaust survivor at all. He had fled Warsaw as soon as the Germans entered the city, spent time in various parts of the Soviet Union and enlisted in the Polish Anders Army, with which he arrived in the then Palestine in 1942. On Sunday a reporter came to interview me. My mother was in the room and he spoke to her as well. The next day the headline over the interview was: YORAM SHEFTEL'S MOTHER: 'THEY ARE ALWAYS THREATENING ME.' The subhead was '*I'd be happy if Yoram left this case, I don't have a day's peace.*'

The tests and intensive treatment continued for a week. The final diagnosis was that the eye had been seriously damaged: the cornea's protective membrane had been completely destroyed, and there was high internal pressure. It was chronically inflamed; the various medications did not improve its condition. It was still misshapen. Every time I took the bandage off my eye I felt miserable. Dr Ilsar, who cared for me devotedly, showed me close-up photos of the eye towards the end of the week. It was a horrible sight. Only with difficulty could one see that it was an eye.

Among the many people who visited me while I was hospitalized was Esther Yisrael, known to everyone as Eti. Pretty and kind-hearted, Eti has been my closest female friend for more than ten years. When I learned that I would have to make daily visits to the Hadassah Hospital's outpatient clinic for further treatment and observation, and since I could not drive for a while, Eti offered to drive me each day from Tel Aviv to Jerusalem and back. She took leave from her job at her own expense for this purpose, and for two weeks chauffeured me, helped me change bandages, administered eyedrops and did everything else that was necessary. She had always dreamed of appearing in a magazine feature, and this injury was my opportunity to make it come true. I arranged an illustrated article in *Ha'olam Hazeh*; the photographs showed her treating my eyes and also leaning against my Porsche, in which she drove me to the hospital.

In spite of Eti's pleasant company, I was depressed. I didn't even want to visit Demjanjuk. After consulting Nishnic I decided to submit another request for a postponement, this time until the beginning of 1990. We also agreed that I would travel to the US at the beginning of February so we could decide on our course of action. It was a month before I was able to drive again. My left eye was bandaged the whole time. There was almost no one who did not recognize me when I walked down the street, and the usual hostile, disgusted stares were directed at me. Even the bandage did not mitigate the antagonism. Now awareness of the 'man in the street's' hatred for me made me feel even worse.

By the beginning of January there had still been no improvement, and I told Dr Ilsar I wished to consult another doctor. He took this in good part, and even recommended Professor Blumenthal, director of the Ophthalmology Department at Sheba Hospital, who also had his own prestigious clinic. After a comprehensive examination and the removal of accumulated contamination, Professor Blumenthal announced categorically that there was nothing more he could do for me. When he heard that I would soon be leaving for the US, however, he recommended that I visit Professor Kenneth Kenyon's clinic in Boston. Kenyon had developed a special operation for cases such as mine, and was the only doctor in the world who performed it. Blumenthal supplied me with a referral.

It was mid-January by the time I got around to visiting Demjanjuk, and even then I did so entirely without enthusiasm. Demjanjuk had been kept up to date on my condition during his weekly phone calls to his family, so he knew in advance when I was coming. He was excited, and seemed truly happy. He greeted me by saying, 'I'm glad to see you, but sorry that it's with the bandage on your eye. They killed Eitan, and at his funeral they tried to finish you off as well.' He squeezed my hand fiercely and tried to embrace me, but I evaded his grasp,

'I'll get better, and the bandage will be gone soon,' I said. 'I'm not in the best of spirits these days, but that won't affect my determination to go on.'

'And what does your mother say?' Demjanjuk asked. 'I read in the *Jerusalem Post* that she would like to see you resign as defence attorney, I read she's afraid you'll be killed.'

'I love and respect my mother very much,' I said, 'but in this matter, as in a number of others, my view differs from hers, and I will do what I think is appropriate.' I told him about the idea I had begun to consider – that I argue the appeal by myself. I would not be able to find an Israeli attorney, especially after Eitan's death and my injury. And I was firmly opposed to a foreign attorney because I was convinced that, beyond not being of the slightest help, he would in fact be a hindrance. Demjanjuk answered as usual: 'On all those matters I leave the decision to my family. I'll accept whatever they decide.' I also told him about the request I had filed for an additional postponement, and about my trip to the States. Demjanjuk again shook my hand warmly, and said he hoped that 'when you come back it will be without the bandage'.

On 5 February 1989 I went to the Supreme Court. Shaked and Bainwall expressed sincere interest in how I was. I told them about my medical condition and hoped they would not oppose my request for a postponement. They promised they would not. We entered Chief Justice Shamgar's chambers; the five judges and the Registrar were already in their places.

I opened by explaining that as a result of my injury, I was unable to do virtually anything with regard to the case. I was about to travel to the US for special medical care, which I hoped would bring about an improvement in my left eye. There was no way I would be able to present the appeal pleadings three months hence, especially if I had to handle the entire case myself. I ended by saying: 'If the honourable court believes that a postponement until 1 January 1990 is too long, I am prepared this very moment to resign my position and to turn the case over to a court-appointed defence attorney.' Deputy Chief Justice Menachem Elon asked, in a critical tone of voice: 'Why have you not brought in another Israeli attorney during the two months since your injury?' In reply to this manifest display of insensitivity, and because of the tone in which the question had been asked, I said obstinately, with no undue politeness, 'If Your Honour thinks that at the door to my office there is a long line of attorneys shouting, "Sheftel, let me join, Sheftel, take me," then I have to disappoint you. No one is anxious to join me.' I explained that I had contacted other lawyers whom I thought might agree, and been firmly rejected by all of them. 'His Honour the Chief Justice asked to know whether a few months hence the court would not find itself faced with a situation in which I would give notice that I was still unable to argue the appeal. My answer is that, unless I am attacked again, I am convinced that on any date after 1 January 1990 I will be prepared, either alone or with another attorney, to report to the court and argue the appeal.'

The floor was given to the prosecution, and Shaked said drily: 'Paul Chumak still appears on the list of the appellant's attorneys, and he can assist Mr Sheftel. There is no need to search for another attorney. The prosecution is prepared to agree to a short delay of not more than two months from the date set for the hearing.' They would agree to a postponement until the beginning of July. I was furious, since Shaked knew very well from his conversations with me that Chumak's involvement in the case had already ended. Furthermore, he had told me only a few minutes ago that he would agree to the postponement. I managed to keep my composure and explained that the previous postponement had been given solely to allow the appellant to obtain the services of another attorney, and that we had returned to the *status quo ante*. All that had happened to me and the late Dov Eitan since the beginning of December was sufficient to justify granting an additional extension.

Chief Justice Shamgar announced that, in accordance with the defence's request, the appeal had been postponed until 1 November 1989, and that the hearing schedule then would be as previously determined. My request was thus answered nearly in full, and I was satisfied. I thanked the judges for their consideration of the appellant's needs, and they wished me a full and speedy recovery. I was furious at Shaked and left without exchanging another word with him and Bainwall. This postponement paved the way for another, and in the end the appeal was set for 14 May 1990.

In March 1990 the evidence showing that Ivan the Terrible had been Ivan Marchenko, not Ivan Demjanjuk, began to emerge – slowly, steadily, unstoppably. It was possible to unearth this evidence only because the Communist government in Poland had collapsed and the Soviet regime was disintegrating. So Yehezkeli, who had tried to blind me and prevent me from defending Demjanjuk, actually brought about a delay in the appeal, and this delay made it possible to discover the evidence providing absolute proof of Demjanjuk's innocence. A modern version of the story of Balaam, I thought to myself.*

I watched with interest the disgraceful way in which the authorities dealt with Yehezkeli. While in hospital I said in a newspaper interview that 'Even though, according to the law, what Yehezkeli did to me is defined as intentional grievous bodily harm – a crime that carries a maximum sentence of twenty years – he will be put on trial for a lesser crime, and he will get a light sentence.' My prediction was soon borne out. Yehezkeli was charged with actual bodily harm, a crime with a maximum sentence of seven years. The prosecution asked the Jerusalem District Court to detain him for the duration of the trial, but the hearing on detainment was a total farce.

It was held on 13 December 1988 before, of all people, Judge Tal. The press reported that Tal had not hesitated to free Yehezkeli even

---

* Balaam, an enemy of the children of Israel, intended to curse them but in practice he blessed them instead.

after the latter refused to express contrition and to promise not to harm me again. Yehezkeli, who had begun to consider himself some sort of 'national hero', had contemptuously rejected Judge Tal's request, adding derisively: 'I am prepared to apologize only to Mrs Shabtai.' Despite this, Judge Tal rewarded him with release on bail.

In the State of Israel, judges have detained hundreds, perhaps thousands, of defendants for the duration of their trials, even when the charge was burglary or selling a packet of hashish. It would seem, then, that for Judge Tal such crimes are more serious than trying to blind and disfigure a defence attorney as punishment for his decision to represent an accused man. This, however, was not the end of the farce. Judge Tal delayed Yehezkeli's release by twenty-four hours to allow the prosecution to appeal his decision to the Supreme Court. But the prosecution didn't bother to avail itself of this option, which shows that it had not really seriously intended to have Yehezkeli detained.

As expected, I was asked to comment on this. I did not hesitate to use the strongest possible language: 'To illustrate the significance of the court's decision, the following rhetorical question should be asked: What would have happened if Ed Nishnic, Demjanjuk's son-in-law, had poured acid into the eyes of one of the Holocaust survivors who had been a witness for the prosecution, causing damage like my injury, and he was brought before Judge Tal for a hearing on a petition to detain him for the duration of the trial? And if, during that hearing, he had brazenly rejected Judge Tal's request that he express regret, and instead of promising not to repeat his offence had stressed that the prosecution witness had falsely accused his father-in-law? Under such circumstances, would Judge Tal have released Nishnic on bail?'

At the trial itself, the prosecution's misconduct was even worse than at the bail hearing. Yehezkeli admitted the crime and was convicted on the basis of his confession. The sentencing hearing was set for 24 May 1989, before Judge Ezra Hadaia, whose son had helped me rinse my eyes. It is routine, before this type of hearing, for the prosecution to attempt to gather evidence to convince the court of the serious nature of the defendant's crime. Collecting medical certification of the damage done by the defendant and evidence of the victim's suffering are things the prosecution does almost automatically in such cases. Yet these rules did not apply when Demjanjuk's defence counsel was the victim. Ten days before the sentencing hearing no one from the District Attorney's office had contacted me, either to summon me as a witness or to obtain documents demonstrating the seriousness of my injury.

Obviously my forecast that the prosecution would want to sweep the entire event under the carpet was about to be realized. I decided to intervene and wrote a sharply worded letter to the Jerusalem District Attorney, Uzi Hasson. I criticized his failure to request documents that could serve as evidence in Yehezkeli's sentencing hearing; I insisted on being called to testify; and that the prosecution submit evidence through me to prove how serious my injury and its consequences were. I warned that if there was not an immediate and positive answer to my demands, I would not keep quiet.

A few days later attorney Avia Alef from the District Attorney's office called me to set up an urgent meeting for 18 May, a week before the sentencing hearing. I brought the many documents I had and, after protesting that the meeting would not have taken place if I hadn't sent my outspoken letter, I presented them to Alef. She examined them and said they would be most useful to her, and we agreed that I would be called to testify.

So, on 24 May 1989, I reported to Judge Hadaia's courtroom in the Jerusalem District Court. The press was well represented, and Miriam Eitan had also come. My testimony lasted for about half an hour, during which various medical certifications were submitted to the court, including the cost of an operation I had had in the US in February. I described the physical suffering and the serious damage done to my eye. I reminded the court of Yehezkeli's boasts and his public threats to attack me again, and mentioned also that he had no compunction about entering my elderly mother's home on false pretences and making threats on my life. I glanced occasionally at Judge Hadaia's face, and got the impression that he was listening with great interest and taking my words seriously. When I left the stand I felt I had been able to frustrate the prosecution's plot to let Yehezkeli off with no serious penalty.

I remained to hear the prosecution's and defence's sentencing arguments, which began immediately after my testimony. The sentence was not handed down that day, but on 14 June. Yehezkeli was sentenced to three years' imprisonment and was ordered to pay me damages of $5,000, plus another $6,000 to cover my American operation. I heard of the sentence in the States, where I had gone for another lecture tour, and was satisfied. Yehezkeli's appeal to the Supreme Court was rejected. He served his full sentence, with a third off for good behaviour.

I had landed in Cleveland on 10 February 1989. My eye was still bandaged and my pockets were filled with bottles of eyedrops. Nishnic and Johnny welcomed me warmly, and said again how sorry they were for what I had endured in recent months.

The next day, after we had eaten breakfast together in the hotel, we went to the defence fund's basement headquarters. I began by saying:

'In the wake of Eitan's death and my injury, there is no chance that an Israeli attorney of any stature will consent to join me. All the candidates I have approached have rejected the proposal outright. You know my views on the participation of a foreign attorney, especially during the appeals stage. We are now almost nine months before the appeal hearing, and for the first time I feel I have enough time to prepare properly and to assume the burden of arguing the entire case by myself.' Nishnic and Johnny were surprised at this: I had never spoken about it in such an open and determined way, though I had hinted at the possibility during our phone conversations since I came out of hospital.

Nishnic asked, 'Are you sure, especially after your injury, that you can handle it physically?'

'I am sure that within two or three weeks I'll be completely back together mentally, and I'll find the physical strength with no trouble,' I responded with confidence. I added, 'It's not an easy job to argue a case like this for two straight weeks before the Supreme Court. But I presented the summations to the district court almost entirely on my own, and that took nearly two weeks. I'm convinced I can do in the Supreme Court what I did in the district court.'

Johnny interrupted: 'There's a reasonable chance that a prominent American lawyer will agree to join the defence in the end.'

'Under no circumstances,' I replied firmly. 'I have no strength nor desire to begin teaching the whole case to an American attorney. I'd also have to give him a comprehensive course in Israeli law. That's just not in the realms of possibility.' Finally, after an hour's exchange, we reached complete understanding: I would argue the appeal myself.

Nishnic said that, since I would be the only defence attorney, it was necessary to ensure my safety from criminals like Yehezkeli. They suggested I live in the US or Canada until the appeal hearing began, at their expense of course. I rejected the idea out of hand. 'Whilst I will appear alone in the appeal, I must be in my office to prepare for it properly. I will need to write a great many drafts, and have them typed in Hebrew, before the argument reaches its final form. Nor will I leave my mother alone in Israel for such a long time. I will not allow Yehezkeli to frighten me, or make me run away across the ocean.' Nishnic tried to insist: 'Just think what would happen if someone were to hurt you a week before the appeal.' I asserted: 'If I am prepared to take the risk and, instead of running away from the case, assume additional responsibility, you too will have to live with that risk.' Nishnic and Johnny realized they would have to let the matter drop.

I then told them about my plan to fly to Boston for a medical consultation on my left eye. Before I could finish my sentence Johnny cut me off: 'Of course, we assume financial responsibility for everything to do with your injured eye.' When we came up from the basement for lunch, Irene and Lydia hugged me and launched into an excited conversation on the turbulent events since the previous December. We sat around the table for two hours. I spent the remainder of the weekend resting, with occasional meetings and interviews with the Cleveland media. On Monday morning Johnny took me to the airport, and I landed in Boston at about noon.

Professor Kenyon's clinic was in a twelve-storey building of clinics and operating theatres for eye injuries. Some of the best eye specialists in the world worked here, and Kenyon's clinic, affiliated to the Harvard University medical school, was one of the most important in the building. Professor Kenyon, a man of average height, very energetic, in his early forties, was waiting for me. After exchanging greetings – he said *shalom* as if to hint at his Jewish origin – he examined my eyes with a magnifying glass. Then he asked me to tell him how the injury had occurred.

When I finished, Professor Kenyon said, 'I read about you in the papers, but I didn't realize that you were the Israeli who was supposed to come to my clinic today. It's horrible to have incurred such an injury just because you've been brave enough to undertake the defence in such a trial. In just a minute we'll see how we can help you.'

I spent the next two hours undergoing a series of examinations conducted by his assistants. About half an hour after these were over, Kenyon entered the examination room and said in a conversational, business-like tone: 'I recommend you be operated on this coming Thursday. The operation will be conducted simultaneously on both eyes. In your left eye, the cornea's protective membrane, the epithelium, has been completely destroyed. The only way to repair it, and pave the way for rehabilitating the whole eye, is to transplant living cells from the epithelium of your right eye. The transplanted cells will be accepted by the left eye and reproduce until they create a new epithelium. The operation, called a limbal autograft transplantation, will take place under general anaesthesia and will last three or four hours. There is a very high probability of success, more than ninety per cent. It will take a day for you to recover, and afterwards you'll have daily check-ups in our clinic for a week.'

I was stunned. I had assumed I had come for an examination and advice, and suddenly I heard that both my eyes would be operated on, immediately, in a foreign country. All this without any friends or relatives to care for me and be with me after the operation. It was a very frightening scenario; I expressed my fears to Professor Kenyon. He explained that this was an operation he himself had developed, that he had performed it thirty-one times, all successful. It was unfortunate I had not come to him earlier, since it was most desirable to perform the operation within ten days of the injury. He made me feel much better when he said that in any case there would be no damage to the right eye, and emphasized that he personally would perform the operation from start to finish. I found myself being persuaded.

I asked how much it would cost. Kenyon's answer again surprised me. 'The hospital's operating-room costs will be between $5,000 and $6,000. I myself will not accept any payment for performing the surgery.' I expressed my deep gratitude for this noble gesture, but with typical Israeli-Jewish chutzpah I asked if I would be able to pay the hospital in instalments. I was aware of the huge financial difficulties faced by the Demjanjuk defence fund, and I wanted to reduce the pressure on it.

'Will a thousand dollars a month be all right?' Professor Kenyon asked cheerfully.

'Of course, and thank you again,' I answered.

Then he asked, 'Will we see you on Thursday?'

'In principle the answer is yes, but I want to sleep on it. I will call tomorrow morning and notify you of my final decision.'

Back in Cleveland Johnny offered to accompany me and stay with me in Boston until I recovered from the operation. Nishnic called some time after I had gone to my room at the hotel. 'Shefy, are you sure about what you're doing? Johnny told me it's an operation on both eyes, a very complex and innovative operation. Don't you think it's too much of a risk, especially since it involves operating on the healthy eye?' His concern touched me, and I thanked him. I explained my positive impression of Professor Kenyon and said I was not ignoring the risks, so I had not yet given a final positive answer. 'We will respect your decision and stand by you, but think very carefully, it's really a fateful decision,' Nishnic said.

The real problem was actually the question of operating on a healthy eye. I was quite troubled by the possibility that I would wake up from the operation and discover that my good eye had also been injured because the scalpel had been a fraction of a millimetre off. The fear grew as time passed since my consultation with Professor Kenyon. But, I thought, this tiny risk to my right eye might pave the way for the recovery of my left, and was a risk worth taking. When it comes down to it, flying to Cleveland is also a risk, as is driving a car or crossing the street. Everything a man does carries a certain risk, but we do these things every single day.

I am a 'lone wolf'. Throughout my life I have made a point of taking important decisions by myself. I did not call anyone in Israel to get their advice. I weighed the pros and cons over and over again, and a few hours later I decided to do it.

When I woke up in the morning, I called Dr Kenyon's clinic at once and informed his secretary of my decision. I could barely sleep that night, in fear that I would wake up from the operation blind.

Thursday morning was spent in a long series of examinations to test my body's fitness to undergo the operation. I put on a hospital gown and was taken down a maze of corridors into the operating theatre. Professor Kenyon was waiting there and in a soothing voice promised me that I was in good hands and that everything would be fine. 'I only hope I'll be able to see when I wake up,' were my last words before I was put under. I just caught his reply: 'Both eyes will be bandaged when you wake up, but you'll be able to see a bit from the bottom edge of the bandage on your right eye and that's how you'll know that you're not blind.'

When I woke up in the recovery room, I felt a piercing chill. My mouth was dry. Immediately I nudged up the bottom edge of the bandage on my right eye. I could see. 'I'm not blind,' I whispered to myself. Then I called out, 'I'm cold! I want something to drink!' Within seconds a nurse was at my side, putting a sponge soaked in water to my lips and telling me that the chill would pass in a few minutes.

After about an hour and a half, during which I began to feel more normal, I was taken into another room. I heard Johnny say happily, 'Shefy, I've spoken to Professor Kenyon. He told me that, as far as one can say anything immediately after an operation, he believes it all went well.'

'Johnny, the most important thing is that I can see in my right eye,' I said with great emotion. 'I feel very tired; I want to sleep.' Johnny said he would stay at my bedside for a while to make sure I was all right. I was asleep within minutes.

The next morning I felt fine, as if I had not been operated on at all. My right eye's field of vision was blocked, but I could see downwards because the bandage was not attached to my cheek. At noon we returned to Professor Kenyon's office, and I thanked him whole-heartedly. He removed the bandages and examined my eyes for two minutes. 'Within three or four days your right eye will return to its previous condition,' he said. 'As for your left eye, the process of the epithelium's regrowth will take about a month. It will begin within the next few days, and our daily examinations will tell us if we're going in the right direction. The operation itself proceeded without a hitch.' He explained to Johnny and me how to care for the eye ourselves, with several kinds of drops and ointments.

We stayed in a hotel in one of the Boston suburbs. Johnny cared for me devotedly, applying eyedrops and ointment and changing bandages. Within a few days we were able to begin taking enjoyable trips around Boston. On 23 February we came in for the last check-up. Professor Kenyon glowed with pleasure. 'About half the cornea is already covered with the new epithelium. It's growing much faster than expected.' I kissed him. 'You are simply phenomenal, and a *mentsch*,' I said. Kenyon then gave me instructions for the days to come, and supplied additional drops and ointments as well as a detailed letter to Professor Blumenthal with precise instructions for further treatment. Finally, he asked me to attend the clinic any time I was in the US.

There were some minor complications in the regrowth of the epithelium. It 'went on strike' and refused to grow in a small area in the centre of the cornea. But after about a year it grew to cover the entire cornea and the eye gradually returned to normal. In July 1990, during one of my further visits to his clinic, Kenyon informed me that my left eye was almost fit and would soon be ready for a cornea transplant, which would completely restore the vision. Towards the end of 1990 the eye regained a normal appearance, with the exception of a small scar near the pupil.

In mid-March 1989 I resumed my preparations for the appeal with full vigour. It was now definitely agreed that I would argue it alone. I was convinced that I was ready and able, even with only one healthy eye.

12 · A Precedent

As early as the trial's second week it had been obvious to me that the press coverage was no more than a smear campaign based on a prejudgement of Demjanjuk. The inevitable result was hostile public opinion about us. Doron began urging me to lodge a formal criminal complaint against the press as a whole, or at least one newspaper. The media coverage was, almost without exception, a gross violation of the principle of *sub judice*, enshrined in Israeli law; this principle forbids the publication of anything liable to affect the outcome of a trial.

I have found the Israeli press repugnant almost from the time I was old enough to have an opinion on it. As far as I am concerned, it is vulgar, shallow and ignorant. It blurs the line between fact and opinion, loves gossip and tends to prejudge. There are of course exceptions, but that is how I see the picture as a whole. These faults, as well as many others, were apparent in the daily reporting of Demjanjuk's show-trial. Doron was well aware of my opinions about the press, and agreed with most of them; he thus had a hard time understanding why I did not adopt his suggestion at once.

The truth is that I thought making such a complaint would be tantamount to admitting that the attacks were hurting me. In all my contacts with the national press I continued to display disdain for all journalists; there were some I refused to speak to at all. I referred to them as the court sycophants, with a smile that expressed a mixture of contempt and indifference. My behaviour bore fruit. When these reporters realized that their attacks were not making me angry, they began to speak of the perverted enjoyment I got out of this smear campaign, and about how I had become a hated man. For this reason, and this reason alone, I persisted for many long months in opposing Doron's suggestion.

The event that finally changed my mind was the discovery that the judges were themselves busily collecting every item of media filth about the trial. If some, or even one, of those responsible for the material in the press albums of Levin and his colleagues were to be tried and convicted, this would discredit the entire proceedings. When else has anyone heard of a court case in which the presiding judges, who also decide the question of guilt or innocence, occupied themselves for its duration by reading press reports that prejudged the defendant?

My huge workload, and all the various dramatic events, were such that only during the break in the trial caused by the meeting of the Zionist Congress did I have time to submit, on 8 December 1987, a criminal complaint against the newspaper *Yediot Aharanot*; one of its journalists, Noah Klieger; and its Editor, Dov Yudkovski. Though submitted in my name, it had been drafted largely by Doron. He estimated that there would be no choice but to petition the Supreme Court, sitting in its capacity as the High Court of Justice. Doron was sure I would win. Attached to the complaint were twenty-four articles written by Noah Klieger and published in *Yediot Aharanot* during the course of the trial. I could have filed a similar complaint against every daily newspaper in Israel, as well as against Israel Television, the Voice of Israel and the Israeli defence forces' radio station. On Doron's advice, however, I decided to focus on Klieger's articles, which we thought were the most serious examples of their type.

All these articles exhibited, in various forms, a presumption that Demjanjuk was Ivan the Terrible, defamation of the defence's expert witnesses and vilification of me for serving as defence attorney. For instance, in an article that appeared on 25 February 1987 under a headline that speaks for itself – FACING THE EXECUTIONER – he said, 'Yesterday, forty-five years on, Pinhas Epstein appeared on the witness stand in Binyanei Ha'uma, facing the executioner himself.' A piece published on 23 April, headlined YORAM SHEFTEL, HOW CAN YOU EXPLAIN THE CONTRADICTION, asks: 'How will Yoram Sheftel explain serving as defence attorney in the Demjanjuk trial, of all trials, if he really is a loyal and devoted Jew?' The headline MISSION IMPOSSIBLE, on 14 August, stood over the following: 'During the four days of hearings in the Demjanjuk trial in Jerusalem, the defence has suffered two more harsh blows . . . So there can be no doubt that the defence, which was in a difficult situation to begin with where the Travniki document is concerned, is now finding itself having to choose between two impossible options.' Each and every one of the twenty-four articles was a blatant and arrogant violation of the law.

The police responded to the complaint exactly two weeks later: 'After investigating the complaint, the police have decided not to pursue their investigations, because no actual violation of the law is involved.' Nothing shows so well as this response how the performance of Israeli law-enforcement officials – the police and the State Attorney's office – is infected by distortions of the law that border on actual corruption, in every matter touching on the Demjanjuk affair.

This statement was signed by Chief Superintendent Moshe Mizrahi, head of the Investigations Division of the Tel Aviv police. He was not only a senior police officer but also a lawyer by profession. He had served for years as a criminal prosecutor for the police, and had appeared in court in many thousands of criminal cases. He knew very well what every first-year law student knows – that these articles amounted to criminal acts, violations of the principle of *sub judice*. Only a warped person could conclude that 'no actual violation of the law is involved'.

We decided to submit an 'administrative' appeal, to the Attorney General, Yosef Harish, against the police's decision not to act on my complaint. The appeal, also written largely by Doron, stated: 'In the humble opinion of the undersigned, there must be a really incomprehensible measure of mental deficiency, insensitivity and bad judgement to conclude, as this decision does, that there is "no actual violation of the law involved" ... The decision is not only so unreasonable as to intimate that it was made under the influence of improper considerations; it also clearly contradicts Supreme Court precedents and clear legal criteria, established in cases of less serious violations.' The appeal was sent to the Attorney General on 28 December 1987, the day I led Judges Levin, Tal and Dorner to admit in the courtroom, on record, that they had indeed collected in their chambers everything published in the Hebrew press on the trial while it was in progress, and that they had read these publications, supplied to them under the terms of a contract with a cuttings agency.

Klieger's articles were, of course, among those appearing in the albums in the judges' chambers. These two actions were thus connected and meant to supply the basis, in the eventual appeal to the Supreme Court, for the argument that judges who collect and read such articles on the defendant before them, for the entire length of the trial, are disqualified from passing judgement on him. This alone should have been sufficient to bring about the disqualification of the entire process and the reversal of its verdict.

As expected, the Attorney General did not rush to respond to the appeal. Three months to the day after it was submitted, Doron and I drafted another petition. It stated that 'If, within a short time, I do not receive a decision on the matter of the administrative appeal, I will interpret it only as a rejection of the appeal and I will have to petition the Supreme Court for suitable remedy.' Magically, within less than a week, the Attorney General replied in person: 'I have considered your appeal and examined the investigation file. However, under the circumstances, including the extensive coverage the Demjanjuk trial has had and the deeply emotional nature of the reports of the trial, I have decided not to instruct Israel Police to continue investigating your complaint. I therefore see no reason to accept your appeal.'

Despite the judicious attempt to circumvent the real question – the fact that all the articles were a blatant violation of the law – the Attorney General's response was both completely incorrect from a legal point of view and motivated by corrupt considerations. His answer cannot otherwise be understood. After all, the Israeli public prosecution had filed charges in the past against reporters for single articles with the slightest hint of opinion concerning the innocence or guilt of a defendant. And here the Attorney General, head of the state prosecution, was saying to all intents and purposes that when a man charged with Nazi crimes is tried in the State of Israel there is to be *no* enforcement of that law of *sub judice*. If that is the case, something is rotten in the State of Israel's rule of law.

Now the way was open for a petition to the Supreme Court to revoke the Attorney General's decision and instruct him to bring the publishers of the unlawful articles to justice. On 12 April 1988, less than a week before the verdict on Demjanjuk was announced, this petition was submitted. Doron was my attorney.

The petition was tersely written, only three pages long. It contained a concise progress report since the submission of my original complaint. Attached to the petition were photocopies of all the articles that were the subject of complaint. The petition said of the Attorney General's decision that it 'suffers from extreme unreasonableness and fundamental distortion, based on entirely irrelevant and alien considerations, inasmuch as it says in practice that for a subject on which the reporting is of "a deeply emotional nature", as in the Demjanjuk trial, the media are not governed by the law.'

No one could dispute the fact that the twenty-four articles amounted to a criminal violation, and that their publishers should be indicted and convicted. We were, however, faced with a double difficulty. First, since the establishment of the State of Israel no one had won a petition to the Supreme Court with an attack on the Attorney General's discretion in charging a person with a crime. Even when it disapproved of the Attorney General's decisions, the Supreme Court had always avoided intervening, because of what it termed the 'broad discretion' that the law allows the Attorney General. Only in cases where it could be proved that the Attorney General reached his decision corruptly or with 'extreme unreasonableness' would the court intervene in his discretionary powers. We decided to forgo the corruption argument, even though we were both convinced that it was actually the real reason for the

Attorney General's decision; taking such an extreme position would probably rouse the court against us. What remained was, then, the second cause, 'extreme unreasonableness', but we guessed that the Supreme Court would not easily reach a decision that the Attorney General's considerations could be defined as such.

The second problem was the argument we expected the respondents to make: to try to play on the Supreme Court's sympathies for the principle of free expression, arguing that if they were brought to trial the freedom of the press, which the Supreme Court had protected devotedly since the state was founded, would be irreparably infringed.

The preliminary hearing before the Supreme Court, sitting as the High Court of Justice – on whether there was good cause to issue an order instructing the Attorney General to explain why he should not put Klieger and his colleagues on trial – was set for 18 May. Harish had submitted his response to the court six days earlier, and explicitly acknowledged, for the first time, that the twenty-four articles were *prima facie* violations of the law. He cited three reasons for his decision not to bring the publishers to trial: 'Despite all that we have said of Klieger's articles, even if taken together they do not create any doubts about the proper judicial conduct of the trial'; 'The Attorney General did not see fit to ignore the fact that the subject of this trial is the subject of strong emotions, and that these may lead to extraordinary expressions'; 'the special personal circumstances of Noah Klieger, a Holocaust survivor'. These feeble excuses proved conclusively that those who had encouraged the media campaign against Demjanjuk and me were the members and head of the state prosecution office. Each line of Klieger's articles helped to fan the flames and make the public think that Demjanjuk's acquittal was not on the cards. The people responsible were serving the prosecution, and for that reason it decided not to bring them to justice.

The hearing on the order lasted less than two minutes. Justice Moshe Beiski, who headed the bench, turned to the Attorney General's representative and said, 'Since there is a consensus that an infraction of the law has occurred, it is clear that an order should be given.' He ordered the Attorney General to reply within forty-five days. The press coverage of the hearing was extremely modest.

About a month later the Attorney General submitted his brief reply to the order. He asserted that 'Because of the policy of restraint and balance that the Attorney General sees fit to apply to the relative weight of these two values, of the integrity of the judicial process on the one hand and freedom of expression on the other, he has not seen fit to change his position, which is principally based on the special circumstances of the matter.'

The hearing on the petition itself was set for 17 July. This was very good timing for me: it was possible that the court would rule on the matter before beginning to hear Demjanjuk's appeal, then set for 5 December. If we were to win, we would be able to make use of the ruling in the appeal hearing. Eitan also thought success with the petition would be of great help in the appeal, especially in the argument about the district court's misconduct.

A long series of postponements then ensued, and the hearing was finally set for 8 June 1989. At that time the appeal, after two postponements of its own, was set for 1 November 1989. Doron assumed the greater part of the labour of preparing the argument, although we consulted regularly on its structure and substance. Doron also made the entire argument for the petition in court, while I sat at his side. The hearing was held before Justices Gavriel Bach, Avraham Halima, and Theodore Or.

Doron focused on two main issues. The first was the Attorney General's principal assertion that he was not charging Klieger *et al.* because it had not been proved that the articles had actually impaired the judicial process being conducted against Demjanjuk. This, we claimed, was devoid of any legal content, since the law of *sub judice* did not demand any such proof. The second issue was the Attorney General's reasons, which were so immaterial as to fall into the category of being 'blatantly capricious', so invalidating his decision. The court accepted the arguments.

Klieger's attorney argued that I had given interviews to the press during the trial, and that therefore 'my hands were not clean' and I was not 'worthy' of receiving remedy from the court. Doron was prepared on this point, but the court did not discuss it on the grounds that it was required 'to judge the petition on its merits'. The Attorney General's representative tried to demonstrate the logic and wisdom of the reasons used and to demonstrate at least that they were not illogical to the point where the Supreme Court had to intervene in the decision.

Doron's argument was so persuasive that even the respondents' attorney complimented him. We were in an excellent mood when the hearing was over but, since no one in Israel had ever won such a petition, we did not expect to win. I tend to be pessimistic about the result of every trial I take part in, even when I am convinced that not only right, but the law as well, is on my side.

Now the months of waiting for the verdict began. I was especially preoccupied by the question of whether it would be handed down before the appeal hearing began, now postponed to 14 May 1990, which increased the likelihood that the decision on the petition would come first. At the beginning of November 1989 my office received notification that the verdict would be handed down on Thursday 16 November.

On the appointed day Doron and I drove to Jerusalem. We were quite tense, and consoled ourselves by recalling that the argument we had made in court had been of a very high calibre. Even if we lost, we would probably not be required to pay costs. When we entered the Supreme Court's Courtroom 1, we were surprised to see the media well-represented. Justice Bach addressed us, and after checking to see that the representatives of the other parties were also present, he began to recite, very slowly: 'By majority vote we have decided...' Doron and I exchanged glances. It was clear that there was at least a minority opinion in our favour. Then came the incredible surprise: '... to accept the petition. We have decided that the Attorney General's reasoning is without foundation ... the judgement will be given to the parties immediately, for their examination.' I could barely keep myself from jumping with joy. Doron was also delighted.

We were overwhelmed by our fantastic success. The first microphone pushed towards me was held by the Israel Defence Forces' Radio correspondent. I referred him to Doron, as my attorney. But Doron, as is his wont, refused to say a single word into a microphone. Since I am much less choosy than he about this, I agreed to give my reaction to the verdict. 'This is the first time since the state was founded that a petitioner has won such a petition against the Attorney General, and for that I thank my attorney in this petition, my partner Doron Beckerman,' I said emotionally. 'The judgement proves the justice of my argument about the media's criminal behaviour – and this includes your radio station – with regard to the entire coverage of the Demjanjuk trial. But the prosecution itself is even more guilty than the press, because it egged the criminals on, if only by not bringing them to trial for prejudging Demjanjuk's case. The prosecution's support for the media lawbreakers has been so wide-ranging and absolute that the Attorney General, in his desperate attempt to avoid taking them to court as a result of my complaint, did not hesitate to make use of reasoning that the Supreme Court's verdict has just described as "without foundation". And, most important, Demjanjuk's judges, by their explicit admission, read this criminal material in their chambers every single day throughout the course of the trial.'

I made similar comments many more times that day, and every time gave me great satisfaction.

The press began reporting at length about the precedent-setting decision. Law professors analysed it; the weekend papers devoted entire pages to reporting the ruling; the headlines told the truth at last: IMPORTANT CONSTITUTIONAL RULING; SUPREME COURT ORDERS INVESTIGATION OF PRESS REPORTS ON DEMJANJUK TRIAL; NEW PRECEDENT, HARD QUESTIONS. The pointed criticism in the ruling, of both the Attorney General and the contemptible coverage of the trial by *Yediot Aharanot* and Klieger, was quoted again and again. I could not have been happier. The only thing that bothered me was that all the attention was directed at me; the press did not give Doron the credit he deserved for having argued the entire petition in court.

That evening Nishnic had called me at home. 'You did it!' he exclaimed. I gave him a brief rundown of the important points in the verdict and their useful implications for the argument we would make in the appeal itself. With each word my spirits rose to the skies. 'I'll call Doron to thank him right away,' Ed promised when we hung up.

There were several reasons for my feeling so wonderful. First, the verdict was a heavy blow to the Attorney General's prestige; as I have noted, this was the first time since the establishment of the state that his discretionary judgement on such an important matter had been nullified. Second, one of the newspaper reporters who had led the campaign of incitement and slander had been declared by the Supreme Court, just as I had argued from the first week of the trial, to have broken the law. Third, the press, which had tried so hard to hurt me, ended up making me the first petitioner to win such a case, resulting in a ruling that will be taught to generations of constitutional-law students at Israeli law schools as 'the Sheftel rule'. Fourth and most importantly, the victory, together with the admission by Levin and his colleagues that they had collected and read press clippings during the trial, could only mean one thing: that for the entire length of the trial Demjanjuk's judges had intentionally exposed themselves to inflammatory material which prejudged the defendant. Of course, this alone was sufficient to disqualify the entire proceeding, so I had another weighty argument for the appeal.

Nearly a year passed before charges were finally filed against *Yediot Aharanot*, Dov Yudkovski and Noah Klieger, and the case was only decided on 17 May 1994 – with the conviction of the three defendants for violating the rule of *sub judice* – even though it could have been ruled on in less than an hour. This was due to the endless delaying tactics used by the defendants' lawyers, fully assisted by the Tel Aviv magistrate who was trying the case.

This was the first important setback for the prosecution in the Demjanjuk affair. With this ruling, I actually began to believe we had a meaningful chance of winning the appeal. Just a small chance, but a small chance is not the same as no chance at all. I had just seen proof of that.

13 · The Appeal

By the time I returned from my operation in the US in March 1989, it had been agreed that I would argue the entire appeal alone. I have never enjoyed my work so much as during this period. Serenely and at my own pace, I devoted several hours each day for fourteen months to drafting and honing my arguments. For the first time since becoming Demjanjuk's defence attorney, I was not pressed for time.

I travelled to North America and western Europe seven times in connection with the case, and also to Romania and the Far East for holidays. Instead of the endless turbulence of the previous two years, my life was tranquil. The press had almost completely stopped covering the affair, and the hostility towards me faded. The Supreme Court decision on my petition was also rendered during this period. In short, it was a wonderful time.

Now I could increase my familiarity with the huge amount of material. Since I knew that I would be alone on the defence bench, I devoted much thought to organizational preparation for the hearing. It was important that I be able to locate any document or quote that I needed quickly, especially in response to questions from the justices.

The appeal notice constituted the foundation of the argument; it was more than a hundred pages long. An additional, separate binder contained supplementary arguments, relating to each section and subsection. The two binders together contained some 650 pages.

I also prepared binders containing the prosecution and defence exhibits in chronological order. Each binder had a table of contents that set out the subject-matter and number of each exhibit, the date it had been accepted as evidence and the page of the record in which the decision to accept it had been made. Two further binders contained photocopied pages from the court record that I might need during the argument. This was in addition to the quotes from the record included in the binder of supplementary material, which I intended to submit to the justices at the end of my arguments, to serve, along with the appeal notice and the record of the Supreme Court hearing, as an aid to the court in finding its way through the maze of my argument.

Yet another file was to be submitted at the beginning of the argument to each one of the five justices. This contained a selection of quotes from the court record and the exhibit file, arranged according to each of the substantive sections of the argument; likewise, I prepared a separate collection of quotes and cross-references to pages of the court record, demonstrating the misconduct of the judges in the lower court.

None of these preparations would have been possible without Tzvia's proficiency and her perfect familiarity with the endless complexities of the case. The prosecutors, despite their staff of lawyers, apprentices and clerks – a total of a dozen people – confessed to me that there was no comparison between their level of organization and ours.

Because of my injury, as I have noted, the appeal hearing was delayed, to 1 November 1989. On 12 September 1989, the Supreme Court had decided, after a five-hour meeting, to acquiesce to an additional request I had submitted for a delay until 14 May 1990. Here is how it happened.

There were quite a few anti-Semites amongst the North American Ukrainian community who lent their support to Demjanjuk. Their goal was not only to help Demjanjuk, whether or not he was Ivan the Terrible, but first and foremost to paralyse completely, or at least interfere substantially with, the functioning of the Office of Special Investigations. The OSI had been established in the late 1970s within the American Department of Justice in order to expose, denaturalize, extradite or deport all the Nazi collaborators who had emigrated to the United States at the end of the war, and who had hidden their war crimes from the American immigration authorities. Most of the OSI's opponents' activity was disseminating false propaganda, and their accusations were for the most part lacking any factual basis. With the Demjanjuk affair, however, they had a real catch.

In mid-1985, one of the activists discovered by chance that OSI agents habitually threw documents into the garbage cans of the McDonald's restaurant opposite their offices on K Street in Washington DC. He removed a plastic bag full of OSI documents from the dustbin. From that day onward, for two years, the contents of the K Street bins were carefully monitored, and more than twenty-thousand documents were collected. Some time later, most of these were sent to Nishnic and Johnny, who diligently studied and sorted them over the course of several years. Hundreds of the documents came from Demjanjuk's file in all its stages between the years 1976 and 1986.

On 12 July 1989 I set out for a vacation in the Far East that took me to Thailand, the Philippines and Singapore. After all the traumatic events I had been through since the summer of 1986, this was probably the most enjoyable vacation in the east I have ever spent. When I reached Manila a fax was waiting in my hotel telling me to call Nishnic urgently in Cleveland because new and important documents had been discovered. Nishnic, excited as usual, told me that among the 'garbage-can documents', as we called them, were two which proved that OSI officials had actually forged Otto Horn's identification of Demjanjuk as Ivan the Terrible. 'There are definitely further documents,' Nishnic continued enthusiastically, 'that the OSI is concealing from us, and we are about to file a suit against the OSI through John Broadly, to get them handed over to us.'

'Send me the documents immediately,' I said. 'If there is really something in them, when I return to Israel I will submit a request for them to be accepted as additional defence evidence in the appeal, and ask for another six-month postponement.'

A few minutes later the two astonishing documents were in my room. During the trial, the prosecution had told the court it did not have the memorandum written during the identification procedure conducted by the OSI with Otto Horn in Berlin on 13 November 1979. Instead of this, three affidavits, all from 1986, were submitted. The affidavits, which contradicted one another on some points, were signed by two OSI agents, George Garand and Bernard Dougherty, and described the photo-spread procedure conducted with Horn seven years previously, during which he had allegedly identified Demjanjuk's 1951 photograph and the Travniki photograph as pictures of Ivan the Terrible.

The first of the two documents transmitted by Nishnic was a detailed memorandum, signed by George Garand and dated 15 November 1979. I saw immediately why it had been thrown into the garbage, why it had for ten years been 'non-existent', and why three false statements had been composed instead of it seven years later. Garand's memo indicated clearly that when the 1951 photograph and Travniki photograph were shown to Otto Horn he had not identified either of them as pictures of Ivan the Terrible. Furthermore, he had not even pointed to either of them as photographs of someone he knew. Horn had actually selected two other pictures among those presented to him as people he might have known during his time in the SS. Only after receiving a broad, blatant hint from the OSI men did Horn finally choose the pictures he had been summoned to choose.

The second document was even more remarkable. It was an internal memo written by Michael Wolf, Deputy Director of the OSI. It was undated, but referred to a meeting held on 2 July 1986 at the American Embassy in Beirut between Wolf, OSI Director Neil Sher and Bernard

Dougherty. Wolf writes that Dougherty had confessed to him that when he signed his affidavit in May 1986 he had no recall of the photo spread conducted with Horn in November 1979. Dougherty claimed he had signed the affidavit at the request of attorney Gavriel Finder, one of the many members of the Israeli prosecution team. He had explained to Finder that he had no memory of what had happened at the photo spread seven years previously. The affidavits, of course, did not mention Finder, nor the fact that Dougherty had no memory of the events he described. In other words, the three affidavits that Dougherty and Garand had sworn were true in 1986 were actually fabrications, meant to create a false picture of Demjanjuk's identification as Ivan the Terrible by Otto Horn. And this had been done in consultation and co-operation with the Israeli prosecution team. The false affidavits were submitted to an Israeli court with the purpose of deceiving it into finding that Otto Horn had identified Demjanjuk as Ivan the Terrible. The manufacture of deceptive evidence by officers of the law in both countries makes one's blood run cold. I read the documents over and over again. At first I was afraid I must be misconstruing them, but their content was totally clear.

I called Nishnic back: 'This is really explosive. The Supreme Court will accept it as additional defence evidence in the appeal. As soon as I get home I'll submit a petition on this matter to the court, with a request for postponement attached. My guess is that both will be approved.'

I returned to Israel on 17 August 1989. A week later I submitted my two requests to the court, using emphatic language to convey the significance of these two documents. At the hearing, on 12 September, the result was everything I could have expected, but two things left a bad taste in my mouth. The first was that, while Shaked did not object to my request, and could not object to accepting the two documents as evidence, he did not hesitate to refer to my claims that they demonstrated the fabrication and concealment of evidence as 'slander that I do not want to be drawn into a debate about'. Then, objecting to the postponement request, he argued that 'the defence's tactic is delay at any price'. At the end of my response to Shaked I remarked: '... and the prosecution's tactic is the gallows at any price, even at the price of sacrificing the truth.'

The second matter that disappointed me was the position of the justices (there had been a change in the bench – Justice Halima, who was close to retirement, was replaced by Justice Ya'akov Maltz). I had expected that the court would not content itself with postponing the hearing, but would also order an immediate inquiry into whether there was a basis for suspicion of fabrication of evidence and deception of the lower court. But my expectations were disappointed.

In February 1990 evidence began emerging that the real Ivan the Terrible was a man called Ivan Marchenko. However, by the date the appeal hearing began this evidence had not yet consolidated into clear and unambiguous proof. That happened only after the end of the appeal hearing, and reopened the entire appeals process.

Towards the end of April 1990, three weeks before the appeal hearing began, Nishnic called to inform me that Peter Yatzik was refusing to transfer to the family tens of thousands of dollars that had been collected by the defence fund's Canadian branch. Yatzik justified this by saying that in his opinion the Supreme Court should be asked to postpone the appeal for another year, so that the family could fire me and retain the services of Ramsey Clark, who had served as Attorney General under President Lyndon Johnson. 'I want to make it absolutely clear to you,' Nishnic went on: 'we will not allow Mr Yatzik, despite the great assistance he has rendered, to decide who will be our lawyer, and I hope that you understand that we would not dream, not only of replacing you, but even of bringing in an extra person.'

'Since this touches on me personally, and since I would under no circumstances want you to continue to keep me as a defence attorney simply out of sentimental awkwardness, and since Ramsey Clark is a very well-known legal figure, I would prefer you to consult with Broadly or other attorneys before you reach a final decision.'

'I have already consulted Broadly,' Nishnic interrupted me. 'He was surprised to hear that Ramsey Clark was even prepared to consider taking on such a case at such a late stage. He recommended rejecting the idea outright, but we didn't need to wait for his opinion anyway. We have absolute confidence in you.' I ended the conversation by thanking him for that great confidence. Yatzik and his friends, who had joined forces with Dr Miroslav Dragan, a fanatically anti-Semitic Ukrainian-American physician, did not give up easily, and even wrote to Demjanjuk directly about it. But the Demjanjuk family refused even to consider it. This episode brought home to me what great faith and hope Demjanjuk and his family had in me, and that I had to do all I could not to disappoint them.

I began to transfer all the material connected to the appeal to the office that had been set aside for me in the Supreme Court building. Four days before the beginning of the hearing, my phone rang; Paul Brifer was on the other end. 'I've come to Israel to attend the appeal. I'd love it if we could meet first.' This was a very pleasant surprise.

When we met, Brifer asked if I would be willing to hear his comments on my arguments if he conveyed them during the breaks. I told him his comments would be very useful. For the two years since the end of the trial Brifer had come to Israel twice, and was aware of all the new developments. His advice was always beneficial, and I was sure he could be of help to me during the appeal.

On Saturday I spent long hours with Johnny and Brifer at the American Colony. I outlined the subjects I was going to argue in the appeal, and the way they would be presented, focusing on nine major subjects. The first was the court's lack of jurisdiction to try Demjanjuk on the charge of genocide; the second, the court's misconduct during the entire length of the lower-court trial; the third, the identification; the fourth, the Travniki document; the fifth, the contradiction between the survivor-identification witnesses' testimonies and substantive details in the Travniki document and the Danilchenko statement; the sixth, the Travniki photograph; the seventh, Demjanjuk's alibi and the historical testimony relating to it; the eighth, the evidence just emerging that Marchenko, rather than Demjanjuk, was Ivan the Terrible; the ninth, the contingency argument on the severity of the sentence. I showed them the thick binders containing the 650 pages of arguments I had prepared on these subjects, and explained my organizational preparation for the courtroom. When I had finished, Johnny said enthusiastically, 'It makes me feel good to know that this time a well-prepared and comprehensive argument will be made for my father, from beginning to end.' Brifer, whose comments were naturally of greater weight, said: 'Shefy, you have prepared a very good argument, and put the emphasis on the major legal points under dispute. I am convinced that when you speak you will have the judges' serious attention. That, of course, is on the assumption that the hearing does not descend to the level of the lower court.' I only hoped I would be able to plead the arguments as well as I had prepared them.

On Sunday 13 May I visited Demjanjuk. A month earlier he had turned seventy. He had been held at the Ayalon Prison for over four years, and for more than two the spectre of the gallows had haunted him. During this period I had visited him once or twice a month. The visits, which generally lasted for about an hour and a half, had become routine and boring; I couldn't get any help from him in the preparation of the appeal argument. But I felt an obligation to visit him regularly, especially since for the past two years he had had almost no visits from family members, because of the cost involved.

I arrived at his cell shortly after his wife and son had left. As soon as I entered he said: 'Sheftel, Johnny tells me that you've prepared really good and interesting things for the appeal.'

'I always promised to do the best I could and to prepare a good and thorough argument on the level required by a case like this,' I responded. 'I'm happy that you and your family think I've kept my promise.'

There was no point in explaining the details of the argument to Demjanjuk. So we sat together for about an hour and a half and chatted, as we usually did, about this and that. Nevertheless at times we touched on the appeal, and Demjanjuk said he was optimistic about the result. As usual, I avoided raising any great hopes. We parted with a handshake, without any real suspense or excitement, as if we were not just hours away from the appeal that would finally decide his fate.

After a short conversation with Johnny and his mother and another talk with Brifer, I went to my room to conduct a kind of rehearsal for the first day of the hearing. The subjects I was to argue the next day were the lack of jurisdiction and the improper conduct of the lower court. I went to bed at close to midnight, so excited that I had little real hope of falling asleep. While I was confident of the quality of my argument, I knew very well that not everything one prepares on paper sounds good when it is spoken in a courtroom. The thought that this was the final judicial proceeding, and that if the appeal were not accepted my client would be put to death, was not a soothing one. Visions of being present at Demjanjuk's execution again began to pass before my eyes.

My professional fate, as well as Demjanjuk's personal one, would be decided during this appeal. This feeling had sharpened over the last two years. If the Supreme Court ruled that Demjanjuk was Ivan the Terrible, I would have no future as a lawyer. My name would be tarnished for ever by having been Satan's attorney, and with such a stain on my record I would find it almost impossible to function in the legal profession. This was not like having one's life taken, of course, but it was having the essence of one's life taken. Apparently, others thought the same way. One of the reporters covering the appeal wrote an article headed: SHEFTEL FIGHTS FOR HIS LIFE. He commented: 'At times it seems as if an invisible thread connects, if not Sheftel to Demjanjuk, then Demjanjuk's interest to Sheftel's interest. It is as if he is fighting a battle for himself as much as he is fighting for Demjanjuk's life.'

During the few sessions that had already been held in connection with the appeal, dealing with the acceptance of additional defence evidence, the judges had been attentive and their attitude towards me positive. But I was concerned as to how they would receive the long and difficult argument I was about to present. Still, I was more confident tonight than on the night before the trial had begun. The events of the past three and a half years had fortified me, I had become a more experienced and much better lawyer than I was at the beginning of the

Demjanjuk affair. It was with these thoughts that I fell asleep at five in the morning, only to be woken a short while later by the alarm.

At seven o'clock, Johnny, Vera, Paul Brifer and I ate breakfast together. I was tense, but I saw no need to hide my feelings, as I now felt confident and close enough to these people. Johnny and his mother were very tense and every so often I noticed them casting hopeful glances at me. Brifer saw himself, to a certain extent, as my chaperon, and gave me warm words of encouragement.

Johnny and I left our cars in the judges' and prosecutors' parking lot at quarter to eight, and went straight to the defence offices. Dozens of policemen were stationed in the building to keep order, but there was none of the hubbub in the corridors that there had been in Binyanei Ha'uma. Tzvia and Doron arrived, then Ilana Alon, legal correspondent for the weekly magazine *Ha'olam Hazeh*. In covering the original trial she was the only reporter not to follow the line taken by the media as a whole. She always took great care to report events as they happened, accurately assessing their significance. Because of this I had consented to her being in the defence office.

Ilana was witness to a scene she later described in an article: 'Before the trial began, in the improvised defence offices in the court building, Tzvia Weiss succeeded in removing from Sheftel's finger the gaudy bead ring that he always wears, but she could not persuade him to let her remove his bead bracelet, which peeked out from his shirt cuffs during the trial.' Before Tzvia removed the ring, I thanked her for all she had done: 'Without you I would never have got to the appeal in such an organized way.'

I wore dark glasses during the entire hearing, even though my eye had almost healed. The glasses were to be a standing reminder to the court of the dire consequences of the media's incitement against me.

We headed for the courtroom at a quarter to nine. As I came in I noticed a group of photographers standing in a half-circle before Demjanjuk, who had been brought in and was sitting in the special cell prepared for him. I went up to the prosecution table and shook hands with the five attorneys, led by Shaked and Blatman. The latter had already left his position as State Attorney, but had asked to take part in the prosecution arguments in the appeal. The cameras continued to flash until after a few minutes Demjanjuk got sick of the show and shouted at the photographers in Hebrew: 'What do you think you're doing?' A moment later the court Registrar, Judge Tsur, appeared and ordered the photographers to leave the courtroom, then I could go to my desk at the far end of the hall and exchange a few words with Demjanjuk.

I surveyed the courtroom. It was completely full, but it had a maximum capacity of eighty, so this said nothing about public interest in the proceedings. Many members of the national and international press were in the hall. Most of these did not return in the days that followed. Some did not even bother to return after lunch on the first day. Courtroom 1 was fairly dilapidated. It was about ten yards long and six wide. The judges' bench, which took up almost the width of the room, was made of dark wood, and behind it were five high, old chairs of brown-painted wood. Close to the entrance, on the right, was the appellant's cell, about two yards square, its walls made of the same wood. Demjanjuk sat inside, two policemen flanking him and two interpreters behind him. Even though the atmosphere in the hall was nothing like the carnival spirit of Binyanei Ha'uma, I was very nervous, playing with the many binders on my table in order to calm myself down.

At precisely nine the bailiff gave his cry and the door to the judges' chambers opened. Justices Eliezer Goldberg, Aharon Barak and Ya'akov Maltz, Deputy Chief Justice Menachem Elon and Chief Justice Meir Shamgar entered. When they and the public had taken their places, the Chief Clerk, Shmaryahu Cohen, who sat at a table just below the judges' bench, announced: 'Criminal Appeal 347/88, appellant John Ivan Demjanjuk; respondent the State of Israel.' Chief Justice Shamgar turned to Demjanjuk and asked, 'Are you John Ivan Demjanjuk?' Demjanjuk replied, 'Yes.' Then the Chief Justice turned to me: 'Mr Sheftel, you may proceed.'

After a few opening words and a concise survey of the issues I would raise during the hearing, I began to present my argument on the lack of jurisdiction. It was not by chance that I had chosen to begin with this subject. It is customary to begin an appeal with this issue, if relevant, but I had other reasons too. First, I wished to win the court's serious attention right from the start, with a business-like and persuasive legal argument; second, the decision of Levin and co. on the court's jurisdiction to try Demjanjuk for the crime of genocide was a gross legal error, and it was possible to show this with a simple, relatively uncomplicated legal argument.

I argued this issue for two hours. For the first two or three minutes my voice trembled slightly as I was so very tense, but slowly I began to feel relaxed and confident. I kept glancing at the judges and was certain that they were absorbing what I was saying, that their interest was roused and that I was making a good impression. When I completed this argument, the judges declared a break. While they were still filing out of the hall, Yonah Blatman came up to me, shook my hand and complimented me on my argument. Brifer approached, and his broad smile showed that he too thought it had gone well. The most excited of all was Johnny. 'Shefy, it was a real pleasure to sit in the courtroom and hear you speak,' he said in the defence office, where we all spent the half-hour in high spirits. Many reporters tried to get in, but we locked the door. But the nicest surprise was still to come.

When the hearing reconvened, Justice Goldberg addressed a question to me: 'In your opinion, Mr Sheftel, would it be possible to try the appellant for murder, as stated in the extradition order, instead of for the crimes in the original charge sheet?' This was a sign that my argument had made a real impression and that the judges had begun to think that it might not be possible to convict Demjanjuk on the charge of genocide set out in the charge sheet, but rather only on the charge of 'regular' murder. The difference is vast, because the sentence for murder is life imprisonment, not death. Justice Goldberg apparently forgot for a moment that it would not have been possible to try Demjanjuk on the charge of murder, because the statute of limitations had run. In Israel, the statute of limitations for murder is twenty years, while Demjanjuk had been put on trial twenty-three years after it had expired. Goldberg's comment gave me great satisfaction, but before I could open my mouth to respond Blatman rose and said: 'The appellant may not be tried for murder because it is covered by a statute of limitations.'

I went on to the question of the conduct of the lower court; the argument lasted seven hours, into the following day. I had been waiting impatiently for this moment for over two years; it was like a fire within me. Using quotes from the record and citations from Supreme Court rulings, I denounced the ludicrous way in which Levin and his colleagues had conducted the trial, hoping to show the Supreme Court that it was this conduct, and not (invalid) evidence, that was the real reason for Demjanjuk's conviction and death sentence. I wanted with all my heart and soul to settle my account with Levin, all on the basis of undeniable facts, for his overtly biased treatment of me and the defence as a whole.

I discussed each of Levin's most prominent delinquencies, supporting each claim with quantities of quotes from Levin and his fellow judges. Despite the rage blazing within me, I managed to include several humorous asides that brought smiles to the justices' faces. One of the newspapers wrote that

> Attorney Sheftel succeeded in riveting the Supreme Court justices. He entertained them and even brought a rare smile to the face of Justice Aharon Barak. Anyone who was at the Demjanjuk trial in

Binyanei Ha'uma could mark the huge difference between what happened there and what is happening now in the Supreme Court. The justices of the Supreme Court, with serious expressions, listen attentively and do not interrupt the defence attorney. As a result, Sheftel is succeeding in making an excellent legal argument that fascinates both judges and public.

Even though I was voicing the sharpest criticism that a lawyer had ever directed at judges (one of whom was a Supreme Court justice), none of the five justices interfered or tried to disrupt my arguments.

I paid special attention to Chief Justice Shamgar's face, as a representative of the entire judicial system. He was far from pleased, to put it mildly, with what he was hearing. The more audacious my arguments were, the more shocking my examples (such as the scandalous press albums and their significance), the more obvious it was that the Chief Justice would prefer not to hear them. Yet he did not interrupt me a single time.

At the end of the first day I was very encouraged, not only because I had made a good argument but also because I was already convinced that I could continue to put my argument to the judges and keep their attention. I ended my presentation for that day with the statement that 'The inference to be drawn from all this can only be that all the conclusions – especially the conviction and, of course, the sentence – resulting from such a process must be declared void. With all due respect, this must unfortunately be said of the lower court. A trial in which all these things, or even ten per cent of them, happened, was not a due process but a perversion of justice. Thank you very much.'

The next day I opened with a description of Levin's behaviour after the verdict was handed down. I meant the unprecedented lecture tour he made from coast to coast of the US, less than a week after he had sentenced Demjanjuk to the gallows. His lectures had referred to the trial over and over again, especially the verdict, all while the verdict was still subject to review on appeal.

I proceeded to the identification issue, the heart of the appeal argument. I went over it in great detail for an entire week, breaking it down into its elements and subsections. The judges asked plenty of questions, and they were generally relevant, constructive and useful. They even helped to make my argument by drawing to my attention matters that concerned them.

Each day's hearing lasted about seven hours. From the second week they went straight through from nine till three, with two half-hour breaks. So there were fewer hours available to both sides, and Chief

Justice Shamgar announced that the defence would be given two additional days to make its arguments, if needed. I took advantage of the offer. At the end of the first week Vera Demjanjuk returned to the US, thanking me emotionally for my efforts.

As the hearing progressed I grew so calm that I felt as if I was arguing any normal appeal. Sometimes, however, I did get carried away by my tendency to be sarcastic. But Brifer would bring it to my attention during one of the breaks, and I would get back on track. The relaxed, business-like atmosphere continued throughout my arguments. True, here and there Justice Elon would ask a fairly aggressive question or make a somewhat hostile remark, but this was nowhere near Levin's level of antagonism. The Supreme Court had never devoted as much time to hearing a criminal appeal as it did to Demjanjuk's: another sign that under the leadership of Chief Justice Shamgar the Court was determined to conduct a hearing that would not only be fair but would also look and sound fair.

When I sat down after ten days of arguments, Shamgar said to me, 'Thank you very much, Mr Sheftel. I think it only correct to thank you in the name of the bench for your thorough and comprehensive argument, which will certainly help us in reaching our conclusions.' I could never have *dreamed* of hearing such words from Levin and his colleagues.

Not everything, however, was rosy. There were clear signs that the justices were having serious trouble grasping the obvious. This was especially apparent in the questions and comments they raised over the identification issue. When I was discussing the testimony of Shlomo Helman, Chief Justice Shamgar commented: 'From his handwriting and signature, it seems to me, without my of course being an expert on the matter, or expressing an unambiguous opinion, that Helman seems to have been mentally disturbed.' Shlomo Helman was one of the survivors who had known Ivan the Terrible very well, and who had observed him more than all the other survivors who had testified. He had died before the beginning of the trial in the lower court, and his statement from 1976 had been submitted as evidence. The statement showed that he had not been able to identify Demjanjuk's picture as that of Ivan the Terrible when it was presented to him, whilst he *had* been able to identify Federenko as a guard from Treblinka. Helman's inability to identify Demjanjuk as Ivan the Terrible was sufficient to raise a reasonable doubt as to whether Demjanjuk was Ivan the Terrible, and Shamgar's comment was an indication that the judges were trying to repress that doubt.

This was not the only comment of its kind – there were worse. Even though there were already two pieces of evidence in the court file indicating that Ivan the Terrible's name had been Ivan Marchenko, and even though none of the survivors who had identified Demjanjuk as Ivan the Terrible had claimed that his surname was Demjanjuk (they simply did not know his last name), Deputy Chief Justice Elon remarked during my pleadings on this issue: 'What importance is there to Ivan the Terrible's name when they identify a photograph of the appellant as being the picture of Ivan the Terrible?' At various points during the arguments on the identification issue and on Marchenko, all five justices made this comment, in different forms. At first I found it very hard to understand their question – after all, if Ivan the Terrible's name was really Ivan Marchenko, and the appellant's name was Ivan Demjanjuk, then the only possible conclusion was that the identification of Demjanjuk's photograph as that of Ivan the Terrible was fundamentally in error and he should be acquitted. Again, some words of Haim Cohen's from four years back echoed in my ears: 'There is always a danger that we will convict . . . because psychologically we cannot do otherwise.' The judges' comments were proof that, even though they were conducting the hearing with impartiality, their feelings were apparently preventing them from reaching the logical conclusion indicated by the facts before them.

Shaked began his arguments after a one-day break. He too could see, at least with regard to the atmosphere in which the hearing was being conducted, that this time it was a completely different story. He was also more aware than anyone that there were many difficult questions for which he had no real answers. In his opening statement he said something that he repeated whenever he had to provide a response to such a problem: 'The attempt to find logic in this type of question is an attempt to find logic within madness, and that is very difficult.' Such a cynical answer was merely a combination of demagoguery and an appeal to emotion: he continued to hold that when the subject was an accusation involving Treblinka, there was no need for legal explanations. The word 'Treblinka' must elicit such strong emotions that it could sweep aside accepted legal standards for deciding a criminal case. Shaked was well aware that Demjanjuk's conviction could be sustained only if the court ignored such standards.

Another problem for him was those findings in the verdict that found against the defence case above and beyond the prosecution's requirements. So at the appeal Shaked was forced to argue certain points from a position diametrically opposed to that he had held in the district court. This was, of course, somewhat embarrassing. And now the judges – with the exception of Deputy Chief Justice Elon – also asked him difficult and awkward questions throughout the length of his arguments, and (as he himself said when he began) he did not always have reasonable answers.

As expected, Shaked repeated the major points he had made two years ago, except that this time he was addressing the verdict and not the evidence. During his arguments, which ended on 20 June, further evidence on Ivan Marchenko was submitted. Aware of this, Shaked put the Marchenko issue at the end of his arguments. He based himself on various comments the justices had made during my own presentation. 'If I understand correctly, there are no photographs of Marchenko in which one sees, first, that he is a different person to Demjanjuk, and second that he looks so similar to him that one might make a mistake. So what remains is speculation within the tiny area of the names Demjanjuk and Marchenko, both of which are linked to the appellant.' Later such pictures were discovered, and it was shown beyond the shadow of a doubt that the name Marchenko has absolutely no connection to John Demjanjuk. But even without these facts, how could anyone seriously argue, beyond any reasonable doubt, especially in a case in which the prosecution was demanding a death sentence, that Demjanjuk was Ivan the Terrible when the court file already contained two detailed statements indicating that the family name of Ivan the Terrible was Marchenko? Is that 'speculation within a tiny area'?

The national press had a difficult time changing its habits in its coverage of the hearing. Reports were less venomous and inaccurate than those emerging from Binyanei Ha'uma had been, but were still far from fair and reliable. If ever a judge took exception to something I had said it was prominently and gleefully noted as a 'reprimand'. Still, this time the reader could form some impression, if tenuous, of what was actually going on in the courtroom. The headlines related that SHEFTEL, IN SUNGLASSES, ATTACKS CONDUCT OF TRIAL; SHEFTEL: 'STATE OF ISRAEL HAS NO RIGHT TO JUDGE DEMJANJUK FOR GENOCIDE'; SHEFTEL: 'PHOTO SPREADS LIKE A BLACK PERSON AMONG WHITES'; SHEFTEL: 'DEMJANJUK IDENTIFIED IN UNACCEPTABLE PROCEDURES'; SHEFTEL: 'TRAVNIKI DOCUMENT CANNOT BE TRUSTED, SOVIETS ARE EXPERT FORGERS'. The prosecution arguments in contrast were presented as facts: PREMEDITATED MURDER CHARGES ALSO INCLUDE GENOCIDE; TRAVNIKI DOCUMENT TURNS DEMJANJUK INTO SS MAN; QUALITY OF WITNESSES' MEMORY VERY HIGH; WITNESSES IDENTIFIED DEMJANJUK CLEARLY AND ABSOLUTELY; PROSECUTION REFUTES APPELLANT'S ALIBI. Occasionally, however, reports were worded in such a way that the reader could understand that these were just claims and not facts. The judgement against the Attorney General concerning Noah Klieger's articles was the basis of the change in the media's reports. This change could be seen clearly in an article published during the appeal:

As I have told you before, my dear *sub judice*, I am smaller than the youngest of the judges, than the most insignificant of the prosecutors, and I do not pretend to understand the arguments and their quality well ... but Courtroom 1 in the Supreme Court is not like Hall 2 in Binyanei Ha'uma. And what can I say, *sub judice*, after Yoram Sheftel's effort to re-create the atmosphere of those days for the court, and with the crimes of the media added to the sins of the lower court, but that things are different here in the Supreme Court?

During the prosecution's arguments my pressure at work was like the days of the trial. The defence has the right to say the last word in the appeal, and during the course of the hearing Chief Justice Shamgar notified me that I would have three days for this. Shaked's complex argument went on for three weeks, and what made it even harder to prepare a concise rebuttal was the knowledge that I could refute every single one of his claims. After each day's session was over, I would take a break of about two hours to eat and rest then sit in my hotel room and work into the small hours of the night, preparing a written answer to all the prosecution's arguments from that day. I would then fax this to my office so that Tzvia could type it first thing the following morning and fax it back to me for proof-reading. So by the time the prosecution finished making its arguments I already had a typed and almost complete response to each point, and even had time to polish it up over the weekend before my concluding argument.

I began to make my rebuttal on Tuesday 26 June. This time the court was less at ease and less patient with me, particularly Deputy Chief Justice Elon, whose comments began to remind me of Levin's. When I again reviewed the Marchenko issue, I said something risky: 'I do not, with all due respect, have to prove that the appellant is definitely not Ivan the Terrible. Yet I have a hunch (and all my other hunches in this case have turned out to be true) that before the verdict is handed down we will prove this also. More evidence is on the way, and we will yet prove categorically that the appellant is not Ivan the Terrible.' The judges understood full well that I was taking on a challenge: to prove definitively that Ivan Marchenko, not Ivan Demjanjuk, was Ivan the Terrible.

With this in mind, I requested that the verdict not be handed down before 1 January 1991, so that I would have six months to keep my word. The court did not decide immediately on my request, and on 28 June, at close to two in the afternoon, it looked as if the appeal hearing into Demjanjuk's case had ended. All that now remained was to await the verdict.

14 · The Turning Point

I had mixed feelings when the first stage of the appeal proceedings was over. The court had devoted more time to this case than to any other criminal appeal ever; the judges allowed me to present my arguments without interruption, and listened attentively; I was sure that I had argued well; and I was absolutely certain that the sum total of the evidence before the court mandated a verdict of not guilty. Yet I had grave doubts that this was sufficient to bring about Demjanjuk's exoneration. The evidence and arguments I had presented to the court raised much more than reasonable doubt as to his guilt, but it was still no more than doubt, rather than proof positive that Demjanjuk was *not* Ivan the Terrible.

I was not required to bring such proof. But as the appeal progressed, and especially as it drew to a close, I sensed that I needed it. We had to clear the 'emotional hurdle', and I was more and more convinced that only if Demjanjuk could prove unambiguously that he was not Ivan the Terrible would he be found innocent. At that time I was already certain that this was possible and that the key to such proof was Ivan Marchenko.

On 21 February 1990, the Supreme Court heard my motion to examine a witness in Germany. A few days before, unrelated to this request, I had received the transcript of a film about Demjanjuk's trial and conviction prepared for the CBS television programme *Sixty Minutes*. It had been recorded back in the summer of 1988, but when the appeal was postponed so was the broadcast. CBS's patience finally ran out in February 1990 and they decided to schedule it. The transcript revealed that in 1988 the TV crew visited the village of Volka Okgrolnik, half a mile from the site where the Treblinka death camp had operated. According to testimony presented in the trial, the guards from Treblinka had frequently gone drinking and whoring in this village. The CBS reporters tried to find out if anyone in the village had known Ivan the Terrible, operator of the gas chambers at nearby Treblinka.

They were sent to an elderly woman called Maria Dudek. According to the villagers, she had been a prostitute at the beginning of the 1940s, and the Treblinka guards had been among her clients. The CBS crew asked if she had known Ivan the Terrible; she responded decisively in the affirmative, and even added that he had been a frequent and regular customer for a year. He would also buy drink, mostly vodka, at a shop/tavern run by her husband, Kazhimezh Dudek, who was also her pimp. When they asked if she knew Ivan's name she responded without hesitation: Ivan Marchenko. They asked if she was sure, since an Israeli court had recently convicted one Ivan Demjanjuk of having been Ivan the Terrible from Treblinka. Maria Dudek again replied firmly that she was a hundred per cent sure that Ivan the Terrible's name was Ivan Marchenko, and absolutely not Ivan Demjanjuk. The old woman was unwilling to say this in front of the camera, on the grounds that she did not want to declare to the world, towards the end of her life, that she had been a prostitute. As a result, the crew decided that the CBS anchorman would relate her story.

My joy was unbounded. No one will be able to say, I thought to myself, that the defence has cooked *this* evidence up. The fact that this important proof had been discovered by an entirely neutral body with CBS's reputation gave it great credibility. I conferred with Nishnic on the phone and we decided to travel to Poland after the court session of 21 February, to form an opinion of Maria Dudek and ask her to appear as a defence witness.

On 21 February, although the session dealt with other matters entirely, I divulged to the court that the defence had very reliable information on the existence of *prima facie* evidence that could overturn the verdict. I announced that it was my intention to travel shortly to an eastern European country, to review the testimony personally. I added that, if the bench desired, I would be happy to give more details in chambers, in the prosecutor's presence. Under no circumstances did I want it made public that I was going to meet Maria Dudek, as early publicity would sabotage the entire action. The court evinced great interest in my announcement and summoned the counsels to chambers. There I explained the general nature of the evidence, emphasizing that it could overturn the conviction by itself.

On 2 March 1990 Nishnic arrived in Israel, and a week later we took a direct flight to Warsaw. There we immediately contacted an elderly professor, a former editor of various Catholic journals, who was to serve as our interpreter. We soon discovered that the man was an out-and-out anti-Semite. The next day we set out with the professor in a dilapidated Polish-made cab to the village of Volka Okgrolnik, about sixty miles from Warsaw. This was the very route taken, with horrific suffering, by the half-million Jews from the Warsaw ghetto who were sent to Treblinka. They were packed into cattle trucks without food or water, and tormented endlessly by the Ukrainian guards whose job was to shoot anyone who tried to escape the death that awaited them at journey's end.

These thoughts stayed with me throughout our drive. I fell into a profound gloom, only worsened by the idiocy being spouted by the anti-Semitic professor. He held forth in praise of the Polish people, most of whom – he argued – had come to the *help* of the Jews during the Holocaust. These lies aroused my argumentative instincts, and I repaid him with interest. 'It was not for nothing that the Nazis built their death camps in Poland,' I told him. 'They did it because there is no other nation so riddled with anti-Semitism as the Poles. Only your church's hatred of the Jews can compete with the people's.' The heated argument had one positive aspect: the hour-and-a-half trip passed very quickly. We were still swapping accusations when the cab reached the centre of Volka Okgrolnik. The village was typical of eastern Poland. There were decrepit houses made of wood, rotting both inside and out, with no running water. A chilly sense of poverty pervaded every corner. This was socialism in its full glory.

Passers-by directed us to Maria Dudek's home. In the yard we found her sister Elizabeth, a woman of about sixty-five, milking a cow. She welcomed us graciously and said that her sister would soon be back; and returned to her cow. A few minutes later Maria entered the yard: a thin woman of about seventy, five foot two inches tall, white hair peeking out from under her kerchief. Most of her teeth were missing; her clothing was scant and ragged; and she was shod in worn, black rubber boots.

We presented ourselves and our reason for coming. As Maria began to understand, her face reddened. I could feel her apprehension. She burst out: 'I made a big mistake when I agreed to talk to the American television. There are lots of other people who knew Ivan Marchenko. Why are you hounding me?' I changed tack and tried to get her to repeat for us what she had said to the CBS crew, which she did after much effort on my part. Then we showed her a series of pictures, including Demjanjuk's, and asked whether she could see Ivan Marchenko among them. After a lengthy examination she responded with a categorical no. I pointed to Demjanjuk's picture and asked her if that was Ivan Marchenko. The old woman again responded firmly in the negative.

All my pleas that her testimony could save a man called Demjanjuk, convicted of being Ivan the Terrible, from certain death fell on deaf ears. One could actually understand this old peasant woman who had no desire to tell the world that she had once been a prostitute and that Ivan the Terrible had been one of her customers; in spite of my disappointment I was very impressed by her sincerity and conviction, and I had not the shadow of a doubt that she was telling the truth. It was during these minutes with her that I became absolutely and totally convinced, as opposed to simply having a gut feeling, that Demjanjuk could under no circumstances have been Ivan the Terrible.

When I saw that I had no hope of changing her mind, I had another idea. I knew that simple villagers like Dudek gave much credence to the opinion of their local priest. I decided to cut short the conversation with her and locate him. I presented my idea to Nishnic and the professor. The latter agreed that it was excellent, so we bade Maria and her sister farewell, promising – to their displeasure – that we would be back. We soon found the priest at a church near the town of Małkinia, five miles from the village. This town too had been a station on the way of torment of the Jewish victims taken from Warsaw to Treblinka. The priest acquiesced almost immediately to our request for help, and agreed to accompany us to Maria's home that Sunday. He had to be in the village that day in any case to say Mass, which Maria Dudek would attend.

We returned to Warsaw disappointed but not despairing. The professor and I arranged that next day we would go to the Glovna Komisia. This is the Polish abbreviation for the Commission for the Investigation of Nazi Crimes Committed on Polish Territory. The Communist regime in Poland had collapsed by now, and we hoped this time to find people more co-operative with our attempt to locate documents. To our surprise – perhaps because of the professor's presence – we were courteously received by two members of the commission, Sanishinski and Mikulski. We told them we wanted photocopies of all the material Glovna Komisia had on Ivan Marchenko of Treblinka. The officials promised to do all they could to help, and we said we would return the coming Monday.

On Sunday morning we arrived in Volka Okgrolnik just as Mass was ending. Nishnic, the priest, Dudek and I returned to the old woman's house. Along the way I asked the priest to emphasize to Maria that her Christian conscience required her to agree to testify, since she could save a fellow Christian from being mistakenly hanged. I chuckled to myself at the use I made of the term 'Christian conscience'. After all, just half a mile from where I stood a death camp had operated, product of the combination of the Nazi regime and the anti-Semitism that Christianity, with its so-called conscience, had fostered for the first 1,900 years of its existence. But what else could I do? We needed this elderly provincial Polish priest, so we had to dredge pearls of wisdom from that bed of clichés, the laws of the church he represented.

Unlike on our previous visit, we were invited into Dudek's home. The hut was virtually unfurnished; there was no running water, no electrical appliances, no gas; and it was lit by a single electric bulb. There was a pervasive bad odour. Maria served us tea made with water boiled on a kerosene lamp, and inedible cookies. She showed us photos from her days of splendour, as she called them: she was dressed in expensive clothes and furs, with jewellery at her neck and on her hands. These were the days when she sold her services to the Ukrainian guards, coming to her, I reflected, on their breaks from the systematic murder they engaged in not far from the hut where we sat. The clothes and jewels had presumably been purchased with the fees she got from the guards, money the Ukrainians had stolen from the Jews they slaughtered.

We drank the murky tea and the priest launched into a long homily (I received a whispered translation from the professor), a plea to her sense of charity and Christian duty to give evidence of all she knew about Ivan Marchenko, to save the life of the Christian Ivan Demjanjuk. Maria's expression, very similar to four days before, dispelled any hope that she would be convinced by the priest. In fact she rejected his entreaties indignantly. In despair, he asked if she would change her mind and agree to testify if the bishop were to tell her to. She vigorously opposed this as well, but added that if Lech Walesa or the Pope were to order her to testify she would be unable to refuse. Had there been no other choice, I would have found a way of contacting one of them to make the retired prostitute give evidence. But in the end this was unnecessary, because we uncovered much better proof of Ivan the Terrible's true identity.

With Maria Dudek's dramatic declaration of the conditions under which she would consent to testify, I knew we had reached a dead end. I signalled to the priest that there was no point in continuing. We rose and said goodbye to Maria; she was only too happy to be rid of us for good. Then I decided to do what I had promised myself I would not – to pay a visit to the memorial at Treblinka.

I have always had an aversion to visiting Holocaust memorials, especially the death camps. It is humiliating that vile goyim were able to murder six million Jews while every Jewish organization stood on the sidelines and did almost nothing. The knowledge that not only was the world silent but also that the leadership of the Jewish people did not lift a finger makes it impossible for me to face the horrors of the Holocaust. Yet as I left Dudek's house I felt a sudden need to visit the site of one of the most horrible of the Nazi death factories for slaughtering the Jewish people.

The memorial is a forest clearing of about one and a half square miles. In contrast with camps like Auschwitz, nothing remains of Treblinka. Scattered across the site are rocks that look like gravestones, each engraved with the name of one of the communities, small and large, whose inhabitants were brought to this very place and, mostly, murdered within an hour of their arrival. In the centre of the site is a huge cairn with inscriptions in Hebrew and Yiddish. The entire site is in very good taste; I was pleasantly surprised with the thought and effort the Poles had invested in building such an impressive memorial.

With the vast knowledge I had gained about Treblinka during the trial, I could easily reconstruct the camp, its barracks, gas chambers and the 'pipe' through which some nine hundred thousand Jews were sent into the chambers while being horribly tormented by Ivan the Terrible and his comrades. The whole time I was there I saw in my mind the horrors that had taken place just where I was standing. Especially clear in my imagination were the terrible sights on the loading dock, where the dozens of cattle trucks stopped. Less than an hour after the trains arrived by the dock, the bodies of thousands of Jews – men, women, the old, children – were thrown out of the gas chambers to be burned by Jewish slave labourers like prosecution witnesses Epstein and Rosenberg. For an hour and a half I trembled and shivered, though the sun was shining and I was warmly dressed. These dreadful feelings were deepened by being in such a place in the company of two goyim, one of them an anti-Semite.

Another thought struck me: the Holocaust did not happen in grey, but in green. The green forest all around, the grass that sprouted everywhere, the birds whose singing could be heard constantly – all this must have looked and sounded the same at the time of those nine hundred thousand murders. I recalled a line from Bialik's famous poem 'In the City of Slaughter': 'The sun shone, the trees bloomed, the slaughterer slew.'

Despite all these feelings, I had no moral doubts about defending Demjanjuk. It was now totally clear that Demjanjuk was not Ivan the Terrible. The irony was that I had first been persuaded of this at a distance of less than half a mile from Treblinka. There I promised myself that nothing would keep me from proving that Epstein and Rosenberg, even though they too had been where I was standing and had seen with their own eyes the horrors they described in their testimonies, had erred in their identification of Demjanjuk. Demjanjuk had never been where I was standing. The monster whose loathsome deeds had been described by Epstein and Rosenberg went by the name of Ivan Marchenko, not Ivan Demjanjuk. At that moment, however, I had absolutely no idea how I would keep this promise.

The real breakthrough came from a totally unexpected quarter. We arrived at the Glovna Komisia offices to find Sanishinski and Mikulski waiting for us. They announced that their search of the document catalogue had turned up two documents mentioning 'Ivan Marchenko' as a guard at Treblinka, both testimonies from another Treblinka guard named Dimitrenko. Locating these documents in the archives would take some time, but the two promised that as soon as they were found copies would be delivered to us, along with official certification that the copies were accurate. Then one of them pronounced the most significant sentence I had heard since becoming involved in the Demjanjuk affair: 'If you really want to know who Ivan the Terrible is – not who the judges in Jerusalem ruled he is, but who he *really* is – you must go to the city of Simferopol on the Crimean peninsula, to the court where the trial of Federenko was held in 1986. There, in the case file, you will discover all the material you need about the real identity of the two gas-chamber operators at Treblinka.'

I was stunned; clearly this was something serious and substantial. There were documents in the Soviet Union proving that Demjanjuk was not Ivan the Terrible, and the Soviets were concealing their existence, even though they realized that another man was going to be hanged for being Ivan the Terrible. We made every effort to squeeze more details out of them, but they wouldn't volunteer another word.

A few weeks later, when the Supreme Court began to hear the appeal, Nishnic received a message from Glovna Komisia: the documents had been found. Yet it turned out that they added nothing to the information contained in another statement already before the judges. The new documents showed only that Marchenko had been a guard at Treblinka, without specifying his crimes there. (They related to crimes Marchenko committed in the surrounding villages in his free time.) They were submitted as additional evidence in the appeal hearing, but they didn't constitute a complete breakthrough.

We left Glovna Komisia with a sense that the trip to Poland had been worthwhile. The next day we flew back to Israel, ready to start planning our trip to Simferopol. I would also submit a request for an additional postponement of the appeal hearing to give us sufficient time to obtain all the evidence showing that Ivan Marchenko was Ivan the Terrible. On Monday 7 May 1990, exactly a week before Demjanjuk's appeal hearing was supposed to begin, the court convened to hear arguments on the request to postpone. The official grounds were to allow the defence to persuade Maria Dudek to appear as a witness. We could not mention our planned trip to the Soviet Union because we could not prove to the court that there were indeed documents there that could lead to Demjanjuk's acquittal on all charges. Furthermore, I feared that any mention of our intentions would lead to further Soviet sabotage of our efforts.

To my utter astonishment and great delight, I discovered as soon as this hearing began that the judges had contacted CBS on their own initiative and asked for the full transcript of their film. The transcript, including Maria Dudek's claims, was thus before the judges. This initiative showed that they understood the importance of this turning point in the trial.

I began by detailing the facts according to Maria Dudek, my meeting with her and her total refusal to testify for the defence. I concluded by saying that the subject was so important that it was inconceivable that the defence not be given another chance to persuade Maria to testify. During the course of the hearing it emerged that there was yet another piece of evidence naming Ivan Marchenko as Ivan the Terrible: recorded in 1986, also in Poland, from none other than Kazhimezh Dudek, who had died in 1987. Dudek said in his statement that Marchenko had told him 'without shame' that he, along with another guard called Nikolai Shelaiev, operated the gas chambers at nearby Treblinka. Dudek mentioned that he knew Ivan the Terrible because he had frequently come to his shop to buy liquor. The only thing he forgot to mention was that Ivan also slept with his wife.

In response, Shaked argued that Demjanjuk's name was not simply Demjanjuk, but rather Demjanjuk-Marchenko. He took this from the form Demjanjuk filled out in 1948 to request refugee status, where he had recorded his mother's maiden name as Marchenko. Shaked suggested that when Demjanjuk left Treblinka to visit the local villages he had used the name Marchenko to hide his identity; or that he may have used the name Marchenko at Treblinka itself for the same reason.

Despite the fundamental difference of opinion between us, Shaked and I agreed during this hearing that Dudek's statement would be submitted as defence evidence. The court would also note that Maria concurred with her husband that Ivan the Terrible's name was Marchenko. In return, I had to withdraw the postponement request; the hearing would begin as planned on 14 May.

The Marchenko thesis was still a weak link at this point in the appeal. The information about Ivan the Terrible's name had been furnished by people outside Treblinka (the Dudeks); while guard Dimitrenko's testimony mentioned that Marchenko had been a Treblinka guard but related only to crimes in the nearby villages. According to all legal criteria, the Dudek and Dimitrenko testimonies should have been sufficient to create the reasonable doubt necessary to acquit a defendant in a criminal trial. But in the Demjanjuk affair, even at the Supreme Court, we needed much more.

On Sunday 8 July I landed in Cleveland. On the way to the hotel Nishnic expressed his great satisfaction with the progress of the appeal hearings. Later, at an Italian restaurant, I explained that everything depended on the success of our visit to the Soviet Union. 'Only the testimony of guards from Treblinka, taken decades ago,' I said, 'will be enough to ensure an acquittal in the appeal.' We finally decided that Johnny and Jaroslav Dobrovolski (an American lawyer of Ukrainian extraction who knew Ukrainian and Russian well and assisted the family greatly) would come with me to carry out two missions. The first was locating documents to prove unequivocally that Marchenko was Ivan the Terrible. The second was to get an official document showing Demjanjuk's mother's maiden name, which we knew very well was not Marchenko.

At that time Israel and the Soviet Union still did not enjoy full diplomatic relations, and it was very difficult for Israelis to get permission to visit Russia. We decided to go to Washington DC and take advantage of the office of Ohio Congressman James Traficant. Traficant had given us a lot of help, including discovering the forgery and fraud of the OSI and their accomplices in the Israeli public prosecutors' office. Traficant and his staff were very obliging and promised not to let the Soviet Embassy alone until they issued the permits. Each of us submitted his visa application separately, stating the purpose of our trip as visiting relatives. We assumed that revealing our real intentions would ruin any chance of getting visas. I spent a week in the US and Canada on a lecture tour, and after a few days' rest in Holland I returned to Israel. Only at the end of August did Nishnic inform me that the visas had finally been issued. Johnny and Dobrovolski set out first; there was no point my joining them in the provincial town of Kuzhiatin, where they went to get certification of Johnny's grandmother's maiden name.

I set out three days later in the early morning, with great excitement, on a Tarom (the Romanian airline) flight from Tel Aviv. After changing planes in Bucharest I landed at exactly three p.m. in Moscow. I had visited Eastern Bloc countries a number of times – Romania, Yugoslavia, Poland – and gathered many impressions of life and government in the Communist world, but I was hugely curious about the original, from which the cancer had spread to so many corners of the globe. I encountered corruption as soon as I arrived, at the passport-control desk. A soldier gestured at me. I asked him in Russian, 'What do you want?' and he quickly asked, 'Do you have a packet of American cigarettes?' I said I had. (I don't smoke, but experience of eastern Europe had taught me that a packet of Western cigarettes can work wonders; I had armed myself with several cartons.) The soldier said, 'If you give me two packs, I'll see that they don't open your suitcases and you get through control in half a minute.'

'If you can really do that,' I said, 'I'll give you a third pack.' We both kept our promise.

Minutes later I was in a cab on my way to the Russia Hotel, next to the Kremlin walls. The road from the airport to the city is about fifteen miles long, and filled with potholes, and the vehicles using it were primitive and decrepit. I felt as if I had been transported back to the 1950s. Still, it was possible to sense the spirit of *glasnost* even in the taxi: the driver had no qualms about cursing the entire Soviet leadership. He went on at great length about Gorbachev's family tree, repeatedly emphasizing his foremothers' affiliation with the world's oldest profession. When he heard that I was from Israel, he said that until then he had only heard of Jews fleeing from Russia to Israel. Now he was seeing someone who had come *from* Israel *to* Russia. Soon we reached the famous Gorky Street. It looked miserable, neglected, filthy and with many empty shops. The passers-by were dressed the way our grandparents dressed in the '40s and '50s. On every corner the red flag waved. In the vicinity of the Kremlin there were many Party offices, and every windowsill had a red flag stuck on it. Despite the grass that sprouted here and there, everything looked grey and cold.

The taxi stopped at the entrance to the Russia Hotel. The building was as shoddy as it was huge; the lobby was swarming with prostitutes. It looks, I thought to myself, as if socialism makes at least the whores diligent, if they report for work as early as four in the afternoon. It took sixty minutes to fill out forms and get the key to my room. The boy who carried my suitcase offered me fifty roubles per dollar, ten times the official rate, an offer I could not refuse.

When I finally reached my room I wanted to wash my face, but the tap came off in my hand. The shower head also came off in my hand. The telephone, on the other hand, worked. I spoke to Johnny, who had had no trouble locating his grandparents' marriage licence from 24 January 1910. The names of the couple were Nikolai Kosmovitch Demjanjuk and Juliana Nikonievna Tabachuk. An official Soviet seal verified the document. This was the end of Shaked's 'explanation' (which we had always known to be incorrect) that Demjanjuk's mother's maiden name was Marchenko. Johnny was excited, as was I. 'If we succeed in Simferopol like we did in Kuzhiatin, this will be the most successful trip of our lives,' I said. 'So it will,' Johnny replied, elated.

The next day I arrived after a six-hundred-mile flight in Zaporozhye, a mouldy industrial city of one million souls with a smog-obscured sky. When I reached the hotel, named after the city, I began to miss the Russia. Johnny and Dobrovolski arrived a few minutes later, and I asked to see the marriage certificate at once. Zaporozhye was the nearest large town to the village where a Treblinka guard called Nikolai Malagon lived. He had also claimed, in a statement given to the Soviet authorities in 1979, that Ivan the Terrible's family name was Marchenko. The Soviets had passed this statement to the OSI, and like many other such statements it had been maliciously hidden from Demjanjuk, his lawyers and the courts in Israel and the US. After two meetings with Malagon it was clear that the man was completely senile and could remember little about Treblinka.

On Tuesday 3 September we went to Simferopol. It looked much like Zaporozhye, only half the size. The Moscow Hotel, unworthy of the name 'hotel', was our home for the next two days. Awaiting us in Simferopol was attorney Yuri Ivazian, who had helped Johnny and Dobrovolski at the Kuzhiatin offices. The four of us decided to go to the district court building the next day to ask the name of the judge who had presided at Federenko's trial, and to try and meet him in his chambers.

When we arrived at the courthouse, we learned from the concierge that the judge's name was Oleg Tatunik, and his office was on the second floor. A friendly young secretary sat in his anteroom. On the wall facing her was a large picture of John Lennon, not the sort of decoration one would expect to see in a Soviet judge's office. Yuri asked if we might be admitted to see him. 'All of you?' she asked in surprise. 'Yes, all of us.' Without bothering to ask who we were or what we wanted, she went into his chambers. Two minutes later she returned and said, 'The judge will see you in five minutes.' I could not believe my ears. One could not get into a judge's office so easily in the West, especially if one's identity and purpose were not known.

The judge himself opened the door and invited us in. His room was simple, but large and well cared-for. The floor was spread with small rugs, and a large bookcase stood along the wall, along with some fairly ugly pictures. Yuri presented us and gave a brief explanation. Then I said in Russian, 'I am certain this is the first time an Israeli attorney has been in your chambers.' Judge Tatunik, a balding man with glasses, in his mid-forties – friendly, even a little shy – smiled and said, 'You are, of course, correct.' I shook his hand warmly. 'As attorney Ivazian has told you, I am the defence counsel for Ivan Demjanjuk, whose appeal is currently being heard in the Israeli Supreme Court. Demjanjuk has been convicted and sentenced to death because the court ruled that he is Ivan the Terrible, the operator of the gas chambers in the Treblinka extermination camp. We know for certain that Ivan the Terrible's name was Ivan Marchenko. This March, in Poland, I was told explicitly by members of the Commission for the Investigation of Nazi Crimes Committed on Polish Territory that the file on Fyodor Federenko's trial, which took place before Your Honour, contains many documents that prove that Ivan Marchenko and Nikolai Shelaiev were the operators of the gas chambers at Treblinka.'

This was not entirely accurate. In Poland I had been told only that Federenko's file contained documents showing who Ivan the Terrible really was, not that his name was Ivan Marchenko. I said what I did to make Judge Tatunik think I knew exactly what the file contained, so that it would be hard for him to deny it, if it *were* true. 'That's right,' he responded. I doubt I was ever happier than when I heard this. With difficulty I overcame my elation and in a dry, matter-of-fact voice I managed to say, 'You mean that Your Honour has such material and that it is in Federenko's file?'

Judge Tatunik confirmed this. 'In the file on Federenko's trial we collected many statements and excerpts from statements from many trials held all over the Soviet Union about the Nazis' crimes in Treblinka. These statements were all taken from guards at Treblinka and they tell not only of Federenko's crimes but also of those of other Treblinka guards. In many of the statements attached to the file there is mention of the two criminals who operated the gas chambers. If I am not mistaken, the statements give their names as Ivan Marchenko and Nikolai Shelaiev.'

I was ecstatic, as were Dobrovolski, Yuri and especially Johnny. The face of Judge Levin began dancing before my eyes, regarding me with one of those sinister looks so typical of him during the trial. I heard myself saying, 'Here, Dovele. This is the fruit of the show-trial you so eagerly presided over. Soon your name will be in disrepute all over the world.' Through this daydream I could hear Johnny asking the judge, 'Can you order the file to be brought to your chambers so that we can photocopy the documents and submit them as evidence in my father's appeal?'

The judge's response cut my daydream short. 'I'm afraid that, despite *glasnost*, the procedures here are still not as they are with you in the West. Federenko's file is a KGB file, and the regulations are that at the end of the trial such a file does not remain in the court archives. It goes back to the KGB and is kept in its archives in the city where the trial was held.'

I immediately recovered and asked, 'Would you be able to request that the KGB bring the file to your office, so we could photocopy the documents?'

'With pleasure,' he replied. 'I will even call the KGB offices in your presence and ask them to bring the file tomorrow.' He picked up the telephone on his desk and within minutes was speaking to a man from the KGB. We were not asked to leave the room and could hear the judge ask for the Federenko file to be brought to his chambers at ten the next morning. After this brief conversation the judge told us: 'Come back here tomorrow at ten, and the file will be available to you. I'll see to it that the public prosecutor's photocopier in the next building is also made available. The courthouse has no photocopier.'

Audaciously I asked, 'Would Your Honour be prepared to certify for us with his signature and the court's seal that the photocopies are faithful to the originals?'

The friendly judge agreed: 'With pleasure, although the documents in the file are also photocopies, with certification that they are identical to the originals.'

It seemed like a dream. Everything went so smoothly and quickly, there was no reason to doubt that the next day we would have the evidence that would turn the conviction on its head. We sat with the judge for another half an hour, chatting about all manner of things. Finally we parted with warm handshakes, expressing our most heartfelt thanks. When we left the building, the four of us embraced, then we began dancing in the middle of the street.

That evening some relatives that Johnny had contacted arrived at the Moscow Hotel. It was a very emotional encounter. We all sat in the hotel restaurant and were served a disgusting meal, to the accompaniment of dance music. The men amongst Johnny's relatives quickly got drunk and conversation with them became impossible. Dobrovolski and I agreed that we had 'done it', Demjanjuk would win his appeal; it was only a question of time.

The next day at exactly ten o'clock we arrived at Judge Tatunik's office. The moment we entered I could tell from the look on his face that something had gone wrong. He told us, 'You did not leave me a telephone number where I could reach you, so I was unable to inform you that, half an hour after you left, the KGB called back to tell me they would not be able to bring the file to my office without a permit from the Ukrainian KGB's headquarters in Kiev.' This was an unpleasant surprise. We realized that we were still a long way from achieving our goal. Judge Tatunik invited us to sit down, and we conferred on what measures we should take. I asked if he could issue a court order requiring the KGB to bring the file to his office. He replied, 'In this matter also our procedures differ from yours in the West. As a judge I do not have the authority to issue orders to the KGB.'

In the end we decided to request a face-to-face meeting with the local KGB authorities to try and persuade them to allow us to photocopy the necessary documents. Judge Tatunik was so considerate that he even called their headquarters again to find out if they would agree to see us. To our surprise, they did. Tatunik explained how to get there, about ten minutes' walk from the courthouse.

I was more and more excited. Just a year ago, I would never have imagined that I might visit the Soviet Union, let alone that a Soviet judge would see me in his chambers, and with such conviviality. Now I would soon be at a KGB office! Before we parted I asked the judge to allow us to be filmed together, with my camcorder. He gladly agreed to this as well. Johnny was the cameraman and added an explanatory soundtrack.

An hour later we entered the Simferopol KGB headquarters. It was the most magnificent and best-kept building in this neglected city. It was three storeys high and about twenty-five by ten yards. The façade was brown, with red flags waving everywhere. It was thrilling, and I could see that Johnny and Dobrovolski felt as I did. Of all of us it was Yuri, who had lived all his life in the KGB's shadow, who did not seem at all tense. As we opened the door, facing us was a huge statue of Dzerzhinski, founder of the KGB. A wooden counter divided the foyer for almost its entire width, and three receptionists sat behind it. On the right-hand wall was a stone memorial plaque engraved with the names of about thirty KGB men from Simferopol who had fallen in the Great Patriotic War, as the Soviets call World War II. I was shocked and angry as I read the names: the first was Polonski and the last Levinstein, and all those between were ones like Zalmonowitz, Geller and Kagan – all Jews. The best of Jewish youth in Russia, the cradle of Zionism, had sold itself and its soul to the Red Devil.

As these thoughts passed through my head, Yuri had some words with the receptionists, who knew about the strange delegation scheduled to arrive in their building. Yuri informed us that the city's KGB chief himself would meet us. I wanted to pinch myself to be sure I wasn't hallucinating.

The room to which we were shown was completely white and had no windows or openings of any sort. A fluorescent bulb emitted a pale white light. Sitting in the near left-hand corner, in civilian clothes, was the KGB chief. Four chairs were arranged in a straight line facing him; there was no other furniture in the room. The man looked about fifty years old; he was thin, almost completely bald, his temples grey. There was nothing frightening or unpleasant in the way he looked. He wore grey trousers and a long-sleeved white shirt. As soon as we entered the room he noticed the video camera and commented, 'I hope you have not filmed anything since you entered the building.'

'Of course not,' I responded.

He invited us to sit, and then spoke without waiting for us to introduce ourselves. 'I've spoken to Judge Tatunik, and I know from him who you are and why you've come, so you needn't tell me. Unfortunately, I cannot help you, not because I don't want to, but simply because I can't. I must receive advance written permission from Kiev. That is what regulations demand.'

I cut him off: 'If that is the case, how is it that in your phone conversation with Judge Tatunik, only yesterday, while we were in the judge's office, you agreed to have Federenko's file brought to his chambers? Did the regulations change overnight?'

'The regulations did not change. It was not I but one of my men who spoke with Judge Tatunik. When I learned of the conversation, I called the judge myself and informed him that the promise to bring the file to his office had been made by mistake. I made it clear to the judge that without written permission from Kiev it cannot be done.'

I tried another angle. 'It could be that permission will be granted months from now. Can you expect us to tell the Supreme Court of Israel that it must wait until you and your superiors in Kiev arrange the matter in accordance with regulations? In the mean time Demjanjuk is liable to hang for being Ivan the Terrible, even though you and your superiors in Kiev know very well that he is the wrong man. Is this not the kind of special instance in which it is best not to be so bureaucratic, but to let us photocopy the evidence we so badly need? After all, we are not talking about secret documents. The trial itself was public.' I added: 'Unless you are not saying what you really think, and you are actually interested in seeing Demjanjuk hang for being someone he isn't.'

He responded to this last point: 'If that was what interested me and I wanted to see you fail, I would not bother to meet you. I can only act in accordance with the regulations to which I am subject. Just as the Supreme Court in your country cannot adapt itself to us, we cannot adapt ourselves to it, whatever the consequences might be.'

I tried again: 'Yet if the regulations are so clear, how is it that yesterday someone on your staff agreed to bring the file to the judge's office?'

'He simply made a mistake,' the man replied drily. I interrupted again.

'If he spoke to the judge, he must be a fairly senior person, since you wouldn't let a novice speak with the President of the court. How could he have been mistaken about such a basic regulation?'

I made out the slightest hesitation in his face, but he recovered immediately. 'I cannot and do not want to explain why he made a mistake, but he made it and I will not repeat it.' It was clear that the conversation had reached a dead end. Yuri made an attempt, but could not budge the KGB officer. At one point Yuri lost his temper and said angrily, almost shouting, 'There's nothing you can do about it, we'll get to that material whether you want us to or not.' The officer did not respond to this outburst. I thought to myself that a year earlier Yuri would not have dreamed of speaking so bluntly to a KGB official. Now it was Johnny's turn to try an emotional appeal: 'I can't believe they'll hang my innocent father because we have to wait for a permit from Kiev.' This did not sway the man either. I was amazed at the mixture of inflexibility and good manners he displayed. An hour went by and it was clear that we would not be able to photocopy the documents. The KGB man accompanied us to the staircase that led to the entrance. A minute later we were outside.

Yuri said, 'Don't worry. Rukh, the Ukrainian national movement, will not rest until we receive the material. I'm certain we'll get it in time to prevent your father's hanging.' Johnny was disappointed and despairing. Only yesterday we had been sure that we would leave Simferopol with our prize and we had danced in the streets. Now we would leave empty-handed.

This sense of disappointment was unjustified, however. I explained why as we walked: 'Look, we received confirmation, even if it was only oral, from the President of the Simferopol District Court, that in the file from Federenko's trial there are dozens of statements from Treblinka guards, according to which Ivan Marchenko was Ivan the Terrible. True, we haven't yet obtained those statements, but they definitely exist and we know where they are. The key to Demjanjuk's acquittal is in our hands.' Yuri concurred, and repeated his promise that come hell or high water he would get the statements from the Federenko file.

In the evening we boarded an Aeroflot flight for Kiev. There we spent three days, and Yuri began taking steps to get access to the material. Exactly a week later I asked Shaked and Bainwall to lunch at a restaurant above the Tel Aviv marina. I naïvely supposed that the recent momentous developments would persuade Shaked and his colleague that the state could no longer defend Demjanjuk's conviction for being Ivan the Terrible. The three of us spoke affably, and I told them the story of my remarkable trip to the Soviet Union. To make it easier for the prosecution to back down I said, 'I'm also prepared to produce a letter signed by Demjanjuk and his family, stating that if the prosecution does not oppose our appeal they will forgo any demands for compensation of any sort from the State of Israel.' I didn't have the family's authority to say this, but I had no doubt that I could easily persuade them to agree.

Bainwall responded belligerently: 'What about Sobibor? And what about Travniki? Will Demjanjuk confess to that?' I could not believe my ears. Even though Demjanjuk was not Ivan the Terrible, unless he confessed to having been a concentration-camp guard he would be hanged. For the first time since we had met, almost four years earlier, I was filled with contempt and disgust for Shaked. At that moment I understood that Shaked would never admit that the prosecution had made a serious error in accusing Demjanjuk of being Ivan the Terrible, and that this error had disgraced the entire Israeli judicial system. He was prepared to take any position, however hateful, to avoid admitting his mistake. His machinations after that meeting amply confirmed this judgement.

I responded more calmly than I felt. 'Demjanjuk will never admit to having been at Sobibor or Travniki. He stands by his story that he was never at those camps, just as he has consistently claimed for the last fourteen years that he was not Ivan the Terrible. You are well aware that had it just been Sobibor and Travniki you would never have asked for his extradition to Israel, just as you did not request Federenko's extradition. So trying now to make it a question of Demjanjuk having allegedly been a regular guard is absurd, grotesque.' I said this forcefully, but with no trace of hostility. We sat there for another hour and a half while I made every effort not to poison the atmosphere, but we reached no real understanding. From that meeting onward, as the case became ever worse for the prosecution, Shaked's actions became more and more appalling.

In the mean time, I petitioned the Supreme Court to accept the marriage certificate as additional evidence. The hearing on my petition was set for 12 December 1990. Even though the court had not officially acceded to my request that the verdict be postponed to 1 January 1991, this meant the verdict could not in fact be handed down until after that date.

Since my first visit to the Soviet Union there had been dozens of telephone calls between Kiev, Cleveland and Tel Aviv concerning the documents in the KGB's possession, until a breakthrough finally seemed to be possible. Among the people the Rukh movement managed to enlist was Alexander Yemets, then chairman of the Ukrainian Parliament's Committee on Human Rights. The intervention of such a person could not be ignored. On 11 December 1990 Yemets and the committee's counsel, Nyoma Sokol, examined some of the documents in the Federenko file, which had been transferred from Simferopol to Kiev for the purpose.

The next day Yemets faxed a report to Cleveland, addressed to me on the official stationery of the Ukrainian Parliament. Nishnic refaxed it to my office: Yemets and Sokol had seen about a quarter of the dozens of statements from Treblinka guards contained in the file. They had not come across the name Ivan Demjanjuk. They had, on the other hand, found Ivan Marchenko's name again and again, cited as the man who operated the gas chambers at Treblinka along with Nikolai Shelaiev. Yemets mentioned several statements in particular, noting the guards' names and the date each statement had been recorded. All were from the late 1940s and early 1950s, and all stated explicitly that Ivan Marchenko had operated the gas chambers at Treblinka. Yemets quoted the statement of guard Piotr Nazerovitch Goncherov, recorded on 6 March 1951: 'He [Ivan Marchenko] was Ukrainian, I don't know where he was born. He served in the Red Army and was taken prisoner by the Germans and then went to the Travniki training camp. From there he was sent to Treblinka, where he served as operator of the diesel engine that sent the gas into the gas chambers and also took part in tormenting and shooting Jews. He was tall, solidly built, broad-shouldered, with a dark complexion, round face and long nose.'

So authentic evidence, collected and scrutinized some forty years previous to the Demjanjuk verdict, existed to mock all 444 pages of the judges' decision. Nishnic told me that Yemets would return to the KGB's Kiev archive within the week, to photocopy all the Federenko-file statements relating to Marchenko as Ivan the Terrible.

On 15 November 1990, Shaked had submitted a petition, with my consent, to postpone the 12 December hearing, because he had been called up for army reserve duty until the 21st. The hearing was rescheduled for 31 December; it looked as if I would be able to present all the evidence proving Demjanjuk's innocence, on the very last day of the half-year during which I had requested a verdict not be given.

It was impossible to trust the Soviets, however. I was worried that for some reason the evidence Yemets had examined might suddenly 'disappear'. To reduce this risk as far as possible, I quickly leaked the substance of Yemets's report to the local and foreign media. The press reports were disappointingly inconspicuous and sceptical. But the main thing was that the material in the KGB cellars, and the fact that it had been seen by a respected Ukrainian MP had been made public. Before leaking the report to the media I called Shaked and Bainwall's office to notify them of the pivotal developments. There was no reply. Nishnic called and expressed this fear that someone in Israel would intercept the evidence somewhere on its way to my office; so I decided to go to Holland and have the material sent to me there. This I did on 16 December 1990, staying with my friends Peter and Henzi in Deventer.

Two days later Peter's telephone rang, and I heard Nishnic's agitated voice: 'I just received a fax for you from Yemets. He writes that yesterday he was informed that all the evidence in the Federenko file was sent to Moscow to be presented to an official Israeli delegation. So he couldn't see it, and of course not photocopy it.' I realized that the 'official delegation' was none other than Mr Shaked and Ms Bainwall. Shaked, instead of going for reserve duty as he had told me and the court, had gone secretly to Moscow. This was why there had been no answer from his office when I called, several times, before travelling to Holland. I asked Ed to call me again in three hours.

Now I called Shaked's home. His wife, a lawyer herself, answered. 'May I speak to Micky?' I asked.

'No,' she answered, 'he's on holiday.'

'And when is he returning?'

'In a few days.'

'Where is he on holiday?'

'That's not important, you can't get him there by phone anyway.' That was the end of the conversation. I called Bainwall at home. Her husband answered, the resulting conversation being almost identical to the one with Shaked's wife. Now I was sure Shaked had gone to Moscow to sabotage my plans. He did this secretly, lying to me, although for four years I had informed him in advance about each of my foreign trips and almost every step I had taken in Demjanjuk's defence.

I was furious. I called his wife back. As soon as she answered I said, 'Is Shaked's vacation in Moscow and did he go there with Bainwall instead of to the Army?'

'You said that,' she replied.

'When I say something,' I responded, 'I generally know what I'm talking about.' I then called Ilana Alon at *Ha'olam Hazeh* and told her what had happened. I advised her to call the Justice Ministry press officer to get his reaction to certain information she had just received. When I called her back half an hour later she told me, 'The ministry spokesman refuses to confirm or deny or comment in any way on the information, on the grounds that the ministry does not report its employees' trips overseas.' We both agreed that this evasive answer was, to all intents and purposes, confirmation that Shaked and Bainwall were in Moscow.

Nishnic called back and I told him about all my phone conversations. Shaked was obviously studying the material in the Federenko file in Moscow. Nishnic was extremely worried, afraid that the material might be destroyed, or that the Supreme Court would refuse to wait until it reached us and would hand down its judgement. I calmed him down: 'Given the new circumstances, there is no chance the court will hand down its verdict before it gets the Federenko material. The publication of the contents of the Yemets report is a guarantee that the statements will not be destroyed. As much as he would like to, Shaked cannot deny the existence and the substance of this material.'

When I returned from Holland on 24 December Shaked was home again. He had read the contents of Yemets's letter in the press, as well as my version of the circumstances surrounding his secret trip to Moscow. I called his office; Bainwall answered. 'You should be ashamed of yourselves,' I said immediately. 'For years I've been informing you in advance of every move I make, even though I am not required to do so. I even told you in detail, in advance, about my trip to the Soviet Union, and in return you do this and even use your other halves to mislead me.' Bainwall had the gall to say it was a 'misunderstanding'. I responded angrily: 'You know me well enough not to take me for a fool.' During the course of the conversation she confirmed that they had been in Moscow, and examined dozens of statements naming Ivan Marchenko as Ivan the Terrible. I asked pointedly: 'What's your next step? When will you notify the court that you agree to accept the appeal and free Demjanjuk from prison?'

'First, we've ordered the material from the Soviet Union. When it arrives, it will have to be translated. Then we'll study it carefully and decide.'

Once again I could not believe my ears: 'You haven't brought it with you? Did you return empty-handed on purpose, to begin wasting time in the hope that Demjanjuk will die in the meanwhile? What do you mean, study the material? You spent a week in Moscow, and I know exactly what material we're talking about. What is it that requires such detailed study when the material speaks for itself?'

'We did not bring the material because we intend to submit an official request by the State Attorney's office to the Soviet States Attorney's office.'

I interrupted: 'OK, it's clear that you intend to launch a series of dirty tricks with the goal of, if not preventing, at least delaying as long as possible the shame and humiliation you will have to endure when it becomes clear how absurd it has been to accuse Demjanjuk of being Ivan the Terrible.'

After this I decided that I could no longer maintain any contact with them; it was the last conversation I had with Shaked or Bainwall.

I decided to submit an immediate petition for Demjanjuk's release from prison, since the prosecution concurred in the fact that there were more than twenty statements from Treblinka guards naming Ivan Marchenko as Ivan the Terrible. Under these circumstances – I stressed in the petition – when it was already clear that Demjanjuk's acquittal was inevitable, there was no reason to keep him incarcerated until the final judgement was handed down – something that could take a considerable time. I never thought that this petition would be accepted. I did it to add a dramatic element to the hearing, to show the court that we were speaking of a crucial turn of events that made Demjanjuk's conviction totally untenable.

Yemets's report and my conversation with Judge Tatunik made it clear that the guards' statements must also address some photograph of Marchenko. I was convinced that Marchenko's photograph had been identified as the picture of the gas-chamber operator from Treblinka. Likewise, it seemed that some of the statements must contain some reference to Marchenko's age, his place of birth and other personal details that would make it impossible for Demjanjuk and Marchenko to be the same person. I therefore decided that at the hearing I would act as if I knew these things for a fact, from the documents themselves. If my guesses were correct, Shaked would fall into the trap and be forced, on the court record, to confirm these facts exonerating Demjanjuk.

On 31 December the Supreme Court convened to hear about the new developments. The court accepted as evidence the Soviet document confirming the contents of Demjanjuk's mother's marriage licence, specifying her maiden name as Tabachuk and not Marchenko. Many of the comments of the judges, especially President Meir Shamgar and his deputy Menachem Elon, indicated that they were trying their best to find some fault in the document and so discount its value. Therefore even this document was not enough to save Demjanjuk from the gallows. Only the documents in the Federenko file could do that. It was again proved, for the umpteenth time, that even the Supreme Court had trouble discarding the case's emotional baggage. As long as Demjanjuk's innocence was not proven categorically, he would never be anything other than guilty.

In the section of the hearing devoted to the Federenko file, the judges were especially impatient. Justice Goldberg firmly refused to allow me to relate the chain of events that led me to the discovery of the material. I nevertheless succeeded in reporting the major facts at the basis of my request to release Demjanjuk forthwith, and only then could I argue without interference.

My ruse succeeded. Shaked had to admit that the Federenko file contained a picture of Ivan Marchenko, identified as the photograph of Ivan the Terrible. Likewise, he said on record that, according to the material he examined in Moscow, Marchenko had not been born in the same district as Demjanjuk, and that his age and many other details distinguished him from Demjanjuk. In any ordinary criminal appeal such admissions by the prosecution would be enough to bring about the immediate release of the appellant from prison. Were the prosecutor for some reason not to consent to the release, the bench would order it over the prosecution's protests, censuring them for lack of integrity.

The hearing itself was not concluded that day. It was postponed, at my request, to 9 January 1991. It was then further postponed to 14 January, but did not take place on this date either. I had to undergo an urgent operation and the Gulf War led to further disruptions of the court calendar, so the hearing was put off until 26 February.

This session was a faithful repetition of its predecessor. The statements had still not arrived from the Soviet Union. Enquiries made on our behalf by intermediaries in Moscow revealed that Shaked had secured a commitment that no material would be handed over to us by the Soviet public prosecutor before being given to him. Shaked hoped in this way to come out of Demjanjuk's acquittal with clean hands, able to say that the prosecution had given the defence the material that paved the way for the defendant's vindication. There really was no limit to his chutzpah and cynicism. As expected the court rejected the petition for Demjanjuk's release from prison, on the grounds that 'the information before us is not sufficient to justify such a decision'. As for the new material from the Federenko file, the judges declared: 'The learned defence counsel and the learned prosecutor have informed us that they are now making efforts to obtain the material in the Soviet Union in order to ask for its submission to the court. Both have requested that we defer handing down judgement in the mean time. We accede to the request to defer our decision for a time. We instruct that either of the parties wishing to submit evidence to the court do so within ninety days.'

Two things were now clear: first, no judgement would be made in the appeal until the court had studied the material in the Federenko file; second, the prosecution had decided to engage in a stalling action, to delay judgement as long as possible. They hoped that Demjanjuk would die in prison before the judgement was given, since that would put a freeze on the entire case.

At the beginning of March 1991 evidence from the Federenko file finally reached the prosecution, but Shaked did not notify me or the court of this. As a result I was forced once more to submit a request that the hearing be postponed. I also asked the court to apply directly to the Soviet authorities and request that the material be sent immediately to the court secretariat. The continuation of the hearing was put off until 6 June. A few days before this, the prosecution submitted its rebuttal to my petition. Among other things, it said: 'The Soviet public prosecutor has acquiesced and handed over to the prosecution copies of statements, evidence, etc. found in the file from the trial of Nazi criminal Fyodor Federenko, conducted in 1986 in the Soviet Union. This is not, however, sufficient to give a full picture of the subject and there is need for supplementation and examination of additional material that exists not in the said Federenko file but in other files.' This was a gross deception of the court. As I saw when the material was finally handed over to me, it did contain a 'full picture'. The statements in the Federenko file meant that no court in the Western world could convict Demjanjuk of being Ivan the Terrible. The prosecution's claim that there was a need for 'supplementation' was mere filibustering.

During the 6 June hearing, Shaked announced his intention of setting out the next day for another trip to the Soviet Union. He said he intended to go through fifteen thousand documents gathered for him in Moscow, among them all the evidence presented during a series of trials held in the Soviet Union concerning Treblinka. Shaked claimed that he was going to examine each and every one of these documents. He did not deny that all the Marchenko material from the Federenko file had been in his possession since March.

I opposed the further delay vehemently. I asked that the hearing be put off for only the briefest period, so that the prosecution could hand the material over to me and I could submit it as additional evidence from the defence. Immediately thereafter a date could be set for hearing further, and this time final, arguments. I emphasized that all the prosecution's actions, and especially the new trip to Moscow, were nothing more than stalling devices being used precisely because the picture painted by the documents in the Federenko file was completely clear. I also argued that the court could not determine that there was a need for further material to 'clarify the picture' when it did not have before it the material supposedly needing clarification. But my words fell on deaf ears. The court agreed to the prosecution's demands, contributing to a delay of many months more.

Demjanjuk was not present at any of these hearings. From time to time, of course, I updated him about the earth-shaking developments. He was especially happy when I showed him the document confirming his mother's marriage certificate. 'I told you all along my mother's maiden name wasn't Marchenko,' he said with a smile of victory. After the 6 June session it was clear that the next hearing would revolve around the evidence in the Federenko file. I decided to request of the court that from this point forward Demjanjuk be brought from prison to attend every hearing (which involved a certain amount of organization). This should increase interest in the sessions and so make the media and the public realize the dramatic turning point the case had reached. The Israeli media, which had previously rushed to pass judgement on Demjanjuk as Ivan the Terrible, were in turmoil over the reversal that was beginning to be apparent. As a result, they made every effort to disregard the facts that were coming to light. The Gulf War only made this easier.

June passed and I still hadn't received the evidence from the prosecution. Even my petition to the court that I be allowed to submit the documents from the Federenko file (which unlike the prosecution I had not yet seen) did not expedite the delivery of the papers. The prosecution presumed to defy Justice Shamgar, President of the Supreme Court, who had expressly ordered on 6 June that 'It is important to the court that at our next session Mr Sheftel be in a position to address the existing material. I therefore request that this intervening period bring about a situation such that at our next session Mr Sheftel may address the merits of this material [sic].' It was determined that the next hearing would be on 14 August 1991.

Nishnic, Johnny, Demjanjuk and I decided that if by the end of July the prosecution had not passed all the material to me then Demjanjuk would start a three-day hunger strike. It was agreed that I would then convene a press conference to explain his reasons for taking such exceptional action. This would expose the scandal and hit the news internationally. The prosecution would then be forced to give me the material.

I estimated that the mere threat of a hunger strike would be sufficient, so I contacted a reporter and leaked Demjanjuk's intention of launching a hunger strike in the near future should the prosecution not immediately give me the evidence from the Federenko file. The reporter called Shaked the next day to get his reaction, and even asked why he was not handing over such important material to the defence. Shaked refused to comment, but the next day he wrote a letter, which reached me on 24 July, saying, 'The translation and typing have been completed and I am making available to you copies of the Russian and Hebrew versions of the statements from the Federenko file.' (The translation of twenty-two statements thus took five months. At this rate, Levin should have given the defence some twenty-five years to prepare for the trial, and that only to complete the translation of the evidence. Yet the defence had had to go over all hundred thousand pages of the documents within three months of their being submitted to O'Connor.) The most despicable paragraph in Shaked's letter came at the end. 'Despite the fact that the said material is in my possession and was the greater part of this time in translation, proof-reading and typing, and while it naturally passed through many hands, not a shred of its contents was leaked nor appeared anywhere in the press in Israel or elsewhere before it was passed on to you and accepted as evidence in court. It is my hope that this will be the case in future as well.' The prosecutor who had conducted a show-trial in a theatre in front of the national media was asking for a press moratorium. I was burning with anger. At the beginning of next week, I vowed, the material, in full, would be brought (legally, via a petition) to the notice of the local and world media.

The next day I reported to the state prosecutor's office in Jerusalem to collect the material. Within an hour I was at home in Tel Aviv, excited, tearing open the envelope. Minutes later I was trembling with emotion. In my wildest dreams I had never imagined that there would be so much material and that it would offer such firm proof.

Take, for instance, the statement of a guard named Sergei Stefanovich Vasilienko: 'Marchenko Ivan, the operator of the motor of the gas chambers in the Treblinka camp. The Jews in the work crews called him Ivan the Terrible. He was noted for his great cruelty to the people during the process of their extermination. He beat them with obvious enjoyment, with whatever came to hand, however he wanted.' Vasilienko was presented with the pictures of two guards in SS uniform – one short with a pistol in his hand, the second tall and unarmed. Vasilienko was asked if he knew the men, and answered, 'The picture shows guards of the SS forces in the Treblinka camp. Takchuk is the one holding a pistol in his right hand. Next to him is the operator of the motor of the gas chambers, Marchenko Ivan. The two of them have been photographed in the uniform of the guards in the SS forces.' This picture was also shown to Ivan Takchuk himself, who said, 'I had my photo taken with the operator of the gas chambers at Treblinka – Marchenko Ivan.' Marchenko, as he is seen in the picture, was tall and broad-shouldered, i.e. not dissimilar to Demjanjuk. Now I knew not only that Demjanjuk was not Ivan the Terrible, but also why he had been mistakenly identified as him.

The gist of all the statements was similar. It took me about two hours to read them, the image of Judge Levin dancing before my eyes the whole time. Again and again I imagined myself addressing him: 'These statements, Dovele, are a fitting answer to all your dishonourable behaviour during the trial.' I admit without shame that, happy as I was about the impending acquittal of Demjanjuk, I was even happier that I was about to bring shame and disgrace on the panel of judges that sentenced him to death. Levin's many angry outbursts, both in the courtroom and in chambers, ran through my memory. Time and again I heard myself telling him, 'Now, Dovele, you'll have *really* good reason to be angry.' In all my years of legal practice I had never been so happy and satisfied as in those precious moments; and from time to time I recall them nostalgically.

When I had finished reading the statements and calmed down a bit, I called Nishnic in Cleveland. He answered immediately, tensely: 'Shefy, is that you?'

'Yes, Ed. We've done it, in spite of the OSI, in spite of the Israeli prosecution, in spite of Levin.' I added, 'Ed, just as I told you before judgement was given in the lower court that I was sure your father-in-law's fate was sealed, so I'm telling you now, with the same certainty, that Demjanjuk will be acquitted and that the Supreme Court will declare that he is not Ivan the Terrible. The material I've just finished reading is amazing, beyond all our expectations.'

Nishnic responded with great emotion: 'That's great, that's great, I don't believe it, finally the truth has come out, and fourteen years of hell are coming to an end.' I then gave him an overview of the contents of the statements. 'What's the next step?' he asked.

'On Sunday or Monday I'll submit a petition for the immediate release of Demjanjuk, principally to be able to make public the full contents of each and every one of the guard statements, where they deal with Ivan Marchenko, Ivan the Terrible. My petition will quote the statements verbatim. Since the petition itself becomes a public document as soon as it is submitted, it can be quoted by reporters without violating the *sub judice* rule.' I also told him about the section of Shaked's letter asking me not to talk to the press. When he heard this, Nishnic burst out, 'Not leak them to the press? We'll make an international scandal out of this!' I promised to send him photocopies of the statements in the original language, and our conversation ended.

Now I called Doron. I asked him to come to my house immediately and see the material with his own eyes. He arrived a few minutes later, and without preamble I showed him the relevant sections of the statements. He is of a much more restrained temperament and more cautious in his evaluations than I am, but after only fifteen minutes he said, 'The case is closed! With material like this every court and every judge, even Levin, would acquit Demjanjuk and rule that he is not Ivan the Terrible. There's absolutely no doubt about it. You are about to win the appeal.'

Over the weekend I read the material over and over, until I knew the sections dealing with Marchenko almost by heart. I drafted the petition for Demjanjuk's release, also noting that it would be fitting for all those responsible for him spending more than five and a half years in prison to apologize to him and compensate him for his great suffering. On Tuesday the petition was sent to the Supreme Court, and it was reported at length in the international media. In the evening Nishnic called to tell me how much the reports had encouraged him and the family, and that all were now eagerly awaiting Demjanjuk's release.

At the end of June, in the midst of all this excitement, I met Tali Ofri. With every passing week I sensed that my single days were coming to an end. Her beauty and intelligence were so fascinating that every day she succeeded in diverting my attention for long hours away from the adventure of the Demjanjuk affair to the wonderful adventure of life with her. On the evening of Tuesday 13 August we went to the American Colony Hotel to spend the night before the court session. I wanted Tali to be with me during these hours. I felt she had become part of me, and could not contemplate appearing in such a session without her being there. I knew that this session would be especially dramatic, and I guessed I would argue well and make a great impression on her.

In the morning we made our way along the corridors of the Supreme Court to Courtroom 1. Cameras flashed around us all the way. I could not and did not want to hide the satisfaction and pride that I felt, both because of the event and because Tali was at my side. All the fuss reminded me of Binyanei Ha'uma during the first stages of the trial. As soon as I entered the courtroom I sensed the tension. Demjanjuk himself was already there, and several photographers were taking his picture from every angle. Just after nine the judges entered the room and took their seats. The suspense was palpable. President Shamgar gave me the floor. To give the session drama from the start, I opened with the words, 'This is the day we have hoped for.' I explained my statement, emphasizing that the material that would be submitted as evidence completely and incontrovertibly changed the direction of the case. 'From this point forward,' I declared, 'it will be impossible to have any doubt that the verdict convicting Demjanjuk is without foundation. This is because Ivan Marchenko, who has no connection with the appellant, is Ivan the Terrible.'

I was asked by Justice Goldberg if it would be possible to call as witnesses the guards who had given the statements I was basing myself on. I said not: 'They have all been executed or died.' I quoted some parts of the statements to convey their dramatic import first-hand. As I spoke I glanced continually at the judges' faces, and it looked as though these facts were having the required effect. I read on, the quotes becoming an unambiguous set of testimonies, and I discerned a mixture of astonishment and disappointment in their attitude.

At the end of this part of my speech I referred the court to its decision of February 1991 not to free Demjanjuk forthwith from prison, because 'the information before us is not sufficient to justify such a decision'. 'Now there is such information, more than is necessary. Now it has been made perfectly clear to Your Honours that the appellant is not Ivan the Terrible and that he never set foot in Treblinka. There can be no escaping the need to release him from prison forthwith.'

Many of the journalists, especially the foreign ones, were naïvely convinced that Demjanjuk would be freed that very day. Some of them even thought that the verdict of acquittal would be given on the spot. I myself knew better. Although convinced that Demjanjuk's exoneration was assured, I believed that, precisely because of this, the prosecution would be doing everything it could to stall, and the court would co-operate. It would be hard for the court to accept the new reality, especially that of a disgraceful show-trial conducted under the aegis of a Supreme Court justice, Dov Levin. That trial had now become a farce, and it was a disaster for the prestige of the Israeli legal establishment. I had said all this to Nishnic and Johnny, who were naturally very disappointed. Demjanjuk himself was more optimistic than ever. Just before this hearing he had told me in Hebrew, 'Sheftel, pretty soon I am going home.' I answered, 'You're going home, but it won't be soon.'

At the end of my speech I attacked the prosecution for claiming there was additional material in the Soviet Union that could change the picture. I stressed – not because I knew, but only because it was a logical assumption – that 'In the Soviet Union there are dozens of other statements all of which, like the ones before Your Honours, state clearly that Ivan Marchenko was Ivan the Terrible.' The issue of the additional material, I went on, had been raised for one reason: to stall the appeal for as long as possible because the prosecution hoped that during the delay the appellant would die. Even though further material from the Soviet Union could be of benefit to the defence, we were willing to do without it and take the risk of the court judging solely on the basis of the material presented to it that day. Either way, the prosecution wanted judgement to be postponed until such material could be submitted, but this should not be at the expense of the appellant's time.

Tali had been sitting behind me the whole time. When we left the courtroom together, she told me that she had been enthralled. I refused all the requests for interviews; I wanted to rest and share my feelings with Tali about what had just occurred. I was walking on air when she complimented me on my arguments and said, 'It was simply amazing to see the power of your appearance.'

The hearing reconvened at noon and the floor was given to Shaked. He began by saying that even if Demjanjuk were not Ivan the Terrible, the petition to release him from prison should not be granted because he had been a guard at Sobibor and Travniki. Thus began a new stage in the prosecution's decline. The court's immediate reaction to Shaked's argument was encouraging. Justices Goldberg and Barak asked, one after the other: 'Is counsel abandoning Treblinka and persisting with Sobibor and Travniki?' Shaked did not respond directly. He could not possibly admit that he had erred in naming Demjanjuk as Ivan the Terrible, but because of the new evidence and the great impression it had made on everyone, he could not continue to claim that Demjanjuk *was* Ivan the Terrible. As a result, he tried to ignore the question. To my surprise, the judges did not press him. Shaked continued to flog the Sobibor/Travniki issue and argue that this was sufficient reason not to release Demjanjuk. I made every effort not to interrupt, though this was an argument unbefitting any decent public prosecutor. Travniki and Sobibor, as Shaked himself had claimed in his opening arguments, were nothing but links in the testimony of the survivors in their identification of Demjanjuk as Ivan the Terrible. I.e. Travniki and Sobibor were simply stations along Ivan the Terrible's way to Treblinka. Now that the prosecution had realized that Demjanjuk was not Ivan the Terrible, this supporting evidence must fall also. Otherwise, what would it support?

The lower court had, it may be recalled, grossly violated the legal requirement to try Demjanjuk solely for the crime for which he was extradited – that is, murder. Now Shaked was trying to compound his offence. He proposed to the court – for the first time at appeal – to convict Demjanjuk of having been in Sobibor and Travniki. The express ruling of the federal court in Cleveland providing for Demjanjuk's extradition to Israel said: 'These same affidavits and supplementary statements also are sufficient to place the respondent at the site where the alleged crimes occurred, namely the Treblinka camp in the years 1942– 43 ... Pursuant to Article XIII, the respondent may be extradited to

Israel only to stand trial for the offenses for which this court has certified that there is a probable cause to indicate that the respondent committed the crimes.' This paragraph is repeated ten times in the Cleveland court's decision, in various wordings. Thus Demjanjuk may be tried in Israel solely for the crimes attributed to him at Treblinka, and even then only on a charge of murder.

Moreover, Shaked was making this argument without anyone to testify to having seen Demjanjuk in Sobibor or Travniki. It was not only that no such witness was available; of the dozen Jewish survivors of Sobibor throughout the world who had been questioned from 1976 onward, by both the American investigators and the Israeli authorities, none had identified Demjanjuk's picture as that of a guard from Sobibor. Yet these facts did not stop Shaked, and at the end of his speech he excelled himself by asking for a postponement of several months in order to submit additional documents – 'to complete the picture', he said.

The court decided, of course, to accept all the statements from the Federenko file as additional defence evidence, but it also decided to postpone the hearing for four months, to 23 December 1991. So Demjanjuk would sit in jail for over a year from the date on which the prosecutor had seen with his own eyes more than twenty statements clearly indicating that the defendant was innocent. No such thing should be possible in any decent judicial system.

After several more postponements Shaked finally submitted, on 6 February 1992, a petition for the acceptance of additional guards' statements as evidence, taken from among the fifteen thousand pages he had examined in Russia. His material consisted of thirty-eight statements from Treblinka guards, some of whom had already given other statements in the framework of the Federenko case. All were similar in substance to the statements from the Federenko file, and all stated explicitly that Ivan Marchenko had been Ivan the Terrible. There were now sixty pieces of evidence indicating Demjanjuk's total innocence.

One of the statements, dated 20 December 1950, was from Nikolai Shelaiev, Marchenko's partner in the operation of the gas chambers. Shelaiev, captured by the Soviets, convicted and executed in 1952, stated:

> Ivan Marchenko, I do not know his father's [first] name, was born in 1911 in Dnepropetrovsk, not a Party member, married; among his children there was one son who was at that time, 1943, nine years old. He was conscripted into the Red Army at the beginning of the war for the motherland [the Soviet Union], and served in the Army as a private. Description: tall; black hair; brown eyes; thin face; large,

narrow, straight nose; an inconspicuous diagonal scar on his cheek; solidly built; square shoulders; erect gait. I first met him in September 1942 and worked with him as operator of the motor that emitted exhaust gas and transferred it to the gas chambers, where the people were killed.'

I noted the following important points in this statement and others: Ivan Marchenko had been born in the Dnepropetrovsk district, while Ivan Demjanjuk had been born in the Vinitsa district. Marchenko was born in 1911, whilst Demjanjuk was born in 1920. Marchenko had fallen prisoner to the Germans in 1941, whilst Demjanjuk had been taken prisoner in 1942. Marchenko was married and a father of three, one nine years old in 1942/43, whilst Demjanjuk was in those years a childless bachelor of twenty-two. Marchenko had a diagonal scar on his cheek, whilst Demjanjuk had no scars on his face. All this, of course, was in addition to the difference in the names and other physical features apparent from photographs of the two men.

We were not idle during these developments. At the 15 January 1992 session Shaked submitted Marchenko's personal SS file as evidence. This had been handed over to us only a short while previously, even though he had had it since his second visit to the Soviet Union in June 1991. The document contained many details about Marchenko, including his date of birth, district of residence, native village and marital status. These agreed with the details in the many guard statements.

Nishnic decided to go to the Soviet Union to see Marchenko's wife and children, in the village of Seryovka, in the Dnepropetrovsk district. He found the Marchenko home without difficulty and discovered that Marchenko's wife had died just a month before. One of the daughters, Katarina Ivanovna Kovalenko, born in May 1941 – two months before her father enlisted in the Red Army – lived there with her husband and children. Nishnic introduced himself and explained his reason for coming. The daughter expressed her full willingness to co-operate, and it was quickly verified that she was indeed the daughter of the SS man whose file Nishnic had. Her father had been born in this village in 1911, as the file stated. He had been married with three children on the date the file was opened, 1 November 1941; Katarina Kovalenko had a brother and sister born before November 1941. She showed her birth certificate to Nishnic, proving she was the daughter of Ivan Marchenko. Katarina then showed Nishnic her father's wedding photograph, and told him that they had not heard from him after his enlistment in the Red Army. She was shocked when she heard what crimes were attributed to her father. She broke down in tears, saying it was good that her mother had died a month ago and not had to hear these horrible accusations. She was also able to relate that when she was still a girl, in the late '40s and early '50s, KGB men had often come to their home, confiscating all photographs of her father except for the wedding picture she had shown to Nishnic. The KGB had never explained why they took her father's photographs, or what he was suspected of.

Katarina would not give Nishnic the original photo, but agreed to allow him to copy it, along with her birth certificate. Furthermore, she signed a statement confirming that the wedding picture was of her father, Ivan Marchenko, and that she was the daughter of the man whose personal details were in the SS file. She promised to consult with her sister and, if she agreed, to send the photograph to Nishnic. Nishnic did receive the original in the end, signed on the back by Marchenko's daughter to certify that this was her father's wedding picture. At the court session of 25 February 1992 the picture, birth certificate and statement were accepted as defence evidence, despite the vigorous opposition of the prosecution. Still the judges refused to free Demjanjuk from prison. They ruled bluntly: 'We see no reason to change our position on the matter of the petition to release the appellant from detention.'

This was unprecedented. The State of Israel had never left a man in prison, even for a day, in the face of evidence discovered after his conviction that had even five per cent of the value of this evidence. Demjanjuk had now been imprisoned in Israel for six full years. It is doubtful whether our Supreme Court had ever made such an unjust decision as this brief one not to free Demjanjuk. Moreover, the judges decided to allow the prosecution to waste more time, ostensibly to locate additional evidence in the Soviet Union. As if this were not enough, it revoked its intention of hearing final arguments from 29 March.

In the time available to me I studied closely the statements from the Federenko file and formed a picture of how the KGB had conducted its interrogations about Nazi crimes in Treblinka. I concluded that somewhere in a KGB archive in the Soviet Union there must be an investigation file labelled IVAN MARCHENKO; and in it there must be all of the statements taken during the KGB inquiry into him; and I supposed it would contain dozens of statements dealing with Marchenko's identification in one or more photographs in the KGB's possession. These assumptions were based on two things: first, immigrants to Israel from the Soviet Union whom I had met, some of them attorneys by profession, confirmed my surmise; the second was Shaked himself. When he submitted Ivan Marchenko's personal SS file to the court,

Trawniki, den 1.11. 19

Personalbogen Nr. 476

Name: Martschjenko
Vorname: Iwan   Vatersname: Iwanowitsch
geb. am: 2.3.11   in Serhijowga / Dnjepropetrowsk
Nationalität: Ukrainer
Staatszugehörigkeit: UdSSR
Beruf: Bauer
Stand: verh.   Kinderzahl: drei
Mädchenname der Frau: Katharina geb. Krauwtschenko
Mädchenname der Mutter: Aksania geb. Beretjatka

Militärdienst — Waffengattung: Infanterie
Letzter Dienstgrad: Soldat   Dienstzeit: 27.5.41–10.7.41
Bemerkungen:

Sprachkenntnisse: ukrainisch
Besondere Fähigkeiten:

Grösse: 174 cm
Gesichtsform: oval
Haarfarbe: schwarz
Augenfarbe: grau
Besondere Merkmale: Narben im Genick

rechter Daumen

Obige Angaben werden belegt mit:
1.)
2.)
3.)
— auf Grund eigener Angaben aufgenommen
Aufgenommen durch:
Unterschrift:
Dienstgrad: Hptw. d. Schupo.

Ivan Marchenko's SS personal file, isued on 1 November 1941

he mentioned incidentally that it came from the KGB's investigation file on Ivan Marchenko.

It was time to make another move. At the 25 February session I argued that, even though I needed no additional evidence to persuade the court of Demjanjuk's innocence, the defence knew, and it was desirable that the court also know, that there was more material in the Soviet Union that could point to the same conclusion. To quote the court record: 'This is the place to emphasize that, in addition to the material that the prosecution was obliged to deliver to me before this session, there also exist in the Soviet Union dozens of additional statements of guards from Treblinka, each of which, without exception, identifies Marchenko in SS uniform as Ivan the Terrible.' When the court asked where they were, I explained that they could be found 'in a file labelled "Ivan Marchenko", kept in the cellars of the KGB in Kiev'. I pointed out that I did not want to submit these statements as further evidence, because the defence was satisfied with the material already in the court file.

Unfortunately, Shaked and the bench pounced on this finding. Shaked asked to travel once more to the Soviet Union to find Marchenko's KGB file. The court's favourable decision concluded: 'In any case the results will be reported to the court in writing, no later than sixty days from today.' No wonder I was worried. Even though the court file now contained sixty statements pointing to Ivan Marchenko as Ivan the Terrible, I feared that the stalling game that had been going on for the last fifteen months would never end.

In April 1992 Shaked went to the Ukraine, which had just won its independence. It was his fourth trip to what had been the Soviet Union. He assumed, from the conviction with which I had presented my story, that the existence of the statements in the Marchenko file was an established fact; and he was afraid to come back without this identification evidence. This time he 'suddenly' succeeded in finding all the identifications of Ivan Marchenko's picture as that of Ivan the Terrible, identifications that his sharp eye had 'somehow' missed during his three earlier trips.

On his return Shaked reported to the press on the evidence he had brought from the Ukraine. 'The KGB archives contained no evidence that would help Demjanjuk,' the newspapers told their readers on 20 April, based on the false information Shaked had given them. Only three weeks later, in a statement to the Supreme Court, Shaked said that 'The state hereby submits all the evidence photocopied for it by the prosecutor's office in Kiev and having as its source the KGB file of Marchenko Ivan Ivanovitch. This file was handed over to representatives of the prosecution for their study during their last stay in the Ukraine.' Afterwards he listed twenty statements, most of which were about photo spreads in which Marchenko's SS-file picture was identified as Ivan the Terrible.

One of these statements was Nikolai Shelaiev's identification of Marchenko's picture from a group of three. It contained the following language:

> I identify with certainty in picture number three Marchenko Ivan, who is well known to me. I first met Marchenko Ivan at the Treblinka death camp, where he had arrived from the city of Lublin, more than a month previously. Marchenko already worked there at Treblinka as the operator of the motor of the gas chambers, or, as they were called, the 'butchers'. Upon my arrival in this camp I was also appointed to the post of operator of the motor and I quickly came to know Marchenko ... Marchenko Ivan, at the time of his work in the Treblinka death camp as operator of the gas chambers, was of the rank of guard, wore a German uniform of the SS guard forces, and was armed with a rifle. His job as operator included: ensuring that the motor was functional, that it gave off fumes, which were transferred to the gas chambers, in which those sentenced to death were brought by force by the Germans in trainloads; to open the valves of the gas pipes after women, children, men and old people were put into the chambers; likewise to help the guards put in victims who displayed resistance ... During the period of his work in the death camp – for a year or more – Marchenko put hundreds of thousands of people through the gas chambers with the help of the Germans and the guards ... During the final days of the month of March 1945 I saw Marchenko come out of a brothel in the city of Fiume. At this time he no longer served with the Germans, but was with the Yugoslav partisans and had arrived for a furlough. He invited me to a nearby restaurant, where he began to tell me about his flight from the Germans. Marchenko told me that he had no intention of returning home, and that he wished to remain in Fiume, where he had a Yugoslav girl, whom he was thinking of marrying and having a family with. This girl was connected to the partisans, and would receive data on the Germans from him. After this meeting I never saw Marchenko again and never heard anything more of him.

Now it was clear why Ivan Marchenko never returned home after the war and why contact with him had been lost since his enlistment in the Red Army.

So it was that even before the final arguments began the judges had before them eighty statements from thirty-seven guards from Treblinka, all of them indicating Demjanjuk's absolute innocence of the crimes of which he had been accused and convicted. In my wildest dreams I never thought that such a great volte-face would occur. Demjanjuk's acquittal was now certain, even before judgement was rendered. The unbelievable had happened.

15 · The Demjanjuk Affair

It was now obvious that the workings of the Israeli prosecution and the OSI's machinations with Otto Horn's 'identification' of Demjanjuk amounted to a conspiracy to counterfeit and conceal evidence, with the purpose of deceiving Israeli and American courts. During the lower-court proceedings it was already clear that the OSI had criminally kept definitive evidence from the defence and the courts. And an order by a federal district court in Washington, issued over the OSI's objections, required that this evidence – a collection of statements, the most important of which was Danilchenko's – be handed over to the Demjanjuk family. When the defence finally received this material, it was apparent that it had been kept under wraps for some eight years.

While I have always been sceptical of the honesty of governments in general, I never imagined (until the beginning of October 1991) that the American authorities could possibly have known for certain, but concealed for the whole thirteen-year period in which legal proceedings were conducted against Demjanjuk, that Ivan Marchenko was the real Ivan the Terrible. My conversation with Judge Tatunik in the first week of September 1990 revealed that during the American proceedings the Soviets already knew that Demjanjuk was not Ivan the Terrible. Even though those proceedings were aimed at proving just that, the Soviets chose to remain silent. They were not interested in helping a Ukrainian. Moreover, even when Demjanjuk was extradited to Israel and charged with being Ivan the Terrible from Treblinka – meaning the death penalty if he were to be convicted – the Soviets said nothing. This silence continued when Demjanjuk was convicted and sentenced to death. There is of course nothing very surprising about such criminal behaviour, since this was a regime that in its seventy years of existence had been directly responsible for the murder of tens of millions of innocent people. The question is: What was the connection between the behaviour of the American authorities and the criminal silence of the Soviets?

Among the thousands of documents that OSI agents threw in the dustbins on Washington's K Street were several that made passing reference to a certain cable sent in August 1978 by the American Embassy in Moscow to the State Department in Washington. The cable was about the OSI's case against Federenko. These documents roused Nishnic's suspicions at the beginning of 1991; he guessed that the reference was to evidence that could prove Demjanjuk's innocence. Once the OSI's involvement in Otto Horn's forced identification of Demjanjuk was revealed, Congressman Traficant applied to the State Department in February 1991, under the Freedom of Information Act, to be provided with a photocopy of the August 1978 cable and other documents.

On 3 May 1991 Traficant received a reply from Janet Mullins of the State Department. She could provide him immediately with some of the documents he had requested, including the cable, and attached them to her letter. The rest, Ms Mullins explained, required co-ordination with the Department of Justice. When Nishnic read the cable, and especially when he realized that important parts of it had been blanked out, he had no doubt that material pointing to Demjanjuk's innocence was being concealed.

The cable referred to certain evidence the American Embassy in Moscow received on 11 August 1978 from the Soviet public prosecutor's office, material relating to the Soviet investigation of Federenko. American Justice Department officials had asked the Soviets to provide it to facilitate an appeal they were preparing against a Florida Federal District Court decision of 25 July 1978. This decision had rejected the OSI's request to revoke Federenko's citizenship. The cable noted that a hundred pages of documents from the Soviet investigation file on Federenko were attached. This was all in the section of the cable that had been released. Yet the blanked-out part contained something even more important, for it detailed the type and character of the material contained in those hundred pages.

Thus, in August 1978 the OSI had in its possession a hundred pages which, we later found out, demonstrated Demjanjuk's innocence. These had been deliberately kept from Demjanjuk's attorneys and, obviously, from the courts as well. This was done in order to secure, under false pretences, Demjanjuk's denaturalization, extradition to Israel, trial and execution as Ivan the Terrible, when these authorities knew for certain that he was not the right man. Nishnic was certain of this, but I had a hard time believing that the American authorities could have behaved in such a way.

Traficant wrote again to Ms Mullins at the State Department, demanding that she provide him with the full cable, without omissions. He did not receive this until 7 October 1991. The previously

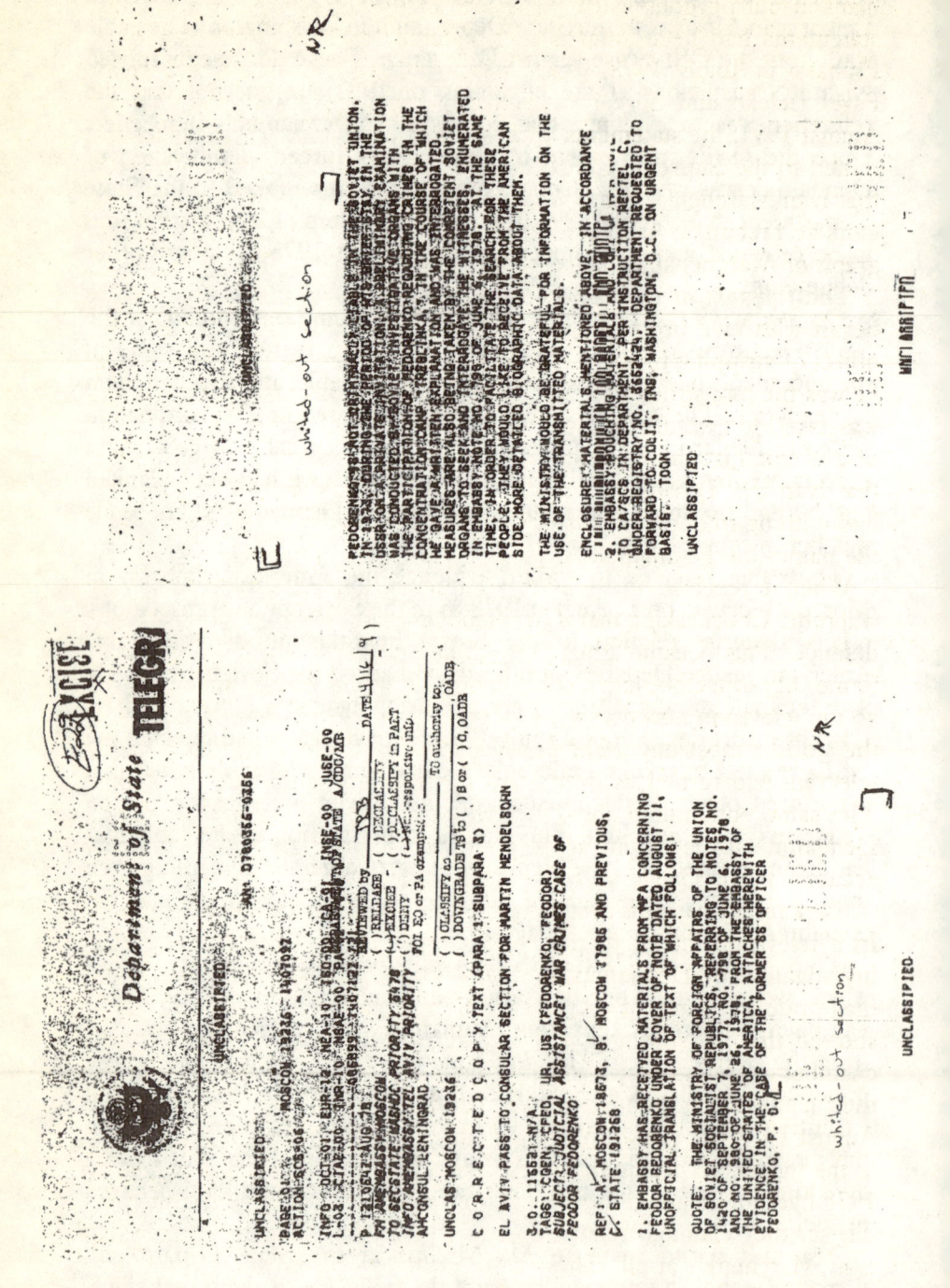

The censored cable

blanked-out portions listed the names of the Treblinka guards whose statements had been amongst the material received by the American Embassy in August 1978. The names included guards Ivan Shevchenko, Pavel Leleko and Sergei Vasilienko. Seven weeks previously, on 14 August 1991, the statements of these three camp guards had been submitted to the Supreme Court in Jerusalem; they stated unambiguously that Ivan Marchenko and Nikolai Shelaiev were the gas-chamber operators at Treblinka. As quoted above, Vasilienko also identified a photograph of Marchenko as being of Ivan the Terrible.

The full text of the cable revealed the contemptible plot in full. It began with civil proceedings against Demjanjuk in the US, with the object of stripping him of his American citizenship on the grounds that he was the monstrous Ivan the Terrible. Afterwards an American court was asked to extradite him to Israel. Now it was clear beyond a shadow of a doubt that the American authorities had known this entire time that Ivan the Terrible was a man called Ivan Marchenko, a man who had nothing to do with Demjanjuk. This disgraceful cover-up deserves the name 'the Demjanjuk Affair'.

When I received the full text, I quickly drafted a petition to the Supreme Court asking that it be included as additional evidence for the defence. This became a huge sensation, and the media began flocking to me. My office became a point of pilgrimage for correspondents from all the television networks with offices in Israel, and for reporters from the world's most important newspapers. Tzvia remarked that a single telegram had turned us from a law office into a radio and TV studio. The same commotion surrounded Johnny and Nishnic in Cleveland. Demjanjuk turned from accused to accuser, and now his American accusers in the OSI were in the media's dock.

As generally happens in such cases, publicity led to further revelations. In a television interview attorney George Parker, who led the OSI's investigation of Demjanjuk in 1978–80, verified the cable and even made public a page of the investigation diary he had then kept. This showed that in November 1979 Parker knew that the Treblinka gas-chamber operators were Ivan Marchenko and Nikolai Shelaiev. He knew their names from the material that had been received with the cable in August 1978. He thus refuted the fantasy the OSI had started purveying to the media, according to which the material that reached it in August 1978 had not included the full texts of the statements but only excerpts. These, they claimed, related only to Federenko and did not mention Ivan Marchenko at all. These false claims made it even clearer that there had been a shameful plot, whose perpetrators were now trying to cover their tracks.

UNCLASSIFIED

PAGE 01 MOSCOW 19236 140709Z
ACTION SCA-06

INFO OCT-01 EUR-12 NEA-10 IGO-00 CA-01 INSE-00 JUSE-00
L-03 CIAE-00 INR-10 NSAE-00 PA-02 /045 W
                                     ------086899 140712Z /21
P 120504Z AUG 78
FM AMEMBASSY MOSCOW
TO SECSTATE WASHDC PRIORITY 6478
INFO AMEMBASSY TEL AVIV PRIORITY
AMCONSUL LENINGRAD

UNCLAS MOSCOW 19236

CORRECTED COPY TEXT (PARA 1 SUBPARA 3)

EL AVIV PASS TO CONSULAR SECTION FOR MARTIN MENDELSOHN

E.O. 11652: N/A
TAGS: CGEN, CFED, UR, US (FEDORENKO, FEODOR)
SUBJECT: JUDICIAL ASSISTANCE: WAR CRIMES CASE OF
FEODOR FEDORENKO

REF: A. MOSCOW 18573, B. MOSCOW 17986 AND PREVIOUS,
C. STATE 191268

1. EMBASSY HAS RECEIVED MATERIALS FROM MFA CONCERNING
FEDOR FEDORENKO UNDER COVER OF NOTE DATED AUGUST 11,
AND NO. 980 OF JUNE 26, 1978, FROM THE EMBASSY OF
THE UNITED STATES OF AMERICA, ATTACHES HEREWITH
EVIDENCE IN THE CASE OF THE FORMER SS OFFICER
FEDORENKO, F. D. AMONG THESE MATERIALS ARE EXCERPTS
FROM THE MINUTES OF INTERROGATIONS IN THE CASES OF
UNCLASSIFIED

UNCLASSIFIED

PAGE 02 MOSCOW 19236 140709Z
SHEVCHENKO, I.S., LELEKO, P. Y., STREL'TSOV, A. I.

UNCLASSIFIED

UNCLASSIFIED

KOROTKIYE, D. N., YEGER, A. I., AND VASILENKO, S. S.,
WHO AT VARIOUS TIMES FROM 1944 TO 1962 WERE SENTENCED
BY MILITARY TRIBUNALS TO BE EXECUTED FOR PARTICIPATING
IN THE EXTERMINATION OF PEOPLE IN THE DEATH CAMP
"TREBLINKA". THE SENTENCES WERE CARRIED OUT.

FEDORENKO IS NOT CRIMINALLY LIABLE IN THE SOVIET UNION.
IN 1973, DURING THE PERIOD OF HIS BRIEF STAY IN THE
USSR ON A PRIVATE INVITATION, A PRELIMINARY EXAMINATION
WAS CONDUCTED BY SOVIET INVESTIGATIVE ORGANS WITH
THE PARTICIPATION OF FEDORENKO REGARDING CRIMES IN THE
CONCENTRATION CAMP "TREBLINKA". IN THE COURSE OF WHICH
HE GAVE A WRITTEN EXPLANATION AND WAS INTERROGATED.
MEASURES ARE ALSO BEING TAKEN BY THE COMPETENT SOVIET
ORGANS TO SEEK AND INTERROGATE THE WITNESSES ENUMERATED
IN EMBASSY NOTE NO. 798 OF JUNE 6, 1978. AT THE SAME
TIME, IN ORDER TO FACILITATE THE SEARCH FOR THESE
PEOPLE, THEY WOULD LIKE TO RECEIVE FROM THE AMERICAN
SIDE MORE DETAILED BIOGRAPHIC DATA ABOUT THEM.

THE MINISTRY WOULD BE GRATEFUL FOR INFORMATION ON THE
USE OF THE TRANSMITTED MATERIALS.

ENCLOSURE: MATERIALS MENTIONED ABOVE, IN ACCORDANCE
WITH INVENTORY, IN 100 PAGES. END QUOTE.

2. EMBASSY POUCHING MATERIALS AND COPY OF MFA NOTE
TO CA/SCS IN DEPARTMENT, PER INSTRUCTION REFTEL C,
UNDER REGISTRY NO. 3652494. DEPARTMENT REQUESTED TO
FORWARD TO COLIT, INS, WASHINGTON, D.C. ON URGENT
BASIS. TOON

UNCLASSIFIED

UNCLASSIFIED

The full cable

In December 1991 another cable was found, thanks again to Congressman Traficant's untiring efforts. This one had been sent on 29 July 1981 from the OSI to Glovna Komisia. It was the OSI's response to Glovna Komisia's request for all the Federenko material in American hands. The cable mentioned that the Soviet documents in the OSI's possession had not been made public. (This was because they led to the conclusion that Demjanjuk could not be Ivan the Terrible.) The OSI recommended to Glovna Komisia that it apply directly to the Soviets, and helpfully listed the statements in their possession, with the names of the camp guards who had provided them and the date on which each had been recorded by the KGB. The cable mentioned, among others, three statements from Pavel Leleko, two from Alexander Yeger, one from Sergei Vasilienko and one from Nikolai Malagon. These statements do not refer only to Federenko's crimes; they principally concern the deeds of Ivan Marchenko, identifying him as Ivan the Terrible. The cable explicitly notes too that these were complete statements, refuting the OSI's claim that only excerpts of the statements had been in their possession all this time.

Given all the facts in the cable, it was easy enough to discover that all these statements, with one exception – a total of six – were exactly those that had been submitted and accepted as defence evidence in the appeal. This cable was also the subject of an additional petition, drafted in the strongest possible terms, that it be accepted as evidence. The cable proved that the Polish authorities had also been partners in the international conspiracy against Demjanjuk: it had been addressed to Sanishinski and Mikulski of Glovna Komisia, the two officials who had told us in March 1990 that the material relating to Ivan the Terrible's true identity could be found in the file on Federenko's case in Simferopol. With the discovery of the second cable, it was clear that the two of them had had the evidence that Ivan Marchenko was Ivan the Terrible.

As the Supreme Court's next session (set for 23 December 1991) approached, we knew that the Demjanjuk Affair, which had begun in August 1978, was a scheme concocted by at least three countries – the Soviet Union, Poland and the United States. At the same time the OSI's motives for this odious deed were revealed. Among the public documents of the American Congress is a letter sent on 25 August 1978 by Congressman Joshua Eilberg, chairman of the House of Representatives' Subcommittee on Immigration, to Griffin Bell, then US Attorney General. It was sent less than two weeks after the cable and its accompanying material had been sent from Moscow to Washington, and a month after the American prosecution had lost the first round in its legal battle to denaturalize and deport Federenko.

UNCLASSIFIED

Department of State TELEGRAM

UNCLASSIFIED
AN: D810384-1069

PAGE 01 STATE 200108
ORIGIN OCS-06

INFO OCT-00 ADS-00 EUR-12 L-03 JUSE-00 /021 R

DRAFTED BY EUR:OGDECCS/EUR:GAFOURLENSKI
APPROVED BY CA:POES/RESICADIPALAIDO
JUS/OSI:CGINZIEMS
DESIRED DISTRIBUTION
JUS/CRIM:RYTN
--------------------000514 292552 /71

P 292166Z JUL 81
FM SECSTATE WASHDC
TO AMEMBASSY WARSAW PRIORITY

UNCLAS STATE 200108

E.O. 12065: N/A

TAGS: CGEN (FEDORENKO, FEODOR)

SUBJECT: JUDICIAL ASSISTANCE: WAR CRIMES INVESTIGATIONS
(OSI: IN-2-42-F71)

REF: STATE A-142 OF FEBRUARY 3, 1981

1. ON BEHALF OF THE DEPARTMENT OF JUSTICE; OFFICE OF
SPECIAL INVESTIGATIONS (OSI), PLEASE CONVEY THE FOLLOWING
TO THE MAIN COMMISSION FOR THE INVESTIGATION OF HITLERITE
CRIMES IN POLAND:

2. WITH REFERENCE TO THE RECENT MEETING BETWEEN MICHAEL
WOLF OF THE OFFICE OF SPECIAL INVESTIGATIONS (OSI) AND
MESSRS. SANISHINSKI, MUSIOL, AND MIKULSKI OF THE MAIN
COMMISSION, A REVIEW IS NOW BEING MADE OF WHAT MATERIALS
SHOULD BE SENT TO FULFILL THE MAIN COMMISSION'S REQUEST IN
THE CASE OF FEODOR FEDORENKO, BORN 1907 IN SIVASH, UKRAINE,
AND NOW STATELESS, RESIDING IN PENNSYLVANIA. OSI IS NOW
UNCLASSIFIED

PAGE 02 STATE 200108
POUCHING A COPY OF THE OPINION OF THE UNITED STATES SUPREME

UNCLASSIFIED

COURT IN THIS CASE. ALL OTHER RELEVANT MATERIALS IN THE
PUBLIC RECORD WILL FOLLOW AS SOON AS POSSIBLE.

3. OSI ALSO HAS SEVERAL STATEMENTS BY SOVIET CITIZEN
WITNESSES; HOWEVER, SINCE THESE STATEMENTS ARE NOT OF
PUBLIC RECORD, OSI SUGGESTS THAT THE MAIN COMMISSION
CONTACT THE SOVIET AUTHORITIES DIRECTLY FOR THESE
STATEMENTS. THE WITNESSES AND DATES OF TESTIMONY ARE
AS FOLLOWS:

DOROFEYEV, NIKOLAY YAKOVLEVICH   4 JAN 78
SAVENKO, YAKOV KLIMENT'YIVICH   8 JAN 78
MALAGON, NIKOLAY PETROVICH   18 MAR 78
SHEVCHENKO, IVAN SEMENOVICH   18 SEP 77
LELEKO, PAVEL VLADIMIROVICH   26 NOV 77
LELEKO, PAVEL VLADIMIROVICH   20 FEB 78
LELEKO, PAVEL VLADIMIROVICH   21 FEB 78
STREL'TSOV, ANTON IVANOVICH   1 MAR 78
KOROTKIKH, DMITRIY NIKOLAEVICH   21 APR 80
YEGER, ALEKSANDR IVANOVICH   2 APR 80
YEGER, ALEKSANDR IVANOVICH   7 APR 83
YEGER, ALEKSANDR IVANOVICH   18 APR 80
VASILENKO, SERGEY STEPANOVICH   18 SEP 81
FEDORENKO, FEDOR DEM'YANOVICH   11 NOV 76 (?)
FEDORENKO, FEDOR DEM'YANOVICH   13 NOV 73
KUZ'MINSKIY, ANANIY GRIGOR'YEVICH,
  AND FEDORENKO, FEDOR DEM'YANOVICH   18 NOV 73
FEDORENKO, FEDOR DEM'YANOVICH   17 NOV 73

4. YOUR CONTINUED ASSISTANCE IS APPRECIATED. HAIG

UNCLASSIFIED

The cable of 29 July 1981 from the OSI to Glovna Komisia

Reports have reached me that deficiencies have become apparent in the preparation of the case of the U.S. v. Demjanjuk, a denaturalization proceeding against an alleged Nazi war criminal now living in Cleveland, Ohio.

I wish to express my strong concern over the possible inadequate prosecution of the case. A repeat of the recent Federenko adverse decision to the government's case in Florida would nullify and gravely jeopardize the long and persistent efforts of this Subcommittee in ridding this country of these undesirable elements ...

The creation of a Special Litigation Unit [the OSI] within I.N.S. was established to bring expertise and organization to this process. This Unit should be fully entrusted with these cases.

I would strongly urge you to place the direction of the proceedings of the DEMJANJUK case in the hands of the Special Litigation Unit. We cannot afford the risk of losing another decision.

The thrust of this letter comes, of course, in its last line. The letter was forwarded by Bell to the officials of the OSI, who felt that their future would be threatened by another lost case. Were they to lose the Demjanjuk case, the new office that was their employer would be liquidated, so they decided to conceal evidence they had received less than two weeks earlier. It was clear to these officials that the material would lead to the very outcome that Congressman Eilberg had so bluntly warned against: they would lose the case, and their jobs.

This was confirmed by Alan Ryan, who headed the OSI from its establishment until 1981. In an interview in an Alabama newspaper in 1991, he said in reference to the Demjanjuk trial: 'It was one of the first cases we tried, and we were very much on the line. If we had lost that case, we probably would have had very short lifespan.' Thus, the OSI conspired to shorten Demjanjuk's life in order to lengthen its own.

It is worthwhile to note just how far the OSI officials went. John Martin, Demjanjuk's lawyer at the time of the denaturalization trial in Cleveland in October 1982, wrote a letter to Alan Ryan demanding that Ryan hand over all the documents touching in any way on Demjanjuk's trial that the OSI had received from West Germany, Poland, Israel and the Soviet Union. Martin received a reply from attorney Bruce Einhorn, a member of the prosecution team in the denaturalization trial: 'All relevant and discoverable documents in the Government's possession have already been made part of the record of these proceedings. As a result of those documents, and other evidence, your client was denaturalized.' Einhorn had no compunction about lying baldly and concealing information that had been in the OSI's possession for four years.

Memorandum

Subject: Release of Material From Our Files on John Demjanjuk

Date:

To: Martin H. Sachs
Trial Attorney

From: Bruce J. Einhorn
Trial Attorney

This will confirm our discussion regarding your request for information concerning what the effect would be if we were to agree to the release of our Demjanjuk files pursuant to several pending FOIA requests.

I am familiar with the facts of the Demjanjuk case because I was the lead attorney on it. I am also familiar with the fact that we are currently providing judicial assistance to the State of Israel in their investigation and prosecution of Demjanjuk, who was extradited there this past February.

I can state unequivocally that we should oppose release of our files for the following reasons:

1. Concern over the integrity of the Israeli prosecution and of fairness to the defendant -- release of our material now would, in all probability, reveal (and could easily undermine and prejudice) the Israeli prosecution strategy.

2. Conversely, there is the expected publicity that would naturally attend the release of certain (and oftentimes dramatic) material. The release of such material could well be expected to infringe upon and prejudice the defendant's right to a fair trial by inflaming public opinion and outrage.

3. We have a lot of "background" material in the files which has been supplied to us either by individuals whose identities we would want to protect or which was prepared by OSI (or AUSA) attorneys. OSI investigators and historians also prepared at the direction of the case attorneys, much material including investigative reports, that appears in the case files.

4. There is no way we can determine at this time what material, if any, could be called from the files and/or sanitized for release to the public.

The OSI internal memo

The media's excitement about these developments reached its peak on 23 December 1991, when the court convened to hear my petitions as well as Shaked's request for a further postponement of the hearing (another step in the delaying tactics he had pursued time and again during the previous year). The atmosphere in the courtroom was electric. It was clear the trial was making a 180-degree turn. Demjanjuk was present, as during the previous session.

The day before, when I had visited him in his cell, Demjanjuk repeated the statement he had made many times since October 1991: 'They should be ashamed of themselves, how can that happen in a democratic country like America, that they do such a horrible thing to a simple man like me?' He was very optimistic that his release from prison was imminent, and when he was brought into the courtroom he said in Hebrew to the journalists who crowded round him: 'Pretty soon I'm going home.' For my part, I knew before the session that Shaked was continuing energetically with his stalling game, putting off the submission of the new material he had brought from the Soviet Union after his June trip. I therefore had no illusions that Demjanjuk would be released soon.

I opened my statement with: 'Your Honours, up until 7 October 1991 the defence believed, through a mixture of large doses of foolishness and naïvety, that the appellant's denaturalization, his extradition to Israel, his being put on trial in Jerusalem, his being found guilty and sentenced to death were all the result of mistaken identity. This is not the case. Since that date it has become clear that we are not dealing here with a case of mistaken identity, but rather with a plot that was planned step by step, move by move. I will enumerate these steps in my arguments.'

The court, which only four months ago had seen the evidence proving how preposterous Demjanjuk's conviction had been, apparently found it difficult to digest the new findings that this had all been a frame-up. Throughout the session the judges made hostile comments to me, with the court's Vice-President, Justice Elon, taking the lead. I soon realized that the Supreme Court did not want the plot, with all its disconcerting implications, to be uncovered in its courtroom. President Shamgar even hinted at this when he said, 'I request that the gentleman concentrate on his arguments and not on attacking parties who are not present before us.'

The true story nevertheless became more and more undeniable, and President Shamgar was soon asking Shaked if he had any objection to the bench accepting the cables for its examination only. Shaked did not object, and the documents were submitted for the justices' perusal. (The decision to accept the two cables and their accompanying documents as additional defence exhibits was handed down later, on 15 January 1992.)

In this same session I demanded again that the court order Demjanjuk's immediate release from prison. The justices' emotional difficulty with this case resurfaced. Justice Goldberg commented: 'Would the appellant's release at this stage not be tantamount to handing down a judgement? In releasing him, the court expresses its opinion that the appeal is essentially correct ... Is it proper thus to hand down, to spit out a decision to release, without looking deeper into this material?' At the time of speaking, Goldberg and his colleagues had before them more than twenty statements from Treblinka guards, all positively indicating that the verdict convicting Demjanjuk had been in error. I was unwilling to give in: 'The material that has been before the honourable court for the last four months and one week is sufficient for a determination that the appellant is not Ivan the Terrible. This material, as Your Honours can see, establishes absolutely that Ivan the Terrible, the operator of the gas chambers at Treblinka, was Ivan Marchenko, a man with no connection at all to the appellant Demjanjuk.' But it was no use.

Shaked was given the floor. First he took pains to deny any involvement by the Israeli prosecution in concealing the material that had been before the American Justice Department since 1978. He claimed to have first seen this material a year ago, on his first trip to Moscow. He also tried to minimize as far as he could the significance of this material having been kept from Demjanjuk's lawyers in the US and Israel.

The Israeli media were in top form again. Instead of discussing the evidence presented to the Supreme Court and its far-reaching significance, press reports were devoted to the bench's hostile comments to me during the hearing. Only the foreign press presented the serious business of the court that day.

Before the next session Shaked submitted a petition for the acceptance of additional prosecution evidence that would, he claimed, show that from October 1943 Demjanjuk was a guard at the concentration camp near the city of Flossenbürg. This was another scandal, since Demjanjuk had of course been extradited to Israel only to be tried for crimes he allegedly committed as Ivan the Terrible of Treblinka. Now, realizing that the state prosecutors had got Israel embroiled in the most embarrassing trial in its history, he was doing his best to prove that, even if Demjanjuk were not Ivan the Terrible from Treblinka, he had at least been a concentration-camp guard elsewhere. He hoped thus to diminish the ignominy somewhat. The fact that the court had blatantly to exceed its mandate if it was to determine that Demjanjuk had served as a camp guard elsewhere was of absolutely no consequence to Shaked.

On 15 January 1992 the hearing on Shaked's petition to submit additional evidence began. The hearing lasted two and a half hours, during which I of course voiced my firm opposition to the submission of the documents, but the court decided to accept them. Then the judges heard Shaked's request for an additional postponement of the proceedings, on the grounds that the prosecution had not yet managed to translate all the evidence Shaked had brought with him from his second trip to the Soviet Union. A full seven months had not been enough to translate and type a few dozen documents. I objected to this as well, both because by Shaked's own admission this additional material contained not one document connecting Demjanjuk with Treblinka, and because it was inconceivable that the translation of such a small amount of material could take so long. But this request was also granted, and the next hearing was set for 25 February.

The result of both these sessions was the acceptance of evidence which proved that since 1978 the American authorities had been concealing evidence that could have demonstrated Demjanjuk's absolute innocence of the crime that had condemned him to the gallows. The material proved that three countries had taken part in framing Demjanjuk – the Soviet Union, Poland and the United States. But had the Israeli government and its state prosecutor's office also been involved in this conspiracy?

The cable of 12 August 1978 was sent not only to the State Department in Washington but also to the American Embassy in Tel Aviv. The cable was addressed to Martin Mendelson, a lawyer who was then running the OSI's litigation department. He had come to Israel at the beginning of August 1978 for consultations with top officials in the Ministry of Justice regarding the Demjanjuk and Federenko cases. (This may be learned from a cable Mendelson himself sent from Tel Aviv to the OSI's offices in Washington on 8 August 1978.) Could it really be that Mendelson did not reveal to his Israeli interlocutors the contents of the documents he had received from Moscow, documents relevant to the subject of his consultations with them? An additional document, the precise contents of which have still not been made public, raises suspicion that the Israeli legal authorities were partners in the plot against Demjanjuk. A letter headed 'Potential Difficulties in the Demjanjuk Case and Recommendations for Solving Them' was sent from Israel Police to none other than Martin Mendelson. The letter is dated 24 August 1978, less than a week after Mendelson returned from

Israel to the US, and less than a fortnight after the material from the American Embassy in Moscow was sent to the State Department in Washington and to Mendelson in Tel Aviv. Could the 'Potential Difficulties in the Demjanjuk Case' be anything other than the material sent from Moscow? And could the 'Recommendations for Solving Them' relate to anything other than concealing that material?

Before the reader reaches any conclusion, I would like to draw his attention to an internal OSI document from 1986, written by Bruce Einhorn to another OSI attorney, Martin Zachs. Nishnic had submitted a suit to the federal court in Washington, demanding that the OSI immediately turn over to him all material in their possession relating to the Demjanjuk trial. This internal memo expresses 'concern over the [public] integrity of the Israeli prosecution . . . release of our material now would, in all probability, reveal (and could easily undermine and prejudice) the Israeli prosecution strategy . . .' The document concluded that the OSI would oppose handing the material to the Demjanjuk family. It was written after Demjanjuk's extradition to Israel, but before his trial began. The reader may now decide whether or not the Israeli legal authorities collaborated with other parties in concealing evidence connected to Demjanjuk.

As if this were not enough, the German weekly *Stern* published a shocking revelation on 5 March 1992, proving unmistakably that the Israeli prosecution concealed crucial information about the Travniki document's being a forgery; the Israelis had had the full co-operation of the German police and Ministry of Justice. The article states that on 23 January 1987, three weeks before the show-trial began, Superintendent Amnon Bezaleli took the original Travniki document for examination at the German police force's main criminal-identification laboratory in Weisbaden, known by its initials as the BKA. Bezaleli, it will be remembered, was the head of Israel Police's document-examination laboratory and the prosecution's central witness on the Travniki document. According to *Stern*, the BKA, after a cursory examination, told Bezaleli that this was a counterfeit document forged in a more or less amateur way. The laboratory analysts addressed the following points, among others: the face in the photograph, which the prosecution identified as Demjanjuk's, had been pasted on to the uniform using photomontage techniques; the picture was not originally attached to the card, but had been transferred from another document; there was no match between the seal on the Travniki picture and that on the document itself. The analysts did not have time to compare Demjanjuk's known signature with the *Demjanjuk* signature on the Travniki document, but even more serious revelations appear in the rest of the article.

Dr Louis Ferdinand Werner, head of the BKA, informed Bezaleli of the results of the preliminary examination in a private conversation. Bezaleli consulted people from the state prosecutor's office in Jerusalem, then announced to Werner that all tests on the Travniki document should be halted at once. Even when Dr Werner told Bezaleli that with the results of further tests, which would take no more than two weeks, he would be able to provide a comprehensive report on the document and its faults, the Israeli position did not change. Bezaleli took the document and returned to Israel with all due haste. Dr Werner wrote a memo in the wake of these events, in which he said, 'Regarding this case, the experts' doubts will be subordinated to political aspects ... the discovery of true facts in this case is not what is important here.' When *Stern*'s correspondent had presented this information to Shaked and asked for his reaction, he made no denial. 'We base ourselves on our experts' opinions and continue to consider them persuasive,' he said. Dr Werner's memo lay hidden for years in a German safe.

So for years Shaked and Bezaleli, with the help of the German authorities, concealed vital information: that the world's most authoritative and reliable body for determining the authenticity of documents from the Third Reich needed only a cursory examination to state unequivocally that the Travniki document was no more than an amateur forgery. I believe the reader will need no further assistance in deciding whether the Israeli public prosecutors knew throughout the Demjanjuk show-trial that Ivan Marchenko was Ivan the Terrible.

Calling the entire affair 'Operation Justice' could only be termed cynical. Israel Police's special investigation team was called the Justice Team; the wing in which Demjanjuk's cell in the Ayalon Prison was located was called the Justice Wing; the shameful show-trial was nicknamed Justice 1, and the appeal Justice 2.

There is no escaping the fact that the public prosecutor's office and the special court conducted a show-trial of Demjanjuk. Not only was the wrong man put on trial; the whole affair began with a despicable plot, an international conspiracy of five countries – the Soviet Union, Poland, the United States, Germany and Israel. The first three knew for certain, for many years, even before Demjanjuk was extradited to Israel, that he was not Ivan the Terrible. The fourth, Germany, did not volunteer anything about the faults in the Travniki document. Was the Israeli state prosecutor's office, in addition to its manufacture of Otto Horn's 'identification' and concealing the truth about the Travniki document, also a partner in the conspiracy that created this disgraceful sham? Based on all the facts before them, my readers may decide.

16 · The Final Appeal Hearing

After Shaked returned from his fourth trip to the Soviet Union and reported to the Supreme Court, the appeal's closing arguments were finally scheduled for 1–4 and 8–9 June 1992. A year and a half of deliberate foot-dragging by the prosecution (not prevented in any way by the Supreme Court) had come to an end at last.

The job of preparing the summations was most enjoyable and I did it at a leisurely pace. I was under no pressure; a few hours' work each day was sufficient for me to prepare a thorough and exhaustive argument. Each of the documents I was basing myself on should alone have been sufficient to turn the lower-court verdict on its head and to present the public prosecution's position as erroneous.

As the date of the hearing approached, interest began growing in the foreign media. Since I had plenty of time, and since at this point I was also willing in principle to talk to the press, I granted almost every request for an interview. Because of these interviews – and especially because of the facts I emphasized in them – the foreign journalists soon began to see how Demjanjuk had fallen victim to a plot of unprecedented scope. The Israeli media, understanding that the change of direction in the case had shown their work up as a farce, kept a very low profile.

The Demjanjuk family's excitement was also growing. Demjanjuk himself was somewhat indifferent, at least in appearance. Johnny was the only member of the family planning to attend the hearings; the stream of contributions to the defence fund had dwindled to a trickle as time had passed, and it was not financially possible for other relatives to accompany him.

On Sunday 31 May I went to the Moriah Plaza Hotel in Jerusalem, where I was to stay during the hearing; Johnny and Dobrovolski were already there. I was completely calm and relaxed, and did not feel I needed to make any great effort to bring the appeal hearing to a successful conclusion. I spent two hours presenting the main points of my summation to Johnny and Dobrovolski. When I had finished, the three of us agreed that the defence had never faced an easier task than the one now before it.

Their principal concern was that the Supreme Court would decide to convict Demjanjuk on the alternative charge of having been a guard in other camps. I estimated that if the Supreme Court were to ignore the rules of jurisdiction, extradition and criminal procedure, and decide to examine the accusation against Demjanjuk on its merits, then he would certainly be convicted: disregarding these rules would certainly lead the court to disregard the weakness of the evidence at the foundation of this charge as well. Still, I believed there was only a slim chance that the Supreme Court would disregard extradition law, if only because this was liable to be a serious blow to Israel's status and prestige, at least outside her borders.

I told Johnny and Dobrovolski that there was absolutely no chance that the court would free Demjanjuk at any stage before handing down its final verdict. Emotionally and psychologically, the judges were simply incapable of such a thing, in spite of the clear facts, substantive law and precedents of cases in which new evidence favourable to the appellant (of much less weight than that found in Demjanjuk's case) had been discovered after conviction.

Even though I expected to have an easy time of it, I couldn't get to sleep till about three in the morning. At breakfast the three of us were in a lively mood. Except for a little excitement, I had never felt so relaxed, tranquil and sure of myself before a decisive court hearing.

This time I was not given an office in the court building, nor did I need one. As expected, the media turned out in full force. Doron repeated his opinion that Shaked would declare that he consented to the appeal, since the evidence before the court was sufficient to establish doubt that Demjanjuk was Ivan the Terrible. The prosecution would concentrate solely on the argument that Demjanjuk should be convicted on an alternative charge, and on trying to persuade the court that it had the jurisdiction to consider this. But I was sure Doron was wrong, given the behaviour of Shaked and his superiors so far. Even though they were as convinced as I that Demjanjuk was not Ivan the Terrible, they would not be able to admit that the charge against him was, at best, an error. So they would not let it go. If we had brought Ivan Marchenko himself to the courtroom, and he admitted that he was Ivan the Terrible, even that would not have been enough for the prosecution.

On the dot of nine, the five judges entered the packed courtroom. Chief Justice Shamgar said good-morning and gave me the floor. 'Your Honours, exactly two years ago, towards the end of the defence arguments before this honourable court, I said the following, which appears on page 1,821 of the appeal record: "I do not, with all due respect, have to prove that the appellant is definitely not Ivan the Terrible. Yet I have a hunch (and all my other hunches in this case have turned out to be true) that before the verdict is handed down we will prove this also. More evidence is on the way, and we will yet prove categorically that the appellant is not Ivan the Terrible." I am happy to report to you that we have kept this promise fully, down to the last word, via eighty statements from thirty-seven camp guards, all of which declare that Ivan Marchenko and not Ivan Demjanjuk is Ivan the Terrible.'

I then proceeded to present my arguments throughout the day. This time I was asked almost no questions by the judges. When I glanced at them the impression was that they were listening attentively, that my argument that there was not the slightest possibility of letting the conviction stand was penetrating their consciousness. Towards the end of my speech I said, 'As yet the prosecution has not withdrawn its charges, and this makes it in effect the defender of Ivan the Terrible, since it is arguing that Ivan Marchenko is not Ivan the Terrible, even though it is clear, according to eighty items of evidence, that Marchenko is in fact that monster. The prosecution has thus become defence attorney for the real Ivan the Terrible. The prosecution has adopted such a disgraceful position because our establishment is unable to accept responsibility for an error and its consequences. There is no such convention in our public life.'

During that day I also presented the two most important chapters of my final argument – jurisdiction and identification. The next day, at close to noon, I ended with the words: 'As a result, the appellant should be fully acquitted of the charge of being Ivan the Terrible, and the court should not even enter, because of the rules of jurisdiction, into a discussion of any other charge. Thank you for your attention.' Chief Justice Shamgar thanked me and adjourned the session.

When I had sat down I considered that I would never have imagined, five and a half years ago, that at the end of the judicial process I would be in the position I was now in. In sixteen years as a defence attorney I had never made an argument that was so well supported by the evidence, both quantitatively and qualitatively.

Now at last the Israeli media began changing their tune; they could not continue to misrepresent the evidence. 80 STATEMENTS SHOW THAT IVAN MARCHENKO IS IVAN THE TERRIBLE said one headline. MUCH EVIDENCE FROM USSR INDICATES THAT DEMJANJUK IS NOT IVAN THE TERRIBLE said another. Yet another newspaper proclaimed, over Marchenko's picture: EVIDENCE UNEARTHED IN USSR INDICATES THAT THIS MAN IS IVAN THE TERRIBLE.

Shaked and his superiors, however, would not give in. Shaked began his summation with: 'We have indeed been asking ourselves these questions for two years, investigating, erasing from our minds what came before and trying to re-examine the subject, and when I say we, I am speaking of the State Attorney, the former State Attorney, the members of the prosecution team and myself. We have sat down every so often, re-examined the material, reanalysed it, and we have in full cognizance reached the decision that there is no reasonable cause, given the current state of affairs in the case, to change our minds ... The fact that the name Marchenko appears many times in many statements is entirely negligible, because the names come from the KGB interrogator, and the guards being interrogated confirm this rather than dispute it ... We therefore do not feel that the weight of the identifications by the survivor-witnesses is reduced ... In such a case the court still has to find in the most reliable and truthful way, which is according to the survivor-witnesses.' In the end, summing up the prosecution's position, he said, 'Standing against the prosecution is a profusion of paper from the Soviet Union ... and I have at least tried to explain to the court our position, our assumption, our evaluation ... It is impossible, from these papers, to reach a finding of doubt.'

Shaked made these embarrassing remarks on the basis of a ridiculous theory. Two of the guards caught and interrogated by the KGB in 1944 had named Ivan Marchenko and Nikolai Shelaiev as operators of the gas chambers at Treblinka. Subsequently KGB agents had got hold of Ivan Marchenko's personal SS file. These two events led them to believe that Ivan Marchenko and Nikolai Shelaiev had been the operators of the Treblinka gas chambers. As a result, Shaked maintained, when Nikolai Shelaiev was caught in 1949, the KGB forced him to confess that he had operated the gas chambers at Treblinka and that Ivan Marchenko had been his partner. So it also went, according to Shaked, with each of the guards that had been interrogated after 1944. The conclusion he drew from this fairy tale was that all the guards' statements should be disregarded and that the court should determine beyond any reasonable doubt that Ivan Demjanjuk was Ivan the Terrible.

Shaked's argument brought the prosecution to a nadir, in terms of both professional honesty and the quality of the argument expected from a public prosecutor in the Supreme Court. It should be recalled, however, that State Attorney Dorit Beinish and her predecessor Yonah Blatman had vetted every word Shaked said. Furthermore, Attorney General Yosef Harish, whose position made him responsible for the state prosecution, had also approved this embarrassment of an argument.

A chill ran down my spine. Now, any low anti-Semite could, if he wanted to, argue that the Jewish state's prosecution was unable to act in accordance with legal criteria in any trial that involved the Holocaust. The argument that Shaked made in the Supreme Court, at the behest of his superiors, was no more than a sordid attempt to commit cold-blooded judicial murder. The intended victim was Demjanjuk; the subterfuge the prosecution used to carry out its evil scheme was the argument, which it knew to be false, that Demjanjuk was Ivan the Terrible; the weapon was not a pistol or a knife, but Shaked's tongue. If ever a state prosecutor dares voice, in the Supreme Court, arguments with just a fraction of the foolishness of Shaked's arguments, he is silenced by the bench. The justices do not allow prosecutors making unfounded arguments to complete their pleadings. But Shaked spoke for three full days. The bench, Justice Barak in particular, asked hard questions and made serious comments, but they allowed him to carry on.

Shaked did not restrict his arguments to the issue of Ivan Marchenko. As expected, he also demanded that the court convict Demjanjuk of crimes of genocide he allegedly committed in Sobibor. This part of Shaked's pleading brought even a justice as easygoing as Barak to the point of losing his temper. Barak interrupted time and again, with comments like 'Was Demjanjuk extradited for having been a camp guard? Having been a camp guard is not a crime in America. Was a trial conducted on the question of whether he had been a guard at Sobibor? There are dozens of Jewish witnesses who were in Sobibor and who do not identify him. Has anyone called them? Do we know anything about Sobibor? Now we are changing the focus from Treblinka to Sobibor. Does he not at least have the right to defend himself?' But Shaked went on arguing the alternative charge.

There was no doubt that the prosecution had decided to make this move only when they began to realize that they had involved the State of Israel in an embarrassing show-trial of the wrong man. On 3 April 1992 the newspaper *Ma'ariv*, in a quote from 'a senior prosecutor close to the case', beneath the headline GETTING DEMJANJUK DOWN FROM THE HANGING TREE, said, 'So the most important thing now is at least to prove that Demjanjuk was part of the Nazi extermination machine ... otherwise ... we will be making a great contribution to the new world-wide movement of those who deny the Holocaust took place.' Here was a 'senior' member of the state prosecution admitting in public that the motive for Shaked's argument was at base political, not judicial.

Shaked made a very bad impression on the observers in the courtroom, especially the Israeli press. They were all expecting him to pull some sort of rabbit out of his hat, but as his arguments went on it was clear there was no rabbit. Johnny, Dobrovolski and Demjanjuk himself had been very apprehensive before he stood up, but they were soon reassured and their spirits soared. During the recesses we could not help making jokes about Shaked's arguments. Most of what he was saying did not even deserve to be rebutted; this time I would not have to devote more than an hour a day to preparing my response. So once again I was able to grant almost every request for an interview. Finally, after five and a half years, there was almost universal acknowledgement that Demjanjuk was not Ivan the Terrible. I was very, very happy.

On Tuesday 9 June I began my rebuttal. It was the last day of the summations. Tali, my fiancée, sat just a foot away. My self-confidence was at its height. I was about to mow Shaked's argument down without even bothering to address every detail. As a parting shot I tried to explain to the court the extent of the superficiality and duplicity needed to convict Demjanjuk of being Ivan the Terrible on the basis of inadmissible photo spreads, the sole evidence against him since the case began. I asked Chief Clerk Shmaryahu Cohen to display enlargements of the photographs used in the photo spreads in the courtroom, so that I could illustrate my point.

The judges entered and as usual Chief Justice Shamgar wished everyone a good morning. Shaked asked for permission to complete his presentation on a matter that had slipped his memory the previous day, and then I took the floor. I opened with the jurisdiction issue. For the umpteenth time I pointed out that the US courts that had judged the matter of Demjanjuk's extradition to Israel, whose records I quoted, had ruled explicitly that he could be extradited only for the crime of murder, and this only with regard to crimes committed in Treblinka. The prosecutor was deliberately ignoring this and requesting, despite the lack of jurisdiction and for the first time on appeal, that Demjanjuk be convicted also for his alleged complicity in genocide, which is a different crime to murder, allegedly committed outside Treblinka. Utter silence reigned in the courtroom. The judges were giving me their full attention.

I went on to discuss the identification issue and the profusion of evidence indicating that Marchenko was Ivan the Terrible. 'The prosecutor says that there were several Marchenkos and Nikolais at Treblinka, and he latches on to various fragments of statements to back up this ridiculous claim. I will not go over the prosecution's argument step by step, because to do so would take this absurd argument much more seriously than it deserves. And if there *were* any basis for the theory that the prosecution is now presenting, it would pull the carpet out from under his witnesses' identification testimony. After all, they were in close quarters with Ivan the Terrible for an entire year, sometimes as close as a yard from him, and they say there was only one Ivan the Terrible – the appellant, they claim – and one Nikolai, and that only these two operated the gas chambers. If the prosecution now claims that there were several of them, he invalidates that testimony.'

Addressing the photo spreads that had been the basis for the conviction, I said: 'Being a pessimist, I never dreamed that I would have eighty statements showing that the appellant is not Ivan the Terrible. I said during the lower-court trial that we would never know if the survivors identified the appellant because he is Ivan the Terrible or because he looks similar. As a pessimist, being proved wrong is always for the best. I said we would never know, but today we know with complete certainty that the survivor-identification witnesses chose the appellant's photograph by mistake because it was fairly similar to Ivan Marchenko. This is exactly the argument I made more than five years ago, and which Professor Wagenaar and I tried to explain to the lower court. Where we failed the KGB succeeded, producing eighty statements from camp guards at Treblinka that lie before you, Your Honours, together with the personal SS file of Marchenko.' I concluded my argument on this point by saying: 'Just because the prosecutor is unable to admit his dreadful mistake, the court should not be penalized by having to hear such baseless arguments as the ones heard here these last three days. Does the prosecutor himself believe even one word of what he said?'

The last chapter of my argument dealt with the issue of what weight could be assigned to the evidence for the other charges on which the prosecution demanded that Demjanjuk be convicted. Again I stressed the unassailable fact that there was not one witness who had identified Demjanjuk's picture as being of a guard at Sobibor. Furthermore, none of the Jewish survivors of Sobibor who had been interviewed over the years, all over the world – in Israel, the US, Brazil and Australia – had identified Demjanjuk's photograph as a guard familiar to them.

I completed my five and a half years of appearances in the Demjanjuk affair before one o'clock, ending with a request: 'It took the lower court precisely two months from the end of the summations to hand down the verdict according to which the appellant was to be sent to the gallows. I believe it would be fitting, and this I request at the behest of the appellant, that, because of the long years this trial has been going on, the verdict be given in approximately the same period used by the honourable lower court.' I was apprehensive, after the prosecution's stalling and delaying tactics of the past year and a half, that there would also be stalling in handing down the verdict. Unfortunately, these fears proved well-founded.

Chief Justice Shamgar adjourned the hearing of the Demjanjuk case. 'I thank the representatives for their arguments,' he said. 'With this the hearings have come to an end, and we will now recess to study the material and to reach our verdict.' The study of the material, as it turned out, was not a brief matter: the court needed more than a year before it deigned to produce a verdict. Again it was clear how difficult Israeli judges, as honourable as they might be, find it to render a not-guilty verdict in such a trial, even when they have seen evidence that establishes unambiguously the defendant's innocence.

A great commotion rose up around me at the end of the session. I took Tali by the hand and we strode, happy and satisfied, out of the building. I was surrounded again by reporters and photographers. I gladly answered all their questions and stressed that not only had Demjanjuk's absolute innocence been proved but it was also proved that the entire affair was actually a conspiracy. Johnny, Dobrovolski, Tali and I went to the hotel; Tali and I quickly packed our belongings and took our leave of the others. Within minutes we were on our way to her parents' village, so that we could enjoy those wonderful moments together, and the magnificent feeling that enveloped us both.

The turn-around in the trial was so undeniable that it was even reflected in the national press, by the same reporters and commentators who had served as the prosecution's mouthpiece for five years. There were occasional articles, some written by members of the academic community, calling on the prosecution not to wait for the verdict and to withdraw the charges immediately. It was hard not to wonder where all the authors of these articles had been for the last year and a half. Finally *Ha'aretz* could tell its readers in a headline that ISRAEL MAY ASK US COURT TO CHANGE EXTRADITION PROVISION AGAINST DEMJANJUK. Another headline described the reversal as THE VICTORY, NOT THE FAILURE, OF JUSTICE. The media eventually began reporting on the darkest aspect of the Demjanjuk affair, the conspiracy. The headlines proclaimed SEARCH FOR THOSE AT FAULT IN US; INCREASING PRESSURE ON US JUSTICE DEPARTMENT CONCERNING DEMJANJUK EXTRADITION CASE; THE DEMJANJUK AFFAIR – THE END? US MAY SOON CALL ON ISRAEL TO FREE DEMJANJUK; THEY THREW THE BOOK AT US. A few days later an article was published under the headline TRAVNIKI DUD, listing the many facts that indicated that the Travniki document was a forgery. But the piece that pleased me the most was an editorial in *Ha'aretz* that called on the prosecution to consent to the appeal before the verdict was announced, and to refrain from any attempt to divert the hearing towards conviction on another charge. This was the newspaper that, in an editorial published after the verdict in the original trial four years ago, justified with great pathos both the conviction and the death sentence, stressing that they had been handed down at the end of an 'exemplary' trial. I said to myself again and again, Who would have believed it when I joined the case, or even just a year ago?

17 · From the Gallows to Cleveland

Secretly I hoped that the verdict would be rendered before 7 September 1992, the date of my wedding, and would be a kind of wonderful wedding present. But July and August went by and there was no sign of a verdict.

I was in regular contact with the Chief Clerk of the Supreme Court, Shmaryahu Cohen. When I told him I was leaving for a honeymoon in the US immediately after my wedding, he asked for my travel dates, because he wanted 'to ensure that the date announced for the verdict won't be during the time you are in the US'.

'Should I take that to mean that the verdict will be rendered soon?' I asked.

'Yes, you should,' he said.

We returned from honeymoon at the beginning of October, and there was still no verdict. It was now four full months since the end of the hearing. My patience was running out, and towards the end of the month I wrote to Chief Justice Shamgar:

> My client's appeal of the verdict of the honourable special district court has been before the honourable Supreme Court for some four and a half years. Five months have passed since the hearings in my client's appeal were concluded, and to the best of my knowledge the honourable court has yet to announce the date on which its decision in the appeal will be rendered ... I should emphasize that, for more than a year, from 14 August 1991, the court file has contained more than twenty statements, including photo identifications, from which it is clear that Ivan the Terrible was no other than Ivan Marchenko, who has no connection at all with my client ... My client is seventy-two and a half years old and at this point has spent a tenth of his long life in jail on the groundless supposition that he is Ivan the Terrible. By any standards that is an unacceptable perversion of justice ... I believe, with all due respect, that the proper way to put an end to this unacceptable travesty of justice is to render my client's verdict within the next few days. If the court cannot produce a fully

reasoned judgement by then, in my humble opinion it might act as the honourable court has in many other cases in the past, by rendering a verdict but issuing its reasons at a later date.

Chief Justice Shamgar responded promptly with a brief letter, containing the following language: 'The reference to a four-and-a-half-year trial is not appropriate. Perhaps you have forgotten that there were no few petitions and requests for delays and for stays of the verdict, which the court acceded to, in order to enquire into the matter fully.' Even though the Chief Justice did not answer the arguments I made in my letter, I decided to wait until mid-December.

On 17 December I wrote to Shamgar again, addressing also his response to me:

His Honour's reply stated that the lengthiness of appeal process results, among other reasons, from no few petitions and requests for delay on both sides, to allow a full inquiry into the matter. I find it only proper to note, with all due respect, that this should expedite the rendering of the verdict all the more, because the requests for delay all related to evidence, in the end submitted during the appeal, that was maliciously concealed for years from the appellant and his attorney, and so the appellant, through no fault of his own, suffered an almost unprecedented travesty of justice and undue hardship.

At the end I wrote: 'In conclusion, the gap between the short time needed to reach a decision to send the appellant to the gallows and the time needed now to decide the appeal, when it is clear that the appellant should be reprieved, is liable to mean that, even if justice is done to my client, it will not be *seen* to be done.'

Again the terse response was not long in coming. 'Thank you very much for your letter. I have considered it and I can assure you that there is no needless delay.' But there was no answer to my question as to why the court had refrained for all those long months, despite the unambiguous material before it, to render an early judgement that Demjanjuk was not Ivan the Terrible, providing the justification for its decision at a later date. I had no doubt that the real reason for this was the 'emotional difficulty' for the honourable justices of the Supreme Court in making an immediate decision in such a sensitive case.

It was necessary to make a dramatic move to draw public attention to this unreasonable state of affairs. I knew what had to be done: Demjanjuk must stage a three-day hunger strike. I would call a press conference when it began, for the foreign press in particular, and explain the reason for the strike: the unreasonable delay in rendering the verdict. I was certain that such a step would get much media attention and would considerably hasten the handing-down of the verdict. At this time I also learned that the verdict had not even reached the writing-up stage, and the matter was simply lying unattended.

When I told Demjanjuk about my idea of a hunger strike, he immediately agreed that it was the right thing to do. However he stressed that, as with all other matters, he would leave the final decision to his family, and follow their wishes.

I discussed the matter by phone with Johnny and Nishnic. For the first time we disagreed about something important. They did not dispute the need to make the public aware of the court's failure to produce a verdict, but they opposed the means, for two reasons. The first was that it might lead the prison authorities to impose all kinds of sanctions against Demjanjuk. They might go as far as poisoning his food when he resumed eating, so that any illness (or worse) could be attributed to the strike. He might be killed, they thought, precisely because everyone had known for two years that Ivan the Terrible was someone else. Whilst I could understand their fears, they seemed baseless, not to mention paranoid, to me.

Their second reason was connected to an interesting, almost unheard-of legal procedure then under way in the US. As a result of a huge wave of publicity since October 1991 around the revelations that American Justice Department officials had known the entire time that Demjanjuk was not Ivan the Terrible and had maliciously concealed the evidence for this, Chief Justice Gilbert Merritt of the United States Court of Appeals for the Sixth Circuit, in Cincinatti, volunteered to issue an order to investigate whether Demjanjuk's extradition had been obtained by the OSI through fraud upon the court. The order was issued on 5 June 1992, during the last summation hearing in the appeal in Jerusalem, and paved the way for an inquiry that included hearing testimony. This process was now in full swing, and Nishnic and Johnny feared that Demjanjuk's hunger strike would be interpreted as an attempt to influence this proceeding, which they did not want. This concern too was unfounded, since I planned to call a press conference to explain the reasons for the strike in detail, and none of these had to do with the legal process in the US.

It took me more than two months to persuade Johnny and Nishnic to accept my recommendation. When they had finally agreed, I suggested Demjanjuk launch his hunger strike on 1 March 1993, the day he began his eighth year in an Israeli prison. About a week before this date

I issued invitations to most of the foreign correspondents in the country to a press conference at the Moriah Plaza. As expected, the announcement made the news, both in Israel and overseas. I chose to leave all the explanations for the press conference itself, so that it would be well attended.

I visited Demjanjuk a day before the strike and conference. He was in high spirits, and was eager to play his part. He had great hopes for the strike, although he repeated something he had often said to me in recent months: 'I don't believe they'll let me leave this cage, no matter what happens!' When we parted, I promised to visit him within the next forty-eight hours, to see how he was holding up.

On Monday 1 March, at ten a.m., I arrived at the Moriah Plaza. Despite the great publicity, the hall was empty. I was afraid that the whole exercise would fail. Happily, however, within a few minutes dozens of reporters and photographers began filing in, and in the end there were some seventy media people there.

I opened with an announcement briefly surveying all the injustices Demjanjuk had suffered from the day of his extradition to Israel exactly seven years before. I emphasized the abnormal and contradictory standards in the timetable the judicial system had adopted in Demjanjuk's case – that is, the speed with which his conviction and sentence had been given on the basis of such dubious evidence, in comparison to the length of time the Supreme Court was taking to give its verdict, even though it had before it a large amount of evidence demonstrating unequivocally that Demjanjuk was innocent. 'These standards,' I said in conclusion, 'when taken together with the serious perversions of justice in the Demjanjuk affair, are what lie behind the decision to stage a three-day hunger strike.' Afterwards I was asked many questions demonstrating the correspondents' great interest. Nobody left the press conference before it ended.

The strike proved to have been the right thing to do. For the next ten days the media devoted plenty of space to Demjanjuk, emphasizing the long time that had passed since the end of the hearing without a verdict being rendered. One article worth mentioning is that written by Ran Kislev in *Ha'aretz* on 9 March 1993. Under the sarcastic headline THEIR HONOURS' HONOUR, he wrote: 'The Demjanjuk case has not ended and that is bad . . . What has delayed the verdict for nine months? No new material has reached the justices, and what remains for them is to consider the existing material, to think and to draft their judgement. Can it be that they simply do not have the time? . . . Or perhaps, God forbid, they are afraid to issue the verdict because of its problematic nature?' This criticism of the country's highest judicial institution showed that it was not just the trial that had made a U-turn, but also the media, in the Demjanjuk affair.

The success of the press conference and the ensuing attention angered officials in the Ministry of Justice, of course, and they began issuing statements against me: I was reproached for not observing the principle of *sub judice*! There was no end to their chutzpah. The prosecution team, who had for months devoted all their energies to staging a shameful show-trial; who had encouraged open media incitement against Demjanjuk, his witnesses and his defence attorneys, blatantly violating that principle, were suddenly rolling their sanctimonious eyes to heaven in fear for the integrity of the judicial process. Moreover, there is of course no connection between a press conference at which an attorney explains that his client has decided to stage a hunger strike because of the injustice he has suffered and a violation of *sub judice*.

At the end of January the Ukrainian Ambassador to Israel, Yuri Scherbak, visited my office. He wanted to learn first-hand about the evidence in the case and if the press reports (that Ivan Marchenko and not Ivan Demjanjuk was Ivan the Terrible) were true. Like everyone before and after him, the Ambassador was utterly astonished when I presented him with the major documents from the KGB files. He read and reread the statements taken by the KGB forty years earlier, and examined the pictures of Marchenko identified in the statements, uttering cries of astonishment the whole time. 'Unbelievable, unbelievable!' he exclaimed. Nor could he understand why, with such decisive evidence before the court for such a long time, Demjanjuk was still sitting in prison. I now hoped to use the Ukrainian Ambassador to keep up the media momentum. I estimated that he would agree to visit Demjanjuk in jail, which would return Demjanjuk's case to the public eye. I could then appeal again to public opinion about the intolerable delay in rendering the verdict.

A few days later I received permission for the visit from the Prison Service. On Monday 7 April Ambassador Scherbak, his assistant and I arrived at Demjanjuk's cell; Demjanjuk, of course, had been notified in advance. He was very moved by a visit from such a highly placed official. As a Ukrainian nationalist he did not forget to tell the Ambassador how privileged he was to have such a guest now that the Ukraine was an independent state, free of the Soviet yoke. During the warm, relaxed conversation, which went on for about two hours, the Ambassador suggested to Demjanjuk that he take advantage of his right, under the laws of the free and independent Ukraine, to request Ukrainian citizenship. He promised to look after the request himself and to take it personally to the country's President, Leonid Kravchuk, for a swift decision. As expected, this offer, and the visit itself, roused much media interest, and Demjanjuk's case returned to the headlines for a few days.

Around this time I learned that the preparation of the verdict was now in high gear, and that the announcement was not far off. Towards the middle of May 1993 rumours began to spread that the date was very close, and would be towards the end of June.

During the long wait for the verdict an unpleasant development occurred in my private life. Tali, 'the woman of my dreams', turned out shortly after our marriage to be a *femme fatale*. Life was an endless, insufferable nightmare. I had felt for more than six months that separation was inevitable, and at the beginning of June I was finally persuaded to put an end to my failed marriage. Just as I had been without a wife in the theatre at the beginning of the case, so I would be at the final session.

On 28 June Shmaryahu Cohen notified me that the verdict in Demjanjuk's appeal would be handed down on 14 July at nine in the morning, and that a public announcement to that effect would be made within a few days.

The next day in the US, Judge Thomas Weiseman, who happened to be Jewish, rendered his verdict in the inquiry into whether Demjanjuk was the victim of a plot. At the heart of the judgement, which filled 210 pages, were the following determinations. First, 'the statements of former Treblinka guards and laborers recently obtained from the Soviet Union constitute an harmonious chorus which inculpate a man named Ivan Marchenko as the Ivan who worked at the gas chambers, and thus exculpate Mr. Demjanjuk from those specific crimes'. Second, from 1978 the American Department of Justice had in its possession evidence transferred to it from the Soviet Union that showed that Ivan Marchenko was Ivan the Terrible. Third, this material had not been given to Demjanjuk and his lawyers while legal proceedings were being conducted against him in the US, even though the goal of these proceedings was to prove that he was Ivan the Terrible.

Judge Weiseman therefore determined that it would be appropriate to examine the possibility of reinstating Demjanjuk's citizenship and revoking his extradition to Israel. If any further proof was needed that no court in the civilized world would convict Demjanjuk on the basis of the evidence the defence had uncovered (and which had been before the Supreme Court for two years), this verdict provided it.

I quickly informed Johnny and Nishnic about the date of the appeal verdict. They were delighted, of course, and immediately began making preparations to come to Israel – 'this time', as Johnny said, 'to take Dad back home'. But a few days later Shmaryahu Cohen called me again to tell me that the date had been put off 'because of problems involving external technical factors over which the court has no control'. He would, he said, let me know when a new date had been set. Johnny and Nishnic were hugely disappointed.

In the mean time there was a surge of speculation about the verdict. An army of sycophants tried to explain to their readers that even if Demjanjuk were acquitted – something they thought unlikely – he could still be convicted on other charges. One reporter even wrote with absolute confidence that Demjanjuk would be sent to the gallows, because if there were any intention of acquitting and releasing him the court would have done so long ago. It seemed the Israeli press had forgotten that just a year ago, after the summation arguments in the appeal, its definitive opinion had been precisely the opposite. As for me, I gave anyone who asked me the clear prediction that any result other than Demjanjuk's acquittal and release from prison was impossible.

On Saturday 17 July, I received confirmation from a reliable source that my prediction of the verdict was correct. The person who told me this had the information from two sources who knew the contents of the verdict first-hand. I learned that the verdict filled some four hundred pages, and that its conclusion was a unanimous acquittal of Demjanjuk by the five justices, and a decision not to convict him on any other charge.

I was overjoyed at the news, though not at all surprised. Since the veracity of my information was certain, I decided to take two particular measures as if the acquittal verdict had already been given, something I had never done in the past. First, to relieve the tension for the Demjanjuk family, I gave them the information I had about the upcoming verdict. They had no doubt that it was true and were able to relax a bit. Second, I decided to prepare for Demjanjuk's swift and orderly exit from Israel immediately after the reading of the verdict. So on Monday morning I headed to the Ukrainian Embassy. I had developed excellent relations with Yuri Scherbak and his assistant by now, and I intended to take advantage of them to ensure Demjanjuk's smooth departure from Israel.

While I was still deep in conversation with the Ambassador, Tzvia called. 'Sheftel, Shmaryahu just called and announced that the verdict will be handed down on Thursday 29 July, at nine in the morning.'

'That means Demjanjuk is going home next Thursday,' I responded, 'and I am just now sitting with the Ambassador to arrange it.' The Ambassador and I concluded that Demjanjuk would write a letter in his own hand requesting asylum in the Ukraine after his acquittal, and the Ambassador would see to the matter personally.

To my surprise, the media suddenly began writing about me in a friendly way, and two newspapers published long feature articles. The headline of one was THERE IS ONE WINNER IN THE WHOLE AFFAIR, AND THAT IS YORAM SHEFTEL. The second headline was similar, with the subhead debating whether James Caan or James Woods would play Demjanjuk's lawyer in the movie about the affair.

Johnny and Nishnic were to arrive in Israel the following week, and they intended to visit Demjanjuk every day. I thus wanted to make my own visit before they came, to allow them as much time as possible together by themselves. Demjanjuk awaited me with great anticipation, and he looked nervous. As soon as we sat down, I told him, 'You should know, this Thursday you will be acquitted by a unanimous decision of all five justices, and they have also decided not to convict you of any other crime. I have been telling you that for two and a half years, but up until now it has been a prediction. Now I am telling you a fact. The results of the verdict were leaked to me by an unimpeachable source, and I have no doubt about it.' Demjanjuk was clearly happy to hear this, but his reaction was not at all that of a man who has just been told he has escaped the gallows after living in its shadow for over five years. He said, 'Sheftel, I hope very much that you are right. Actually, I am sure you are right. Congratulations,' but he said it apathetically. Afterwards I told him about the agreements I had reached with the Ukrainian Ambassador to ensure his rapid departure from Israel, and he expressed his great satisfaction with this too. I explained that we would see each other next in court, and that a day or two after the verdict was given we would take our leave of each other. We chatted for about an hour and a half, with the Russian-language Voice of Israel on his transistor in the background. We parted with a handshake, and I promised again that the information about the verdict was entirely reliable.

The days passed quickly. Johnny and Nishnic landed at Ben-Gurion on Monday the 26th, at three in the afternoon. We shook hands and embraced. Johnny and Nishnic kept repeating excitedly, 'We've come to take Dad home,' and within minutes they were heading for the Ayalon Prison to visit Demjanjuk. The next day Johnny, Nishnic and I saw the Ukrainian Ambassador and his assistant at the Embassy. The Embassy would issue Demjanjuk a transit permit and a visa, and on Sunday 1 August, at two-thirty p.m., he would leave Israel with his son and son-in-law on a direct flight to Kiev.

On Wednesday afternoon, after giving interviews to various representatives of the media, I was in the office with Tzvia and Doron, discussing various matters, when suddenly Tzvia asked, 'Tell me, don't you think there's at least a fraction of a chance that he won't be acquitted?'

'No, I don't,' I answered. 'Only one result is possible and that is acquittal. It will also be unanimous. There will be no conviction on any other charge, and that decision also will be unanimous. Yet I am also sure that the court will find that Demjanjuk was a camp guard at Flossenbürg, Regensburg, Travniki and Sobibor. It will stand solidly behind all of Dovele and co.'s misconduct, and will say the survivors should be believed and the identification procedures were performed carefully. The acquittal will be on the basis of doubt alone, and they will send Demjanjuk home from the gallows with regret, because there is no other option.'

Nishnic and Johnny arrived in the office later, after visiting Demjanjuk. We went to a department store and bought him some trousers, a shirt, a sports jacket and a suitcase. Then we headed for the hotel in Jerusalem. On the way I could see that, despite our purchases, Nishnic and Johnny were still extremely worried. They had noticed that various unusual security devices had been installed in Demjanjuk's cell in the last few days, and it looked as if arrangements were being made for his execution. I explained to them that the prison staff did not know what the decision would be, and were simply preparing for either outcome. This explanation did not entirely reassure them. They interrogated me over and over again about the reliability of the information I had received, and only when we reached our rooms were they persuaded that there was no cause for concern.

The media furore was already at its height, and when we entered the hotel several television crews charged at us. We gave brief answers to their questions and went upstairs. I unpacked my suitcase, washed my face and sat down on the sofa. I began to munch on a juicy apple, letting my mind wander. I felt no tension or excitement, and my tranquillity was surprising, despite my certainty about what was to happen the next day.

I called my mother. She was very excited and burst into tears. In the end she wished me success, and expressed her hope that Demjanjuk would be acquitted and released immediately. She repeated this in the same emotional way the next morning at seven-thirty, when I called her just before leaving for the court.

I had dinner with Johnny and Nishnic in the Italian restaurant near the hotel. When I got back to my room I was overcome with a feeling that had been growing within me for several weeks, that this affair had lasted for too long and that I was beginning to get sick of it. For the first time since I began my involvement in the trial, I felt that if it went on any longer I would not have the strength to continue. I was glad the whole thing would be over the next day.

I undressed and got into bed. Scenes from the previous six and a half years began passing before my eyes: my first meeting with Demjanjuk and O'Connor, the opening session of the show-trial, some of Levin's outbursts, Eitan's death, my eye injury, the meeting with Maria Dudek, the meeting in the chambers of Judge Oleg Tatunik, the turning-point session in which I had submitted the first documents paving the way for Demjanjuk's acquittal, various newspaper headlines from over the years, the shouts and screams in the theatre hall after Levin and his colleagues sentenced Demjanjuk to the gallows. It was all mixed up, pictures merging into one another and reappearing in odd combinations. For a while I tried drowsily to put the pictures into some sort of order, and then I fell asleep.

The wake-up call roused me at six, and at quarter to seven the three of us were in the dining room. Johnny and Nishnic were very tense. I tried to amuse and entertain them, with some success.

We parked at the Supreme Court and headed towards the door, where Tzvia and her son Aviram, Doron, his girlfriend, and my friends Eyal and Vali were waiting for us with representatives from the Ukrainian Embassy. We all walked into the packed courtroom together. Demjanjuk was already in his place; Shaked and Bainwall had not yet arrived. Johnny and Nishnic were seated in the second row, and the rest of my companions in the row behind them. The photographers were busy taking Demjanjuk's picture when I approached him, shook his hand and told him that within the hour his acquittal would be announced. He responded as he had before: 'I hope you're right. Actually, I am sure you are right.' I sat down, perfectly serene. But then I walked over to the press bench, where I was asked if I was still sure that Demjanjuk would be acquitted. For the umpteenth time I answered unambiguously in the affirmative.

At precisely nine the judges entered and took their places. Without any preliminaries, Chief Justice Shamgar's voice broke the silence with the following: 'Our verdict in this appeal is . . .' The law requires an appeals court to announce its decision immediately in the case of an acquittal. I remained completely calm, but I could not prevent a slight smile from appearing at the corner of my mouth. Levin's image danced before my eyes, castigating me in one of his typical outbursts. Yes, yes, Dovele, I said to him in my mind, that which you most feared has come to pass, and no accolade that Shamgar may shower on you now can diminish by so much as one per cent the dire shame of your verdict.

I returned my attention to what Chief Justice Shamgar was saying:

'We acquit the appellant by reason of doubt of all the charges in the charge sheet, which involve his identification and his activity in the Treblinka extermination camp, as the man known in the camp as a guard called Ivan the Terrible, all of which is detailed in the verdict. The verdict also addresses the question of whether there is cause to convict the appellant of another charge on which his guilt has been shown by the facts that were proven in court as cited in Articles 184 and 216 of the criminal procedural code of 1982. For the reasons set out in the judgement, we did not find it appropriate to convict the appellant of any other charge at this point in the matter. Our verdict is unanimous.'

I glanced at Demjanjuk. Even now he looked as if what was happening had nothing to do with him. Later on he even yawned, his mouth wide open, as he listened to Chief Justice Shamgar, whose speech was being simultaneously translated for him. Johnny, on the other hand, could not hold back his emotion and started crying, while Nishnic's face showed that he was deeply moved. Shaked was as red as a tomato, obviously hugely disappointed.

As was only to have been expected, Shamgar immediately began justifying all the actions and decisions of the court whose verdict he had just reversed, as well as all the work of the prosecution and the police, who according to all five justices had conducted themselves appropriately and honestly. When I realized that this was the substance of his speech, I stopped listening and began to exchange glances with my friends and with the journalists, some of whom did not hide their great disappointment at the outcome.

The reading of the synopsis of the judgement took two hours. As soon as the justices left the courtroom, and in accordance with a prior arrangement, the security people encircled me, Johnny and Nishnic, and we were taken to the next-door room so that we could discuss our reactions to the verdict undisturbed. When we were left alone in the room, the two of them embraced me with all their might, and Johnny said, 'We did it, Shefy, you won a glorious victory, and my father is going free as a result.'

After a brief consultation we decided that we would not be too excited in public about Demjanjuk's acquittal and release. We would point out that he had been held in an Israeli prison for more than seven years, more than a tenth of his life, simply for being someone he was not. So all the verdict had done was end a long-running injustice. Likewise, we would express our displeasure at the Supreme Court's decision, despite the quality and quantity of unambiguous evidence, to acquit Demjanjuk solely on the basis of doubt.

After about fifteen minutes we emerged, surrounded again by about twenty policemen, to the mob of journalists waiting for us in the foyer. But we were forced to retreat: the reporters and photographers rushed at us so violently that we had no choice but to ensconce ourselves once more behind the glass doors of Courtroom C.

We went out through a side door into the courtyard. There, after much effort, and in the midst of hysterical shouts from frenzied reporters through which my voice could barely be heard, I managed to say the following: 'I said many times during the last two and a half years that there would be no choice but to acquit Demjanjuk, and that he could not be convicted of any alternative crime. And this is exactly what the Israeli Supreme Court has just decided. In the face of all the evidence before the court, there was no escaping this result. Therefore, as well as seeing the verdict as doing the appellant justice, we see as an *in*justice the court's failure to release him two years ago, when the bulk of the material that paved the way for his acquittal was already before the court.' I repeated this in English. Because of the clamour and the endless shouting I could not respond to questions in any orderly way. In the mean time the atmosphere around us was becoming thicker and more hostile. Holocaust survivors and hooligans who were unhappy with the verdict were screaming at us. So the policemen led us to our cars, and within a minute we were on our way to the Moriah Plaza Hotel, with a police escort.

Doron and my other guests had reached the hotel some time ago. Everyone was very excited and joyful. I gave interviews all afternoon and evening, about forty altogether, to the electronic and print media, national and foreign. So did Johnny and Nishnic.

I enjoyed every minute of that day, loving it more as time passed. I became more and more aware of the significance of the beating I had given the Israeli prosecution that had initiated and directed the show-trial against the wrong man. I felt ever more content that the verdict rendered by Levin and his colleagues was now worth less than the paper it was written on, and that this was being heard and seen at that very moment literally over all the world.

The morning's headlines were varied. Some of them quoted Demjanjuk: 'I MISS MY WIFE AND CHILDREN.' Over a picture of Demjanjuk, in which he was grinning from ear to ear and holding the prison release form, was the caption *Innocent by reason of doubt, shortly to be deported*. In contrast, a headline quoted one of the witnesses, a Treblinka survivor: 'I ASK MYSELF IF IT WAS WORTH STAYING ALIVE.' Another headline stated: SHOCK AND ANGER AT THE VERDICT. But then there was the opposite: CELEBRATIONS IN DEMJANJUK'S HOME TOWN, and another about the reaction in the Ukraine: UKRAINE: 'IN THE END JUSTICE WON'. As for what awaited Demjanjuk, one headline quoted me: A COUNTRY HAS ALREADY AGREED TO ACCEPT DEMJANJUK. Yet another heralded the wild smear campaign that would be launched against me a week later: SHEFTEL, YOU ARE A MURDERER.

The Supreme Court's verdict almost merits a chapter to itself. The five most respected judges in Israel faced no easy task. They *had* to acquit Demjanjuk of the charge of being Ivan the Terrible and not convict him of any other charge. Convicting Demjanjuk of being Ivan the Terrible would have necessitated his execution, and created a huge international scandal that would have done great damage to Israel, especially to its judicial system. Convicting Demjanjuk of another charge on appeal, a charge on which the lower court had not been asked to try him, would have had the same result. Moreover, it would have been a gross and blatant violation of international law; the extradition treaty between Israel and the US; and Section 24 of the State of Israel's extradition law. All of these explicitly forbid the arrest or prosecution of an extradited person on any charge other than that for which he was extradited. And, of course, Demjanjuk had not been given any opportunity to defend himself against an alternative charge. Such a conviction would also have engendered conflict with the American judicial system, the kind of conflict Israel, and especially its Supreme Court justices, would like to avoid. Therefore, the court could not do anything other than acquit Demjanjuk and release him.

The most vital interest of every institution is its own existence. An institution's good name and professional integrity are always an existential interest, and all the more so with a court system, which has no assets other than its good name, its integrity and its professionalism. The most serious mistake a court can make is to sentence someone to death for crimes he did not commit. This is exactly what the judges in Demjanjuk's show-trial did, and the Supreme Court had to reverse that verdict. However, precisely because of this same dereliction, at the centre of which stood Judge Levin, himself a Supreme Court justice, the Supreme Court's verdict had to lend its full support to each and every one of the lower court's improprieties, and to each of its legal and factual determinations. For this reason and this reason only, the Supreme Court verdict was worded as it was.

As will be recalled, the late Judge Dov Eitan was convinced that the defence argument on the lack of jurisdiction to try Demjanjuk for crimes of genocide was utterly incontrovertible (because Demjanjuk had been extradited to Israel to stand trial for murder). The Supreme Court's acceptance of this argument would be an admission that Demjanjuk had been held illegally in prison for seven and a half years. That was an impossible admission to make, particularly in the context of what was manifestly a show-trial. Such a scenario could cause serious, irreversible damage to the entire judicial system, which the Supreme Court heads and symbolizes. For this reason, the verdict spent twenty pages on the legal technicalities of the jurisdiction issue, finally reaching the following construction: since the crime of murder, according to American law, means causing death with malice aforethought, and since this notion is also included in the crime of genocide, then

> according to our approach, the offence that is the subject of the extradition order in the extraditing country is not a 'different offence' to the one that is the subject of the trial in the requesting country if the elements of the first are contained in the second. According to this approach, there is no need for all the substantive elements of the crime in the extraditing country and the requesting country to be identical for the offence in the requesting country not to be a 'different crime' to the crime in the extraditing country. It is sufficient that the elements of the first crime are included in the elements of the second crime. It makes no difference if the second crime [in the requesting country] has additional elements of its own.

In this section of the verdict there are quotes from many precedents by foreign courts and from the jurisprudence of foreign scholars. Yet none of them provides any support for the odd thesis constructed by the appeals court in order to grant the Israeli judicial system the intrinsic authority to try Demjanjuk for an entirely different crime to the one for which he was extradited. Not only do the precedents cited provide no support for this; there is not a single precedent or scholarly article published during the last 250 years in the Western world that provides any support for the Supreme Court's position. The court deliberately refrained from quoting the explicit words of the Cincinatti Federal Appeals Court, which ordered Demjanjuk's extradition to Israel: 'Although these allegations would certainly appear sufficient to support a charge of genocide against... Demjanjuk... until the United States and Israel amend the extradition treaty to include a crime of genocide ... genocide does not provide a basis for extradition.'

The Supreme Court's decision on the jurisdiction issue was also no doubt affected by the fact that Israeli judges face enormous emotional difficulties in ruling that they have no authority to try a man standing before them accused of being Ivan the Terrible. Neither is the Israeli legal community capable of this, and the torrent of articles that have appeared in the press since the verdict was rendered has not included a single criticism of this baseless finding.

The verdict covers 405 pages, more than half devoted to the identification issue. Here also the court faced a difficult dilemma, as it had to make two contradictory determinations. On the one hand, the court had to establish that it was reversing the district-court verdict that Demjanjuk was correctly and lawfully identified as Ivan the Terrible. Such a determination means that three judges, one of them a Supreme Court justice, sent to the gallows a man who did not commit the crimes of which he was convicted. On the other hand, the damage to the judicial system was all the greater when this was done in the framework of a show-trial. As a result, it was clear that if the Supreme Court reversed the conclusions of Levin and his colleagues on the identification issue, it would have to mitigate this by lending its full support to everything the lower-court judges said and did not say, did and did not do, on this issue.

Thus there were 214 pages of validation of the entire identification process, with all its improprieties. The court found that all the identification witnesses had exceptional and credible powers of identification. It considered itself bound to preserve the honour of the survivors, whose identifications it rejected, although this meant it rejected both the general and the specific arguments regarding the quality and evidential weight of each identification. Even Professor Wagenaar, whose testimony was the most important in the trial, especially in light of the material discovered in the Soviet Union, had to be discredited by the Supreme Court. The contents of his testimony were presented as an amateur and trivial set of baseless assumptions.

The court found it appropriate to go into the finest detail of each identification, to create an impression that the identification process had been kosher. Yet in the end it ignored everything written on those 214 pages, and acquitted Demjanjuk. In contrast, the section dealing with the reasons for Demjanjuk's acquittal filled only thirteen pages. This bizarre state of affairs will ensure that every unbiased jurist who studies the verdict will treat it as a ridiculous legal document, meant first and foremost to obscure a fact that cannot be obscured – that Demjanjuk was clearly the innocent victim of a show-trial. No praise of the lower court by the Supreme Court will make any difference, because one question will always remain unanswered: if the survivor-witnesses' identifications were so reliable, and if the identification procedures conducted by Israel Police and the OSI were so perfect, and if all of the findings made by Levin and his colleagues were so correct, how was it that 'something' went wrong and the wrong person was sent to the gallows?

The answer given to this question in the verdict – that the new evidence discovered after the conviction and submitted during the appeal was the reason for the acquittal – does not answer the real question. After all, if everything had been so good and correct, the evidence that Ivan Marchenko was Ivan the Terrible would never have been found.

The amount of time, the length of the testimonies and the number of pages of the court record devoted to the Travniki document by the lower court were even greater than those devoted to the identification issue. It was therefore unthinkable that the Supreme Court would subvert the lower court's conclusions on this. Furthermore, a finding that the Travniki document was authentic could not contradict Demjanjuk's acquittal, since it contained nothing that tied its bearer to Treblinka in general or to Ivan the Terrible in particular. The fact that no expert had been willing to state that the signature on the document was Demjanjuk's, while the greatest forensic scientist of the twentieth century concluded unequivocally that the signature was *not* Demjanjuk's, was not sufficient.

This paved the way for the finding that Demjanjuk, even if he were not Ivan the Terrible, was nevertheless an SS camp guard trained at Travniki. This was supposed to create a kind of moral, if not legal, justification for holding him in prison for seven and a half years for being someone he was not. The court in any case had no authority to make this finding, because (even if we assume that it had the authority to try Demjanjuk for the crime of genocide) it only had authority to try him for genocide committed at *Treblinka*, as stated explicitly by the American court that ordered his extradition. In its verdict, the Supreme Court deliberately avoided a decision on this point. This allowed it to discuss the issue of the alternative charge from a theoretical point of view, thus placing the mark of Cain on Demjanjuk's forehead. But the court did rule explicitly that Demjanjuk had not been given an opportunity to defend himself against these alternative charges; therefore, even from a moral point of view, the mark of Cain could never have any force.

On the issue of the alibi and the historical evidence, the Supreme Court went far beyond the ruling of Levin and his colleagues. Just as the lower court had in some instances found beyond what the prosecution had argued, so the Supreme Court went beyond what was stated in the verdict it was defending. While Levin and co. ruled in their verdict that 'the learned defence attorney Sheftel is correct that even if the defendant's alibi is found to be false, it has not been refuted in the precise sense of the word. In other words, the objective external – that is, historical – evidence does not prove that the defendant could *not* have been in Chełm during the period he claims to have been ... and since there is no refutation in its precise sense here, there is no corroboration of this point to the prosecution's case.' On the same issue, the Supreme Court ruled: 'In our view, the set of evidence discussed above at length not only justifies treating the direct alibi as unreliable, but also refutes it entirely.'

So, after reading ninety per cent of the Supreme Court's verdict one must inevitably reach the following conclusion: the identification testimonies determining that Demjanjuk was Ivan the Terrible were totally reliable, as were the identification procedures that preceded them; the Travniki document, which purports to say that Demjanjuk was a guard trained at Travniki and also stationed at Sobibor, belonged to Demjanjuk; Demjanjuk's alibi, in which he claimed that he had been at Chełm and not at any of these places and had done none of the acts attributed to him at those places, was not only unreliable but was also proven false; yet, wonder of wonders, despite all this, instead of sending him to the gallows, the Supreme Court sent Demjanjuk home. How and why could this wonder occur?

The court needed only twelve pages to explain. It was obviously very uncomfortable discussing the single relevant issue – whether Ivan the Terrible was Ivan Demjanjuk, as the survivor-witnesses claimed, and as Judges Levin, Tal and Dorner ruled, or whether he was Ivan Marchenko. This discomfort arose, of course, because they knew very well that they had no choice but to say there *was* a possibility that Marchenko was the man, despite everything they wrote in the 356 pages of the verdict.

Therefore the judges devalued as far as possible the evidence that demanded the acquittal. So, for instance, the verdict stated:

> We did not hear any testimony beyond the written documents [i.e. the eighty statements], that could cast any more light on the documents, beyond what is recorded in them; that is – (1) no testimony was brought from any person that he had had the documents in his possession, to tell us where they came from and the chain of custody from the day they were created; (2) the people making the statements did not testify and were not examined, and it was not possible therefore to clarify or determine anything beyond what is written, although many questions have arisen in this context; (3) we were not given testimony from those who recorded the statements, to build up any

kind of picture of the way the statements were taken and the situation of the person giving the statement at the time he made it. The manner in which the statements were taken and the characters of those who made them and those who took them remains one great unknown for us, which neither party has clarified with acceptable evidence.

The connection between this paragraph and reality was somewhat loose. True, no testimony was brought 'that could cast any more light on the documents', but there was no need for such testimony. The court heard a detailed explanation from me *and Shaked* about all the circumstances of the investigation conducted by the KGB against Nazi crimes in the extermination camps in Poland. According to the legal procedures in Israel, when such explanations are acceptable to both parties, as in this case, there is no need for them to be proved by witnesses; they become facts and as such the court must accept them. The verdict was correct, however, about the second and third flaws in the eighty statements. But for some reason, when the court deliberated on Danilchenko's statement and the rest of the evidence ostensibly linking Demjanjuk to other camps, even though the same flaws existed in all of them, Danilchenko's statement in particular, this did not prevent a finding that Demjanjuk had been a guard at other camps. As for those other camps, the court's finding is not that there is *doubt* over whether Demjanjuk was there, but that he actually *was*. So, according to the peculiar logic of the verdict, evidence of a certain type with certain flaws, if it pointed to Demjanjuk's innocence, was sufficient only to create doubt. But when it indicated Demjanjuk's possible guilt, it was sufficient to make an unambiguous finding against him. No wonder, then, that a man on trial in Israel on the charge of being Ivan the Terrible has trouble receiving true justice no matter what the facts are.

The court made another conjecture designed to reduce the weight of the evidence that so clearly established his innocence: 'It may well be, for instance, that the appellant worked part of the time at the gas chambers and part of the time was replaced by someone else.' This of course ignored the testimony of all the identification witnesses, after devoting more than two hundred pages to giving plenty of weight to their testimony. It was they who had stated in all their statements and testimonies that Ivan the Terrible, along with Nikolai Shelaiev, worked at the gas chambers all of the time.

Make no mistake, like the lower court before it, the Supreme Court would not have hesitated to send Demjanjuk to the gallows on the basis of the deplorable identification testimonies, which it praised to the skies. It went as far as to say: 'We see no reason to overturn the conclusions reached by the lower court in the matter of the conviction.' In other words, had the defence not discovered material that the court recognized as requiring that Demjanjuk be recalled from the gallows, the five most respected judges in Israel would also have sentenced him 'without any ambivalence or doubt' to death, based solely on the impermissibly suggestive photo spreads. All this is doubly serious because Demjanjuk's appeal proceeding in the Supreme Court was not a show-appeal, and the Supreme Court, unlike Levin and his colleagues, was not influenced by the media and the mob.

Yet in the end the court had no choice but to state the following:

> Now that new evidence is before us, in the form of a set of statements from camp guards attributing the operation of the gas chambers to a different guard by the name of Ivan Marchenko, whose photograph looks different from that of the appellant and who is not even similar to him ... in the absence of a reliable and well-founded evidential explanation, their significance cannot rationally be denied. We have received no explanation of the thesis raised in these statements that can harmonize them with the testimony of the identification witnesses on the one hand, or negate their value on the other hand. The lack of a rational explanation for the source and nature of an entire set of testimonies creates a reasonable doubt. Under the circumstances before us, the statements brought during the appeal make it impossible to reach a rational, certain conclusion about the basis for the appellant's conviction ... In the absence of any logical conclusion about the statements, what remains is a tie, a reasonable doubt, and if there is a reasonable doubt the appellant has the right to benefit from it.

Is all this really no more than a reasonable doubt?

The judges devoted dozens of long pages to the identification testimonies and to lengthy and wearisome quotes from the statements of the survivors, despite the fact that, in light of the appeal verdict, they had no value. Yet, in discussing the camp guards' statements, the court found it could present its argument in twelve pages. Furthermore, it took care not to quote a single word from the sections of the statements relating to the identity of Ivan Marchenko as operator of the Treblinka gas chambers. The court contented itself with naming the guards who had identified Ivan Marchenko as Ivan the Terrible. This too is no coincidence, since quoting from these statements would have shown to all that they created not a reasonable doubt as to Demjanjuk's guilt, as the court ruled, but incontrovertible and unambiguous proof of his absolute innocence. No member of the Israeli legal community was honest and brave enough to point out how bizarre a way this was to write a verdict.

If this was the case with regard to the jurisdiction issue, the Travniki document and the identification issue, it was all the more so with regard to the misconduct of the three lower-court judges, Levin in particular. On this issue the court saw fit to say:

> Here it is appropriate to add that we have dealt with the District Court's treatment of the appellant and the defence in various parts of our verdict. In the district court the trial was conducted properly and lawfully, objectively with regard to both sides and, at times, with special regard for the appellant. We find it proper to refer to this fact explicitly, given the claims that the appellant's attorney has made before us, in the appeal petition and orally, with regard to the 'general conduct of the honourable lower court, throughout the appellant's trial, including its attitude towards the parties before it, and especially with regard to applying entirely different standards to the prosecution and to the defence'. The appellant's attorney made these claims at length before us, at times using harsh expressions and an insulting manner that have no place in a court of law. We have examined each claim and have found no truth in them.

The reader has seen how 'proper and lawful' the show-trial as conducted by Levin really was. This section of the Supreme Court's verdict, which makes no attempt to address even a single one of the many disgraceful facts presented to it over the course of seven hours, constitutes unambiguous proof that the thrust of the verdict as a whole is the desire to defend and absolve the lower court. After all, the objective truth is that the unacceptable treatment of the defendant and his defence attorney contributed to the pronouncement of a death sentence on the wrong man. The Supreme Court saw itself obliged to draw a veil over this truth.

The verdict ends with the words 'We call a halt to this matter. Perfection is not the lot of a judge of flesh and blood.' With reference to the 'judge of flesh and blood' the explicit intention of the court was to bring the Demjanjuk trial to a close and adjourn permanently the most needless criminal trial in Israel's history.

But it was not so easy to bring the disgrace of the Demjanjuk affair to an end. On the day of the acquittal verdict, Noam Federman, a young political activist well-known for his clashes with the law, petitioned the Supreme Court, in its capacity as the High Court of Justice, to order the Attorney General to try Demjanjuk for crimes he allegedly committed in other extermination camps. He asked for Demjanjuk's departure from the country to be delayed until after the consideration of his petition. The petition was brought that same day before Chief Justice Shamgar, who refused to suspend Demjanjuk's departure from Israel. The hearing on the petition was set for Sunday 1 August. In the mean time, on Friday, Johnny received the papers his father needed to leave Israel on a direct flight to Kiev on Sunday.

On Saturday afternoon Nishnic, Johnny and I arrived at Demjanjuk's cell for the last time – as I thought. First we had a meeting in my office with Mr Shmulevitch, the legal counsel to the Prison Service, to co-ordinate the arrangements for Demjanjuk's departure the next day. We spent an hour and a half in the cell, where the mood was joyful. Demjanjuk had already packed his things. He received me warmly, thanked me, praised me and even tried to embrace me, but I politely avoided him. Again and again he said: 'If it wasn't for you, they would be taking me out of this cell to hang me instead of to set me free.' I was swept up by the cheerful atmosphere and said, 'Next time we meet it will be in Cleveland.'

When we left the prison, Johnny and Nishnic insisted on having their picture taken with me sitting on their shoulders. We parted and agreed to meet the next morning in my office, before the two of them set off to join Demjanjuk in the police car that would take him from the prison gate to the door of his plane.

They arrived at my office at eleven, but that was fifteen minutes after three Supreme Court justices – Gavriel Bach, Shlomo Levin and Mishael Heshin – issued an order delaying Demjanjuk's departure from the country for ten days. They scheduled a hearing on Federman's petition (Federman had in the mean time been joined by Yisrael Yehezkeli, the criminal who had thrown acid in my eyes) for Wednesday 11 August. Indeed, a halt had been called, but we were not at the end of the road.

This was unprecedented. In contradiction of the final verdict of the Supreme Court, the unanimous decision of five justices that included the statement 'We have decided not to continue proceedings regarding the alternative charges,' a different bench of three justices had issued a staying-order to keep Demjanjuk in Israel 'until a decision is made in the petition for an order nisi', and the order nisi was based solely on the petitioners' desire for a different decision to that made by the Supreme Court in its final, definitive verdict.

As if that were not bad enough, the order was issued without Demjanjuk or even me being invited by the court to argue the defence position on the stay of deportation. The practical significance of such a step was that Demjanjuk had to remain in prison for another ten days. I doubt whether any court in Israel, not to mention the Supreme Court, especially in its capacity as the High Court of Justice, has ever ordered that a person be detained for ten days without that person, or his lawyer, being summoned to voice his position. But the Demjanjuk affair had its own set of rules. No wonder Johnny and Nishnic, especially the latter, were beside themselves with rage.

Over the last few years my office had often been a gathering place for the media, sometimes, as Tzvia had said, turning into a radio and television studio. But all that was nothing compared to what began to happen in my office when the High Court of Justice's peculiar order became known. As if in response to a prearranged signal, foreign and local reporters besieged my office. Sometimes there were more than twenty there simultaneously. Tzvia sighed and pronounced, 'Nothing like this has ever happened before.' In any interviews I gave I stressed the serious perversion of justice involved in issuing such an order, in terms of both substantive and procedural law. I quoted Section 24 of the Israeli extradition law: 'When a person has been extradited to Israel by a foreign country, he will not be arrested and will not be brought to trial for any other offence he committed before his extradition.' I also explained that, since his imprisonment was illegal, Demjanjuk's status from this moment until such time as the order was rescinded was that of a hostage. But I said however that I was certain Demjanjuk would soon be released and be free to leave the country.

Now the media, especially the two mass-market tabloids, launched a savage campaign against me for having brought about the acquittal of a 'Nazi criminal', and in particular for having dared to voice my view that the acquittal verdict did not do Demjanjuk justice. The campaign included biased, false statements from a Ministry of Justice spokeswoman. The tone and the amount of the truth in the statements issued to the press were reminiscent of the Soviet propaganda distributed during the Moscow trials. To complete the picture, and again in keeping with the best Bolshevik tradition, which influenced Israeli public life for a long time, the Minister of Justice (in the Knesset) and the Attorney General (through his spokesman) announced that they intended to open a criminal investigation into my public criticisms of the court, an empty threat that was never carried out.

In spite of these vicious slurs, managed entirely by a defeated and frustrated establishment, every time I went out into the street I encountered many expressions of support and approbation, more than once even from Holocaust survivors. The media frenzy left me entirely indifferent.

On Tuesday 3 August, an earthshaking development occurred in Ohio. The Federal Appeals Court of the Sixth Circuit in Cincinatti decided to allow Demjanjuk to return to the US, to take part personally in the inquiry into the legality of his extradition to Israel. This decision was announced in the midst of a flurry of declarations by spokesmen for the Department of Justice that, despite the acquittal in the Israeli Supreme Court, Demjanjuk would not be allowed to return to the USA under any circumstances. These declarations were prominently quoted by the Israeli press, of course.

The upshot of all this was that those who had wanted to delay and interfere with Demjanjuk's departure to the Ukraine (which his family had agreed to accept as a place of refuge only because there was no other choice, while hoping he would be able to return to Cleveland sooner or later) actually paved the way for Demjanjuk's direct return to his family in Cleveland. Whilst it was not stated explicitly, it was clear that the Cincinatti court was very angry at Demjanjuk's detention in Israel in violation of the extradition agreement with the US and of international law. The American court did not have to address the issue at all, but nevertheless said in its decision:

> Article 13 of the extradition treaty between Israel and the United States, signed December 10, 1962, and effective December 5, 1963, expressly provides that 'a person extradited under the present conventions shall not be detained, tried or punished in the territory of the requesting party for any offense other than that for which the extradition has been granted' ... our previous order in this case was expressly subject to the understanding that Demjanjuk was to be tried only for the charges in the warrant against him and under which he was extradited, that is, charges based upon the allegation that he was 'Ivan the Terrible of Treblinka.' The doctrine of speciality forbids him from being tried on any other charges.

The Cincinatti court repeated this statement three days later in another decision. This state of affairs created the possibility of collision between the Israeli and American judicial establishments, and in circumstances that would show everyone that the Israeli side was in the wrong. The Minister of Justice's spokesman blustered that Israel was not bound by the decisions of the American court and would decide the issue independently. But in practice these two federal-court decisions had an immediate and decisive effect on the position taken by the Attorney General in the Supreme Court.

In the mean time, a long list of petitioners had joined Federman and Yehezkeli. The most prominent were eight of the eleven Sobibor survivors living in Israel, the World Jewish Congress, the Organization for Holocaust and Heroism Heritage, the Second Generation of Holocaust Survivors, and Ephraim Zoroff, representative of the Israeli Weisenthal Centre. Zoroff made his living as a Nazi hunter, but for more than two years he had avoided taking any measures to find out where Ivan Marchenko – Ivan the Terrible – was and what had happened to him. Yet he, like the State of Israel, had significant information that could help solve the riddle, in the evidence revealed by the defence. It should be stressed that the man after whom the Weisenthal Centre was named, the legendary Nazi hunter Simon Weisenthal (who now has no connection to the centre), stressed in an interview he gave to the French newspaper *Libération* that the Demjanjuk affair should be brought to an immediate end and Demjanjuk allowed to return to his family in Cleveland.

All the petitioners demanded that Demjanjuk be tried for being a guard at other concentration and extermination camps, at Sobibor in particular. They ignored the legal situation that prevented this, and their arguments were drafted with a large measure of demagoguery. So, for instance, a petition submitted by attorney Shafir Shilansky (son of the former speaker of the Knesset, Don Shilansky), lawyer for the Weisenthal Centre, contained the following gem: 'The petitioners see the failure to try respondent 3 [Demjanjuk] as in effect granting pardon and clemency to all Nazi criminals now alive everywhere in the world.' Similar nonsense could be found throughout all the ridiculous petitions.

The World Jewish Congress's petition was submitted by attorney Yehuda Raveh, son-in-law of Gideon Hausner, prosecutor at the Eichmann trial. It contradicted itself in its central argument. First it said that the Attorney General had 'to submit to the American authorities a request to receive their written consent to try Ivan Demjanjuk in Israel for having been a participant in Nazi crimes at Sobibor, Regensburg and Flossenbürg'. Here, of course, Raveh conceded explicitly that without such consent it would not be possible to detain Demjanjuk on these charges. Yet in the following paragraph he demands that 'Ivan Demjanjuk be detained and his departure from Israel prevented until the rendering of a definitive verdict on these charges'. But he himself had stated that such detainment was not possible without first receiving the consent of the United States government!

There was much speculation about what position Yosef Harish would take in response to the flood of petitions. Even though the legal position was crystal-clear, the Attorney General's irresolution, his tendency to contradict himself and the abysmal dishonesty that characterized so many of the prosecution's actions in the Demjanjuk affair made me very unsure of what his response would be.

When Johnny and I visited Demjanjuk (Nishnic had left early on Monday morning) on Friday 6 August, I told him unequivocally: 'The delay in your departure is only temporary, and you will soon leave this cell – but this time you will be on your way to Cleveland, not the Ukraine.'

'I really hope that you are right this time too,' he answered.

On Tuesday the 10th Johnny picked me up from my office in the afternoon, and we drove once more to the Moriah Plaza Hotel, where Johnny had been staying all this time. In the late afternoon I spoke with Nili Arad, head of the High Court of Justice division of the State Attorney's office, and learned that even at this late stage the Attorney General had not decided his position. Even so, I was entirely relaxed and calm. The only thing that bothered me slightly was the oppressively hostile atmosphere expected at court the next day.

When Johnny and I reached the Supreme Court parking lot we were immediately surrounded by about ten policemen, who escorted us into Courtroom C, where less than two weeks ago the acquittal verdict had been read. The courtroom was already full and the atmosphere was indeed oppressive. A hostile murmur passed through the crowd as I came in. A few minutes later the judges entered; Demjanjuk himself was not even brought from prison. This hearing was one of the oddest ever to have taken place in the Supreme Court. The justices listened with great patience to the arguments of the convicted criminals Yehezkeli and Federman, whose arguments were entirely inappropriate for such a hearing. Yehezkeli, who claimed to be a Holocaust survivor, half-way through his argument changed the location at which his relations were murdered – the relations he had abandoned as soon as the German Army entered Warsaw, to make his own escape easier. During the trial and appeal, Yehezkeli had claimed again and again that Demjanjuk had murdered his entire family at Treblinka. Now, after the acquittal, he changed his tune and said that Demjanjuk had murdered his entire family at Sobibor. I sat there and thought how horrible and shaming it was for this delinquent to use and abuse his slaughtered family's memory, their blood. Nothing better illustrated the despicable nature of the Israeli media than its turning this detestable man into a national hero.

Raveh proved, should anyone need proof, that he was nothing like his father-in-law, whom he made a point of referring to at the beginning of his speech. Among his arguments was the claim that: 'Since the Supreme Court found that Demjanjuk was a camp guard, he is not a human being, and therefore does not enjoy the legal rights of a human being.' When I saw the level of the arguments presented by the petitioners in response to me and to Nili Arad – who had announced at the beginning of her speech that the Attorney General had no intention of submitting an alternative charge sheet against Demjanjuk – I was finally sure that all the petitions would swiftly be rejected.

I was very pleased with the position taken by the Attorney General, no less than I had been with the acquittal verdict itself. For more than two years Shaked had declared in and out of court that the state had sufficient evidence to convict Demjanjuk of alternative charges, and that the courts had the power to try him on these charges without exceeding the terms of the extradition. Now another representative of the Attorney General was saying the opposite. The Attorney General's view, expressed in both his written response and in the hearing, was that 'the original order on his extradition was given on the assumption that Demjanjuk would be tried only for the charges in the extradition order concerning crimes attributed to him as Ivan the Terrible from Treblinka, and therefore the rule of speciality forbids charging him with crimes other than those for which he was extradited'. There can be no doubt that he took this position as a result of the two decisions pronounced a week earlier in Ohio. Two and a half years late, the Attorney General had finally recognized the correctness of my argument on the rules of jurisdiction and extradition. I was even more pleased when I heard Arad say, 'The public has no interest in opening proceedings against Demjanjuk on alternative charges if in the end there is no certainty that he will not be acquitted of those as well. An additional acquittal would look like a débâcle and we cannot rule out such an acquittal.' The truth came out at last: the Attorney General was forced to acknowledge that he did not have hard evidence to prove any alternative charge against Demjanjuk. Everything Shaked had previously said in his name on this subject was baseless and lacked the support of substantial evidence. But the most astounding point in this grotesque hearing was that all parties involved – myself excluded, of course, but including the three justices – shared an erroneous and legally invalid assumption that, had the Attorney General wished to press other charges against Demjanjuk, he was free to do so, even though this ran counter to the explicit and final ruling of the Supreme Court verdict.

The tedious hearing went on for about five hours, at the end of which Justice Shlomo Levin declared: 'Our decision will be rendered shortly.' On Sunday I was informed by the court clerk's office that the decision would be given on Wednesday 18th. On that day a 'delegation' from

Cleveland landed in Israel: Johnny, Nishnic, Congressman James Traficant and four private bodyguards.

I had no doubt that all the petitions would be rejected unanimously. I had voiced this view to Johnny the previous week, stressing that I was as sure of this as I had been that Demjanjuk would be acquitted unanimously in his appeal. So the entire Demjanjuk crew was sure that on Wednesday 18 August the final green light would be given to Demjanjuk's departure from Israel. A ticket was purchased for him for Thursday morning's Delta flight to Cincinatti, with a short stopover in Paris.

The arrival of the delegation, and especially of Congressman Traficant, attracted attention in the media, and many journalists descended on the American Colony Hotel – the 'defence citadel' – to which we had all happily returned thanks to a one-off contribution to fund the delegation's costs there. On Wednesday morning, for the third time in less than three weeks, I entered Supreme Court Courtroom C, members of the delegation in my wake. I was quiet and relaxed as if none of this had anything to do with me. The composition of the audience was also familiar – media, Holocaust survivors, curious onlookers. A few minutes after nine the three judges entered. Justice Gavriel Bach opened, and without any preliminaries announced that all the petitions had been rejected unanimously, although they had not been unanimous 'in their reasoning'. The most important paragraph in the judgement stated: 'The implication of the arguments before us is that the Attorney General believes, under these circumstances, that it would be necessary to hear the trial from the beginning, and even to broaden it, while the likelihood of obtaining conviction is, in the opinion of the Attorney General, small. We cannot say that this consideration is groundless.' So, less than two weeks after the ruling that Demjanjuk had been a camp guard stationed at Sobibor (even though, as will be recalled, the Supreme Court also recognized that he had not been given a proper opportunity to defend himself against this finding), the same court ruled that it found it necessary to justify the opposite view on the part of the Attorney General. The mark of Cain that the Supreme Court had stamped on Demjanjuk's forehead had faded within three weeks.

Yet even now the disgrace of the Demjanjuk affair was not at the end of the road. As soon as Justice Bach had finished speaking, Shilansky rose and asked that Demjanjuk's deportation be delayed still further, so that he could study the decision and decide whether an additional hearing should be held before a bench of five or more justices, to review the decision just announced. An additional hearing is an exceptional procedure that takes place only when a judgement of the Supreme Court given by three judges establishes a precedent that contradicts an earlier precedent, or that sets 'a difficult, new and important precedent'. Even when these conditions exist, there is no requirement that an additional hearing be held, and the decision is at the sole discretion of the Chief Justice, or another Supreme Court justice before whom the request to hold the hearing is brought. When the request is granted, two judges (or in rare cases even more) are added to the three on the original bench. The hearing before them deals with the specific question defined as deserving an additional hearing.

The three justices were startled by the request, and I expressed my total opposition to the continued illegal detention of Demjanjuk in prison. The bench decided that the request would be brought before Chief Justice Shamgar that same day. Within the hour the Chief Justice announced the following decision: 'I hereby order the stay as requested, until a decision on the request, which will be given after a hearing before all representatives. The hearing will take place on Friday 20 August 1993, at nine a.m. in Courtroom C.'

The next day I went to visit Demjanjuk with Johnny and Nishnic. The mood was joyful. I gave him a detailed explanation of what had happened in the High Court of Justice hearing and what could be expected the next day in the hearing before Chief Justice Shamgar. I told him I believed that this would be the last session in which the court would discuss his case. I added, 'I am seventy-five per cent sure that early on Saturday morning you will leave this cell, never to return.' I further explained that even if his departure from Israel were delayed, to allow the petitioners to submit their requests for an additional hearing, I had no doubt that the result would be a confirmation of the High Court of Justice ruling that had rejected the petitions. When we parted two hours later, it was as if it were Demjanjuk's long-awaited exit from Israel.

That afternoon Johnny, Nishnic, Traficant, the bodyguards and I were sitting in the delightful garden of the American Colony Hotel when, to our surprise, our old friend Paul Brifer walked in. I embraced him and he said, 'I came to see the consummation of your great victory. Tomorrow will be the court's last session regarding Demjanjuk, when the final decision on his release will be made, and I wanted to be present for the great moment.' Brifer joined us and for several hours I told him all that had happened in the case and in my own life in recent weeks. Brifer was happy for me in the way a father enjoys his son's success; he saw himself, with good reason, as an important participant in all these great events.

On Friday the courtroom was overflowing and the atmosphere, until the Chief Justice's entrance, was like the two previous hearings. The composition of the crowd was also as usual. I considered it a good sign that Chief Justice Shamgar would be presiding over this hearing. The single legal issue under consideration in all the petitions that had been rejected was whether the Attorney General's decision not to charge Demjanjuk with alternative offences was so unreasonable as to justify intervention from the High Court of Justice. As will be recalled, the first time since the founding of the state that the Supreme Court decided to overturn a decision by the Attorney General was in my petition against the Attorney General and the media. The court had handed down a majority, rather than a unanimous, decision. Then also there had been a request for an additional hearing, a request that Chief Justice Shamgar had rejected even though the ruling was unusual and had not been unanimous. Therefore I guessed that Shamgar would find it difficult to order Demjanjuk's continued detention for the purpose of submitting petitions for an additional hearing, when previously, with an identical legal issue at stake under circumstances that on the face of it provided better justification for such a hearing, he had decided against.

My speech centred on the argument that it was already manifestly clear, according to the legal criteria on which such petitions are judged, that there was not the slightest chance of the request for such a hearing being granted. Therefore, it would be unreasonable to continue to delay Demjanjuk's departure from Israel, now that all the petitions to try him on alternative charges had been rejected unanimously, and after he had been kept in prison for more than twenty days after his acquittal. I submitted to the Chief Justice his ruling of three years ago, in which he had rejected the request to hold an additional hearing on the verdict in my petition against the Attorney General and the media. The attorneys for the various petitioners, Raveh in particular, accepted that their motion to delay Demjanjuk's departure should be judged according to the likelihood of their requests for an additional hearing being granted. But they argued there *was* a high probability that their requests would be granted. The hearing went on for about an hour and a half, after which Chief Justice Shamgar declared a recess. He instructed all parties to remain in the courtroom, because his decision would be rendered quickly.

Surrounded as usual by policemen, I made my way into a side room. Within minutes the Demjanjuk delegation and Brifer had joined me. I was very optimistic. I figured that, particularly in light of Shamgar's concluding words, he intended to reject all the requests to delay departure. Otherwise, he could have immediately extended the stay order by several days, until his decision was announced. I was very happy, and we all discussed the technicalities of Demjanjuk's journey the next day. Representatives of the American Embassy, who were supposed to issue his travel documents, were also present, as was attorney Shmulevitch from the Prison Service. We all finalized the details together for Demjanjuk's smooth departure from Israel's borders.

At almost eleven-thirty we were called into the courtroom to hear the decision. It was short and, contrary to expectations, retained Demjanjuk in Israel for the period during which petitions for an additional hearing could be submitted – fifteen days, less the two days that had passed since the High Court of Justice verdict. The bottom line said, 'I have therefore decided – without taking any position on the requests for an additional hearing and their likelihood of success – that the enforcement of the deportation order will be delayed until the end of the period for the submission of requests for an additional hearing.' At the end of this period Demjanjuk's departure would be delayed for yet another fifteen days, so that the Attorney General and I could respond to the petitions. The essence of the Chief Justice's decision was, then, that Demjanjuk would spend at least another month in prison.

I was extremely disappointed, and Johnny, Nishnic and the rest of the party even more so. We decided to hold a brief press conference at the American Colony. With Ed and Johnny sitting on either side of me, I made no attempt to conceal my profound disappointment with the decision and its practical consequences. I stressed, nevertheless, that the decision was but a technical one and there was no indication that, in the end, there would actually be an additional hearing on the High Court of Justice decision. I reiterated my certainty that, in light of the two Supreme Court verdicts in which eight out of the court's twelve justices had ruled that Demjanjuk should not be put on trial for any alternative charges, nothing could prevent Demjanjuk returning to the US within a few weeks. This time, however, I took care not to specify a precise date. The press as usual tried to present my announcement as presumptuous, and on Sunday the headlines reporting the press conference said SHEFTEL: 'I'LL WIN AGAIN.'

After the press conference, it was decided that the delegation would return immediately to the States, and come back to Israel only when it was conclusively clear that the legal procedures had ended and Demjanjuk was irretrievably on his way to the airport.

The petitioners, as expected, did everything to lengthen Demjanjuk's prison stay for as long as they could. They submitted their motions for an additional hearing on the last day possible, so the order forbidding

Demjanjuk's departure was extended until a decision was reached on the petitions.

We had fifteen days to submit our response, but did so within five. By now I was depressed and tired of the case, and my main desire was to see it brought to an end at last. For this reason Doron assumed the major burden of preparing the brief, which filled eight pages. I tried to get the state prosecution to submit its response before the fifteen days had passed, but to no avail. The file was transferred to Justice Or's chambers only on the eve of Rosh Hashanah. Happily, he did not need much time to issue his decision.

On 19 September the radio news programme reported that Justice Or had decided not to grant an additional hearing. In his twelve-page decision, he rejected all the petitioners' arguments, concluding:

> In the eyes of many, the acquittal of the respondent and the failure to put him on trial on other charges is hard to accept. Yet, as I have tried to make clear above, the matter does not justify an additional hearing. The result is that the requests for an additional hearing are rejected. On 2 September 1993 I decided to freeze the deportation order against the respondent until the rendering of a decision on an additional hearing. With this decision, the stay of deportation is terminated.

The next day's headlines declared: HIGH COURT OF JUSTICE DECIDES CONCLUSIVELY TO FREE DEMJANJUK; DEFINITE: DEPORTATION; AFTER 7½ YEARS, DEMJANJUK GOES FREE. But there were also silly ones, including MURDERER CERTIFIED VIRTUOUS.

After explaining to Nishnic that this decision was absolutely final, and that there could not be anything more, it was decided that their entire party would set out immediately for Israel, and that a ticket would be purchased for Demjanjuk for Wednesday 22 September, on El Al's one a.m. direct flight to New York. We had to arrange a non-stop flight because the French authorities had announced they would arrest Demjanjuk if he landed in France. It is doubtful whether they would actually have done so, but we did not want to put them to the test.

On Tuesday morning, after once again co-ordinating with Shmulevitch, I arrived at Demjanjuk's cell to bid him farewell – for the very last time. As I walked into the cell, scenes from my first encounter with Demjanjuk, more than six and a half years previously, began to dance before my eyes. I reflected that the last thing I had imagined then was that our final encounter would be before he left for home, rather than before he went to the gallows. This thought gave me enormous satisfaction.

Demjanjuk himself, who knew of the recent developments, including the arrival of his son and son-in-law and others to take him home, from the radio and his guards, was in good spirits and for the first time expressed his certainty that he would leave the cell where he had lived for over seven and a half years alive. He burst into song again and again, repeating the Hebrew words 'I'm going home.' I sat with him for about an hour and explained the arrangements for his departure. He again expressed his heartfelt thanks to me for the fact that instead of being executed he was returning to his home and family in Cleveland. We parted with a warm handshake. Demjanjuk was moved; I cannot say the same for myself. At noon I was already in my car, on the way to my office, and thence to a press conference I had scheduled for one o'clock at the Tel Aviv press association's building.

It was on that very day that this book was released in its Hebrew edition, and the press conference had been called to mark its publication as well as the end of the legal side of the Demjanjuk affair in Israel. It was perfect timing. Once again I could have no complaints about my *mazel*.

As the press conference was in progress, Nishnic, Johnny, Traficant and two private security guards landed at Ben-Gurion and went over to my office. They arrived at three and, after saying their goodbyes to Tzvia and Doron, they collected me – at Nishnic's request – to go to a Tel Aviv restaurant specializing in traditional eastern European Jewish food. We spent the next two hours gorging on *gefilte* fish, chopped liver, *farfel*, *kreplach* and other delicacies. The mood was euphoric.

At about six-thirty we all set out for the Ayalon Prison to meet Shmulevitch, to get confirmation that all was ready for Demjanjuk's departure that night. At the same opportunity, by prior arrangement, Johnny, Nishnic and Traficant entered Demjanjuk's cell for half an hour, among other reasons to give him the bullet-proof vest they had bought for him to wear on his way home from jail. A convoy of cars and vans full of reporters and photographers accompanied us there, and back to the Plaza Hotel in Tel Aviv.

Johnny and the rest of the party were to be at the airport at eleven p.m. As a lawyer there was no need for me to go too. Even though the climax, when six and a half years of effort would be crowned with success, was approaching, I was again surprised by how relaxed I felt. Time passed quickly and at half-past ten we all went down to the lobby. I embraced and said goodbye to Johnny, Nishnic and Congressman Traficant. They again thanked me warmly and promised that we would meet again in Cleveland, this time together with 'my client'. A few minutes later the merry company set out for the airport. It was then that

I began feeling tense. Perhaps something would frustrate Demjanjuk's departure from the country at the last moment.

I got into my car, turned on the radio and began to drive aimlessly, to pass the time. There was a report from the prison gate every few minutes, and a little after midnight came the announcement that Demjanjuk had left the prison in handcuffs in a Prison Service car heading straight for the airport. (This scene was photographed on the front pages of all the newspapers next morning.) Minutes later there was a sudden announcement that a man named Nahum Weisfish had, at the very last minute, submitted a new petition to delay Demjanjuk's departure. I held my breath. The announcer continued: Justice Eliahu Matsa had refused to issue a stay of deportation. So that final hurdle was cleared. Just after one in the morning the newsreader related that El Al flight 001 had taken off for the United States and that Demjanjuk was on board. A huge wave of relief broke over me. 'Finally it's over,' I muttered.

The last stumbling steps of the Demjanjuk affair received the following expression in the next morning's headlines: THE LAST PASSENGER ON FLIGHT 001 BUSINESS CLASS TO NEW YORK: JOHN DEMJANJUK; DEMJANJUK TOOK NO SOUVENIR FROM THE ISRAELI JAIL; DEMJANJUK WILL TRY TO EVADE DEMONSTRATORS IN CLEVELAND; DEMJANJUK LEAVES ISRAEL FOR US; IN BULLET-PROOF VEST AND SURROUNDED BY POLICE, DEMJANJUK WAS DEPORTED FROM ISRAEL LAST NIGHT; DEMJANJUK – IT'S ALL OVER. My own last word was quoted in one headline: SHEFTEL: 'A REPREHENSIBLE CASE'. One of the tabloids, whose correspondent had not managed to get a seat on the flight, made up a story in which there was more frustration than truth: 'NAZI, MURDERER,' EL AL PASSENGERS SHOUTED AT DEMJANJUK. The rival tabloid said, IN BULLET-PROOF VEST DEMJANJUK FLOWN TO HIDING PLACE IN CLEVELAND, and another headline declared: LEFT NAUSEA IN HIS WAKE.

Yet when I read these headlines, the most important thing for me was that this time we really had reached the end of the road.